TWENTIETH-CENTURY
SOCIAL THOUGHT

TWENTIETH-CENTURY SOCIAL THOUGHT Fifth Edition

R.P. CUZZORT
UNIVERSITY OF COLORADO

EDITH W. KING
UNIVERSITY OF DENVER

Harcourt Brace College Publishers

Fort Worth   Philadelphia   San Diego   New York   Orlando   Austin   San Antonio
Toronto   Montreal   London   Sydney   Tokyo

Publisher	Ted Buchholz
Acquisitions Editor	Chris Klein
Assistant Editor	Linda Wiley
Project Editor	Louise Slominsky
Production Manager	Melinda Esco
Art Director	Jim Dodson

Cover	Copyright © Masao Mukai/Photonica

Address for Editorial Correspondence:
Harcourt Brace College Publishers
301 Commerce Street, Suite 3700
Fort Worth, TX 76102

Address for Orders:
Harcourt Brace & Company
6277 Sea Harbor Drive
Orlando, FL 32887-6777
1-800-782-4479, or 1-800-433-0001 (in Florida).

Library of Congress Catalog Card Number: 94-78728

Printed in the United States of America

ISBN 0-15-501750-0

4 5 6 7 8 9 0 1 2 3 090 9 8 7 6 5 4 3 2 1

Preface

From the Authors: Inspirations and Acknowledgments

Twentieth-Century Social Thought was never intended as a seminal source book in social theory. Any number of other works do that job better and more thoroughly. In the fifth edition of this book, as with earlier editions, we chose to focus on social philosophers and theorists who are controversial figures in the humanistic approaches to social thought. None of these observers of the modern, and now postmodern, era has lacked for critics, but each has stood firm against opponents, arguing his or her case brilliantly and persuasively. The material in this book endeavors to show that social thinkers are involved with profound problems of both a humanistic and a scientific nature. The writings of these individuals demonstrate how their academic concerns led them down interesting theoretical pathways that were crisscrossed by humanistic concerns. So, as before, this volume discusses the major works of social scientists who made important contributions to modern social thought. Not everyone represented will evoke the same response from the reader. But we hope that at least one approach and its theoretical applications will find special favor or meaning for each person who studies this material.

A Remarkable Opportunity

It was our rare and remarkable opportunity to be able to make contact, and hold telephone and written exchanges and discussions, with three of the illustrious social scientists presented in this volume—Robert Merton, David Riesman and Elise Boulding. These world-renowned sociologists were most generous in providing their expertise, their advice, and most importantly, their current work and writings for inclusion in the fifth edition of *Twentieth-Century Social Thought*. When contacted by the authors, the octogenarian Robert Merton responded with articles, reprinted chapters, as yet unpublished works, and the following supportive advice:

> I have gone over the chapter (for the fifth edition) on my own work and, as you see from the enclosures, suggested some corrections, clarifications and additional source materials (correspondence to Edith King, January 25, 1994).

Similarly, David Riesman responded to the authors' request with letters and materials filled with details, information, and an extensive bibliography on his current writings and work in higher education. Further, David Riesman wrote that he was happy to learn that Elise Boulding was to be included in the new (fifth) edition, since "I have such high regard" for her work and scholarship (correspondence to Edith King, November 30, 1993). Finally, the inspiration and encouragement provided to us by Elise Boulding was extraordinary. Because she, as well as the authors, reside in the Denver-Boulder, Colorado area, we were able to get together several times during the months of formulation and preparation of the new edition. Boulding furnished us with her articles, papers, background documents, books, and most importantly, the support and reassurance that is so essential in such projects.

About the Organization of the Fifth Edition

The fifth edition of *Twentieth-Century Social Thought* is similar to the fourth edition in that the authors present *applications* of the social theories discussed in each chapter. These applications are designated by the heading "Encounters with Social Thought" and represent material developed and written by the authors specifically for this book. Each chapter concludes with a section labeled "Putting Social Thought to Work," which contains queries that challenge the reader to engage in further provocative thought about social issues. Further, it was our intention to include more than merely one illustrious woman social thinker and feminist. In the fifth edition, the work of Elise Boulding joins that of Margaret Mead for examination, application, and additional consideration in the "Putting Social Thought to Work" section.

Acknowledgments

Our workload was aided by the invaluable assistance of our departmental staff associate, Deborah Shepherd. The editors at Harcourt Brace College Publishers lent continual support and advice. To them, Ted Buchholz, Chris Klein, Linda Wiley, and Louise Slominsky, as well as Melinda Esco and Jim Dodson, we extend our deepest appreciation. Finally, the chapters of this fifth edition were read and used in courses taught in the College of Education, University of Denver, during the past year. We want to express our thanks to these perceptive individuals who assisted us in evaluating the worthiness of this material.

E. W. K. / R. P. C.   May, 1994

Contents

Chapter 4

Profit, Greed, and Human Misery: Social Theory and Karl Marx

Chapter 5

Sexuality and Social Force: Social Thought and the Contribution of Sigmund Freud

Chapter 6

Symbolic Interactionism and the Work of George Herbert Mead

Chapter 7

The Social Thought of Pitirim A. Sorokin

Chapter 8

The Sociologist in Anger:
The Views of C. Wright Mills

Chapter 12

Theory and Practice:
The Applied Vision of Howard S. Becker

Chapter 13

Sociology as Bad Faith:
The Social Perspectives of Peter L. Berger

Chapter 14

**Life as a Con Game:
The Dramaturgic Vision of Erving Goffman**

Chapter 15

Studying the Commonplace: The Work of Harold Garfinkel

Chapter 16

**Building a Global Civic Culture:
Elise Boulding and Strategies for a Peaceful World**

Chapter 17
Epilogue: Social Thought for a Global Society

Twentieth-Century Social Thought

Chapter 1

Introduction

The Uses of Social Thought
as We Enter the Next Century

❖

It is now obvious that although we have been able to solve a variety of difficult problems in the realms of engineering, medicine, and technology, we are still not much more advanced when it comes to addressing human social issues than we were two or three thousand years ago. The world is still a place of massive suffering. Starvation is a common fate for millions of people. We seem to be incapable of avoiding what appears to be an inevitable confrontation between the great powers—though one hopes that peace talks, despite their bad record, will eventually amount to something. If such a confrontation takes place, there is no small likelihood that most life on this planet will be annihilated. The United States is far from achieving its ideal of full democratic participation, the welfare of its citizens, and continued progress toward a higher form of society. We find ourselves facing crisis after crisis to the point where we feel a growing sense of paralysis as massive social, cultural, and economic forces appear to make any individual effort a mere quixotic tilting with windmills.

We have obtained a kind of mastery over the physical world and, to some extent, over the complexities of biological reality. At the same time, we cannot achieve the kind of wisdom that might enable us to make the greatest use of our lives. We become bogged down in racial, ethnic, and political conflicts. We indulge ourselves, almost to the point of exhaustion, in idle entertainments. We speak of being demoralized. We are not, in a word, capable of dealing with our "simple" social problems as effectively as we are able to deal with "complex" problems (such as, to give just one example, how to get close-up snapshots of the planet Jupiter).

It is something of a paradox that we are more capable of dealing with the mysteries of the universe than we are with the complexities of ourselves and our social systems. More people probably die each day from problems that come from difficulties in establishing effective economic and social systems than from strictly "natural" causes. There is also, possibly, something of a paradox in the fact that many people seem to think it is more important to study those disciplines that deal with technology or "hard science" than it is to study aspects of the social sciences. However, until it is demonstrated that advances in technology have brought about improvements in social relations among people, we shall have to presume it is necessary to study society itself as a problematic feature of human existence.

This book offers the reader overviews of the work of fifteen social scientists and writers concerned with the human condition. We have tried to select writers who are interesting and who, at the same time, have been influential. We have also emphasized the extent to which we think a particular writer's ideas are engaging and thought-provoking. This book is an effort to present to readers first approaching the discipline of sociology a sense of the excitement and perplexity that can come out of a deeper investigation into the nature of human actions than our ordinary commonsense understandings bring us to. We have designed the book to elicit appreciation for the ingenuity various social critics and analysts have shown in their effort to promote a better comprehension of what happens when people join together in communities and of the problems that arise from communal living.

This book is intended to excite the interest of students of the social sciences. That interest, if it is kindled, should lead the reader to the original works of those who are mentioned here and to the original works of many other writers before there can be a better understanding of how complex, tangled, and demanding the study of sociology is when it is taken up with any kind of seriousness.

❖ The Relevance of Knowing Names

Before we move into the organization and structure of the book, we would like to comment on the relevance of being familiar with the names, theories, and major ideas of leading figures in one's field. We suggest that students of social science take the time and trouble to memorize the names of at least some of the authors and books mentioned in the pages that follow. Know who Robert Merton is. Associate his name with manifest and latent functions. Know who Émile Durkheim is and associate his name with concepts such as anomie, the collective conscience, and the distinction between sacred and secular events. A student of literature who is not familiar with the names of such writers as Virginia Woolf, John Donne, Algernon Swinburne, and Ralph Waldo Emerson would be considered unworthy to be called a student of literature. Why social scientists should think they are absolved from knowing the names of leading figures in their own field is something of a mystery to us. Certainly it is important to know the major issues and how these issues have been attacked by different thinkers. But it reveals technical competence and a more sound understanding of these matters for a student to be aware of precisely who is thinking what and when and where and why.

Yet another good reason for knowing names is that it helps bring to mind matters and concepts about which one has a general but hazy sense. Knowledge is something that disappears without use or without constant reminders. One can reinvigorate memory simply by mentioning old, familiar names or works. Furthermore, names provide common touchstones for the student of social science. If, for example, you have read Lewis Carroll's *Alice in Wonderland* and I have read the same book, then, in a most real sense, we have been visitors in the same country. We can communicate better because we have shared that experience. This, at least in part, is why we have a "classical" literature. It is a literature that, because it is shared by such large numbers of people, provides in itself a powerful basis for communication. When you tell a friend you know someone who is a lot like the Red Queen in looks and temperament, you have provided a brief but complex descriptive statement.

With sociological literature, it is much the same. If we are discussing religion and we have both read Durkheim, then we do not have to engage in prolonged discussions to make clear the knowledge we already share. In other words, literature—whether it is classical or sociological—is meant to be read carefully and used to facilitate understanding. It is not something to be read and dismissed. Above all, it is not something to be approached with the attitude that one does not have to get a solid grasp of who developed an idea and where and when it was developed. This awareness is necessary to have a better command of the idea itself. Students today are inclined to think that all they need to know is the general idea of something. It is not enough.

We would also like to make a second comment before we move into the organization of this book. It is our belief that being good social scientists calls for a broad knowledge, on the one hand, combined with a special or particularly preferred mode of interpretation, on the other. The special preference of the student should, we think, come after some investigation has taken place with respect to the various possibilities that exist. In other words, the student should keep an open mind about things. He or she should try out different ideas and see which are congenial to his or her experiences and temperament. But give each new idea a fair shake before rejecting or accepting it.

❖ *Varieties of Social Thought*

There are many ways to approach the study of human social activities. We shall mention only a few at this point to illustrate what we are talking about. There is, of course, the Marxist perspective, which has a large number of followers. There is the structural-functional perspective, which has been strongly influential in American academic social thought. The period following World War II saw the rise of a group of investigators who attempted to construct mathematical models of the workings of social and economic systems. Interactionist theory—specifically symbolic interaction—has also been influential in America and Western Europe in the years following World War II. Quite recently, another major movement in the social sciences labeled critical theory has arisen out of conflict theory to challenge both functionalism and interactionist approaches. In a radically different style, there has been the development of a school of thought known as ethnomethodology. Another approach that has appeared in recent years has been sociobiology. The differences between these perspectives can be quite extreme. The proponents of one school of thought on occasion find it impossible to understand what the proponents of another school of thought are trying to do. For example, statistically oriented social scientists or those endorsing a mathematical approach to the study of social systems generally find it difficult to accept the efforts of a sociologist who espouses an ethnographic, qualitative, or case study method of studying the lives of people.

We mention this diversity of approaches because we believe that a person who is considering moving seriously into the study of human social systems should first become acquainted with the variety of possibilities that exist. Perhaps drawing an analogy will make our point a little clearer: A good artist usually experiments with a variety of techniques and styles before eventually evolving the one that is appropriate for his or her talents and artistic development. There is no reason why an artist cannot establish a single style at the outset and stay with it for the remainder of his or her artistic life. This was pretty much the case with Norman Rockwell, and he was a successful person. However, great artists, such as Pablo Picasso, acquire greatness by examining many styles and techniques and becoming effective with all of them—from the realistic to the most impressionistic and abstract.

We would like to suggest that the situation is similar for students moving into the social sciences. Such students should first attempt to remain as open as possible to the variety of styles, techniques, approaches, and concerns that are recognized in academic centers today. Each approach should be evaluated in terms of its strengths and weaknesses, and the student should acquire a thorough understanding of each. Only then will it be appropriate to select a particular technique or approach as the one most congenial and proper for intensive development. We do not believe that a person should harbor prejudice, contempt, or fear of any particular point of view without thorough examination. After all, a large number of quite intelligent people have endorsed, and attempted to promote, the progress of each of the established academic perspectives that are currently a part of the social sciences.

We would like to suggest that the reader retain, as much as possible, an open mind toward the various arguments that the representatives of different schools of thought have made. Open-minded or not, the reader of social science literature should develop the ability to work within any point of view and to present essays and arguments that show a command of each point of view. Just as the artist spends a lot of time copying old masters while developing a sense of craftsmanship, the student of social science should be able to copy the style and character of a particular school of thought in sociology or anthropology or political science.

It is instructive, in this regard, to read Norman Podhoretz's engaging book, *Making It,*[1] in which he describes his training as a writer at elite English schools. Not only were students asked to write essays in the style of some well-known author, such as Ernest Hemingway, Virginia Woolf, or Thomas Carlyle, but they were also expected to be able to parody, let us say, Hemingway, as James Thurber might write the parody. Few students in American schools—it has been our experience at least—would tolerate such an assignment. Yet without making this sort of effort, one can gain little real working understanding of what a school of thought is all about. The student must attempt to incorporate the style, the perspective, and the understanding into his or her *work*. Anything less is, to use the vernacular, an intellectual cop-out.

We have suggested, then, that it is good for a student or reader of social science to acquire, quite early in the game, a sense of the diversity of thought that exists in the social sciences. The student should move within this diversity, examine it, and begin to make decisions about which point of view is most acceptable. Two or three years is not too long to spend in this kind of examination. Professionalism in the social sciences is, in part, a matter of knowing the range of thinking that exists concerning social issues and what the strengths and weaknesses of each position are. The temptation is to latch onto a single point of view and accept the comfort that singular reasoning offers. We cannot prevent this, but we think it reveals a lack of intellectual character.

To be a serious and well-trained social scientist requires, we believe, a mastery of the extent to which social theories vary in their nature and types. This book gives a limited overview of the extent of this variety without presenting it in such detail that it would ultimately prove confusing. Even though our coverage is necessarily limited, the demands on the good student are severe. The reader is not only called on to note that Max Weber stresses the nature of bureaucratic organization or that Harold Garfinkel is an eth-nomethodologist, but must also constantly keep in mind how each of these points of view is highlighted, in various ways, through its contacts with others. It is not enough, for example, simply to have some idea of what Sigmund Freud was talking about at the turn of the century. One must keep in mind how Freud leads into or away from what Durkheim was talking about. In sum, the reader must retain a comparative sense.

At the same time, we would like to think that studying the ideas of the writers included in this book will have some relevance to more than just academic craftsmanship. The question invariably arises as to whether or not such study is "practical." What can it *do* for people?

The question is not easy to answer. The practical value of social thought derives from the extent to which a person is aware of such thinking and can make use of it. The social essay is generally not pointedly practical. A treatise on repairing a bicycle tire, on the other hand, is purely practical. It is written with nothing more than a practical problem in mind. The social essay is rarely as mundane as an instructional booklet on repairing a tire. The social essay usually covers highly abstract and complex situations. It is rarely written with the idea in mind of some sort of immediate practical application. At the same time, almost any social essayist of stature has written about society because he or she believes such information is important for the society and that it is, in some sense, necessary. Occasionally the practical implications are made apparent by the author. C. Wright Mills, for example, was concerned with the abuses of power and the loss of democratic freedoms in the United States. We cannot think of a more practical human concern.

So it is with many of the writers whose essays and concerns are a part of this book. It is important to understand that the practical use of these studies does not come merely from reading and passing examinations in a college course. No writer presented in this book offers us an instruction manual on how to be a leader, or how to be happy, or how to achieve a great society. Nonetheless, hints for any of these concerns appear in the essays of even the most abstract theorists. It is for the reader (the intelligent and socially sensitive reader) to note them and use them in the circumstances that are unique to the reader.

❖ *Influences on Social Thought from the Industrial Era*

We have organized the essays in this book in a roughly chronological and historical order, beginning with social writers and theorists whose major efforts took place at the close of the nineteenth century and the early twentieth century. As we move with time and events into the twentieth century, we find that World War II had a profound effect on Western intellectuals. Until that time, there had been a growing optimism about the future. The century that preceded the cataclysmic events of war and a worldwide economic depression and then a second global war generated the most exciting sequences of change people had ever experienced. Virtually every major invention and innovation that we now think of as a part of our modern technology had its origins in the Industrial Revolution of the nineteenth century and the modernization and colonization that characterized the early twentieth century. Modern medicine, aerodynamics, the radio, evolutionary thought, Freudianism, Marxism, the gasoline engine, relativity, modern forms of mass production, movies—all came out of this historical period. There was a new hope. The technological successes of the age were dramatized in great "world's fairs" that attracted millions of people. The future appeared to be unlimited. The application of rational thought seemed sufficient to deal with any problem—including problems that came out of trying to organize people into effective communities.

So it was that thinkers near the turn of the century began to suggest that the powerful thoughtways of science should be applied to the examination of human affairs. The problems of individual behavior could be examined scientifically through the development of a disciplined study of psychology. The vagaries of the marketplace would eventually be understood in terms of the development of a more scientific study of economic processes. The political arena could be subjected to a more objective consideration through the development of political science. So it was reasonable that this optimism should eventually be elevated to the fullest extent by suggesting that the entire range of human communal activities could be examined scientifically and that such scientific understanding would enable people to achieve better and more ideal social structures. The new society would be as radically rational and as well designed as a modern jetliner. People would achieve greater efficiency in their social as well as technological efforts. Only time and effort would be needed to develop the necessary research and theory.

The turn of the century must have been exciting for people who were on the thresholds of new knowledge. There was the illusion of advancement. The future was one of progress. Even that most widely damned of all Victorian inventions, Charles Darwin's theory of evolution,[2] was based on the idea that progression was something inherently natural. Darwin set the tone, and down to the present time there are still echoes, very strong echoes, of the belief that progress is inevitable. Darwin said:

> The presence of a body of well-instructed men, who have not to labor for their daily bread, is important to a degree which cannot be overestimated; as all high intellectual work is carried on by them, and on such work material progress of all kinds mainly depends, not to mention other and higher advantages. . . . Progress has been much more general than retrogression.[3]

There were those who were concerned about the excesses that had developed during the early periods of the industrial age. Foremost among these was Karl Marx. He was outraged by the cruelties he saw carried out in the name of industrial progress. At the same time, the vision he offered the people of the world was an extraordinarily utopian one. People would achieve not only a new world of technological riches; they would also come to the point where they would be able to organize themselves into social and economic systems that would abolish class discrimination and the inequities of wealth which were integral parts of the times in which Marx lived. People would no longer exploit each other. There would be no poverty. Struggle and conflict would be reduced to the point where war would be a thing of the past. There is no stronger appeal in the literature of the nineteenth century than that of Marx, and he has had a strong influence on the minds of hundreds of millions of the world's current population.

❖ *A Time of Optimism*

The optimism inherent in Darwin's and Marx's visions of the world was shared broadly by a great variety and number of people concerned with improving the character of modern societies. The Great Depression of the 1930s was a bit of a jolt, but, in the final analysis, it only reconfirmed the belief that careful research and the development of appropriate theory could handle anything that posed a crisis for people. Economic leaders, following the theories of John Maynard Keynes, attempted to curb the economic frustrations of the Depression, and they eventually began to feel that an economy could be rationally manipulated. While this was taking place in the United States, the Russians were initiating a bold experiment in economic control. It was a time of optimism.

This optimism carried into, and a little beyond, the drama of World War II. With the return of American GIs to colleges and universities throughout the country, the future seemed bright. Allied forces had gained the victory. A major threat to democracy had been eliminated. Production levels were high. Education of a high order was being democratized through the GI Bill. Thousands who never dreamed of graduating from college were receiving degrees and going on to graduate school. It appeared, at the time, that nothing could stop our progression toward a more highly technological and civilized world.

Faith in the scientific method probably reached its highest point at this time. The technological wonders that came from scientific research created labor-saving machines and new levels of comfortable living. But there was something still more impressive: Science had won the war. Science was power. The introduction of science into the study of human behavior and human societies could only bring about more powerful forms of society. Science was turned to as a possible means of improving the moral character of humankind.

❖ The Situation in the Social Sciences After World War II

World War II, the very event that had created the great faith in science and the hope for moral progress, was also, paradoxically enough, the event that began to undermine that faith and that hope. World War II revealed just how powerful modern technology had become. It was an intoxicating time. Thoughtful observers, however, were beginning to reconsider what had happened. The war had shown that modern technology is indeed astonishingly powerful. It also revealed that people are possibly not ready for such power. There was now an absolute demand that people become morally wiser and stronger. If they were not any better, in terms of social understanding, than the generation that spawned World War II, there was little hope for the future. It was as obvious then as it is now that World War III would mean the end of civilization.

It was clear, then, that it was absolutely necessary to develop a better sense of humanity. It was necessary to create a social system in which leadership would be able to deal with intricately complex systems and not make serious errors. With each growth in the power of modern weaponry, the consequences of even one serious error were more and more likely to bring the final catastrophic terror. This was the situation the social sciences found themselves in at the end of World War II.

The challenge seemed, at first, one that could be met. The challenge of the war had been met successfully. Again, all that were required, so it seemed, were money, time, research, and the constant application of rational and intelligent thought. There was no problem that could not be solved once it had been formulated properly. If the moral order was a problem, then it would be solved. At the same time, it was not merely a matter of solving a complex problem as a test of human rationality. The point had been reached where the moral problem simply *had* to be solved. People could not continue to conduct their economic, social, and political affairs by following the social, political, and economic practices of the past. The lethality of the older systems of rule and organization had been made frighteningly apparent in the ruin and rubble of the aftermath of World War II. A moving memorial to this fact now stands in Coventry, England, where the magnificent new Coventry Cathedral, built after World War II, stands side by side with the bombed, charred ruins of the venerable thirteenth-century cathedral.

But if the war was a lesson, it was to become a most puzzling one. It was there demanding to be understood. What had caused the Holocaust? As philosophers, artists, writers, social scientists, and political analysts examined the war, they began to discover that here was a matter of such complexity and such peculiar character that it could not be understood in any total manner. There was an especially profound effort to understand what had happened in Germany. There were discussions of the "authoritarian personality," the "banality of evil," "frustration and aggression," the desire to "escape from freedom," and other studies.[4] With the passage of time, however, what took place in Germany and throughout the world appeared increasingly difficult to understand.

Worse yet, whatever lessons had been gained from the examination of the history of World War II appeared to be of little value in improving the moral structure of humanity. The very authoritarianism that had been fought against in Germany appeared in America in the 1950s, as repressive actions were initiated by politicians eager to exploit a growing national fear of Soviet imperialism. Then, only a decade or so later, America became mired in the Vietnam War. Confusion of a profound nature came from this experience: Here was the most technologically powerful nation on earth being brought to a standstill by people who lived in underground tunnels and who got about on bicycles. America's dream of the unlimited value of technology was checked. It made little point to argue that we could have used the technology to, as one general put it, bomb the Vietnamese into one huge parking lot. We found, when the moment came, that the technology could not be used. Science was not enough. To add to the growing pessimism, quasi-scientific "body counts" and statistics were being grotesquely used to offer an apparently rational interpretation of what, by the end of the war, was obviously a mad venture. For mature social scientists of that generation, it was a depressing confrontation with reality.

So, at the international and national levels, there were major social and political movements that could not be ignored and that, at the same time, revealed the importance of social science when it came to moving people in the direction of more rational and certain moral progress. There were some signs, however, from within the social sciences that indicated a growing disenchantment with the older dream of a logical and precise science of human social action. If there was to be a science of human social action, newer writers argued, it would have to be a science quite different in form from that which characterized the natural sciences. The natural sciences, for example, assume that the processes of nature are regular and that these regularities can be uncovered and described. Light, for instance, can be counted to conform, in a most regular manner, to the bending effects of gravity. The effect, in this instance, is astonishingly subtle,[5] but it is regular, and it can be counted on to take place anywhere in the universe and at any time throughout the billions of years of existence of the known universe. It is possible to find regularities in human social systems, but the most obvious ones are just that—obvious. The accomplishment of the natural sciences has been to probe ever further into subtle regularities. The social sciences have had limited success in uncovering subtle regularities. Quite often, a finding that appears strong in one setting is weak in another. It is much as though a law of physics that operated well enough in England in September worked quite differently in Japan in May.

One of the more shocking revelations of the limitations of the social sciences has come to light in the recent inability of modern economics first, to anticipate, and, second, to control, the peculiar circumstance of inflation combined with depression. Economics has been, and remains, the ideal social science. It uses mathematical logic and highly rational models, and it can point to empirical methods that are superior to those used in any other social science. It is the only social science whose practitioners are regularly awarded Nobel prizes. Still, with these advantages, the economic behavior of the nation as a whole has been sufficiently erratic to make economic conditions the major crisis of our age.

As we move into the twenty-first century, then, we have come to a time of reassessment in the social sciences. There is still hope, and there is still a serious commitment, but the problems now seem to be greater than they appeared to be for idealistic intellectuals of the late nineteenth and early twentieth centuries. There have been two major responses to all of this. We might refer to one as the "conservative" response. The conservative response presumes that the older vision was essentially correct; that whatever errors have come about have been human enough; and that all we have to do is to work a little harder, apply a bit more effort, research, and thought, and it will still work out. The conservative response still places its faith in mathematical models; the acquisition of great amounts of empirical data; the use of computers; and rational theorizing employing causal systems, path analysis, and other logical models.

The other response might be called the "radical" or critical response. It tends to reject not so much the hope of the older idealism, but rather the conservatives' emphasis on a limited conception of what constitutes science. Where the conservative response views human actions as intrinsically rational, along with the other basic processes of nature, the critical theorist's response claims that people are forced to solve essentially irrational problems and act in ways that, if rational, are not rational in any ordinary sense of that term. The older conservative social scientists rejected moral questions because they could not be dealt with in terms of scientific analysis. Science never raises the question of what, for example, an atom *should* do under certain circumstances. Science only tries to find out what atoms do in fact do. The conservative approach to the scientific study of human social behavior accepts this attitude. It ignores the issue of what people should do. It attempts to deal with what people do in terms only of what they are in fact doing. What they should do is another matter. But what people are doing much of the time is solving, on their own, the crucial issue of what they should do. The social scientist, in other words, may have bypassed the most serious of all human problem areas. If sociologists or economists or political scientists cannot assist us in making moral decisions, then what can they do? If they help make moral decisions, are they really being scientific? It was a dilemma that, by the end of the 1960s, had become painful. The response of the critical or postmodern theorists has been more open in its espousal of human agency and the empowerment of oppressed groups such as women and peoples of color; at the same time, these postmodern social critics have concentrated more on just how people deal with the problem of being ''moral.''

This sketchy overview leaves us with the following observations. Social science came out of the scientific and technological optimism of the late nineteenth century. A strong belief in the rational control of society, as well as of nature, continued through World War II. The massive horrors of the war, coupled with the debacle of the Vietnam War, however, brought about a tempering of the earlier optimism. The entire world is now in a precarious situation: Nuclear technology has been given over to the making of nuclear weapons. Why are these weapons so important? Why must we keep them when, obviously, they are the most dangerous implements of war ever imagined? The answer is that they remain the last resort for the resolution of social disputes. They are the ultimate sociological device. They are the final sociological argument.

So it is that our inability to create a truly effective social science has placed us in considerable jeopardy. The most serious threat to life on this planet comes neither from the physical universe nor from such biological threats as disease or lethal illness. The most serious threat to life on this planet comes out of our inability to transform our social and political systems in such a manner as to assure coming generations that serious social issues will not be resolved by nuclear forms of argument.

If for no other reason than this, it is essential that we begin to examine our social, cultural, political, and economic systems in a more rational manner—in some new manner. The ancient forms of social knowledge must be respected, but we are now called on to find something even better. To remain caught up in the old ways of thinking about human social and cultural systems is actually dangerous. In this age of nuclear and biological weapons, we find ourselves using social principles that were radical and innovative back in a historical period when material technology was concerned with the problem of how to shape metal. These old ways are no longer completely sufficient. Now, in the nuclear era, we must create a new sociology. We are not as optimistic about how easily this can be done, but the attempt must be made.

❖ About the Social Scientists in this Book and the Applications of Their Ideas

In the chapters that follow, we utilize a roughly chronological format. First, we examine the social thought and commentaries of several writers who began their lives and their social observation in the early twentieth century. These were social thinkers whose lives closed before the beginning of the postmodern era. We then go on to take up the ideas of those who lived to witness the beginnings of the nuclear and microcomputer technology, and we present their observations on the contemporary world scene. Near the close of each chapter is a section devoted to ''encounters'' with social thought which endeavors to present how a particular theoretical point of view or the work of a specific writer can be "used." We have tried to show how versatile theory is by selecting a wide range of applications. We offer theoretical discussions of matters ranging from the American compulsion to travel, to the drug problem, to the role of pets in American life. No topic is too small, nor is any too big. Our understanding of nearly anything can be enhanced by an imaginative application of modern social perspectives. Until we begin to use social theory, it indeed has little practical value. For those who develop an ability to use it, the theory's practicality becomes evident. Following the applications of theory, there is a section labeled "Putting Social Thought to Work" for the reader's further consideration of the uses of social thought.

We need to point out that although it is the proper effort of social scientists to be as scientific as possible without being rigid, it is still true that their subject matter consists of people and their communities. This is a subject that social scientists share with artists, philosophers, essayists, religious thinkers, journalists, and others who are not so totally dedicated to science. It has been traditional in sociology and anthropology texts to make much of the difference between people who are scientifically oriented toward the study of society and those who are not. Embedded in the Western worldview is an emphasis on rationality and the ability to find "explanations" for all phenomena and human actions. Therefore, strong prejudices and antagonisms exist among scientists, including social scientists, toward "mystical" explanations of human events.

As a result, social science and religious approaches to the human scene are in a state of tension. Social science is very much "this-worldly." "Religion" is "otherworldly." Social science is objective. Religion is highly subjective. Social science is concerned with the material world. Religion is concerned with the spiritual world. Social science is analytic. Religion is moralistic. We could go on; however, we do not want to add more fuel to the argumentative fires. Our own sense of the matter is one that is tolerant of both perspectives. There is no serious reason why a person cannot be a good social scientist and devoutly religious. The novelist Andrew Greeley is a Catholic priest and was, at one time, a well-known sociologist and social scientist. There is a place for both social science and religious sentiment in human affairs. Each serves, in its way, to advance the cause of human moral and social improvement.

❖ *The Social Scientist Versus the Humanist*

This book is not an attempt to drive further boundary stakes into the grounds of intellectual endeavor in an attempt to specify the lines separating the domain of the sociologist from that of the humanist. Nor is it an attempt to suggest that sociologists and social scientists are no different from novelists, artists, or romantic philosophers. They *are* different. Moreover, it is a difference that makes a difference.

Though there are considerable differences between literary-humanistic and social science perspectives, we would like to see greater recognition of the fact that each has much to gain from the other. It is possible today for a professor of English to bring further meaning to a body of literature by using the theories, observations, and concepts of the social scientist. It is also possible for a sociologist to use literary examples very effectively as a way of teasing further meaning out of formal sociological concepts.

Sometimes, in an effort to divorce themselves from their humanistic origins, social scientists go to great lengths to hide from others (and perhaps themselves) the fact that they are interested in matters that for thousands of years also interested philosophers, novelists, poets, or artists. In their struggle to achieve scientific respectability, social scientists have, for example, disclaimed an interest in evil: After all, it is an extremely difficult term to define, and it certainly lacks objectivity. They are, instead, concerned with crime and delinquency—defined in strictly operational terms. Rather than show an interest in the "art" of love, they are concerned with family disorganization—measured by divorce rates. Rather than endow people with dramatically heroic or antiheroic qualities, which is the eternal humanistic effort, they seem to prefer talking in terms of bloodless abstractions that remove us, as human beings, from the scene.

In this book, we try to make explicit the implicit humanistic concerns of social scientists. Each of the social thinkers considered in the following pages touches on some problem that has already been deeply examined in humanistic literature, but the social scientist brings a new view. Durkheim's own work, and the works that later evolved from his ideas, looked at faith—particularly religious faith—and attempted to give it a secular place in human affairs. Max Weber examined the loci of power, and, when he was done, the myth of the hero had lost some of its vigor.

The humanistic concerns of Marxism are evident to anyone who has read Marxist literature. Karl Marx was profoundly concerned with the causes and the alleviation of human suffering brought about by the economic exploitation of one group of people by another. Sigmund Freud was concerned with the problem of human suffering brought about by repressive moral beliefs. Freudian theory, in some ways, is pessimistic about the relief of suffering. Even so, it has offered twentieth-century humanity a vision of an ideal form of self-awareness, in which the person is able to achieve higher levels of consciousness and fulfillment than ever known in the past. George Herbert Mead was interested in the relationship between the individual and the greater community. Is the state more important than the individual? Is the individual the more important consideration? It is an old humanistic concern, and one that Mead resolved in a highly innovative manner.

The newer writers included in this book do not, by virtue of their modernity, ignore the older issues of humanistic philosophy. Howard Becker is interested in the complex relationship between those people who are labeled "bad" and those who are labeled "good." Erving Goffman offers one of the most unusual treatments of hypocrisy to be found in modern literature. Harold Garfinkel, more than the others perhaps, seems removed from older philosophical issues. However, one of the central issues in Garfinkel's writing is the problem of the nature of subjective experience and its effect on social interactions. Garfinkel (together with some of his students) has not denied the subjective—as have many modern scientists—and, in this respect alone, his work is relevant to the humanistic thinker as well as to the scientific thinker. Peter Berger is unique among the better-known social scientists of our time in the way he has tried to deal with the problem of freedom. Robert Merton's contributions to the discussions of human social behavior continue to open new vistas for us. Three of the social thinkers whose observations and writings on American society and culture have contributed to our collective self-image are Margaret Mead, Pitrim Sorokin and David Riesman. C. Wright Mills was a constant critic of the institutions of our society and the power they wielded. And finally, Elise Boulding has awakened our conscience to the need to end worldwide conflict, the need to institute a just world peace, and the role that women and men must play in its creation and perpetuation. This quick run-through can only sketch some of the different humanistic themes these writers have developed in their own ways. The list is not exhaustive, and it suffers from the drawback that several writers may deal in unique ways with the same general humanistic concern.

The great concentration on methods that has characterized social science down to the present has caused sociologists to eschew the nonscientific, humanistic approach to problems. Often, in this effort to place barriers between the social scientist and the literary person, the social scientist has lost sight of the fact that actually there is little difference between the central concerns of sociology and those of humanistic literature. This book tries to indicate these common concerns without making any claims that social science is the only way to approach them. We spend too much time, we believe, trying to resolve the problem of whether social science or literature should be turned to for inspiration and guidance in our lives. This way of phrasing the question, so typical of Western forms of thinking, is unfortunate. A more profound question is: How can we use both sociology and humanistic-literary pursuits to improve our condition? Each chapter in the book, therefore, attempts to point up the nature of the humanistic concerns of the social scientists considered here.

We should warn the reader once more, before ending this initial chapter, that it is impossible in a work of this kind to give a realistic presentation of the richness of thought contained in the works of people like Émile Durkheim, Max Weber, Karl Marx, Robert K. Merton, Erving Goffman, David Riesman, Margaret Mead, Elise Boulding, or any of the others presented here. We must, therefore, be content with the hope that we have caught something of the "spirit" of any given author. If we have been successful in this, then we remain confident that the reader will want to find out more about these writers by turning to their original works. Only by going to the source can one understand the full extent to which these theorists displayed the courage and tenacity necessary to remain locked in struggle with profound questions until the questions began to "give a little."

Endnotes

1. Norman Podhoretz, *Making It* (New York: Random House, 1967).
2. Darwin incensed Victorian Europeans, who were shocked and revolted by the idea that they might share a biological affinity with "lesser" creatures, such as monkeys and apes.
3. Charles Darwin, *The Descent of Man*, 2d ed. (New York: Wheeler, 1936; originally published, 1874), p. 137.
4. We refer the reader to such books as the following: T. W. Adorno et al., *The Authoritarian Personality* (New York: Norton, 1969; originally published, 1950); Erich Fromm, *Escape from Freedom* (New York: Holt, Rinehart & Winston, 1963); Elie Wiesel, *Night* (New York: Hill & Wang, 1960); Hannah Arendt, *Eichmann in Jerusalem: A Report on the Banality of Evil* (New York: Viking, 1963); and Bruno Bettelheim, *The Informed Heart: Autonomy in a Mass Age* (New York: Avon, 1971).
5. A beam of light aimed at the earth's horizon bends only a third of an inch over a distance of 4000 miles as a result of the earth's attraction. See Nigel Calder, *Einstein's Universe* (New York: Viking, 1979), p. 45.

The Sacred and the Profane

An Introduction to Émile Durkheim

❖

❖ The Invisible Social World

The social world is "invisible." That is to say, social relationships are not perceived directly by any of our senses; they can only be known by learning the meaning the relationships have for those who participate in them. To a surprising extent, most of us, including a few who should know better, think we can "see" social happenings. For example, when asked if they have ever seen a family, students in introductory courses—along with a lot of other people—quickly, and with few exceptions, reply in the affirmative. Of course they have "seen" families; after all, they have lived in one for the past eighteen or nineteen years.

Although people think they know a family when they "see" one, they really do not. The point is simple to make, and its implications, as we shall presently note, are quite profound. Suppose we observe a young man walking down the street with his arm around the waist of a young woman;

toddling behind them are several children. We immediately think we are looking at a "family." However, this collection of individuals may in no way constitute a family. Perhaps we are looking at an unmarried man and woman who are baby-sitting for a neighbor; or they may be related or unrelated in a variety of other ways, none involving kin associations. We do not know whether they constitute a family unless we ask them or unless we examine credentials that might certify them as a bona fide family.

So substantial is the social world, so deeply does it penetrate into our personal lives, that we begin to think of it as being in some way substantial. But it is not. Anything that is social is, by definition, not directly perceivable. We can only comprehend it by indirect means. Coming back to our example, we can go further with it: Not only have we never seen a family, we have never seen a student or a teacher. Nor have we ever seen a scientist, a saint, or a sinner. So it is with all socially defined statuses.

We can observe the people who occupy such statuses, but until we are informed that they occupy a certain status and we are expected to behave accordingly, we cannot respond in an appropriate manner. (There are epistemologists and philosophers who would even dispute the contention that we can observe people, but we do not need to go into such cloudy flights here.) The social world is something we can know only by being told what it is. We are vulnerable in this regard. If we are told one thing, we tend to believe it. If we are told something else, we believe that. We can see, immediately, a problem that sociology as a science faces. In other scientific studies, an object is what it is. In sociology, a social object is what we are told it is.

The social world is, then, largely an invisible world, and this constitutes a major methodological problem for the sociologist. This, of course, is not only a problem for the sociologist; every social scientist must cope with it. The cultural anthropologist, for example, is concerned as a scientist with the meanings that different events and things have for people in primitive societies. A true understanding of these can come only from an extensive immersion in the culture. One cannot merely observe what is happening at a physical or behavioral level and fully comprehend its anthropological value.

The "invisibility" of the social world, then, confronts us with a problem. Sociology is supposed to be a science, and science, after all, is based on observation. What kind of science is it that devotes itself to an examination of events that are, by their very nature, not directly observable? Worse yet, the events acquire their "reality" by how they come to be defined by those who observe the events.

We shall not belabor this question. Let it suffice, for the moment, to mention that many sciences (high-energy physics, for one) believe that it is valid to rely on indirect observation. The problem the invisibility of social identities poses for scientific sociology must be left to weightier methodological treatises. We will pass it by and move into the more engaging substantive implications of the invisible nature of the social world. However, before we do so, we would like to mention that the same things that make understanding the social world difficult for the social scientist also make it difficult for people going through day-to-day experiences.

❖ Social Influences: Effects and Interpretation

Let us begin by establishing two fundamental and realistic principles. The first of these is that social influences, though not directly observable, produce observable effects. We cannot, for example, directly observe those ideas and involvements that lead people into wars, but we can observe the aftermath of a bombing raid. We can say, then, that even though social forces remain hidden, they are nonetheless "real." They are real because they are real in their effects. If the invisibility of social forces appears to deny validity to the efforts of social scientists, the real consequences of social involvements give their work a scientific justification. Science, after all, is the serious examination of what is real.

It is necessary to mention this first principle because people want to deny the reality of social forces.[1] Apparently they go by the old maxim that sticks and stones can break one's bones, but social meanings will never hurt anyone. We argue, quite to the contrary, that society, though "invisible" and indirect, is powerfully real—and can be malignant as well as benign. The Durkheimian argument for the reality of society is a reasonable one. It is real because it is real in its consequences.

The second principle we must develop before going on is that the invisible and indirect nature of the social realm implies that it can be understood or approached only through interpretation. Only a few years ago, social scientists hoped to be able to do away with interpretation—always a kind of "loose" way of looking at things—and bring social and cultural reality to heel by finding its underlying, fundamental, substantial reality. The effort basically failed. Social reality still remains primarily a problem of interpretation.

Social influences daily confront us with the equivalent of "black box" problems. *Black box problems* are those given to students in electronics who are called on to observe the electrical energies going into and coming out of a mysterious black box and determine what is in the box on the basis of this information. So it is in society. We are given various kinds of information (and, perhaps more importantly, misinformation) about people, and we must reach conclusions about what makes them tick the way they do.

This second principle—that social actions are subject to interpretation—is significant because, paradoxically enough, the form the interpretation of social forces will take comes from society itself. This feature of society gives it a power over the individual it would otherwise lack. For example, if you live within a religious community, social interpretations of events and people will take a religious cast. If you are a modern youth, attuned to, let us say, the content of popular music and songs, the interpretive forms offered by the songs become a part of your way of "seeing" the world around you.

Here is a brief illustration of what is meant by the statement that society provides the form of its own interpretation. In earlier times, persons who behaved peculiarly were likely to be accused of harboring demonic spirits. This was in keeping with the religious temper of the times. Today we would be more likely to say that such a person is "sick." There is surprisingly little difference between the two interpretations of the *What is going on inside the "black box"?* problem posed by the person who is behaving oddly.

Both kinds of interpretations are ways of legitimizing the use of repressive sanctions against the individual. Both interpretations provide society with a justification for imposing penalties on the person who is violating proper standards of conduct. Both interpretations are capable, to a surprising degree, of blinding us to the moral or external or normal features of the actions of the person we believe to be possessed of the devil or sickness. In this way, we are armed by socially authorized forms of interpretation with a rationale for injuring others in the name of keeping them in their proper social place. The surprising thing is that this occurs in even the most sophisticated and knowledgeable of social orders.

If the fact that the social world is veiled or hidden behind interpretive meanings creates problems for the modern social analyst, how much more so must it generate difficulties for people living in simple, early, so-called "primitive" social systems. How did people in simple, early cultures respond to the social "black box" problem? How did they come to grips with complex, indirect, powerful, and invisible forces of social influence?

According to our second principle, they must endow these forces with properties they understand. They must rely on whatever they experience and whatever they know to interpret the invisible domain of human social life. Just as sociology tries to interpret society through the modern rhetoric of science, so must primitive people rely on their beliefs, their culturally given awareness, for social understanding. The end product of the primitive effort is often a mythology populated by supernatural beings or powers. The mechanism inside the black box is interpreted as a spiritual force. This, in a brief and inadequate condensation, is the argument made by Émile Durkheim in *The Elementary Forms of the Religious Life.*[2] This book is considered by Harry Alpert as possibly the best of his works.[3]

❖ Religion as a Form of Sociology

Durkheim claimed that religion is actually a primitive form of sociology; religion is an interpreter of the social order and, as such, is also its fountainhead.

> It is a consistent part of Durkheim's conception of religion that a deity expresses in a personal form the power of the society, a power clearly felt, though not so

consciously defined. God is society "apotheosized"; society is the real God. This identity is adumbrated in the totem animal, a "sacred object"; and more clearly shown in the personal deity, Jahveh, or Zeus. The tribal god is, like the totem animal, often confusedly conceived of as a member of the group; another evidence of the close relationship between group and deity.[4]

Durkheim, despite his agnostic and scientific mentality, held that no society can exist independently of religious forms of sentiment and action. Into any social event there will intrude religious forms of expression. Even science, that especially secular and skeptical human enterprise, is not immune to quasi-religious modes of thought and conduct. Indeed, to the extent that science grows and acquires the character of a "community," we may expect to find it incorporating more "religious" characteristics.[5]

But what are these characteristics? The most essential, in Durkheim's thought, is the quality of sacredness. Every society distinguishes between the sacred and the profane. At lower levels, relatively small communities within the greater society have their communal heroes and events that parallel, in a more subdued fashion, the sacred personalities and literature of the larger social unit. The distinction between the sacred and the profane is crucial and highly relevant to sociological understanding, for it is essentially a distinction between the social and the nonsocial. That which is considered sacred in a society is given its awesome or sacred qualities by virtue of its capacity to represent values, sentiments, power, or beliefs that are shared in common: The sacred object comes out of and is supported by the total society. The profane object, on the other hand, is not supported in this manner. It may possess considerable utility, but it gains its value primarily from the extent to which it is useful to an individual; it has little or no public relevance.

An illustration may clarify what Durkheim was pointing toward. When Babe Ruth was a living idol to baseball fans, the bat he used to slug his home runs was definitely a profane object. It was Ruth's personal instrument and had little social value *in itself.* Today, however, one of Ruth's bats is enshrined in the Baseball Hall of Fame. It is no longer used by anyone in a profane way. It stands, rather, as an object that in itself represents the values, sentiments, power, and beliefs of all members of the baseball community. What was formerly a profane object is now in the process of gaining the qualities of a sacred object. The introduction of religious elements into a secular pastime provides an insight into the nature of traditionally religious structures. Such "shrines" as the Baseball Hall of Fame take on the qualities of para-religious systems.

We might note further, in this regard, that sacred objects, sustained by collective sentiments, gain in value as their collective function is enhanced. We once again can come back to the principle that social forces, though invisible, are real in their effects. In this instance, the real effect is to transform the value of an ordinary wooden bat from its original wholesale price of a few dollars to an assessed real value of thousands and thousands of dollars. (There is a connection between sacred events and marketing dynamics that is implied here, but we do not have time to pursue this rather intriguing link.)

With Babe Ruth's bat, we have purposely selected an illustration that leads us away from traditional conceptions of sacred objects. Durkheim extended the concept of sacredness in such a manner that we come to see the process whereby the profane is transmuted into the sacred in a wide variety of realms. In the case of the bat in the Baseball Hall of Fame, we encounter a profane object undergoing a mild and limited form of transmutation into the sacred: It changes from a private object to a public object. In the process, it becomes distinctive in quite a special way.

The difference between sacred and profane objects has much to do with a comprehension of the nature of religious institutions. The definitive feature of a church or religious institution resides in the fact that the church is an organized body of people concerned with maintaining and responding to sacred objects.

> Thus a definition of religion exists: an interdependent system of faiths and practices relating to things sacred—that is, to such things as are separate and proscribed, faiths and practices uniting all their adherents in a single community, known as a Church.[6]

We respond to the sacred object with a sense of awe and respect. This response may, on occasion, be so overwhelming that we think our feelings come from the sacred object itself. This, argued Durkheim, would be a mistake. The reason is fairly simple. Anything and everything imaginable has, at one time or other, served the purpose of being a sacred object. An object that evokes mysterious and serious responses in one person can generate laughter in another. Sacred objects, in various places and times, have ranged from small bowls of urine or a preserved whisker in a little jar to jade statues and holy texts.

Because an astounding variety of objects may serve as sacred things, and because, in addition, what is sacred in one place is not sacred in another, the awesome character of the sacred object must come from outside itself. The sacred object represents or symbolizes something—a force capable of inducing submission, awe, a sense of personal impotence, humility, and powerlessness. The force that is capable of achieving this in relation to the person, Durkheim argued, is society. Thus, Durkheim came to the conclusion that the sacred object is actually a symbolic representation of social force.

Following in Durkheim's footsteps, a modern sociologist, Guy Swanson of the University of Michigan, has carried the argument further.[7] If the sacred object is a representation of society, and if societies differ in the way they are organized, then the socially held conceptions of the nature of the sacred should vary systematically with the way in which the society is ordered. Regrettably, we cannot explore all of the ideas and facts that appear in Swanson's work. We can indicate something of its spirit and its connection with Durkheim's thinking, however, by concentrating on how Swanson has demonstrated the connection between monotheistic religious beliefs and a particular type of social structure.

God and the symbols associated with God fall in the realm of the sacred. In fact, it is not especially rare to find religions in which the name of God is so sacred it may not be uttered aloud. What accounts for the forms these ideas take? If Durkheim is correct, there must be an association between a given social structure and the conception of God that exists in that society. Swanson has argued that religions organized around the concept of a single God evolved out of societies with particular organizational difficulties that developed as the societies became more complex.

At this point, before we can begin to understand something of the Durkheim-Swanson argument, it is necessary to introduce a qualification. When we talk of "monotheism," we must be aware that we are rarely talking about religious conceptions involving only one God. Usually we are referring to religions that involve a number of gods, spirits, and heavenly beings, with a supreme God or heavenly being standing above this spiritual host.

Instead of using the term "monotheism," Swanson uses the term "high-god religions." Our own Judeo-Christian religious beliefs provide us with a high-god religion of this type. There is not only a supreme God, but there is Satan, also a powerful god, who rivals the ultimate forces of the spiritual world. More significantly, and more notably to the sociologist, Satan is essentially a disruptive force—a constant threat to the solidarity and smooth operation of the community. The intercession of God Himself is usually required to keep Satan from wrecking the life of any individual and the community that the individual serves. We concede that Satan is a more complex personality than he is described as being here. He is not always directly disruptive. For example, in the short story "The Devil and Daniel Webster,"[8] Satan offers wealth, position, and a life of happiness for Webster's soul. Presumably Satan may thereby build up his power within the spiritual realm and then prove even more disruptive later on.

Now we can come back to Swanson's work and rephrase our question slightly: At what point in a society's development does the concept of a high god begin to appear in that society's religious beliefs and practices? (We have used the phrase "At what point in a society's *development* . . ." This makes Swanson sound more evolutionary than the specific facts of his study warrant. We have done this in the interest of making a complicated point in a relatively brief space. Technically speaking, Swanson's study is cross-sectional rather than longitudinal.) Swanson, again on the basis of an extension of Durkheim's thinking, suggests that a high god appears when organizational elements within a society begin to conflict with each other and bring about the demand for a higher authority that can resolve these conflicts.

Thus, a society organized strictly on a kinship basis, where the family is the principal organizing agency and has no other agencies conflicting with it, will have no conception of a high god. The character of the society does not require it. Such a society may believe in a diffused spiritual force, sometimes called *mana*,[9] or it may rely on other religious conceptions, but the idea of a high god will not appear.

Also, for theoretical reasons too involved to go into here, a society comprised of two major organizational groupings will not have a conception of a high god. However, when we get into the realm of three or more major organizational groupings, we move into a situation where one of the groupings must become dominant over the other two and must function to resolve conflicts between subordinate major components of the society. Thus, a society organized into kinship units, which in turn are parts of tribes, which in their turn are parts of a still higher level of organization (such as a kingdom or nation) will be likely to develop a religion that involves the idea of a high god. The concept of a high god is a manifestation of the organizational characteristics of the society.

All of this has been highly speculative and abstract. We are still left with the question: Is there any way of demonstrating whether this is true or not? Swanson's work indicates that there is a way. Moreover, Swanson's demonstration suggests that Durkheim was correct in his speculations.

To test the Swanson-Durkheim theory concerning high-god religions, Swanson obtained data from thirty-nine primitive cultures and examined their social structure and their religious beliefs. With the aid of several assistants, Swanson divided these cultures into those that had religions involving the concept of a high god and those that did not. The cultures were also divided into those having a "simple" social structure involving only one or two sovereign groups and those with "complex" structures involving three or more sovereign groups.

According to the theory, the idea of a high god should appear only in the cultures with complex social structures. Cultures with simple social structures should not have high-god religions. When Swanson ordered his facts, he obtained the distribution of cultures shown in Table 2–1.[10]

So, out of the thirty-nine cultures examined by Swanson, thirty-four conformed to the theory and five deviated. Statistical tests by Swanson indicated that the amount of conformity to the theory was much greater than we might reasonably expect simply by accident. Therefore, the facts do not give us cause to reject Durkheim's general theoretical position.

TABLE 2–1   Social Structure and Religious Belief

High God Religion	*Number of Sovereign Groups*	
	1 or 2 *(Simple)*	*3 or More* *(Complex)*
Present	2 against theory	17 for theory
Absent	17 for theory	3 against theory

Swanson, advancing further the theoretical perspectives of Durkheim, has investigated such other aspects of religious belief as the idea of a morally concerned God, witchcraft, the existence of the soul, and similar concepts. He has found them also to be related to different features of the social structure. We cannot go into these demonstrations here. Exciting as Swanson's research is, we must leave it and return to Durkheim.

❖ *Moral Order and Social Structure*

We began with Durkheim's speculations on religion because they quickly lead us to the heart of his understanding of society. According to Durkheim, the only legitimate approach to a comprehension of the social order is by an examination of morality. Because morality and religious thought are so closely conjoined in primitive societies, the investigation of primitive religious thought can be especially revealing to the sociologist. In modern society, the relationship between moral order and religious practice is more tenuous, but this does not diminish the value of examining moral force as a means of comprehending human social nature.

> But if there is one fact that history has irrefutably demonstrated it is that the morality of each people is directly related to the social structure of the people practicing it. The connection is so intimate that, given the general character of the morality observed in a given society and barring abnormal and pathological cases, one can infer the nature of that society, the elements of its structure and the way it is organized. Tell me the marriage pattern, the morals dominating family life [in a society], and I will tell you the principal characteristic of its organization.[11]

In his doctoral dissertation, published ten years before the above statement appeared, Durkheim presented, at great length, the rationale underlying his claim. This work, entitled *The Division of Labor in Society*, reveals that a superb sociologist can hold views of society as radically different from those of the common people as are the views of physical reality held by the best physicists. We can give a hint of the radical nature of Durkheim's thought by presenting his views on crime.

Crime, Durkheim believed, is a natural consequence of the existence of a collectively supported morality. Crime is therefore a natural part of *any* social order, because any social order requires a collectively supported morality. In itself, this thesis does not seem radical or inventive—but it quickly leads to a more comprehensive understanding of the nature of criminal action than we can arrive at through biological or even psychological approaches.

One of the perplexing aspects of criminal action noted by Durkheim is the fact that it is often action that does not appear to be directly harmful to society, or to any individual. As Durkheim wrote,

What social danger is there in touching a tabooed object, an impure animal or man, in letting the sacred fire die down, in eating certain meats, in failure to make the traditional sacrifice over the graves of parents, in not exactly pronouncing the ritual formula, in not celebrating certain holidays, etc.?[12]

We cannot, then, simplemindedly define crime as action that is directly injurious to the physical safety of the members of a society. There are too many exceptions to such a definition. Even more notable, there are cases of crimes that, though physically injurious, are less seriously punished than crimes that violate an exotic code—and Durkheim makes much of this fact. A modern example of what we are talking about is the fact that a white man in the United States who kills a black man is likely to be less severely punished than a black man who rapes a white woman.

We must give up the whole idea that crime is a simple form of injury to society when we consider further that actions that are capable of completely disrupting the entire society often carry no criminal onus at all. A stock market collapse, for example, can disorganize the social body overwhelmingly, but it is not viewed as a criminal act. (It should be noted here that this is Durkheim's example. The objection might be raised that a market collapse does not involve intent to engage in crime. Durkheim would reply that in all probability, most societies have not, throughout history, been concerned with intent in reacting to criminal action.)

A person may give serious consideration to an action that he or she has reason to believe might result in the deaths of thousands of people, and yet may be applauded as a hero rather than a potential criminal of fantastic magnitude. For example, a story appeared in the *New York Times* about the late president, Lyndon Johnson, stating that he feared that an action on his part might initiate World War III. At that time the horrendous destruction implied by this incident did not lead anyone other than a few extremists, perhaps, to look on President Johnson as a potential criminal of great magnitude.[13]

Crime is not, then, something actually or potentially physically harmful to society. Durkheim asked:

Shall we say [in modifying our conception of crime] that criminal acts are those which *seem* harmful to the society that represses them, that penal rules express, not the conditions which are essential to social life, but those which *appear* such to the group which observes them?[14]

This would seem to be an easy way out of the matter, but Durkheim refused to accept the gambit. There is more to it than that. This solution, appealing though it is, does not really get us anywhere because it does not tell us why societies introduce rules that are apparently useless. The important thing is to find out why various rules are considered vitally necessary, even when no direct connection between the rules and the viability of the society can be ascertained. Why, for example, was the medieval church so morbidly interested in sexual delinquency? Anthropological studies reveal numerous societies that sustained themselves admirably with sexual patterns the church condemned as highly perverse and disruptive. For example, Margaret Mead and Nicolas Calas cited a study that reported the marriage of a Chuckchee shaman to another male in the tribe. The institutional incorporation of homosexual relations did not destroy Chuckchee society.[15]

The problem is resolved if we can comprehend the extent to which Durkheim distinguished between the form and the content of social action. Though an impressive number of rules seemingly have little connection with the efficient operation of a society, they may, through the possibility of their violation, remain as standards of the effectiveness of the moral force of the total society. In this respect, it makes little difference what the rule may be. Indeed, the more powerful the moral force of the total society, the more arbitrary the rules of the system can be and still serve as standards of the strength of that force.

This kind of reasoning enabled Durkheim to make an unusual observation concerning the nature of crime. He asserted:

> We must not say that an action shocks the common conscience because it is criminal, but rather that it is criminal because it shocks the common conscience. We do not reprove it because it is a crime, but it is a crime because we reprove it.[16]

Murder is a classical illustration of Durkheim's argument. Murder receives whatever criminal status it acquires according to the extent to which it is reproved by society, not because murder in itself calls for its own evaluation as a moral affront. There are occasions, even in our own contemporary society where murder (broadly defined as taking the life of another against that person's will) is not reproved and is therefore not criminal. Police, at some times and in some places, beat prisoners to death without arousing any great sense of moral indignation in the communities they serve.

Criminality, therefore, does not inhere within the specific form of an illegal action, but rather in the content of that action when viewed in terms of the affront it offers to the moral conscience of the entire society. Curiously enough, according to Durkheim, the stronger the moral conscience of a society, the more likely we are to find murder less reproved than are acts against the body of rules that exist as the moral authority of the society. Durkheim stated:

> Thus, in lower societies, the most numerous delicts [offenses] are those which relate to public affairs, delicts against religion, against custom, against authority, etc. We need only look at the Bible, the laws of Manou, at the monuments which remain of old Egyptian law to see the relatively small place accorded to prescriptions for the protection of individuals, and, contrariwise, the luxuriant development of repressive legislation concerning the different forms of sacrilege, the omission of certain religious duties, the demands of ceremonial, etc. At the same time, these crimes are the most severely punished. Among the Jews, the most abominable attacks are those against religion. Among the ancient Germans, only

two crimes were punished by death according to Tacitus; treason and desertion. According to Confucius and Meng-tseu, impiety is a greater crime than murder. In Egypt, the smallest sacrilege was punished by death.[17]

Crime is action that has its meaning only because it violates the moral sentiments of society. It is a threat to the integrity of those sentiments and, as a consequence, produces a reaction. It is in the reaction that Durkheim comprehended the distinction between collective force and the nature of the individual. The general reaction to crime is punishment, but the significant thing about punishment is the extent to which it is carried out. No other creatures on the planet have displayed such talent with respect to punishing their own kind as have human beings.

Capital punishment is a case in point. If criminals were to "pay society" for their misdeeds by giving their lives, then it would seem sufficient merely to take their lives in the simplest manner possible—a quick and quiet garroting, perhaps. But this is not done, even in modern and presumably enlightened cultures. There is an institutionalized form of harassment that goes with taking a criminal's life. There are demeaning actions that seem to have the purpose not only of taking the criminal's life but of taking the criminal's humanity as well. Individuals may, for example, spend their final hours in a cell that is lighted twenty-four hours a day. They may remain in the continuous presence of a guard. Their heads may be shaved. They may wear shabby clothes and experience other forms of humiliation. The taking of life is not enough.

One of the most bizarre forms of executing prisoners we have heard of consisted of placing the condemned individual inside a large metal statue shaped in the form of a beast. This form of execution was practiced in ancient times. A fire was then lighted beneath the statue, and the prisoner was roasted alive. What made the execution especially ingenious was that the nostrils of the metal beast were designed as flutelike whistles. The screams and exclamations of the person being roasted alive were transformed into pleasant musical tones. Whether this actually happened or not, it takes imagination and a mentality oddly geared toward the delights of punishment even to think of such a perverted device.

We are now considering one of those simple questions that philosophers are fond of—childish to those who do not question, profound in its implications to those who do. What intrigued Durkheim was this: Why do people carry out severe punishments, of an elaborated and vicious nature, for actions that often appear to have little physical or material consequence? Durkheim's quest for an understanding of how human social systems are held together led him into a lengthy involvement with the problem of punishment.

Our own Western judicial philosophy nicely illustrates the riddles of punitive policies in human communities. For example, there is a peculiar illogic in taking people convicted of the same crime and placing some of them in a hospital because they are "insane" and others in a prison because they are "normal." What we are doing in such instances is confessing that, since an individual is normal, what brought about the commission of the crime is not evidently an inherent serious defect in character. It must, therefore, have been something else, and the only other reasonable thing left is social circumstance.

Here we come to the center of Durkheim's vision. In order for punishment to be meted out, culpability must be established. Social circumstances, however, are defined by the community, and the community does not generally establish itself as culpable. Yet, if a crime is committed, something must be made to account for the wrong action. Since social circumstances cannot be made culpable, it is the individual who is assessed. However, an insane individual is responding more out of individual influences than a normal person. Yet, strangely enough, it is the normal person who receives the punishment.

Therefore, in our culture one can experience the odd sensation of being guilty of being normal. The sane person may be executed, whereas the insane person is sent to an asylum, treated, and then perhaps released. It would seem, if we were being reasonable about this matter, that a person's normality would stand as the greatest argument for not punishing that person.

Current thinking underscores Durkheim's arguments, in that it is evidently based on the idea that a presumably normal person who violates the existing social code threatens the viability of that code, more so than an insane person. Our reaction is not concerned with the welfare of the person who broke the code. Instead, we are concerned with the welfare of the code itself. To the extent that the violator is considered normal and yet is subjected to punishment, he or she must be seen as a sacrifice for the welfare of the many. Durkheim would suggest that this is characteristic of all societies. In one way or another, it is a normal characteristic of human social systems.

For Durkheim, extreme and "irrational" qualities of punishment were a clue to the nature of collective sentiments. People are not only concerned with making criminals "pay" through punishment; they are concerned with making criminals an embodiment of suffering that balances an affront to the moral order.

> It is certain that at the bottom of the notion of expiation there is the idea of a satisfaction accorded to some power, real or ideal, which is superior to us. When we desire the repression of crime, it is not that we desire to avenge personally, but to avenge something sacred which we feel more or less confusedly outside and above us. This something we conceive of in different ways according to the time and the place. Sometimes it is a simple idea, as morality, duty; most often we represent it in the form of one or several concrete beings: ancestors, divinity. That is why penal law is not alone essentially religious in origin, but indeed always retains a certain religious stamp. It is because the acts that it punishes appear to be attacks upon something transcendent.[18]

The power of the moral order comes from the fact that it is a collectively held set of beliefs. That is to say, it is a set of strongly held beliefs shared in common by a large number of people; it lies within the public as well as the individual domain. It is essential to understand that it is the collective nature of the moral order that gives it tremendous influence and that elevates it above any single individual. Indeed, the moral order acquires a solidarity or a kind of reality *sui generis* (of its own kind). For this reason, crimes are more than an affront to the individual. They are a threat to the solidarity of the moral order, and the reaction is beyond anything that might seem reasonable to a dispassionate observer.

Thus it is that we, from our present disengaged vantage point, can feel a sense of horror when we read the punishment prescribed by the ancient Germans for damaging a tree.

> Sacred groves were common among the ancient Germans, and tree worship is hardly extinct amongst their descendants at the present day. How serious that worship was in former times may be gathered from the ferocious penalty appointed by the old German laws for such as dared to peel the bark of a standing tree. The culprit's navel was to be cut out and nailed to the part of the tree which he had peeled, and he was to be driven round and round the tree till all his guts were wound about its trunk.[19]

Whether anyone actually suffered this dreadful punishment we do not know. Certainly history offers us countless examples of people who were made the objects of obsessive punishment. Even if no one actually experienced this gruesome punitive measure of the ancient Germans, it exemplifies what Durkheim was trying to say. From a modern perspective, it seems unthinkable that anyone could want to disembowel a person merely because he or she damaged a tree.

That is precisely Durkheim's point. The reaction hinted at in this old punishment transcends a rational, objective, and individualistic consideration of the matter. The threat is not to an individual sentiment, but to a collectively shared sentiment—and the reaction stems from that collective source, not from an individual source. So it is that we must come to understand crime and punishment as actions and reactions taking place at a collective level.

Durkheim's considerations of crime are actually a means of entering into a greater matter—an examination of the changing nucleus of social order. Repressive punishment occurs when the solidity of a society comes from its collective commitment to a moral order of some kind. By sharing similar beliefs, traditions, and moral sentiments, people are strongly held together by their common morality. Any challenge to the collective sentiments of such societies is met with the full force of an outrage that is sustained not by any single individual, but by an entire community of individuals.

But this form of social integration is in the process of being supplanted by another. The key to this is the fact that repressive punishment has been steadily declining in severity. Taking its place is punishment more concerned with the attainment of restitution than with making an example through torture or vicious punishment.

❖ *The Division of Labor and Social Structure*

If this is so—if we are witnessing the decline of social organization based on moral consensus—then what is the basis of the newer forms of social order? The answer, according to Durkheim, is a social order based increasingly on a complex interweaving of highly specialized and discrete units that together make up an organic whole, somewhat as the separate and specialized organs of the body make up an individual.

It is necessary to mention at this point that Durkheim was careful to probe further than a simple physiological analogy would suggest. Indeed, he went to great lengths to show the limitations of a biological model for the analysis of society. Durkheim stated: "The division of social labor is distinguished from the division of physiological labor by an essential characteristic. In the organism, each cell has its defined role, and cannot change it. In societies, tasks have never been so immutably distributed."[20]

Such a society, organized on the basis of the division of labor, acquires an increasing amount of differentiation between its parts. An idea of the extent of this differentiation in the modern United States can be ascertained by a quick reference to the *Dictionary of Occupational Titles*. It currently lists more than 35,550 job titles.

As this division occurs, the moral basis that forms the common sentiments underlying the society grows broader but does not cease to exist. The violent forms of reaction that characterize its existence in primitive cultures give way to reproval of a more feeble sort. A member of the U.S. Congress who violates the codes of ethics of the Congress, such as they are, is not drawn, quartered, and beheaded. He or she may receive a censure or, at worst, be ousted from office.

Even where society relies completely upon the division of labor, it does not become a jumble of juxtaposed atoms, between which only external and transient contacts take place. Rather, its members are united by ties that extend deeper and far beyond the short moments during which specific exchanges are made. Each of the functions they exercise is, in a fixed way, dependent upon others, and with them forms a united system. Because we fulfill some certain domestic or social function, we are involved in a complex of obligations from which we have no right to free ourselves. There is, above all, an organ upon which we tend to depend more and more; this is the state (that is, the political organization constituting the basis of civil government). The points at which we are in contact with it multiply, as do the occasions when it is entrusted with the duty of reminding us of the sentiment of common solidarity.[21]

A further sense of what Durkheim was trying to tell us can be gained by considering the question of how many people we rely on to get through an ordinary day. For example, how many people make it possible for you to drive home in the evening? If you give the matter a little thought, you see that the number quickly becomes impressively large—on the order of hundreds of thousands. You begin by adding up the people who were involved in: finding, obtaining, and distributing the gasoline you rely on as fuel; designing and producing the windshield, the wipers, and then each of the other parts of your automobile; making and maintaining the road; producing the clothes you are wearing; producing and distributing the food you rely on to get through the day; and so forth.

At any point in time we are sustained, as it were, by an invisible ocean of hands and unheard voices. The more affluent our lives, the more dependent we are on others. We are the dependent creature *par excellence*. Our lives are increasingly dependent on a social order that exists through a complex division of labor. This complex division of labor, of course, now extends outward on a global level, whereas earlier it was more localized.

The division of labor, specialization, the integration of highly differentiated parts—this is a later basis of social solidarity that comes out of and moves alongside the older moral basis. The division of labor is a second ring of force in a nucleus that has the moral order at its core.

This theme, the reality and force of the collectively supported moral order, was dominant in Durkheim's thinking and appeared throughout all his work. It provided the foundation for his masterful investigation into the nature of suicide. So brilliantly did Durkheim execute this combination of theory and research that it is even today lauded as a model of investigation in social science, though Durkheim published the work in 1897.[22]

❖ *Suicide and Its Relation to Social Forces*

But why would Durkheim, a man interested in the nature of social organizations, be concerned with something as individualistic as suicide? The answer is that suicide provided Durkheim with a subject matter that permitted him to carry off a *tour de force*. If Durkheim's sociological perspectives permitted him to bring new understanding to that most individualistic of all acts, suicide, then sociology would be forcefully established as a perspective for examining other features of human actions. How did Durkheim accomplish this demonstration?

It would appear, from a commonsense perspective, that people who kill themselves engage in an act that is about as private and as removed from social approval as can be imagined. For Durkheim, however, the issue was whether or not the intrusion of social influences could be found even here, in this most personal and final moment. If the intruding social forces could be found, then a nice case could be made for seeing people as more than the sum of their biological and psychological natures; they would have to be viewed also as captives of social forces extending beyond them and shaping their private fate.

Here it is worth mentioning that Durkheim is often viewed as an "antipsychological" writer. This is not entirely correct. It is fairer to say that he was concerned with getting people to recognize the value of social as well as biological and psychological factors in human affairs. In order to draw people away from an excessive involvement with psychological approaches, he was occasionally excessive himself. However, the central thrust of his work is toward bringing greater balance between psychological and sociological approaches to human affairs.

Durkheim began his argument by suggesting that perhaps suicide is such an individualistic act it might not be of interest to a sociologist. Anything that would make suicide demonstrably a result of individualistic conditions would, therefore, negate a sociological consideration of the matter. So it was necessary at the outset to consider all individualistic factors to determine whether or not they could account for self-inflicted deaths.

> But is [suicide] of interest to the sociologist? Since suicide is an individual action affecting the individual only, it must seemingly depend exclusively on individual factors, thus belonging to psychology alone. Is not the suicide's resolve usually explained by his temperament, character, antecedents and private history?[23]

Note here that Durkheim began by recognizing the theoretical position he intended to oppose. He was aware that he must develop it thoroughly before he could enter into a discussion of the social perspective he endorsed.

The first psychological argument he took into account was the possibility that suicide is a product of insanity, mental imbalance, or a derangement of a person's abilities. To refute this argument, Durkheim obtained data from hospitals for the mentally ill. He observed that the proportion of women in such hospitals was slightly greater than the proportion of men. This being the case, he argued, we ought to expect suicide resulting from insanity to occur as often among women as among men. Suicide rates indicated, however, that men are three to four times as likely to commit suicide as are women.[24]

Durkheim then examined the extent to which the incidence of insanity varied among Protestants, Catholics, and Jews. He found that Jews were more likely to experience mental disorders than were Protestants and Catholics. However, despite this, the Jewish people had lower suicide rates. From this, Durkheim concluded that suicide varies in inverse proportion to psychopathic states, rather than being consistent with them.[25]

But sanity is only one individualistic possibility. There are others. Perhaps, suggested Durkheim, alcoholism is a factor in suicide. Durkheim quickly discounted this by comparing maps of the distribution of suicides in France with maps showing the distribution of prosecutions for alcoholism. There was no relationship between the two.

If abnormal psychological conditions and alcoholism do not account for suicide, perhaps there are yet other nonsocial influences that do. Race, for example, may have an effect on suicide. Durkheim did not have much racial variation among the nationalities he studied, but he showed great ingenuity in his analysis of the facts that were available at the time. Taking the Germans as a racial type, he observed that in different Austrian provinces the proportion of Germans varied from high to low. (Durkheim used what would today be considered an ethnic or national type and not a racial type. Germans are part of a broader Caucasian racial grouping, which includes most of the people of Europe who were included in Durkheim's data.) If the racial factor were important, Durkheim said, then suicide rates should vary along with the proportions of Germans in the provinces. But the suicide rates behaved erratically in conjunction with Durkheim's racial factor. For example, provinces with high proportions of Germans had both high and low suicide rates. Provinces with low proportions of Germans also had high and low suicide rates. Durkheim concluded that race does not affect suicide.

Yet another class of nonsocial influences remained to be considered. Perhaps the physical environment has an effect on suicide. Possibly climate or weather may determine or at least be associated with self-destruction. Here Durkheim ran into a problem, because the facts did support a relationship between seasonal changes in weather and the occurrence of suicide.

> The monthly variations [in the incidence of suicide] obey the following law, found in all European countries: Beginning with January inclusive, the incidence of suicide increases regularly from month to month until about June and regularly decreases from that time to the end of the year.[26]

But any number of other social activities follow the same law. Railroad receipts are greatest in the summer and lowest in the winter. Accidents increase in the summer and decline in the winter. Crime increases in the summer and decreases in the winter. Durkheim admitted that there was a relationship, but then discounted its significance by claiming that weather is simply associated with human activity in general. Because suicide is one form of human activity, it happens to vary with the weather.

Finally, Durkheim considered the possibility that suicide is a product of imitation or of mass contagion—that a person may commit suicide because it is a fad. The evidence and arguments Durkheim used to dispense with this suggestion are too lengthy to dwell upon here. However, he made a comment that sums up his rejection of imitation as an explanation of suicide:

> Certain authors, ascribing to imitation a power it does not possess, have demanded that the printing of reports of suicides and crimes in the newspapers be prohibited. . . . Actually, what may contribute to the growth of suicide or murder is not talking of it but how it is talked of. Where such acts are loathed, the feelings they arouse penetrate the recital of them and thus offset rather than encourage individual inclinations. But inversely, when society is morally decadent, its state of uncertainty inspires in it an indulgence for immoral acts frankly expressed whenever they are discussed, and which obscures their immorality. Then example becomes truly dangerous not as example but because the revulsion it should inspire is reduced by social tolerance or indifference.[27]

What happens, for example, when people endow their lives with meaning in terms of a code of conduct and then are not permitted to live in the manner they have come to feel is important to them? If, under these circumstances, such a person commits suicide, it is certainly not imitative. It may, to the contrary, be a reaction to a denial to conform to a socially prescribed code.

We have not, in the paragraphs above, done justice to the patience and thoroughness of Durkheim's consideration of views that he felt were in error. We have, through his example, made one point, however. In the examination of human social conduct it is necessary to be as aware as possible of all existing relevant arguments and know the evidence that supports them.

Having considered positions contrary to his own, Durkheim went on to develop his sociological interpretation of suicide. He believed that the cause of suicide lies somewhere in the relationship existing between the individual and the moral order constituting the society of which he or she is a member. This relationship can vary in nature; accordingly, the individual is variously subject to inclinations toward suicide.

First, Durkheim considered the case where the individual is related to the moral order in a normally binding way, but the moral order itself contains within it ideas that make one see oneself as separated from it. For example, it is possible for certain forms of moral orders to place greater reliance on the individual to make the individual responsible for his or her own affairs. In this event, the people do not have recourse to the community when things go wrong. They are personally accountable.

Such people, said Durkheim, will be more likely to commit suicide than will those who believe they can turn to the community for support when they make errors. Suicide coming from this sense of individualism of a belief in freedom from the constraining moral order he called "egoistic suicide." Durkheim felt he had evidence to support this position by observing that suicide rates were higher among Protestants than among Catholics. The former religion places people more on their own, freeing them from institutional constraints to a greater extent and making them vulnerable to the limitations of their own egos.

A second kind of relationship between the individual and the moral order that Durkheim considered was one in which there is an intense binding of the individual to society. In this instance, one is so closely tied into the social group and is so much a part of the moral order that one is willing to give one's life for it. Suicide of this kind, Durkheim noted, still exists in the army and in those cultures that impose ancient forms of obedience. The rite of *hara-kiri* exemplifies this form of suicide. Durkheim used the term "altruistic suicide" to refer to this phenomenon.

The best example of altruistic suicide we can relate is a celebrated incident in Japanese history that occurred early in the seventeenth century and is known as the "Tale of the Forty-Seven *Ronin*." This incident involved forty-seven *samurai* warriors who cunningly avenged the death of their master, a minor lord, who committed *hara-kiri* after being insulted by an official in the *shogun's*, palace. The *samurai* retainers of the *daimyo* killed the official of the *shogun* and then, according to their code, met together in a grove after the assassination. There each of the forty-seven men killed himself.

The distinction between egoistic and altruistic suicide is not always a clear one, yet it seems necessary. The suicide of a person who feels despondent and guilty because of a belief that he or she personally has done a wrong for which there is no absolution seems different in kind from that of the *samurai* warriors who found honor in death.

Finally, Durkheim isolated a third form of suicide, which he called "anomic suicide." Anomic suicide, described in quite unacademic terms, is suicide resulting from the pain or disorientation that comes when we are pushed out of whatever social rut we become accustomed to. As a person matures within a society, he or she comes to develop a social character that is comfortable and acquires a conception of the moral order that gives stability and meaning to the person's life.

Various things can disrupt this. A poor person, for example, may suddenly fall heir to great wealth. Rather than finding the riches a blessing, he or she may feel alienated from former impoverished friends while remaining unacceptable to the established rich—the classic Eliza Doolittle bind. This condition Durkheim referred to as "anomie"—a state of normlessness, of being pushed into a realm where the rules are either ill-defined, contradictory, or lacking. In such circumstances a person, torn away from the regulative influences of society, finds life unbearable. The result is anomic suicide. Durkheim felt that the higher rate of suicide during times of economic crisis and among divorced persons supported his contention.

By relating suicide to social systems, Durkheim validated the sociological perspective in an almost sensational manner. He was wrong in several particulars, but the *tour de force* was accomplished nonetheless. After Durkheim, it became impossible to view the individual as an autonomous being, or society, as merely the individual's biological nature extended over the landscape. Society has peculiar qualities that come about from the nature of social organization itself. Society is a condition *sui generis*. Although society is, in general, beneficial to people, it still exacts a cost. Society enables the majority to live, and, paradoxically, is the cause of death for a minority.

❖ *Durkheim in Perspective*

Durkheim worked at the end of a century of magnificent scientific achievements, two of which should be mentioned here. Above all, the end of the nineteenth century was the age of Darwin; as a result, it was an age when humanity was being placed in truer biological perspective. But the obsession to divest people of their angelic origins led to excesses, until virtually every feature of human endeavor was believed to have its origins in strictly biological conditions. Durkheim's contribution is, then, all the greater when we recognize the extent to which he was moving against a scientific perspective of great respectability. If Durkheim seems excessive today, it is perhaps because he was attempting to counter another excess—that of biologism.

The second scientific feature of Durkheim's era was the value given to observable facts. The scientific ethic of the time was moving radically toward getting people to "put their money on" whatever could be demonstrated to be observably true. Durkheim's contribution is all the greater, therefore, when we understand that he was working within and against the handicap mentioned at the beginning of this chapter—the fact that the social world is not directly observable. By taking observable forms of action, such as suicide or crime, and revealing their connection with social identities, Durkheim gave sociological investigation a new basis in fact, and at the same time laid a course for social investigation that has continued down to the present.

The humanistic implications of Durkheim's work are not easy to assess. To an age that idealistically extolled democratic virtues and the autonomy of the individual, Durkheim gave the tempering concept of anomie: The price of individualism may be anxiety and death. Individuals require social regulation and order. Anomie is the other face of freedom.

In a century that saw the church being rudely elbowed aside by science, Durkheim further undermined the sanctifying rationalizations of religion by saying that God was simply a personification of social force. Yet, at the same time, he also provided the greatest justification for religious doctrine ever granted by a social scientist when he claimed that all societies must have religious commitments. Without religious dedication, there is no social order.

For the humanist concerned with the problem of evil, Durkheim offered little hope. Even a society of saints, he suggested, would identify among its membership those who violate the high standards of that saintly group. Social organization, a necessity of life for human beings, has as one of its properties the differentiation of its parts into the moral and immoral. Just as there cannot be a success without those who fail, there cannot be a good without those who are evil.

The moral order that is the pervasive force binding society together creates, in itself, the evil that is necessary to sustain it. Durkheim's message to the humanist concerned with evil is to recognize that somehow we all share in the process. To the extent that we are human, we are social. To the extent that we are social, we share. Though a judge who condemns an evildoer to die cannot legally condemn himself or herself as well, the judge should never lose sight of the greater matrix of involvements that brought about the evil and in which we have all participated and conspired.

Durkheim devoted his life to the endeavor that people should not lose sight of that greater matrix, which he called the moral order or the collective conscience. For that reason, if for no other, humanists as well as social scientists will long be indebted to him.

Encounters with Social Thought

A Brief Essay on Food

Theory is meant to be used. The profundity, the utility, or the power of theory cannot be appreciated until we draw on it for a greater understanding of the world around us. Theories such as those developed by Durkheim have broad applications. Virtually anything that is socially significant can be understood better by viewing it from a Durkheimian perspective. Although no theory provides a final form of understanding, each of the theories examined in this book can give us a new way of seeing the world. When theory is used in this manner, it leads to one of the finer forms of expansion of consciousness.

In this section of our discussion of Durkheim, we shall apply Durkheim's ideas to a topic selected more or less casually or at random. The idea here is to provide an example of how Durkheimian thinking can be *used*. The reader is encouraged to apply Durkheim's ideas to one of his or her own concerns.

We shall take as a topic for theoretical interpretation the topic of food. The idea is to show that theory can be applied to subjects that are not generally thought of as stereotyped "sociological" topics. Sociology is commonly associated with the study of crime and delinquency, poverty, divorce, and other so-called "social problems." Sociology, more correctly, is the application of social theory to *anything* that is a part of human communal activity. In attempting to apply a given social theory to a particular aspect of communal life, we are called on to exercise what C. Wright Mills referred to as "the sociological imagination."

To be sociologically imaginative calls for a basic understanding of theory and theoretical concepts. In this chapter on Durkheim, we have considered such ideas as collective representations, the sacred and the profane, the power of the moral order, division of labor, anomie, and altruism. These ideas form a kind of fundamental conceptual palette of theoretical "colors" for putting together a different approach to our topic.

At the same time, in working with a theory, it is essential to have a grasp of the primary theme that lies behind that theory. With respect to Durkheim's work, this theme is that a new form of reality comes into being when relatively large numbers of people gather and form communities of different kinds. We shall refer to this new reality as "social reality." Social reality is different from biological or psychological reality. It interacts with people as individuals, but it is not the same thing. What an individual may desire, strictly as an individual, and what the community brings an individual to want as a member of the community can be quite different. With this in mind, we can now turn our attention toward food as a topic.

One quite personal and organic or biological feature of living involves food and eating. What could be more individualistic than getting hungry, finding food, and then eating it? However, Durkheim's argument is that people are transformed, as it were, by the fact that they are immersed in social and cultural forms of reality. So food and eating become not simply matters of individual appetites and inclinations, but also matters of social and cultural forces. As the slogan puts it, we may be what we eat. But what we eat and how we eat happen to be influenced, to a high degree, by how our society is ordered.

To begin with, the modern American typically has an unusual relationship to food: He or she has little idea of how to obtain it in any direct fashion. In a smaller society, with less elaborate division of labor, everyone is engaged much of the time in the quest for food. Food is an immediate and constant concern. In such a social and cultural context, food conveys a different message than it conveys to us.

As food becomes integrated into an ever more refined system in which the division of labor is increasingly refined and elaborated, the typical individual not only loses any sense of how to obtain food directly from nature, but increasingly loses any sense of how to prepare food. For example, one of the simplest forms of food preparation imaginable is the making of pancakes. Nonetheless, prepared pancake mixes are now a popular staple on American supermarket shelves.

The careful preparation of food is no longer a common understanding among families. It has become the sport of those who are possessed of sufficient leisure to indulge in more archaic art forms. The baking of bread is a case in point. Bread is a specialized product prepared in bakeries and sold in mass quantities. When it is made in the home, its preparation acquires much the same social meaning as any other hobby might. It becomes a peripheral rather than a central activity. Food work, like other forms of work in modern complex social systems, is now the unique province of the specialist. The consequence is a society in which more and more people spend more and more time eating outside the home. According to recent estimates, Americans eat more of their food outside the home than within it.

The restaurant is a feature of modern society. It does not appear in simpler societies. Feasting and special food occasions seem to be common, however, in simpler cultures. These are generally a matter of total community participation. Everyone watches as the food is prepared— pigs may be shot with arrows, released to die, and then butchered. In simple hunting societies, a successful hunt may result in the meat from the hunted animals being distributed throughout the village and then eaten. After the food is consumed, the hunt begins once more.

With the introduction of highly specialized professions interacting within an elaborate system of division of labor, the production, preparation, and distribution of food become parts of the more generic process of social specialization. Food, along with other aspects of the society, acquires a unique character and history. No individual, for example, wants a tomato that is unusually hard and tough. However, an industry concerned with shipping soft perishables finds such a tomato to its advantage. As a consequence, we find ourselves living today with hard tomatoes, whether we like them or not. The point is that this kind of tomato has not been called into being by our biological or our psychological natures. It has been called into being by the demands of an increasingly complex socioeconomic system. Keep in mind that Durkheim argued that anything real in its effects is real in itself. The hard tomato is another reminder, and possibly not such a trivial one, that we are embedded within a complex *social* world.

The hard tomato is one form of a more general treatment of food— the creation of food that is long-lasting or well preserved. Various means of preserving food were known from ancient times. The foods so preserved were limited pretty much to those that could be pickled, salted, smoked, or dried. It was not until the end of the eighteenth century that a Frenchman named Nicholas Apport succeeded in preserving a variety of foods by heating them in champagne bottles.

The desire for better-preserved foods came, in part, from the increasing demands being created by well-organized navies and armies. The armies of Napoleon, for example, were so well organized and massive that they could not survive through simple foraging off the land. Problems with respect to provisioning his armies led Napoleon to offer a prize for better food preservation. The point being made here is that the new forms of social organization brought into being new demands, which in turn led to innovations that had previously not been considered.

The simple act of eating consists merely of food being ingested by an individual. All creatures do it. However, among human beings, as food is integrated into larger collective systems, the distinction between eating as a purely individualistic act and eating as highly social action becomes impossible to make. It is, for example, one thing to be walking in the woods eating blackberries that are growing wild. This is a relatively individualistic act. It is something quite different to eat a McDonald's hamburger. The hamburger, as we now know it in America, is an economic, social, cultural, and historical phenomenon. It cannot be understood in purely individualistic terms.

Historically, the hamburger originated in steak tartare from the Russian steppes—raw beef seasoned with salt, pepper and onion juice. German sailors brought the idea to Hamburg, where the meat was seared on the outside, leaving the middle rare. The delicacy was brought to the United States by German immigrants in the early 1800s. At the St. Louis World's Fair in 1904, a desperate food server started tossing meat patties on buns to deal with the large numbers of people clamoring for service, and the fast hamburger was born. It is only three-quarters of a century old. The history is a brief one.

It should be noted that the hamburger gained in popularity partly as a result of the general acceptance in England of Dr. James Salisbury's diet—ground beef three times a day with hot water. The ground beef became known as Salisbury steak. So the hamburger is a cultural phenomenon. More to the point, it is a product of modern mass markets. McDonald's brags that it sells one billion hamburgers every four months. The typical American eats three hamburgers a week.

The hamburger, as a mass-produced food item, is only one of thousands of foods that depend on a massive division of labor and an elaborate socioeconomic structure. Without society as we know it today, we could not eat as we eat today. When we go to a restaurant for our evening meal, the food we are served comes before us without our having to consider anything other than how we will pay the bill. We do nothing. Hidden from our view is the simple fact that the food on our plates is the product of hundreds or, more likely, thousands of individuals working in concert.

So far, we have emphasized the idea of the division of labor and its bearing on food. Within nearly any culture, food acquires traditional characteristics: It may be eaten in traditional forms or prepared in traditional ways, or it may, in itself acquire special prominence as a symbol of the culture or particular social group. Or, conversely, in modern mass marketing systems, a particular food may be sold by associating it with powerful cultural symbols—collective representations, to use Durkheim's expression.

> This local prominence [of the McDonald's chain] throughout the country had been achieved as a result of one of the costliest and most thoroughgoing [public relations] and ad campaigns in American corporate history. A massive apparatus of patty propaganda had made the trademark a household word, placing the McDonald's hamburger—the "all-American meal"—next to the flag, Mom, and apple pie. An unremitting campaign identifying McDonald's with every form of patriotism, community concern, and loudly-trumpeted benefactions had dinned the name into public consciousness. This campaign had been so successful that on the occasion of his seventieth birthday, Ray Kroc [owner of the chain] could happily announce, "I have had the satisfaction of seeing McDonald's become an American tradition."[28]

It is one thing to eat food which is merely healthy and nutritious. It is something else to eat a tradition.

The peculiar interaction between the individual act of eating and the greater social system can be seen in the extent to which eating in America has political ramifications. For example, in the 1970s, a columnist reported that the head of McDonald's contributed $255,000 to the Nixon campaign. The McDonald's operation depends on a low-paid youth labor force of approximately 150,000 to 200,000 teenagers who do it all for America.

The gift was seen by the donor as "some insurance in the free enterprise system." It was looked on by others as an effort to influence high-level decision making in American government to sustain a low-level guaranteed wage. (If each hamburger sold contributed one cent to the "gift," it meant distributing over 25,000,000 hamburgers.) We cannot even eat any longer without its having systemic ramifications throughout the society as a whole. The primitive hunter is responsible to the community and is understood as the bringer of food. In modern societies, few of us know or care where our food comes from or what our consumption of it implies in terms of the distribution of political power.

If we keep our understanding of Durkheim in mind, we begin to see that there is more to simple actions than we may first suspect. For one thing, we are less likely to lose sight of the possibility that biting into a hamburger may be more closely related to how power shifts in America than the ostensibly more collective action that takes place when we all go to the polls and pull a lever on the voting machine.

Putting Social Thought to Work

1. Durkheim was aware of the extent to which social forces are both powerful and, at the same time, invisible or indirect. We cannot "see" society directly. We must always infer it from what little we do see. At the same time, people make inferences about the social character of themselves and others, and acquire a strong sense of certainty about what they are doing. One way they manage this is by relying on abstract religious concepts that function as mythical "maps" of the social order. If this is so, we would expect leaders to make use of religious arguments to sustain their leadership. In what ways do leaders, even in secular contexts, make use of religious devices to sustain their authority? What problems does this suggest with the American ideal of the separation of the powers of church and state? From a Durkheimian view, is such a separation really possible?

2. The effect of the modern secular intellectual quest, particularly in the sciences, has been to destroy myths. The great debate in Victorian England over Darwin's theories centered on the myth of creation. The word "myth" has become a term of invective for ideas repugnant to the mod-

ern secular, empirical mentality. Durkheim argued, however, that society requires myth. What myths are common to the American culture? Why is it often difficult to be aware of the extent to which myth dominates our thinking? What is a myth, anyway?

3. One of the great issues raised by Durkheim was that of the human inclination to engage in complex, elaborate, and intense forms of punishment. Human beings, with few exceptions, might be defined as punitive animals. (Even the mild and peace-loving Zuñi Indians of the American Southwest would, on occasion, hang someone by his or her thumbs.) Americans are certainly not exempt from the punitive motive. We have a history of punishment—from lynch mobs to firing squads. Our literature and mass media are saturated with the vicarious delights of observing punishment being handed out to the "bad guys." What is involved in punishment? Is it possible to construct a human society without punishment? Is punishment simply "human nature"? If so, why are certain cultures excessively punitive and others not?

4. Durkheim shocked people at the turn of the century by suggesting that crime is a natural part of any social order. This sounds cynical. He argued that a society must create criminals in order to sustain a notion of what is "good." Is there an analogy between what takes place in the greater social order and what takes place in colleges or universities? That is to say, is there the possibility that a university is required to create a kind of "criminal" person (worthless, threatening, no good, stupid, anti-intellectual, and so forth) in order to establish its higher standards (students who are good, bright, intellectual, and possessed of "honor"?)

5. Durkheim's concept of "anomie" is a good taking-off point for a discussion of freedom. Durkheim found that people who are "anomic" have a significantly greater inclination to give up on life. But anomie implies that one is "free" of social obligations and restraints. Do people really want "freedom"? What are people really talking about when they talk about being "free"? If people were totally free, would society be possible? Is the concept of freedom merely an illusion? How is the term used politically by men and women of power? What are the possible social effects of having freedom as a political ideal? That is to say, what has a belief in freedom done to the family, business practices, the school, the military system, the political structure, crime, and other manifestations of the social system?

6. We have said quite early in this chapter on Durkheim that science, as it becomes a community, incorporates religious elements much as any other community does. This is especially noticeable in the way science presents itself to the general public. For example, modern public television programs dealing with scientific offerings commonly use religious or quasi-religious music as background music. Science defends

itself as an institution that seeks nothing less than to "explain" the entire universe (despite the fact that science has not as yet explained anything completely). In what ways does science use devices that are necessary for sustaining the morale and the solidarity of the scientific community? Are these devices, in themselves, scientific in nature (logical and experimentally proved), or do they possess characteristics similar to those used by any other human community concerned with problems of integration and morale?

Endnotes

1. A debate has gone on for years among sociologists as to whether or not society is "real." A popular technical treatment of this argument appears in a paper by Charles K. Warriner: "Groups Are Real: An Affirmation," *American Sociological Review* 21 (October 1956), 549–554.

2. Émile Durkheim, *The Elementary Forms of the Religious Life*, translated by J. W. Swain (New York: Free Press, 1954; originally published, 1912). Durkheim's other major works, all published in modern English translations by Free Press, New York, are *The Division of Labor in Society*, translated by George Simpson (1960; originally published, 1893); *Education and Sociology*, translated by S. D. Fox (1956; originally published, 1922—posthumously); *Moral Education: A Study in the Theory and Application of the Sociology of Education*, translated by E. K. Wilson and H. Schnurer (1961; originally published, 1925—posthumously); *The Rules of Sociological Method*, translated by S. A. Solovay and J. H. Mueller (1950; originally published, 1895); and *Suicide: A Study in Sociology*, translated by J. A. Spaulding and G. Simpson (1951; originally published, 1897).

3. See Harry Alpert, *Émile Durkheim and His Sociology* (New York: Columbia University Press, 1939). Alpert's work still remains one of the better reviews of Durkheim's contributions to modern social thought.

4. Charles Elmer Gehlke, *Émile Durkheim's Contributions to Sociological Theory* (New York: Columbia University, Longmans, Green, Agents, 1915), p. 39.

5. A sociological investigation of science as a community can generate pertinent observations. See Warren O. Hagstrom, *The Scientific Community* (New York: Basic Books, 1965).

6. Maurice Halbwachs, *Sources of Religious Sentiment* (New York: Free Press, 1962), p. 23. Halbwachs was one of Durkheim's most brilliant students. In this book he carefully summarized, mostly in Durkheim's own words, the central thoughts contained in *The Elementary Forms of the Religious Life*. We would recommend that a student interested in this subject read Halbwachs and then turn to the more elaborate discussion by Durkheim.

7. Guy E. Swanson, *The Birth of the Gods: The Origin of Primitive Belief* (Ann Arbor, MI: University of Michigan Press, 1960). Swanson's argument—and, more significantly, his data—reveal the current vitality of Durkheim's thinking in modern sociology.

8. Stephen Vincent Benét, *The Devil and Daniel Webster* (New York: Holt, Rinehart & Winston, 1965; originally published, 1937).

9. Swanson, *The Birth of the Gods*, pp. 6–10.

10. Ibid., p. 65. This is a slightly modified version of Swanson's table as prepared by the authors.

11. Durkheim, *Moral Education*, p. 87. In 1887 Durkheim began his distinguished academic career at the University of Bordeaux. This was the first time a French university offered a course in social science. Five years later he moved to the Sorbonne—the University of Paris—where he spent the remaining twenty-five years of his life. Durkheim taught not only social science but pedagogy, and he taught these subjects jointly throughout his career. (See Alpert, *Émile Durkheim and His Sociology*, p. 43.)

12. Durkheim, *The Division of Labor in Society*, p. 72.

13. The reference here is to the May 13, 1967, issue of the *New York Times*: "Washington, May 12. —It may have sounded ominous, but to the White House it was just a regrettable coincidence that no amount of explanation could overcome. . . . What had been for months President Johnson's personal story . . . suddenly broke into print today. . . . On the woman's page (*sic*) of the *Washington Post*—a staple in the news diet of every foreign diplomat here—[a news item] read, 'President Johnson told his daughter, Luci, last June, "Your daddy may go down in history as having started World War III." He felt he had no alternative, he said . . . and he felt he had taken all possible precautions to limit the effects, but there was reason to worry.' "

14. Durkheim, *The Division of Labor in Society*, p. 73.

15. Margaret Mead and Nicolas Calas, *Primitive Heritage* (New York: Random House, 1953).

16. Durkheim, *The Division of Labor in Society*, p. 81.

17. Ibid., p. 93.

18. Ibid., p. 100.

19. Sir James G. Frazer, *The Golden Bough* (New York: Macmillan, 1922), p. 127. Note the discrepancy between Frazer's comment and Durkheim's reference to Tacitus, cited earlier. According to Durkheim, only treason and desertion were punishable by death among the ancient Germans.

20. Durkheim, *The Division of Labor in Society*, p. 329.

21. Ibid., p. 227.

22. Durkheim, *Suicide*. For a work published in 1897 concerning human social nature, this book is astonishingly sophisticated. One need only compare it with more run-of-the-mill social research conducted at the time to see how advanced Durkheim's thought was. This does not mean, however, that Durkheim did not make serious methodological errors. For a balanced review of Durkheim's effort, see Hanaan C. Selvin, "Durkheim's *Suicide*: Further Thoughts on a Methodological Classic," in Robert A. Nisbet, ed., *Émile Durkheim* (Englewood Cliffs, NJ: Prentice-Hall, 1965), pp. 113–136.

23. Durkheim, *Suicide*, p. 46.

24. Durkheim relied to a great extent, in this study of suicide, on what are today called "ecological" correlations. These are tricky measures of association. See W. S. Robinson, "Ecological Correlations and the Behavior of Individuals," *American Sociological Review* 15 (June 1950), 351–357.

25. This is Durkheim's wording. See *Suicide*, p. 72.

26. Durkheim, *Suicide*, p. 111.

27. Ibid., p. 141. What Durkheim has said is that people do not blindly imitate actions that occur around them. Instead, they are more likely to follow or to imitate

actions that are highly valued. But this changes the character of the problem. If this is so, then we must ask why societies come to value particular forms of action and not others. We must also consider the position of the individual with respect to the possibility of attaining valued forms of social action.

28. M. Boas and S. Chain, Big Mac: *The Unauthorized Story of McDonald's* (New York: Mentor Books, 1976).

Chapter 3

Power, Bureaucracy, Money, and Religion

The Views of Max Weber

❖

❖ Introduction

Modern American sociology was strongly influenced by the works of Émile Durkheim and Max Weber. Possibly only Karl Marx had a stronger influence. Without question, these three figures stand as giants among the numerous European thinkers whose writings affected American social thought. Let us first consider Weber's time as it related to Durkheim's career. Weber's reaction to Marx is discussed later.

Durkheim was French; Weber was German. Both were born at about the same time, Durkheim in 1858 and Weber in 1864. Each reached the height of his active career in the years just preceding World War I. Durkheim died in 1917; Weber died in 1920.

Despite their different national identities, Weber and Durkheim had much in common. Both social thinkers gave paramount significance to religion as a historical and human force. In Durkeim's view, religion is a logical

47

necessity. One is forced to recognize and accept its existence, not only because religion is a historical fact, but also because it is logically a social necessity. As Durkheim saw it, the argument is essentially "If society exists,
then religion must exist." For Durkheim, religious sentiments of some kind
are logically necessary for human societies. They are theoretically essential.
No matter what kind of community we are involved with, it establishes its
sacred domains, which generate binding sentiments for the members of that
community.

Weber, with the German scholar's regard for history, approached religion by studying its historical forms in great detail until he reached the point
where he could begin to develop synthesizing generalizations. If Weber is
less exciting than Durkheim, he is more versatile. Durkheim was more narrowly dedicated to sociology. Weber's comprehension ranged across economics, sociology, political science, anthropology, history, and philosophy.

Even so, the differences between the character and intellect of the two
men are less significant than the similarities. Both were thoroughly committed intellectuals, and both were contemptuous of simplistic answers to
human affairs. More significantly, both turned to the moral order as the
fountainhead of social analysis. Both saw religion as a key institution in the
understanding of the social order. Weber was concerned with the specific
political and economic consequences of religious doctrine. He concluded, in
what is generally recognized as his most popular work,[1] that capitalistic economic practice is an outgrowth of ideas contained within Protestant religious
doctrine. Weber examined the pervasive effects of religious thought within
the social structure and traced in great detail the unanticipated consequences
of particular religious beliefs.

Weber's career is all the more remarkable when we note that he spent
nearly twenty years of his adult life disabled by emotional disorders, which
at times left him so enervated that he would sit by the window for hours
picking at his fingernails. He would tell his wife it felt good to do nothing.[2]
The contradictions in Weber's nature and the complexity of the man are
summarized in the following passage:

> Throughout his life, Weber was a nationalist and behaved in the mission of the
> *Herrenvolk*, yet at the same time he fought for individual freedom and, with
> analytic detachment, characterized the ideas of nationalism and racism as justifi-
> catory ideologies used by the ruling class, and their hireling publicists, to beat
> their impositions into weaker members of the polity. . . . He was proud of being
> a Prussian officer, and yet asserted in public that the Kaiser, his commander-in-
> chief, was something of which all Germans should be ashamed. . . . A model of
> the self-conscious masculinity of Imperial Germany, he nevertheless encouraged
> the first woman labor official in Germany and made vital speeches to members
> of the woman's emancipation movement of the early twentieth century.[3]

Weber's scholarship is as complex as his character. Any brief attempt,
such as this, to outline the significant ideas in his writing must preface the
effort with an apology. Yet it is necessary to make the attempt, for modern

sociological thought is grounded in large part in the numerous writings of Weber.

Weber lived in a time and place dominated—or at least strongly affected—by the theories and writings of Karl Marx. There was the hope that just around the corner lay a new utopia, founded in material plenty and a classless society. A politically astute person had to know and had to react to Marxist thought. Weber was a political man and a thoughtful one. Much of his thinking flowed from his reaction to the writings of Marx.

It is certainly an oversimplification, but it is also an aid in reading Weber, to view his writing as an attempt to refute or at least provide greater balance to the emphasis Marx gave to material economic concerns. Where Marx saw the church as an apologist for capitalistic exploitation, Weber saw the church as the matrix of ideas from which capitalism was to evolve. Marx claimed that without capitalism the church was not necessary, Weber argued that without a particular type of religious thought, capitalism could not have come into existence.

❖ Relationship Between Economic and Religious Systems

It is apparent today that both Marx and Weber viewed the historical process too narrowly. Religious and economic systems are not perfectly distinct entities. They are merged and their boundaries are ill defined. It is not really possible to say that one "determines" the character of the other. Both systems influence each other; furthermore, they are both simultaneously affected by changes taking place in the other institutions that make up a society. Even so, it is instructive to examine Weber's work; it stands as an antidote to the popularity of materialistic interpretations of history.

Weber began his speculations on the relationship between economic and religious systems by considering observed differences in economic productivity in Protestant and Catholic districts of Europe. If the former were more productive, he argued, it was not because they had been "freed" by the Protestant Reformation. Quite the contrary, they were under closer religious control.

Moreover, it was not reasonable to argue that the Protestant districts were more economically industrious because they were more materialistic and less "ascetic" than the Catholics in their interests. There were too many exceptions. A number of Catholic districts—in France and Italy, for example—revealed a lusty interest in life and its enjoyments. Many Protestant groups, such as the Mennonites in Germany, were possessed of an austere otherworldliness. It was, said Weber, too simple to say that economic effort is influenced by simple religious acceptance or rejection of asceticism.

Yet the economic picture remained clear: The Catholic areas were less economically progressive. One could not readily forgo the idea that religion has something to do with economic effort. The problem was to find the hidden connection. To do so required an intensive examination of the nature of capitalist doctrines and Catholic and Protestant philosophy and theology.

To summarize the nature of the capitalist spirit, Weber turned to the writings of Benjamin Franklin. Here was capitalism in its most naive and open form of expression—an economic spirit that, incidentally, Europeans found repulsive. One European of the time, writing of Americans, said, "They make tallow out of cattle and money out of men."[4] But the important thing in Franklin's expressions of the spirit of capitalism, Weber held, was to see the *moral* nature of economic advice. This Weberian insight holds for the present-day scene as well. We are possibly inclined to think of economics as a mechanical system operating independently of moral values. Economists are not disinclined to encourage such thinking. However, to divorce economics from the moral order within which it operates is to bypass a profoundly significant aspect of the economic process.

In capitalist economies, the making of money takes on the character of a purpose or an idealized "life-style" rather than a necessity. It becomes a value rather than something that happens by chance or something that wells up out of the avarice of a particular individual. There develops a collective "spirit" advocating the belief that each of us is called upon to make the utmost of his or her life, and, furthermore, that the form this should take is devotion to industry in this world. Along the way, money becomes the measure of industry and prudence, which are moral as well as economic qualities. Weber examined such statements of Franklin's as the following:

> For six pounds a year you may have the use of one hundred pounds, provided you are a man of known prudence and honesty.

> He that spends a groat a day idly, spends idly above six pounds a year, which is the price for the use of one hundred pounds.

> He that wastes idly a groat's worth of his time per day, one day with another, wastes the privilege of using one hundred pounds each day.

> He that idly loses five shillings' worth of time, loses five shillings, and might as prudently throw five shillings into the sea.

> He that loses five shillings, not only loses that sum, but all the advantage that might be made by turning it in dealing, which by the time that a young man becomes old, will amount to a considerable sum of money.[5]

Weber, as he examined the writings of Franklin, concluded that here was something new. There were wealthy men in the past, and there were men of ambition and avarice. But Benjamin Franklin set forth a moral treatise that took the individual to task for not tending to matters of business. To tend one's groats is also to tend to the interests of one's soul. This is powerful stuff. Western religion had not advocated this kind of prosaic sentiment prior to the Reformation. Indeed, as Weber commented, such a state of mind in the medieval period would have been viewed as the lowest kind of avarice and usury. One could not garner a place in heaven by accumulating coins.

Weber established an important point, and we must understand it if we are to appreciate the subtlety of his observations. First of all, capitalism must not be viewed simply as the desire to make money; such a desire in some individuals, Weber claimed, is as old as the history of humankind.

> The *auri sacra fames* [the quest for gold] is as old as the history of man. But we shall see that those who submitted to it without reserve as an uncontrolled impulse, such as the Dutch sea captain who "would go through hell for gain, even though he scorched his sails," were by no means the representatives of that attitude of mind from which the *specifically modern capitalistic spirit as a mass phenomenon* is derived, and that is what matters. At all periods of history, wherever it was possible, there has been ruthless acquisition, bound to no ethical norms whatever. Like war and piracy, trade has often been unrestrained in its relations with foreigners and those outside the group.[6]

Capitalism must be understood as a mass phenomenon. It is a culturally prescribed way of living; it is a complex of ideals. Most interestingly, it is a change in the older moral order. Weber's first point, then, is that we must see capitalism as a moral prescription, widely binding on all members of the society, to advance their individual material interests.

The second important feature of Weber's argument is that capitalism must be seen as a massive encroachment on what might be called a traditionalistic sense of labor or the value of work. It is worth noting that Weber was well aware, before American industrial psychologists documented the matter further, that workers are not always motivated to produce in terms of self-interest. Instead, the inclination on the part of the worker is to accept a traditionally given standard of productivity as sufficient and to produce only enough to meet such a standard. Weber summarized the matter nicely: "A man does not 'by nature' wish to earn more and more money, but simply to live as he is accustomed to live and to earn as much as is necessary for that purpose."[7]

So it was that Weber revealed himself to be concerned with a specific form of a broader problem that is of interest to anyone seriously involved with the social sciences: How does social and economic change occur? How do the massive forces of culture come to be modified? Like other modern social scientists, Weber concluded that the answer must lie within the nature of the social order itself.

To understand social and economic change, we must consider the pre-existing social and economic order. It is the social order that changes itself. (This position, in different forms and versions, is endorsed by most academic social scientists. It is one of the central themes of modern sociology and anthropology.) Any existing social and economic system contains not necessarily the seeds of its own destruction, but rather forces that change its character to the point where it is almost no longer recognizable. Modern

Christianity, for example, despite the conservative nature of religious tradition, is in a number of its modern forms quite a different belief system from Christianity as it appeared, let us say, in Europe in the tenth century.

From Weber's perspective, the growth of capitalism as an economic system was also the growth of capitalism as a moral system. To recapitulate briefly, the problem of the capitalistic transition was (1) to make the acquisitive motive more than a personal eccentricity (it had to be elevated to a moral principle binding on everyone, rather than being the eccentric expression of avarice on the part of a few); (2) to destroy reliance on traditional forms of economic satisfaction and replace those forms with the rational calculation of returns coming from the investment of given amounts of labor and capital. So the question is raised: How was capitalism able to arise out of a preexisting moral order that held the acquisitive motive to be base and vulgar and that accepted traditional standards of consumption and production? This was Weber's concern.

❖ *Action Implications of Protestant Thought*

To resolve the problem, Weber turned to an examination of some of the action implications of Protestant thought. Protestant thought arises out of, and is quite literally, a "reforming" of doctrines long held by the Catholic church. Weber presumed that if people take their religion seriously, then to some extent their actions must accordingly be affected. If this is so, an examination of the moral directives of religion can help us understand how certain kinds of actions come into being. What, then, are the implications of Protestant thought in its relation to capitalism? Weber turned first to an examination of Martin Luther's concept of the "calling."

Luther set forth the idea that individuals should accept their *calling*, their position within temporal society, so long as the calling is legitimate. The idea of the calling served one major purpose. Prior to the Reformation, those activities that most magnified humans in the eyes of God were efforts that essentially involved a withdrawal from the world. In the exercise of monastic asceticism and priestly celibacy, the individual believed it was possible to find a closer identity with Christ and with God.

Luther suggested, to the contrary, that all legitimate enterprises are equal in the eyes of God. Individuals can enhance their own state of grace by meeting the demands of their temporal or worldly callings. Luther was, in a sense, paving the way for the value that we give to professionalism today. Weber was concerned with the extent to which this theological concept and religious argument might have consequences for the economic realm. He suggested that what Luther did was to bring work into the secular realm; after Luther, worldly duties were no longer subordinated to spiritual or ascetic ones. It was the necessary first move toward capitalistic morality. Weber said:

The effect of the Reformation as such was only that, as compared with the Catholic attitude, the moral emphasis on and the religious sanction of, organized worldly labor in a calling was mightily increased. . . . Everyone should abide by his living and let the godless run after gain. . . . But in the concrete calling an individual pursued he saw more and more a special command of God to fulfill these particular duties which the Divine Will had imposed upon him. . . . The individual should remain once and for all in the station and calling in which God had placed him, and should restrain his worldly activity within the limits imposed by his established station in life.[8]

Luther provided a justification for involvement in worldly affairs, but he did little more than that. To see the more profound connection between Protestant thought and capitalistic enterprise, it is necessary to turn to the writings of John Calvin.

It is important, at this point, to introduce an antidote to the oversimplifications that characterize any attempt to summarize Weber's work in a brief space. Weber was not saying that Protestantism, and only Protestantism, is the necessary condition for capitalism. The response of his critics can lead one to think that this is the case. Rather, he was concerned with the extent to which some kind of religious moral order is necessary for the development of particular kinds of economic order:

We have no intention whatever of maintaining such a foolish and doctrinaire thesis as that the spirit of capitalism . . . could only have arisen as the result of certain effects of the Reformation, or even that capitalism as an economic system is a creation of the Reformation. . . . On the contrary, we only wish to ascertain whether and to what extent religious forces have taken part in the qualitative formation and the quantitative expansion of the spirit over the world.[9]

Calvinism, following the momentum established by Lutheranism, continued the process of providing religious justification for worldly concerns and effort. Luther supplied the concept of a calling; Calvin supplied an interest in predestination. If people were placed on this earth as God's creatures, and if God stood infinitely beyond their limited intellectual capacities, then it would be foolish to presume that any kind of effort on their part would place them in a state of grace with God. Only God would know, and God, being far beyond anyone's mind, would not tell.

Thus, one's fate is predestined in the sense that it is out of one's own hands and in the hands of God. Just as one cannot know the specific nature of one's own worldly demise (the form of one's death), one cannot know in advance the form of one's relationship with God. At the same time, Calvin claimed that some—a few—would be among the saved. The rest would fall among the damned.

In this fashion, Weber argued, Calvinism provided the world with a new variation on the older Christian notion of damnation and salvation. Calvin carried the idea of an omnipotent God to its extreme and concluded that salvation has already been determined by God and there is nothing the individual can do about it. More important, there is nothing the church can do about it. The complete elimination of salvation through the sacraments of the church formed the absolutely decisive difference between Calvinism and Catholicism.[10] Weber then went on:

> The great historic process in the development of religions, the elimination of magic from the world which had begun with the old Hebrew prophets and, in conjunction with Hellenistic scientific thought, had repudiated all magical means to salvation as superstition and sin, came here to its logical conclusion. The genuine Puritan even rejected all signs of religious ceremony at the grave and buried his nearest and dearest without song or ritual in order that no superstition, no trust in the effects of magical and sacramental forces on salvation, should creep in.[11]

Not only are magical means useless in the attainment of salvation, but so are any and all other means. It then becomes a curious matter to determine how such an ethic, such a religious point of view, could come to be associated with the worldly, acquisitive, and accumulative spirit that characterizes capitalism. The principal effect of this idea, said Weber, was to throw people into a state of brooding individualism. Torn from the security of the church, of traditionalism, of magic and ritual, the individual stood alone before God, more vulnerable than ever before. Ignorance was a source of torment. One's fate was unknown. Thus it was that individualism became a common affliction and not a specific eccentricity.

But if this idea were carried to its *reductus ad absurdum*, it would produce unbearable anomie and alienation. Rather than stimulating communal development and economic order, it would produce a highly disruptive disengagement of the individual from the affairs of the community. Something had to balance out the individualism of Calvinistic Puritanism by retaining the individual within the communal order. Weber resolved this problem by considering the Calvinist's conception of the ultimate purpose of life.

> The world exists to serve the glorification of God and for that purpose alone. The elected Christian is in the world only to increase this glory of God by fulfilling His commandments to the best of his ability. But God requires social achievement of the Christian because He wills that social life shall be organized according to His commandments, in accordance with that purpose.[12]

Weber's picture of the Calvinist is that of a man or a woman tormented with a concern over the future and where death will lead. The Calvinist stands alone, yet is bound to the community by a sense of God's omnipotence. He or she cannot distinguish the saved from the damned and cannot rely on any device to assure his or her own salvation. Yet there remains a dim light in this ideological darkness. Though Calvinists cannot achieve salvation, they can, through the extent to which they are able to manifest God's glory in this world, convince themselves of their own membership in the elect. They can seek external signs of inner grace. These signs do not completely guarantee a person that he or she is among the saved, but they can help convince true believers that they may be among the saved.

The achievement of Calvinism was that it explicitly brought what had once been a religious or spiritual struggle into this material world. No longer was it necessary for fully dedicated, religious men and women to retreat into monasticism to test the depths of their commitment. They could test their religious commitments in their work, in their calling, and in their daily activities. Weber commented that the effect of the Reformation was to make every Christian a monk for life.[13] More significantly, one became a monk who lived and dwelled within the community, within industry, within the school, and the family. These and other institutions were to be affected accordingly.

It remains now to make the connection between the asceticism of Protestant ideology and the development of capitalism as an economic practice flowing from the greater moral order. The connection is not obvious, because Protestant asceticism, reflecting the more pervasive asceticism of Christianity in general, is inclined to view the acquisition of wealth as morally suspect. One's dominating concern should be the Kingdom of God, not the acquisition of wealth.

However, the fear of wealth coming from Protestant asceticism does not come from the belief that wealth itself is corrupting, but that it promotes a moral relaxation. If one can remain dedicated to the principles of good works and the fulfillment of the glory of God and not be tempted into leisure, then wealth is in no way evil. Indeed, and this is quite significant, it may function as a sign of success in one's calling. It is not wealth that is evil; rather, the waste of time is the true evil.

> Waste of time is thus the first and in principle the deadliest of sins. The span of human life is infinitely short and precious to make sure of one's own election [into the ranks of the saved]. Loss of time through sociability, idle talk, luxury, even more sleep than is necessary for health . . . is worthy of absolute moral condemnation. . . . [Time] is infinitely valuable because every hour lost is lost to labour for the glory of God. Thus inactive contemplation is also valueless, or even directly reprehensible if it is at the expense of one's daily work. For it is less pleasing to God than the active performance of His will in a calling.[14]

Thus, Protestantism, with its roots in early ascetic Christianity and Judaism, latched onto work as an ascetic exercise. In this respect it differs from almost all other monastic rules the world over, according to Weber.[15] Work is elevated to a moral principle, and, moreover, a principle binding on all who aspire to the Kingdom of God. Work is a direct expression of religious fervor. Still more significantly, not all work can satisfy the demands of the Protestant ethic. Only that work is acceptable that directly serves the glory of God, and the glory of God is manifested in the ongoing community and its legitimate interests.

Furthermore, work that is sloppy and ill conceived, even though taxing and tiring, is not sufficient. It may have tried the soul, but it cannot work for the glorification of God. Work that is conscientiously planned, thorough, and methodical is best. In a word, work is given a *rational* quality, through an irrational process. The religious mysticism of Luther, Calvin, and other Protestant leaders generated the idea of rationality in work. The foundations were thus laid for capitalistic modes of thought.

Capitalism, if it meant nothing else, meant the rational use of wealth and the rational use of labor. People had sought wealth before and had worked before; there was certainly nothing new in this. But with capitalism, people were set to the task of calculating gains. In determining the worth of an enterprise, rationalism achieved the level of a socially supported value. Everyone became caught up in the calculated quest for gain.

How, said Weber, could capitalism have come into being unless some kind of moral basis had been laid for it in advance? Because this moral basis was lacking in the religions of other countries—even though they were rich in resources and labor—their economies did not and could not move toward the capitalistic form. Where the proper moral basis exists, capitalistic economic practices are more likely to flourish. (Some writers, such as Robert Bellah, speculate that the code of *bushido* in Japan was influential in promoting the technological and industrial modernization of Japan.)

What has happened to the Protestant ethic in modern times? Observers of the present scene find it laboring under the crushing weight of its own successes. It is ironic, if Weber's thesis is correct, that capitalism not only became independent of its Protestant origins but eventually reached the point where it could challenge values dearest to the heart of the Puritan individualist.

The challenge, when it came, had its origins in two sources. One of these was the rise of the large organization—the development of modern bureaucracy. The other was modern science. In many ways, science is the most rational and possibly the purest extension of ideas contained in the Protestant ethic. At the same time, it stands as the most secular of human institutions and the greatest barrier to a collective return to religious mysticism. In any event, as Weber conceded, once the process leading toward capitalistic morality had begun, it eventually reached the point of being an autonomous system—a system no longer reliant on the older morality that brought it into being.

When we suggest that science is an extension of Protestant thought, we are supported by the works of Robert K. Merton. Merton has argued that a relationship exists between Protestant religious thought and the rise of scientific thinking in Western culture. Following Weber, it makes sense to argue that if Protestantism promoted rationality in business, it also seems reasonable to conclude that it promoted rationality in other spheres of human activity. Essentially, the argument is that if God is all-rational and if God made the world, then the rationality of God will be found in His works. Early scientists of the seventeenth century were, according to Merton, predominantly Protestant and, by virtue of religious training, congenial to the idea of finding rationality within nature itself. No less a figure than Sir Isaac Newton believed that the rationality of God could be found in the rational consistency of His works. This thesis is explored at some length in a later chapter on the works of Merton.

❖ *The Nature of Bureaucratic Organization*

Weber was concerned with the subtleties of the connection between religious and economic moralities. He was also concerned with the consequences of social organization. In particular, he devoted a great amount of time and effort to questions concerning the nature of bureaucratic organization. No sociologist today can discuss this topic without paying his or her respects to Weber.

Indeed, Merton claims that Weber may properly be regarded as the founder of the systematic study of bureaucracy.[16] Weber was interested in bureaucracy because it represents another facet of the process of rationalization—a process that seemed to him to characterize modern society in contrast to "traditional" forms of society. A rational ordering of the economy brings along with it a rational ordering of social relations. The efficiency that now characterizes the productive process also characterizes social organization. In their social lives, people are now "processed" as impersonally and as efficiently as the material resources that are also necessary for production.

Capitalism solved the problem of tearing people away from traditionalistic economic motives and traditional patterns of production. Bureaucracy, in essence, solved the problem of breaking people away from a reliance on traditional modes of power. To see this, we need to consider briefly Weber's conception of the nature of power in its traditional forms and in its bureaucratic forms.

We should warn the reader in advance that any discussion of power in a social context is tricky. The concept of power is surprisingly difficult to define in a social context; no one has achieved a truly satisfactory definition. If we define power as the capacity to make people do things they do not want to do, we have to establish the fact that they do not want to do what we are demanding of them. There is also the peculiar relationship between those in power and those who grant them that power: Leaders, to a surprising extent, must follow in order to lead.

Granting such problems, we define "power" rather broadly as the probability of having a command obeyed by others when they are resistant. Power can be discussed in two quite distinct ways. First of all, power can be seen as having its locus in a particular person or individual. Weber referred to this as "charismatic" power and meant only that certain features may give a person a commanding appearance and cause others to accept the person's dictates as necessary ones to follow. The charismatic individual is believed to be blessed with extraordinary powers. People having such powers are believed to be divinely inspired, possessed of sacred qualities, capable of prophecy, and otherwise set apart from the ordinary run of people.

A second form of power has its locus not within the person, but within the office or status the person occupies. Power derived from occupying a given office does not require charismatic abilities. In fact, charismatic qualities and power derived from an official position can work against each other.

❖ *Charismatic Power*

Charismatic power, as Weber considered it, is reliant on the expressive qualities of the individual. It resides in the flashing eye, the powerful voice, the jutting chin, or some other sign that identifies its possessor as a "born leader." Because charismatic power rests ultimately on the unique impressions of the individual, it has an arbitrary and eccentric quality about it that makes it a potential source of disruption to more rational forms of power utilization. The charismatic leader, as Weber put it, is not congenial to the idea of routine. To the contrary, because that person's power is lodged within personal qualities, he or she exists as a threat to routine and to the established order.

The unstable, eccentric, and individualistic character of charismatic power must be regulated somehow if a permanent and stable power system is to be developed within the community. Weber held that purely charismatic power exists only in the originating moments of new social forms. The need for stability leads to the regulation or, as Weber put it, the "routinization" of charisma.[17]

The necessity for stabilizing power based on the eccentricities of the individual can be quickly seen. If the followers of a charismatic leader are dependent on that person for guidance, how are they to cope with the problems that arise when the leader dies or is incapacitated? How is the quality of charisma to be given continuity beyond the life span of the individual who possesses it? How is the magic of charisma to be retained when the magician has gone? The problem thus becomes one of somehow taking the power-giving qualities of charisma out of the ephemeral nature of the individual and bringing them into the stable and continuous structure of the community. Sources of power that were once the property of a charismatically endowed individual must become the property of the community; they must somehow be incorporated into the routine of communal living. This is the process Weber referred to as the "routinization" of charisma.

The problem of routinizing charisma can be solved in a variety of ways. Weber listed the following as among the more common and significant ones:

1. A search can be initiated for persons who possess signs of charisma similar to those possessed by the leader. If the leader had a cleft between the teeth, then perhaps another person with a cleft between the teeth will also possess some of the charismatic qualities with

which the leader was endowed. Weber referred to the search for the Dalai Lama as an example of this kind of solution. In this instance, a search is initiated for a male child with characteristics that identify him as a reincarnation of the Buddha.

2. The new leader can be sought through divine judgment, revelation, oracles, or the casting of lots. In such instances, the selection procedure is given a legitimacy—an acceptance by the community—and the person who is thus selected is endowed with charismatic qualities. Note, in this context, that there have been cultures in which leaders have been selected by essentially a random process. One wonders whether modern procedures work any better.

3. A very simple and common solution to the problem is to rely on the judgment of the charismatic leader and have that person select a successor. The magician is the person best qualified to select the magician who will follow.

4. A new leader can be established through selection by a council qualified both to determine the charismatic leader and to endow him or her with qualities of leadership by means of special ceremonies. Legitimacy of power rests, in this instance, on the acceptance of a charismatically qualified council and on the impressive and ritualistically correct procedures of ceremony.

5. Another means of routinizing charisma exists in the simple assumption that it can be biologically or hereditarily transmitted; therefore, the charismatic leader can be replaced by his or her offspring, who will be possessed of similar qualities. It should be noted here that such an assumption functions to solve a social problem in the transfer of power, and that it has only a very tenuous connection with reality.

   The community may possess any number of people who are better qualified in terms of talent and energy for the tasks of leadership than is the present leader's offspring. However, to ascribe such qualities to the offspring simplifies what otherwise might prove to be a communally disorganizing process of attempting to rediscover "true" charisma.

6. Finally, the problem of stabilizing charisma can be met by ritualistic transmission:

   > The most important example is the transmission of priestly charisma by anointing, consecration, or the laying on of hands; and of royal authority, by anointing and by coronation.[18]

   Charisma, which is individualistic, disturbing, revolutionary, and eccentric, cannot long remain the organizing force within a community. It calls for routinization, but routinization—whether of a traditional form or a more modern bureaucratic form—introduces a conservative, stable, and collective structure.

Though this statement is severe, it is warranted. There is a tendency for the critical evaluations of the administrative official to take the form dictated by the interests of the bureaucracy rather than the interests either of the individual or of broader moral issues. An example that is not nice, but that makes the point, is the well-known decision of the Ford Motor Company to continue the production and distribution of a certain model of cars, although it was known that they were dangerous. The decision was made on the basis of corporate interests. It was decided that paying settlements to burn victims would cost less than retooling to produce a safer automobile.

3. *Within the bureaucracy, "the typical person in authority occupies an 'office.' In the action associated with his status, including the commands he issues to others, he is subjected to an impersonal order to which his actions are oriented."* The concept of "office" is important in grasping a deeper understanding of the nature of bureaucracy. It enables us, perhaps, to see professors somewhat differently if we recognize them as intellectual officials, or, to put it another way, as officials who are intellectuals. College students acquire a different character when we view them as minor officials—junior bureaucrats within the education bureaucracy.

Because an office requires relatively uncritical acceptance of one's official duties, and because being an intellectual demands a critical sensitivity, the college professor of any intelligence sooner or later experiences the conflicts that come from the opposing demands of bureaucratic passivity, on the one hand, and intellectual rebellion on the other.

Instructors, who are good bureaucrats will, with considerable pride, boast to their students that they have eliminated all personal allusions and anecdotes from their lectures. In such an instance, the instructor is openly recognizing the prior claims of office over any other kind of experience, especially the more disorganizing and less legalistic experiences that arise from one's personal encounters with life.

4. *"The person who obeys authority does so . . . only in his capacity as a 'member' of the corporated group and what he obeys is only the 'law.'"* The educational bureaucracy runs into more problems with this aspect of bureaucratic structure than just about any other. Weber was merely pointing out that bureaucracy has a tendency to restrict performance to the demands of the office. What people do on their own time is their own business. This, again, characterizes an "ideal" bureaucracy. If, for example, the chairperson of the biology department is one of the greatest biologists in the world, then why should it concern anyone that she or he spends off-duty hours passing out pro-abortion leaflets or conducting seminars on the homophobic nature of American society?

A more aggravating problem arises from the extent to which this feature of bureaucracy, within an educational setting, produces "compartmentalization." Students, generally speaking, make very good bureaucrats; they are all too willing to function as members of a corporate group. When this means they must study English 101, Chemistry 201, Sociology 111, and Modern History 202, they do so. Each course is taken, the requirements are met, and the credits are entered in the bookkeeping system. The possibility that there might be a connection among all four courses and that each could be profitably examined from the perspectives of the others is rarely considered. Reality reflects the offices of bureaucracy and is subordinated to them, despite the resulting strain.

5. *"Members of the corporate group, insofar as they obey a person in authority, do not owe this obedience to him as an individual but to the impersonal order."* Weber suggested that within a bureaucracy, allegiance becomes more abstract. College students might, for example, assert their willingness to do or die for old Siwash, but they would consider it absurd to be willing to do or die for President Jones of old Siwash. Recently, over a third of the students in our social science classes were unable to specifically identify Mao Zedong when asked to do so in tests. He was referred to (with obvious guesses) variously as "a Chinese aristocrat," "a South Vietnam political leader," and "an Oriental." The enemy is no longer personalized. Instead, the enemy is looked upon as an abstract condition located somewhere in a misty "they." "They" are held to believe in an equally misty and ill-understood set of ideas called "communism," or "capitalism," or some other "-ism," which "they," in a manner never well defined, will somehow impose on all the mistily "free" people of the world. Weber, had he lived in present times, would have been interested in the extent to which human conflict has become an abstracted process.

6. Within a bureaucracy, *"the organization of offices follows the principle of hierarchy; that is, each lower office is under the control and supervision of a higher one."* This is a fairly obvious comment and does not require much further elaboration in this context. Whether it is a military, political, industrial, educational, or religious bureaucracy, the fact of hierarchy is evident.

There are points in the hierarchy, however, that produce interesting situations. Graduate student assistants, for example, stand between the student body and the faculty in the academic hierarchy. They are not really faculty members, and yet they are very close. This poses a problem for the graduate assistants. Should they treat their teachers as colleagues or as professors? They can easily seem either too formal or too casual. Some graduate student assistants, to avoid the problem, elect to greet their teachers with a noncommittal "Hi" or "Good morning" rather than to commit themselves with a "Hello, Professor Johnson" or a "Howdy, Jane."

There is one other facet of personal greetings and hierarchies that we cannot resist noting. It might appear, at first, that the casual informality of some student-teacher encounters belies the existence of hierarchy. Hierarchy, within a society that strongly abides by democratic values, generates strains. The current attack on the university as a center of "elitism" further illustrates the point. As a consequence, in minor things such as the formalities of greeting and dress, considerable flaunting of hierarchical manners can occur. However, it is a strained form of personalization in which neither real informality or real formality can take place.

7. *"Only a person who has demonstrated an adequate technical training is qualified to be a member of the administrative staff of [a bureaucratically] organized group, and hence only such persons are eligible for appointment to official positions."* The role played by technical competence in bureaucracy is an especially significant one and arises from the more pervasive concern given to the rational pursuit of the organization's ends. If the organization is to attain its goals, then its personnel must be efficient and as competent as possible. Their efficiency is dependent on the extent to which they possess technical competence. The consequence, in an ideal bureaucracy, is that personnel are selected on the basis of examinations.

Within the bureaucracy of higher learning, it is hardly necessary to point to the prevalence of examinations as a means of determining the right to continue in a career. However, some interesting observations have been made concerning the manner in which people are selected for positions in universities when their records are equivalent. Under these conditions, extraneous features are allowed to sway the choice. Usually these features will take into account the extent to which the "personality" of the candidate will be such as to assure a "smooth" operation of the department.[23]

8. *"In the rational type [of bureaucracy] it is a matter of principle that the members of the administrative staff should be completely separated from ownership of the means of production or administration. . . . There exists, furthermore, in principle, complete separation of the property belonging to the organization, which is controlled within the sphere of office, and the personal property of the individual, which is available for his own private uses. There is a corresponding separation of the place in which official functions are carried out, the 'office' in the sense of premises, from living quarters."*

Weber touched here on a property of bureaucracy that has far-reaching ramifications. He was suggesting, albeit somewhat indirectly, that the Marxist doctrines concerning the social employment of property may be only the ideological reflection or aftereffect of a process that had already been established by the bureaucratization of society.[24]

This point, though very profound, hardly needs elaborate documentation or illustration here. It is of more interest to pursue some of the possible implications of the point. For example (still within educational bureaucracy), what are some of the effects of this on the political and social ideology of professors? Is there a liberalizing effect? Does lack of ownership bring about a lowered sense of identification with the institution and a greater willingness to function as a more cosmopolitan intellectual? Does the complete or nearly complete disengagement of the student, *qua* student, from ownership and the acquisition of goods produce a feeling that what he or she is doing is not concrete or personally meaningful?

9. *"Administrative acts, decisions and rules are formulated and recorded in writing, even in cases where oral discussion is the rule or is even mandatory. This applies at least to preliminary discussions and proposals, to final decisions, and to all sorts of order and rules. The combination of written documents and a continuous organization of official functions constitutes the 'office,' which is the central focus of all types of modern corporate action."* Weber was discussing here what C. Wright Mills referred to as the "enormous file." Not only does the bureaucracy record actions taken and the resulting consequences; it also keeps records of policies formed, and it keeps carefully preserved the rules and regulations that give form to the system. All of this constitutes the "file."

Although such files, records, and formally expressed legal definitions of the regulations defining each office provide for a high degree of continuity, they also introduce an impersonal and rigid element into the conduct of office. Paradoxically, it becomes a mark of the good bureaucrat to know how and when to violate the demands of the formal system.[25] An interesting case in point is the following solution to a vexing bureaucratic problem by a professor at a Midwestern university.

The situation consisted, for the instructor, of having to teach classes in an old wooden building that had at one time been a military barrack. The building was a fire hazard, and the classroom itself, with a single exit, was a serious potential catastrophe. The instructor was reasonably concerned. He sent several letters to administrative officials who stood above him in authority. His request that something be done to alleviate the situation was ignored. At the same time, the demands of office called for this class to meet three times a week for a period of fifty minutes each time.

Instead of lecturing, the instructor instituted a program of training in fire drills and fire safety. He spent ten to twenty minutes of each class period taking his students outside the building to a safe place and then returning. This activity was sufficiently disorganizing to call for action on the part of the administration. They could have done several things—one being to chastise or otherwise bring sanctions against the instructor. However, because he was engaging in an action obviously designed to promote the safety of the students,[26] the administration was forced to capitulate. The episode ended happily with a set of fire escapes being constructed for the classroom.

We must bring this discussion of Weber to a close at this point. Weber has been criticized for presenting what, in the final analysis, amount to broad historical speculations and hypotheses. He has been accused of using such general and ideal conceptions that we are made unwarrantedly secure in our feeling that we understand. (For example, when we get down to the specifics of a particular bureaucracy, we may find that it deviates considerably from the picture given us by Weber.) But even if we grant the validity of these criticisms, they still do not detract from the stature of Weber or the value of his work.

Weber remains a significant beginning point for the humanist or social scientist who is seriously concerned with understanding the character of modern society. Few other writers, if any, have so magnificently comprehended the workings of religious, political, economic, and social organizations. Readers should note, as they continue through this book, the extent to which many contemporary sociological writers have been influenced by Weber. Only to the extent that we perceive this influence can we have a basis for evaluating the fullness of Weber's contribution to social thought.

Encounters with Social Thought

The Practice of Medicine

The topic we have elected for our consideration of the uses of theory from a Weberian perspective is that of the practice of medicine—particularly as it is exercised in Western culture. What is sought in these encounters with social thought is to demonstrate the imaginative use of theory. Theory is a form of controlled fantasy. It directs our attention to specific concerns. The further task, of course, is to see whether theory and reality have anything in common. In these applications, we are primarily concerned with seeing where theory might direct us with respect to the sociological imagination.

We shall draw primarily on Weber's arguments as they appear in *The Protestant Ethic and the Spirit of Capitalism*. The basic argument there is that religious ideas permeate economic ideas. The two systems are not discrete entities; instead, they blend into and reinforce each other. In the following discussion, we want to consider the possibility that religious ideas, explicitly or implicitly, give shape and form to the American practice of medicine. Obviously, we cannot go into the discussion in great detail. If the discussion illustrates, in a general way, how Weber's ideas can be used in a different context, then it will have served its purpose.

There is a passage in David Sudnow's *Passing On*[27] in which he describes the broader powers of doctors on call in the emergency room of a large urban hospital. Sudnow reveals how the doctor functions not only as healer but as prosecutor, judge, jury, and, eventually executioner in life-or-death cases. He notes that patients who come into the emergency ward with tattered clothes, alcoholic breath, and other signs of an indigent life are more likely to die during treatment than those who show signs of being affiliated with more reputable middle-class elements. If Sudnow is correct, the doctor is, in addition to making medical judgments, also making moral ones.

There is other evidence of moral selectivity in American medicine. A child of color, in America, is nearly twice as likely to die before its first birthday as a white child. This ratio has remained fairly steady over the past quarter of a century, even though the discrepancy between mortality rates for adult whites and blacks has narrowed significantly.

Before continuing, let us make it clear that we are not interested here in praising or blaming American medicine for its accomplishments or inadequacies. Some of its accomplishments, even in the driest kind of statistical presentation, are nearly breathtaking. American medicine, between the years 1940 and 1975, reduced the number of maternal deaths per 100,000 births from 376 to 12.8. At the same time, the above-mentioned difference between white and nonwhite populations still manifests itself.

The fact remains, however, that for one reason or another, doctors are selective in dealing with patients. The selectivity can take a number of forms. The most obvious one is whether or not a person has medical insurance or some way of paying for services rendered. An operation without complications can now cost many thousands of dollars, exclusive of hospital room payments. Hospital room costs and ancillary tests and medicines have escalated wildly. Selection for medical care in America is made on the basis of ability to pay; at the same time, costs are terribly high. Even a modest medical crisis can bankrupt the typical American family. This is central to the current federal, state, and local governments' frenetic activities toward a form of "socialized" medical care.

Selectivity takes other forms. Doctors of varying religious beliefs can select or reject a patient's claim for care on the basis of moral prejudice. This is the case, for example, when a doctor holding particular opinions refuses to perform an abortion. Despite a concerted effort by federal agencies and the courts, numbers of racial and ethnic minorities are still denied access to good medical care in many areas. A sad example of this happened several years ago when an eminent black doctor, a principal figure in the development of blood transfusion, was denied access to a Virginia hospital. He died.

This business of selectivity is worth examining because it is an additional element in the practice of health care that does not, first of all, have a scientific basis; second, is not in keeping with the moral directives set forth in the Hippocratic oath; and third, has obvious implications for health care. That is to say, to select someone for medical treatment influences the prognosis of the pathology in one way or another. Selectivity suggests the operation of influences other than purely medical ones.

In all of this, we uncover one of the awkward problems confronting the sociologist in any kind of effort to deal "cleanly" with the topic of human social actions. For the natural scientist, many of the phenomena that are of interest are independent from each other, in at least the sense that they "stand apart" from other things. The planet Saturn is not partly melted into the planet Jupiter. Carbon is distinct from hydrogen. When we deal with social phenomena, this is hardly ever the case. Social phenomena are mixed into each other.

At the level of grand institutional systems, such as educational structures, the economy, the military, the family, the church, or medicine, we find that any kind of attempt to distinguish one from the other meets with some success at first, but then eventually it turns out to be quite difficult to push much further. The effort to push the separation into some kind of clear and total disfunction leads to the discovery that it cannot be done.

History offers us a grand example of two major philosophers whose differing opinions resulted from this "sloppy" quality of human institutions. We refer to Karl Marx and Max Weber. Marx promoted a view of the social world in which it was presumed that a relatively clear distinction can be made between institutions. Paramount among these institutions, for Marx, was the economy. It dominates all other systems. It is the controlling or master institution. The church, for example, is, from this perspective, an institution that exists to rationalize prevailing forms of economic practice. Education exists to prepare people for either work as hourly laborers or dominance as members of economic elites. The military is the means whereby economic policy can be put into effect both abroad and at home.

Each institution, from this perspective, has its unique character and serves a central institution, the economy. It is the emphasis on the economic system that is interesting, in that Marxism makes the economy the institutional structure *par excellence.* Modern American policymakers are little different from Marx in this regard. Modern industrial states give preeminence to economic issues; economic advisers are ranked among the most rational and effective within the pantheon of advisers who function in high places.

The Marxists concede that institutions "overlap" in their interests, but they concern themselves with a singular form of the overlap: They are interested in the connection between economic structure on the one hand and all other institutions on the other. They are interested in the overlap between, let us say, the family and the economy, or the school and the economy, or medicine and the economy, and so on. In dealing with this overlap, the influence of the economy on the institution is given great emphasis. The possibility of a causal relationship coming from the other direction is given less attention.

Max Weber, in reviewing the Marxian position, was clearly aware of this restricted conceptualization of what was going on. Instead of giving the economy predominant significance, he dealt with the overlap in institutions by suggesting that the church, for example, may influence the economy even as the economy influences the church.

To make the point, given the power and popularity of Marxist thought in his time, Weber carried his argument as far as he dared. He argued that the form of economy is, in fact, dependent on the church. It was a daring and deep attack on Marxist thought. After the Marx-Weber confrontation, it became more apparent that the interconnections between institutions are not in the least simple.

What does this debate imply when it comes to dealing with the issue of American medicine? It means that medicine, like any other institution, is a part of a complex of institutions. Medicine is influenced by the economy, by educational organizations, by the church, by the family, by the military, by government, and by other major systems at work within the society.

To attempt to reveal the myriad ways in which medicine is influenced by nonmedical structures would require an essay longer than can be developed here. To simplify matters, we shall remain within a Weberian framework and consider a two-institution system—the church and medicine. Keep in mind, as the discussion progresses, that medicine is supposed to be directed, in the ideal sense, to the purely scientific and dispassionate act of dealing with the problem of health. Its proper function is to sustain maximum levels of health for the society of which it is a part. Any action that violates this goal is an action operating contrary to the appropriate practice of medicine and becomes, as a consequence, a problematic concern meriting our interest.

We can begin our Weberian journey into the institution of medicine by noting, first of all, that Weber was a careful historian as well as philosopher. He looked into the early foundations of social systems to gain some idea of how they might have reached their present forms. We can ask, then, what the history of medicine reveals with respect to medicine as we know it now. In what ways do long-established traditions, perhaps no longer meaningful, still operate within the system of medicine?

The father of modern medicine is generally conceded to be Hippocrates (460 B.C.). Hippocrates broke from earlier traditions in which medicine was dominated by priestly practitioners of magic and ritual. For example, the roles of magician and physician were commonly combined in ancient Egypt.[28] Moses, as a case in point, was both a healer and an accomplished magician. To the extent that magic is a matter of controlling perception, the magician-healers probably tried to heal people by controlling their perceptions.

Hippocrates accomplished several things. First, he argued that disease is a disorder of internal physical states. Second, he argued that disease is natural rather than religious or magical. Third, he argued against the blind application of magical techniques: A rationale should be established for any method of therapy. Fourth, the study of medicine is one part of the general study of nature. Fifth, the study of medicine is the study of the body.

This was certainly a breakthrough, as we say, but the Hippocratic system has some further properties that need to be considered. First of all, the Hippocratic mode of thought concentrated on the individual and suggested that the suffering of the patient is to be understood in terms of something "internal" to the person. Medicine today still finds it easier to deal with health problems in terms of treating the individual than in terms of dealing with greater social forces, many of which are murderously lethal in their implications—nuclear war, for example.

Hippocrates stated:

> Things however that are holy are revealed only to men who are holy. The profane may not learn them until they have been initiated in the mysteries of science.[29]

In this statement, there is a mixture of the sacred and the secular. Moreover, it is obviously a statement in which the healer takes on the qualities of a holy person. The priestly form reappears in slightly different guise.

Hippocrates did not have an especially high opinion of the patient. In the *Corpus Hippocraticum*, he stated:

> Indeed, even the attempted reports of their illnesses made to their attendants by sufferers from obscure diseases are the result of opinion rather than of knowledge. If, indeed, they understood their diseases, they would never have fallen into them, for the same intelligence is required to know . . . how to treat them.[30]

What makes this statement especially interesting is that it would seem to imply that one of the best ways to deal with health problems and health care would be to inform the patient as fully as possible—to set up health education systems. Hippocrates never mentioned this possibility. (There are no calls to educate the patient in the *Hippocraticum*.)

The Hippocratic model was by no means a complete break from earlier priestly magical systems of medicine. Consider some further comments taken from Hippocratic writings:

> [I]t is the godhead that purifies, sanctifies and cleanses us from the greatest and most impious of our sins. (*The Sacred Disease*)

In the next quote, notice the reference to the body, as utterly corrupt.

> However, I hold that a man's body is not defiled by a god, the one being utterly corrupt the other perfectly holy. (Ibid.)

The next three quotes place the medical practitioner on a level with the priest: The medical doctor becomes a special intermediary of the gods.

> In fact it is especially knowledge of the gods that by medicine is woven into the stuff of the mind. (*On Decorum*)

> Physicians have given place to the gods. For in medicine that which is powerful is not in excess. (Ibid.)

> The gods are the real physicians, though people do not think so. (Ibid.)[31]

Some five hundred years later, Roman medicine was strongly influenced by the Greek physician Galen, among others. Claudius Galen settled in Rome and was a physician to the gladiators. He later became physician to Marcus Aurelius. Galen was a devoted student of Hippocrates. The religious influence of Galen comes in part from a reliance on the Hippocratic canon, which, as we have already seen, retained religious elements of thought despite its reach toward rationalism.

It comes also from the fact that Galen's way of thinking was especially valuable for the later religious orthodoxy of medieval Europe. Galen's ideas dominated medical thought until the sixteenth century, when they were challenged by Vesalius and then in the seventeenth century, when they were challenged by William Harvey. Galen was useful to the church, for example, in his belief that the mind held power over the body. This fit nicely with the church's position that God, the essence of the soul, was the best medicine for the body.

As an aside, it should be noted that probably the most astonishing medical contribution made by the Romans did not come from men such as Galen, or Asclepiades, or Themison of Laodicea. It came, instead, from the massive public projects that promoted public health. Aqueducts, sewage systems, and bathing institutions were constructed by the Romans throughout the range of Europe. The Roman Empire, if it did nothing else, had the cleanest people in antiquity.

With the fall of the western Roman Empire at the close of the fifth century, and the coming of the Middle Ages, major innovations in medicine ceased. Priests became physicians again along the line of the old Babylonian and Egyptian priest-healers. Superstitious forms of therapy were cultivated. Temple sleep, divination, charms were all resurrected, but in a Christian form.

The shrines of Christian saints became the new healing temples; icons and holy relics became the new charms; Christian prayer became the new form of divination. The god/physicians of earlier civilization (Asklepios and I-M-Hotep) were replaced by the Christ. The god specialist healers of pagan civilization became the Christian healing saints, each with his own disease specialty. St. Sebastian became the healer of pestilence; St. Artemis became the healer of genital afflictions. Often a saint was considered a sacred healer because of the manner in which he or she died for his or her faith. Saint Agatha, the patron saint of nursing women, lost her breasts in the torture which preceded her death. Saint Apollonia, the saintly healer of the tooth-ache, had her teeth knocked out and her jaw broken during torture prior to her death. Saint Lucy, patron saint of ocular pathology, lost her eyes for the sake of her faith.[32]

Famine, plague, pestilence, and war tore at the fabric of medieval institutions. Despite the terror and horror of life in plague- and disease-ridden cities, medicine was constrained by religion. Not until the nineteenth century was there a radical departure in medical practice from the nearly total dominance of priests in medicine of the medieval period. (There were some secular practitioners, and there were Jewish practitioners—an especially interesting case, who were of a quite different philosophy with respect to health practices but were, by virtue of their religious identity, precluded from ready practice within the Catholic or Christian communities.)[33]

From the beginning of the nineteenth century into the twentieth century, astonishing strides were made with respect to increasing the life expectancy of human beings. The major portion of that accomplishment came out of the control of epidemic disease. This accomplishment, in turn, came about largely through the development of public health measures (diet, housing, antisepsis or sanitation, and vaccination).

However, clinical medicine appears to have benefited most as being acclaimed responsible for medical advancements. The reason this is important to note is that clinical medicine, with its emphasis on treating illness after it occurs, is much more in keeping with the Hippocratic tradition than is public medicine. Public medicine in America is, even today, not accorded the prestige or recognition that goes to clinical medicine, despite the fact that a powerful case can be made for public medicine as the major influence in modern health advancements. Garlinghouse puts it this way, in an historical aside:

> Historically, this country has not generally supported the notion of public health. The first installation of a bathtub in the White House by President Fillmore in 1858 was generally viewed as a great extravagance. Cholera, smallpox, typhoid, and tuberculosis continued to threaten the lives of Americans long after preventive measures were well known and widely accepted.[34]

The clinical practitioner is a person who sustains a special control over the patient and the medical profession. Medicine is viewed as the nearly heroic—and, indeed, it is heroic—application of individual effort to the suffering of the patient. Out of this comes, on the one hand, the special relationship between the doctor and the patient. It is a relationship viewed and defended by doctors as having a "sanctity." (The nature of the term should be noted.)

On the other hand, the idea becomes widespread that whatever is accomplished in the realm of attaining greater health among the people is the work of the clinical practitioner. Public medical practice and some forms of health practice that are not directly related to medicine itself (such as, let us say, the institution of set speed limits, which have saved some five to ten thousand American lives a year) do not gain much attention.

American medicine, rooted in the Hippocratic model and afterward emerging out of the religious control of the medieval period, is not by any means a free form of institution, removed from the constraints of hidden traditions. The modern American doctor practices medicine in a manner not too dissimilar from that of priest-healers thousands of years ago. Here is a description of the activities of the secular physicians, the Sunu, of ancient Egypt about three thousand years ago:

> The practice of medicine is so divided among them that each physician is a healer of one disease and no more. All the country is full of physicians, some of the eye, some of the teeth, some of what pertains to the belly, and some of hidden diseases.[35]

The Sunu increasingly specialized and eventually achieved a separate professional status removed from the institution of the lector priests. Garlinghouse goes on to say,

> Among the secular physicians, the specialists treated the aristocracy while the general practitioners ministered to the poor. Their respective pays and statuses were commensurate with that of their patients. . . . One of the Pharaoh's specialists had the title: "Guardian of the Royal Bowel Movement."[36]

The American doctor of today assumes some of the qualities of the priest-practitioner. The locus of illness lies within the patient. The relationship between the doctor and patient is sacrosanct. Illness and the healing of illness are related to status and wealth. Often, the American practice of medicine implies that preventive medicine is not really medicine.

In American medicine, there is a strong strain of Protestant belief, insofar as the patient, *qua* individual, is viewed as the locus of illness and even (in the Hippocratic sense) responsible for it. Illness has some of the properties of sin, just as we are inclined to think that some sins have the property of being illnesses.

The matter ought not to be pushed too far here, and we certainly do not want to suggest that the medical profession is exclusively responsible, but it is nonetheless the case that modern society has easily made the transition from the religious conception of sin to the medical conception of sickness for a variety of conditions that were once the exclusive concern of the religious worker.

Three hundred years ago (indeed, later than that) murder, sodomy, alcoholism, rape, or madness were dealt with as sins. There was possibly much injustice in that. Today we think of them as sicknesses, and there may also be considerable injustice in that, insofar as it implicitly centers attention on the individual as the source of the sickness. Even more significantly, to the extent that the metaphor of evil as sickness extends the influence of medicine into ever-wider domains, the lines that demarcate medicine as a special institutional system within the greater society become less clear.

In this application of Weber's ideas to the field of medicine we have been concerned with showing how Weber can be used to stimulate what Mills called "the sociological imagination." Just as Weber's original work on the Protestant ethic was extremely controversial and remains so down to the present time, we recognize that this foray into applications of social thought on the topic of medicine is more provocative than definitive. However, it is intended to show how theory can generate new approaches to old issues. It is not intended to close off argumentation, but, instead, to direct it into possible new avenues of thought.

Putting Social Thought to Work

1. Americans are inclined to think of being impoverished as an indication of failure on the part of the individual—usually some kind of moral failure. How does blaming the impoverished person for being morally derelict influence the problem of poverty? Poverty is also thought of in economic terms. Weber suggests that economic and moral systems are interlaced elements of a more complete social system. What problems are created by our modern tendency to deal with economics as a separate and isolated matter of markets, labor, and money? Do you think that economic practice is also a matter of moral choice? How would you define the economic morality of modern America?

2. Americans focus on sex as a moral issue. Which do you consider the greater moral problem, sexual promiscuity or the economic exploitation of helpless people? Are they both equally bad? Is sexual immorality worse than economic forms of immorality?

3. Weber was interested in power. What is power? To what extent is a president, for example, capable of exerting influence as an individual? To what extent is a president constrained by the people he or she is supposed to represent? What limits are placed on the powers of a president? Is the president a leader or, instead, the representative of popular sentiments? To what extent must leaders follow? Is it possible to have power without being a member of a powerful organization? If not, then power is latent within the organization and not within the individual. Americans personalize power and indulge in what has been referred to as the "cult of personality." Is power more properly viewed as a sociological than as a psychological quality? What are the implications of the way one resolves this issue?

4. Weber is known as one of the foremost students of modern bureaucratic structures. Bureaucracies are seen as bumbling organizations and bureaucratic workers as ineffectual morons. If you were designing an ideal social system, could you do so without incorporating most of the major features of a bureaucracy-hierarchy, rationalism, officials, tests, communal property, and so on? When you get angry with "bureaucracy," are you angry because it is being bureaucratic or because it is being unbureaucratic? Most students, for example, do not want instructors to be especially "personal." What they really want is for teachers to be "likeable." These are quite different matters. A bureaucrat can be likeable without being personal. Impersonal or "fair" judgment is one quality of an ideal bureaucracy. What are the characteristics of an "ideal" bureaucrat?

5. Weber outlined the diverse effects of Protestantism on Western culture and society. He particularly noted the ways in which Protestantism led toward a capitalistic morality. Weber suggested that it is not possible to achieve a real separation of church and state in other than a legalistic sense. How successful do you believe we have been, in the United States, in achieving this kind of ideal? Do you think we should struggle toward such an ideal? How can you separate church and state? Do you believe the slogan "In God We Trust" should be eliminated from American currency? Is the presence of the slogan on our money an indication that church and state are not separate in the United States?

6. Weber helped bring us the idea of the "charismatic" leader. Most of our entertainment celebrities are charismatic "leaders." How do they compare with governmental leaders who occupy positions of official or routine authority? What are the advantages and disadvantages of each form of leadership? Does a powerful office endow its occupant with a kind of "charisma"? Before taking office as president of the United

States, for example, Harry Truman was considered a dowdy haberdasher without much personal appeal. After becoming president, he acquired a kind of "charisma." Is there the possibility that sociological and psychological qualities have the ability to "mimic" each other? If so, what are the implications for trying to understand human nature?

Endnotes

1. Max Weber, *The Protestant Ethic and the Spirit of Capitalism*, translated by Talcott Parsons (New York: Scribner's, 1930; originally published, 1904). Weber's publications are numerous. The following references indicate the breadth of Weber's interests and studies and, at the same time, may be of interest to students who want to pursue Weber's ideas further: *Ancient Judaism*, translated and edited by Hans H. Gerth and Don Martindale (New York: Free Press, 1952); *Basic Concepts in Sociology*, translated and with an introduction by H. P. Secher (New York: Citadel, 1964); *The City*, translated and edited by Don Martindale and Gertrude Neuwirth (New York: Macmillan/Collier Books, 1962); *From Max Weber: Essays in Sociology*, translated, edited, and with an introduction by Hans H. Gerth and C. Wright Mills (New York: Oxford University Press, 1946); *Max Weber on the Methodology of the Social Sciences*, translated and edited by Edward A. Shils and Henry A. Finch (New York: Free Press, 1949); *The Rational and Social Foundations of Music*, translated and edited by Don Martindale, Johannes Riedel, and Gertrude Neuwirth (Carbondale, IL: Southern Illinois University Press, 1958); *The Religion of China*, translated and edited by Hans H. Gerth (New York: Free Press, 1959); *The Religion of India*, translated and edited by Hans H. Gerth and Don Martindale (New York: Free Press, 1958); *The Sociology of Religion*, translated by Ephraim Fischoff (Boston: Beacon, 1963); and *The Theory of Social and Economic Organization*, translated by A. M. Henderson and Talcott Parsons (New York: Free Press, 1964; originally Published, 1922).
2. Gerth and Mills (eds.), *From Max Weber*, p. 12.
3. Ibid., pp. 25–26.
4. Ferdinand Kurnberger, quoted by Weber in *The Protestant Ethic and the Spirit of Capitalism*, p. 51.
5. Benjamin Franklin, quoted by Weber in *The Protestant Ethic and the Spirit of Capitalism*, p. 50.
6. Weber, *The Protestant Ethic and the Spirit of Capitalism*, p. 57, emphasis added.
7. Ibid., p. 60.
8. Ibid., pp. 83–85.
9. Ibid., p. 91.
10. Ibid., pp. 104–105. This is a slightly modified version of Weber's statement to the same effect.
11. Ibid., p. 105.
12. Ibid., p. 108.
13. Ibid., p. 121.
14. Ibid., p. 158.
15. Ibid.
16. Robert K. Merton et al., *Reader in Bureaucracy* (New York: Free Press, 1952), p. 17.

17. Weber, *The Theory of Social and Economic Organization*, pp. 364–373.
18. Ibid., p. 366.
19. For a penetrating statement of Weber's ideas concerning charisma and bureaucracy, the student should read Reinhard Bendix, *Max Weber: An Intellectual Portrait* (Garden City, NY: Doubleday, 1962).
20. This list is set forth in *The Theory of Social and Economic Organization*. The particular quotations presented here in italics were taken from Merton et al., *Reader in Bureaucracy*, pp. 18–27.
21. A quite ingenious discussion of the transformation of idealism into technical competence by forcing the student to be expedient appears in Howard Becker, E. C. Hughes, and B. Geer, *Boys in White* (Chicago: University of Chicago Press, 1961).
22. Franz Kafka's *The Trial* (New York: Knopf, 1937; originally published, 1925) is one of the better-known depictions of the point being made here.
23. This is documented by Theodore Caplow and Reece McGee, *The Academic Marketplace* (New York: Basic Books, 1958). At one point in the interviews carried out by McGee, a faculty member said, "He played the recorder. That was the reason we hired him." [Interviewer]: "Because he played the recorder?" [Respondent]: "Yes, we thought that would be nice." There is a strong hint here that the respondent, rather unbureaucratically, was pulling the interviewer's leg.
24. A particularly interesting treatment of this theme can be found in Adolf A. Berle, Jr., *Power Without Property* (New York: Harcourt, Brace & World, 1959). See also James Burnham, *The Managerial Revolution* (New York: Day, 1941). Galbraith points out that the meaning of property, where large-scale industrial concerns are involved, is extremely complex. Governmental and industrial interests are so interrelated that it is difficult to establish where the public domain belongs and the private ends. See John Kenneth Galbraith, *The New Industrial State* (Boston: Houghton Mifflin, 1967).
25. This point has been amply documented by sociologists. See Alvin W. Gouldner, *Patterns of Industrial Bureaucracy* (New York: Free Press, 1954), and Erving Goffman, *Asylums* (Garden City, NY: Doubleday, 1961). We understand that postal workers in Britain go on strike by following, to the very letter, every regulation required of postal employees; the resultant mess is sufficient to foul up the delivery of mail. We have also heard the same story told of French bureaucrats.
26. Alvin Gouldner, in *Patterns of Industrial Bureaucracy* (p. 197), points out that administrative officials deal seriously with safety regulations. Gouldner says, "In the main, however, management felt that the most convincing justification for a safety program was the interdependence of safety and production. . . . [T]he major legitimation of safety, work . . . was its usefulness to production."
27. David Sudnow, *Passing On: The Social Organization of Dying* (Englewood Cliffs, NJ: Prentice-Hall, 1967).
28. Material here is based largely on the work of John Garlinghouse, "Ideological and Structural Antecedents of American Medicine," Ph.D. Thesis, University of Colorado, 1978.
29. Garlinghouse (p. 98) quotes from Francis Adams, *The Genuine Works of Hippocrates*, Vol. II (New York: William Wood, 1886), p. 265.
30. Garlinghouse (p. 99) from Adams, p. 211.
31. Garlinghouse (p. 107) from Adams, p. 149.

32. Garlinghouse (pp. 121–122) draws here from Benjamin Lee Gordon, *Medieval and Renaissance Medicine* (New York: Philosophical Library, 1959), pp. 35–36.

33. For an interesting fictional account of early medicine and the complex interrelations between Christian, Jewish, and Persian medical practitioners, see Noah Gordon's novel, *The Physician* (New York: Simon & Schuster, 1987).

34. John Garlinghouse, "Ideological and Structural Antecedents of American Medicine," Ph.D. Thesis, University of Colorado, 1978, p. 195.

35. Garlinghouse (p. 29) quotes from Jurgen Thorwald, *Science and Secrets of Early Medicine* (London: Thames & Hudson, Ltd., 1962).

36. From Garlinghouse, op. cit.

Profit, Greed, and Human Misery

Social Theory and Karl Marx

❖

❖ Malthusian Inevitability

The industrial age introduced new kinds of demeaning experience for great numbers of Europeans. In earlier times they suffered from plagues and war. The industrial age, the age of progress, exacted a price for its benefits in the form of unusual poverty and dull, grinding work. The change was too obvious to go unnoticed by intellectuals of the time. There was something of a paradox to it. How could such a progressive and enlightened period also crush millions of people who somehow found themselves living in the miserable slums of large industrial cities? What accounted for it? Was it necessary? Could anything be done about it? Would the situation improve or simply continue to get worse? Revolutionaries and optimistic intellectuals of the late eighteenth century saw such misery as merely part of a transitional phase that would lead to a greater and more progressive society. Others were less inclined to be hopeful about the future. Among the pessimists was an eighteenth-century economist and minister named Thomas Robert Malthus.

Malthus concluded that the source of such massive misery is located within nature itself. He argued that the simple laws of supply and demand, coupled with the even simpler laws of procreation and the ability of organic populations to increase in a snowballing manner, lead to an inexorable bind. Populations, human as well as animal, should tend to increase to the point where they exhaust their means of subsistence. At this point, as Malthus saw it, population stresses could be resolved only by the wholesale slaughter of warfare, the ravages of disease, and the decimating effects of famine, deprivation, and misery.

We seem to be digressing in this chapter, which is supposed to deal with Marx, by talking about an earlier and much simpler economic argument. However, we would like to stay with Malthus for just a while because the Malthusian argument is so persuasive that to argue against it seems to be the height of folly. Yet we come to understand the great power of Marxism and its tremendous appeal when we counter the optimism of Marx with the dour pessimism of Malthus. So let us simply sketch in a few further comments drawn from Malthus's contentions.

Human populations, said Malthus, have one quite interesting mathematical property: They grow in a geometric fashion. In fact, all populations, whether human or not, possess this property. Malthus meant by this that organic populations, including populations of human beings, double in size over a given interval of time and continue to double with each succeeding interval. This, he argued, is true of any organic population, and it means that nothing in nature can be allowed to grow unchecked for even a moderately long period of time. The reason is elementary: Any population that doubles over a given interval can reach infinitely large values within a finite period.

We might want to stop for a moment at this point. Even if we had never heard of Malthus or of the present concern over the world's population explosion, we could, even if we were only slightly arithmetically inclined, trace out some of the implications of this statement. Suppose, for example, that human populations double every fifty years. (This is a reasonable assumption. Malthus provided data showing that doubling is possible for shorter intervals.) We could begin at the time of Christ with two people and see how long it would take to reach the present world population of roughly four billion souls. The arithmetic is so elementary that we could, with pencil and paper and a small amount of patience, determine the answer in a few minutes: sometime during the sixteenth century. By the middle of the twentieth century we would, at this rate, find ourselves living in a world with a population of over one trillion people—a figure more than two hundred times greater than the present world population.

We can, if we wish, change the interval of time. How many people would be in the world today if we began with two people at the time of Christ and

their numbers doubled every twenty-five years? Malthus made the calculation, and his answer is startling. We would have enough people to place
four persons on every square yard of habitable ground on this planet. Even
so, there would be a surplus. Enough people would be left over to populate
all the planets in the solar system in a similar fashion, and there would still
be a surplus! We would have enough remaining to place four humans on
every square yard of all the planets of all the stars visible to the naked eye
at night—assuming each to be surrounded by as many planets as our own
sun—and we would still have a surplus.

This is, of course, a fantastic figure—a purely mathematical fantasy.
Nonetheless, it fires the imagination and leads immediately to speculation
about what "really" is happening. Since the doubling of human populations
every twenty-five years is not unreasonable, what has happened to the large
numbers we might arithmetically expect? Obviously something has controlled or checked the growth of population. Malthus concluded that devastating checks on population growth are necessary, natural, and inevitable.
Since the checks to population growth involve reduction through famine,
disease, war, and misery, Malthus came to the logical and rational conclusion
that misery is our unavoidable destiny. He did not, incidentally, believe that
population growth could be effectively checked by contraceptive practices.[1]

The model of the world Malthus offers us is a compelling one. The fateful
consequences of Malthusian logic depend, of course, on whether the conditions ascribed to the variables used in the model are in fact true. For example, do human populations necessarily tend to increase in a geometric
fashion until checked by the means of subsistence? Have we today, through
the use of sophisticated contraceptive devices, reached the point where population growth will decline to zero and population size will remain constant?
We can see that it might be possible to check population growth. However,
even our present sophisticated technology looks as though it might be
swamped by the problem, and intellectuals still debate whether or not we
shall soon experience massive catastrophes throughout the world. Setting
such considerations aside for the moment, let us recall that Malthus gave the
century following the initial publication of his essay in 1798 a gloomy argument to chew on.

The Malthusian picture suggests that poverty is an integral feature of
human communities and that it comes out of natural processes, which cannot be corrected by any other than quite extreme and distressing devices.
The poor and starving will always be among us. Why, asked Malthus, worry
about punishing the poor, when nature will do the punishing for us? The
world is the way it is, and we cannot hope to alter it in any significant
manner. Conservative leaders in politics and industry found the argument
of Malthus quite comforting. But there was a response to the fatalistic implications of Malthusianism, and it gained hundreds of millions of adherents
throughout the world. This response appeared in the writings of Karl Marx.

❖ *Industrialization and Human Misery*

Marx was born in a period when the industrial power of Europe was truly beginning to manifest itself. Whether Marx was the greatest social philosopher of the industrial age in purely intellectual terms is difficult to assess. What is less difficult to assess is his political effect. In terms of the numbers of people moved by his work, Marx must be considered, without any doubt, as the greatest social critic and writer of his time. Reformist movements that shook the world and swept up populations numbering in the billions were undertaken in the name of Marx. Rather than shrug Marx off as a kind of anachronistic anomaly, it is necessary to review his work with the thought in mind that, for better or worse, it has shaped human history. The modern world cannot be understood without understanding the appeal of Marx's arguments.

One of the unusual contributions of the industrial age was the appearance of the industrial town. Like few other communities in history, the industrial town offered extreme contrasts in what today would be called lifestyles. It contained, on the one hand, a small minority of people who were able to afford and enjoy the new benefits of an expanding technology, and on the other, large populations of workers whose homes and living conditions were miserable almost beyond belief. There is, even today, a "hidden" population living more miserably than Americans are able to appreciate. Grinding poverty of the variety that appalled progressives of the nineteenth century continues, of course—nicely hidden from the eyes of the affluent suburban American. A visit to the barrios of South America is a searing experience for a person of any sensitivity. Who is to blame for such poverty? As we have seen in the brief discussion of Malthus, one response to the wretched condition of the working population was to attribute the whole business to the cruel workings of a heartless and impassive nature.[2]

The other response was to view the tragedy as a consequence of a flaw in the organization of human affairs. Diligent pursuit of an understanding of human societies and economic systems and how such systems can create unanticipated and excessive brutality might, it was argued, eventually lead to the most ideal of all human conditions—a state in which misery coming from adverse forms of social and economic organization would be decreased to a minimum. Few people in the intellectual history of humankind ever dedicated themselves more to this fundamental aspiration for all of humanity than did Karl Marx. Whether we agree in the final summation with Marx's vision, we must acknowledge that it stands as the most painstakingly rational effort ever made to see through the complexities of entire social systems. Behind the work of Marx was the driving animus of a desire to comprehend the inhumanity of people toward other people.

❖ *Marxist Sociology*

Marx is known, of course, as an economic theorist. His theories, however, have far too many ramifications to be restricted exclusively to the realm of economic analysis. If Marx is an economic theorist, it is only because, in searching for an answer to the problem of human misery, he became convinced that the manifold forms of political, religious, cultural, and philosophical systems under which people live are to be understood in terms of their relationship to the modes of production prevailing in any community at any time.[3] It would seem obvious that a hunting society, with its attendant forms of production and distribution of goods, must necessarily have legal, religious, educational, kin, and other institutional structures quite different from those of a society relying on an economic base employing the use of landed estates, agricultural systems, and barter.

It was an idea that had considerable impact at a time when people were discovering that personal worth could be bought with money. During the feudal period, status was inherited and transmitted through noble blood lines. With the rise of the industrial state, a person could begin thinking about purchasing a sense of importance. The bond between social structure (ideology, values, status, belief, and other nebulous but nonetheless significant features of society) and the economic order was becoming much too apparent for thinkers to overlook. Money has always had a large voice in human affairs, but in the new industrial age its significance became even more marked. It was obvious that money and ideas were connected. The question to be examined was the extent to which money ultimately led to the purchase of social systems inimical to the progress of human welfare.

It is important for the student being introduced to modern social philosophy to understand the essential issue raised by Marxist social thought. We can gain an insight into the problems of sociological investigation if we see the central thrust of Marxist doctrine as being directed toward the end of finding a "substance" in social systems. There are, on the one hand, those who believe that social systems are located within a realm of values, beliefs, ideologies, symbols, linguistic systems, moral codes, doctrines, and other "substanceless" forces. Opposed to this position is the argument that the relations that bind people into greater communal orders are sustained by "lower" or more "basic" conditions.[4] According to this latter position, ideologies and moral codes and such other "insubstantial conditions" are "reflections" or responses to the more substantial conditions that underlie them.

Marx found his "substance" in labor and its use and abuse. Labor creates value. At the same time, Marx was quite aware that the value of a particular commodity is affected not only by its labor input, but by its socially granted merits as well. Labor in and of itself cannot impose a value. The thousands of hours of labor that might go into the building of a useless machine will not generate as much value as a smaller amount of labor that might go into, let us say, the painting of a masterpiece. This example, though crude, is sufficient to make us immediately aware of the problems involved in locating value exclusively within a labor context.

As almost everyone knows today, Marx turned to the economic order as the primal reality determining the ebb and flow of moral and social structures. People are sustained by the extent to which they cooperate in productive efforts to attend to individual and communal needs. This primitive and eternal necessity cannot be ignored. If so inclined, one can dismiss the philosophies of the existentialists or the Christians or the Buddhists and not come to any special grief; however, one cannot ignore the iron laws of the marketplace. Perhaps we do not live by bread alone, but we must obtain bread before we can engage in any other form of activity.[5] Ultimately, Marx suggested, it is the manner in which people obtain their "bread" that determines the way in which they will establish their programs of justice, religion, kinship, education, and other social institutions. The power people gain over one another has its locus in the forces of production.

Marxist sociology, then, is characterized by an effort to interpret uniquely social events in terms of how those events are associated with economic conditions or factors associated with the production and distribution of goods. Marx, writing in 1859, pointed to the mode of production and said that it determines the general character of the social, political, and spiritual processes of life. He argued that it is not the consciousness of people that determines their existence; on the contrary, it is their economic existence that determines their consciousness.[6]

The ringing and often-quoted words at the beginning of *The Communist Manifesto* give us a feeling of the inspirational quality of Marx's message:

> The history of all hitherto existing society is the history of class struggles.
>
> Freeman and slave, patrician and plebeian, lord and serf, guild master and journeyman, in a word, oppressor and oppressed, stood in constant opposition to one another, carried on an uninterrupted, now hidden, now open fight, a fight that each time ended either in a revolutionary reconstitution of society at large or in the common ruin of the contending classes.
>
> In the earlier epochs of history we find almost everywhere a complicated arrangement of society into various orders, a manifold gradation of social rank. In ancient Rome we have patricians, knights, plebeians, slaves; in the Middle Ages, feudal lords, vassals, guild masters, journeymen, apprentices, serfs; in almost all of these classes, again, subordinate gradations.
>
> The modern bourgeois society that has sprouted from the ruins of feudal society has not done away with class antagonisms. It has established new classes, new conditions of oppression, new forms of struggle in place of the old ones.[7]

Economic interpretations of history are still popular and reveal the extent to which the Marxist influence permeates Western thought. Indeed, a lot of Americans who would be shocked to think of themselves as Marxists nonetheless subscribe to a fundamentally Marxist mode of thinking. They think in terms of economic determinism. Following are general examples of the impact of economic interpretations of history and social order.

Charles Beard wrote an interpretation of the founding of America in terms of economic interests and managed to shock a number of Americans who thought American government was grounded in higher ideals.[8] The development of applied mathematics and the growth of science as a unique ideological system are seen by some writers as responses to the growth of a need for more accurate counting procedures on the part of merchants as commercial expansion took place in the fourteenth and fifteenth centuries. Business still remains a tremendous consumer of computer technology, and the computer is essentially a business machine. The growth of exploration in the fifteenth century was motivated less by idle curiosity than it was by the need to expand markets and acquire resources for European countries. As a final general example, we ought to mention that much of the popularity of current discussions of socioeconomic class structures owes its impetus to Marxist thought. In sum, the pervasiveness of Marxist thought within Western social philosophy is greater than we commonly recognize. Anyone who emphasizes the economy as a source of social and ideological change and who views human beings as essentially economically motivated is conceding a central argument to Marx.

❖ *Economic Riddles*

Compared with social theory, the realm of economic study seems closed, nicely ordered, and a proper subject for rational analysis. To a considerable degree, this is the case. There will probably never be a Nobel laureate in sociology, although there are a number of Nobel prize winners in the field of economics. However, the fact remains that economic activity and the more vague and ephemeral forms of social conduct which resist logical analysis are bound together. Several central issues in economic analysis are dependent on a parallel understanding of sociological forces for their resolution. We mention two areas of economic uncertainty here, because we believe that they lead nicely into an appreciation of the problems encountered in Marxist approaches to social systems. These issues also quickly reveal the interdependent nature of economic and more general sociological forces.

The first area of interest has to do with the problem of production and utilization of economic surpluses. It would seem, at first, that the whole idea of the development of economic surpluses would be a simple matter to explain. We all remember the lesson of the story of the grasshopper and the ant. The grasshopper fiddled while the ant stored surpluses against bad times ahead. The value of surpluses is so obvious to us today that the possibility that surpluses are peculiar is difficult to accept. Nonetheless, the economic history of humanity suggests that the acquisition of large surpluses is a unique event. In a sense, true surpluses come about when people are coerced, by one means or other, to produce more than they need as individuals. (Weber used the term "traditional economy" to refer to cases where people work primarily to fulfill immediate needs. American entrepreneurs

occasionally find themselves frustrated in other cultures when they encounter workers who prefer not to maximize their income, but instead work
just long enough to get whatever income will satisfy their needs of the
moment and then stop.)

The second area of interest has to do with the utilization of surplus forms
of wealth. Once an economy possesses surplus goods and materials, means
must be devised of separating people from their individually acquired savings, so that those surpluses can be employed for the benefit of the community. At this point, the crucial connection between the individual and the
state was subjected to a searing commentary by Marx. Marx, more than
anyone else, posed the moral question of how a person's surplus efforts may
be fairly distributed. We shall return to this issue later. Let us first consider
the apparently simple matter of the achievement of surplus wealth.

We are so familiar today with the idea of surpluses that it is difficult to
comprehend the extent to which surplus wealth is, as a matter of fact, a
perplexing economic question. The relationship between need satisfaction
and the acquisition of surpluses is not as simple as might at first be presumed.
In traditional or simple economies, surplus wealth is meager. At the same
time, there is no strong motivation to acquire surplus wealth.

A rather interesting case was observed during World War II in New
Guinea. The people of native cultures living there were astounded by the
wealth of goods and supplies they saw coming from ships and aircraft during
World War II. The natives were convinced that such supplies were coming
from their ancestors and were meant for their consumption and use. Whole
cults were built around the idea of receiving such largesse. These ''cargo
cults,'' as they came to be known, were not grounded in an idea of excess
or surplus wealth. The economy of the natives remained essentially a traditional or subsistence economy.

For example, in the film *The Hunters*, bushmen of the Kalahari Desert
are shown hunting down a giraffe. It takes them over a week to accomplish
their quest. After ritualistically atoning for the ''hole'' they have created in
the world by killing such a magnificent animal, they butcher the carcass,
take home the remains, distribute the food, and eat and tell stories until,
once more, it is time to hunt. In a world where life is difficult and brief, food
is hard to come by, and the acquisition of goods is a serious struggle, there
are reasons why work is limited and surpluses relatively slight.

One of the central concerns of Marxist social thought focuses on the
nature of surplus wealth. Surplus wealth, of course, has reached a sort of
reductio ad absurdum in our society. We not only have surplus wealth to the
point where we suffer from economic ''gluts,'' but we even have ''surplus
labor.'' There is a strangeness in the idea of surplus labor. As David Riesman
has frequently noted, surplus labor actually refers to ''surplus people.'' We
live in a surplus economy. At least an elementary understanding of the nature and character of surpluses—what they mean for people, how they affect
our lives, and the problems they pose—is essential for anyone who seeks to

be informed about the affairs of our time. Having raised the problem of surpluses as an interesting question in and of itself, we would like to set it aside for a moment and turn to another aspect of the nature of surplus wealth. This second feature of surpluses is even more interesting, we believe, than the question of how surpluses came into being in the first place.

This question has to do with how individuals are separated from the surplus goods and services they may produce. Suppose, for example, you have worked hard and industriously for several years and managed to accumulate savings of some sort. These savings, of course, constitute wealth above and beyond the demand of immediate necessities. They are surplus wealth. Suppose, further, that members of the community come to you and tell you that if you give them your savings, it will be to the benefit of all, and you and everyone else will live in a better world as a result. In this baldly simple form, the problem of the separation of the individual from his or her surplus is dramatically clear. What right do others have to your savings or surplus? If they persist, by what devices can they separate you from the results of your effort?

It is immediately evident, although in real situations the matter becomes more complex, that two elemental devices are available for achieving the separation. The first of these is persuasion: You might be talked out of your holdings by members of the community who come to you and plead for your help and assistance. They might add, as part of the persuasive effort, a suggestion that if you give part or all of your holdings to the community, you will be rewarded with nonsubstantial but nonetheless significant honors and elevations in prestige. You can, as it were, purchase a sense of significance. This is one way to be parted from surplus wealth.

The second way others can get your surplus is to take it by force. This, of course, is a time-honored device. Taxation, for example, is a forceful procedure. Two forms of force are commonly employed in the venture of separating people from their available wealth: illegal force and legal force. Both are used toward the same end; the effect is not different. The difference lies largely in the agent making use of force. It is pretty tricky, incidentally, to argue that legal force is good because it works for the benefit of the community and that illegal force is bad because it serves the selfish interests of some crook. The state can take surplus wealth and employ it for evil ends, and a poor person can rob someone and use the stolen money to feed his or her family.[9]

We are interested, at the moment, in the simple idea of how people go about taking someone's excess wealth and what they do with it if they succeed in getting it. This, in a sense, is one of the more dramatic concerns of Marxist philosophy. What are the implications of the relationship between the acquisition of surplus wealth and the application of force necessary for the distribution of such wealth? One of the central concerns of Marxist doctrine is the speculation that force leads to a concentration of wealth in the hands of a few because wealth is capable of being transformed into force.

Therefore, those who are initially successful in acquiring wealth will, at the same time, augment the power needed for gaining greater access to existing wealth. At this point we begin to see that the motivation for the acquisition of surplus wealth may lie in the fact that wealth offers security, in the form of power, to those who obtained control of the economic process. The question of surplus, then, can be explained (at least in part) as the never-ending need for greater and greater security on the part of those who are in positions of power. So it is that people, who in traditional economies produced merely enough to meet their simplest needs, were later transformed into creatures whose needs could never be satiated.

❖ *The Dialectic*

This introduction enables us to move into the more original features of Marxist thought. It would seem, from the discussion above, that the dynamics of the relationship between wealth and power would lead to greater and greater concentrations of wealth in the hands of the very few. There is something to be said for such a view of human social and economic order. There are people whose wealth is so vast that the ordinary person cannot begin to comprehend the magnitudes of power and money involved.[10]

Consider, for example, the wealth and power controlled by someone who approaches billionaire status. If it were necessary to escape from an impending catastrophic situation and one could buy such escape at the cost of a hundred dollars a foot, most of us would not be able to get more than twenty or thirty feet from ground zero. To get a mile away would take over half a million dollars. A billionaire would be able to get almost two thousand miles away. There are currently a few men and women in the United States who control over five billion dollars in private assets. They could, of course, buy their way from the point of catastrophe to a place safely removed ten thousand miles away—at one hundred dollars a foot.

The vast difference between the capacities of an ordinary person and those of a billionaire can be dramatized in a variety of ways, but words cannot fully convey the overwhelming force of great wealth. The rich are quite different from the rest of us—they have lots more money. Money is both power and freedom. So it is that the rich possess greater power and freedom than men and women of ordinary means.

Given the combined forces of wealth and power, one augmenting the other, it would seem that an ever-growing concentration of wealth would be inevitable. The processes of history, from a Marxist stance, produce circumstances in which the legions of the poor continually increase, while the wealthy become fewer in number but ever stronger and wealthier.[11] It is to the credit of Marxist thought that it does not stop here and, like the conservative thought of the Malthusians, conclude that the fate of the great majority of people is to be wretched, miserable, and doomed forever.

Marx was convinced that the historical process would lead eventually to a balancing-out of affairs. The dominant classes or elements that instigate eras of grinding wretchedness are required to dig their own graves by virtue of their excesses. Marx referred to this process as the "dialectic."[12] The dialectic consists of a threefold historical movement in which a given condition, referred to as the "thesis," creates its own opposition or "antithesis." The ensuing struggle between these opposed forces leads to a new state, or "synthesis," which then in turn creates its own opposed conditions. The dialectic is looked upon as a model of cultural and economic change that views history as a dynamic and continuous series of confrontations in which a given historical epoch sows the seeds of its own destruction.[13]

So, if the industrial age produced grinding conditions for the laboring classes, the forces of history would eventually even the score over the longer run. Industrial capitalism would dig its own grave and do it unwittingly. It would be led by its own logic to create those conditions that would bring about a movement toward a noncapitalist state. The dialectic process means the inevitable establishment of a classless society. There is an interesting aspect to this argument. One can quickly see that if the process is inevitable, there should be no need to promote it. Marx's revolutionary propaganda seemed to critics to be a refutation of the dialectic, or at least a possible revelation of a lack of faith in its own vision.

As a brief example of a possible dialectic process, consider the growing awareness of the internal contradictions of a consumer society as we know it. In order for our current economic structure to sustain itself, goods must be produced and distributed for profit. The profit, a form of surplus wealth, is fed back into further production and distribution. The structural demands of this form of economy require rampant consumption. The entire economic process demands constant growth. However, this brings us to a different version of the Malthusian problem with which this chapter has begun. The constant growth of economic goods leads to the same purely mathematical or logical impasse that a constant growth in population leads to . . . infinite quantities in a finite period of time. In sum, constant economic growth is capable of exhausting the finite resources of the planet itself. So, the same economists, industrialists, and developers who promote economic growth are generating those conditions that, over the historical long run, will destroy the economic practices they advocate.

❖ *The Working Day*

All of this is rather abstract and generally known, if not thoroughly understood, by high school seniors. But Marx is famous neither for his political rhetoric (though he was a master of invective) nor for the creation of abstract philosophical systems in the older German tradition. Marx established his reputation, in great part, by penetrating into the picayune, minor, and seemingly inconsequential details available to him. Out of these details, and out of thousands of established and documented facts, Marx began to put together a grand conception of history and of the moment in which he lived. It was with the factual, not the abstract, that Marx overwhelmed readers and won adherents by the thousands. Possibly Marx, more than any other single individual of his time, gave hope to people who sought to ground social argumentation in factual observations.

Marx not only theorized over the nature of labor in its more abstract character; he also described what it meant, in concrete terms, to be engaged in menial labor in industrial England in the nineteenth century. Nothing, we believe, better reveals the extent of Marx's concern with labor than his treatment of the working day.[14] Marx's involvement with the working day achieved two effects simultaneously. First of all, it provided an opening for a treatment of the nature and character of surplus wealth. Second, it presented a shocking description of the wretchedness into which unbridled capitalistic practice had thrown great masses of men and women who were forced to live under its sway during the formative period of modern capitalism.

The working day was divided by Marx into two parts. The first consists of the amount of time it takes a worker to produce the materials and goods necessary for his or her subsistence. The second is a variable period during which the worker produces goods and materials above and beyond whatever is necessary for subsistence. On this elemental foundation, Marx was able to build a structure that leads to an inevitable clash between those who purchase labor (the capitalists) and those who must sell their labor (the workers, or proletariat). Furthermore, this clash results from a strictly rational consideration of their interests by both groups. The worker must determine what is a reasonable working day, whereas the capitalist must determine what constitutes a maximum possible working day. Both the capitalist and the worker, operating within the economic dictates of capitalism, are coerced to respond as they do.

From a Marxist perspective, the capitalist seeks to extend the working day for as long as possible. Workers seek to reduce the length of the working day so that it is not beyond their capacities. But the final resolution of this conflict of rational interests cannot be a matter of rational discussion. In the final analysis, the confrontation between those who labor and those who purchase labor will have to be resolved by the application of force.

> The capitalist maintains his rights as a purchaser when he tries to make the working day as long as possible, and to make, whenever possible, two working days out of one. On the other hand, the peculiar nature of the commodity sold implies a limit to its consumption by the purchaser, and the labourer maintains his right as seller when he wishes to reduce the working day to one of definite normal duration. There is here, therefore, an antinomy, right against right, both equally bearing the seal of the law of exchanges. Between equal rights force decides. Hence is it that in the history of capitalist production, the determination of what is a working day presents itself as the result of a struggle, a struggle between collective capital, i.e., the class of capitalists, and collective labor, i.e., the working class.[15]

This quotation reveals a variety of conceptions basic to Marx's approach toward the examination of social systems. First of all, capitalists are considered dispassionately as operating within "their rights" when they seek to extend the working day in order to maximize surplus wealth, which may then be transformed into profit. Second, workers are also within their rights when they seek to bring the working day within what constitutes a "normal" duration.[16] Third, the clash of two evenly balanced rights makes necessary the use of force.[17] Fourth, and finally, the central struggle within humankind exists not so much between nations as between two necessarily opposed classes of people— workers and those who purchase labor for gain.

There is in this quote, as there is in Marxist doctrine generally, a cold reasoning that looks on the members of the working class as beings caught up in historical forces that demand the working-out of competing interests. There is no condemnation of either side. There is, however, the belief that labor should, and eventually will, exercise the decisive historical force. Marxist morality is grounded in an ethic to which an overwhelming majority of Americans subscribe: Any individual is deserving of the full fruits of his or her labor. Anything less than this is something that falls short of a reasonable conception of a just and fair world.

But Marx's consideration of the working day went beyond a simple calculation of the problems involved in determining what constitutes a proper duration for the working day. The greater part of his discourse was a chronicling of the industrial horrors encountered by working men, women, and children of the nineteenth century. One cannot read Marx at any length without discerning the extent to which his logic was driven by his compassion. Marx understood that capitalists were only exercising a right when they attempted to minimize labor costs by extending the working day to its maximum effective limits. At the same time, the cost of such practice in terms of simple human suffering was not to be ignored in the name of rational economic practice. Here, for example, is one case that Marx presented for consideration in his discussion of the working day. It is worth reviewing because it places in perspective the milieu out of which Marxism arose.

In the last week of June, 1863, all the London daily papers published a paragraph with the "sensational" heading "Death from simple over-work." It dealt with the death of the milliner, Mary Anne Walkley, 20 years of age, employed in a highly-respectable dressmaking establishment, exploited by a lady with the pleasant name of Elise. The old often-told story was once more recounted. This girl worked, on an average, 16½ hours, during the season often 30 hours, without a break, whilst her failing labour-power was revived by occasional supplies of sherry, port, or coffee. It was just now the height of the season. It was necessary to conjure up in the twinkling of an eye the gorgeous dresses for the noble ladies bidden to the ball in honour of the newly imported Princess of Wales. Mary Anne Walkley had worked without intermission for 26½ hours, with 60 other girls, 30 in one room, that only afforded 3 of the cubic feet of air required for them. At night, they slept in pairs in one of the stifling holes into which the

bedroom was divided by partitions of board. And this was one of the best mil-
linery establishments in London. Mary Anne Walkley fell ill on Friday, died on
Sunday, without, to the astonishment of Madame Elise, having previously completed the work at hand.[18]

It must be kept in mind that naturalistic philosophy prevailed in Europe
in the nineteenth century. It seems obvious today to find the causes of poverty within economic systems. Actually, the causes of poverty are not at all
obvious, even within a naturalistic framework. Marx did, however, pretty
much kill the argument that poverty is a moral condition and that wealth,
in and of itself, is indicative of superior moral fiber. What was new in Marxism was not the fact that some people in the world are poor and oppressed
and others are not. What was new was Marx's attempt to find a natural
source of poverty, the *real* focus of oppression. He found it within the economic structure. Ultimately, according to Marx, poverty is a condition coming out of the ways in which the means of production for any given society
are used to meet the needs of the community.

Unlike earlier religiously grounded explanations for the plight of the
impoverished, Marx's theory neither excuses nor condemns poverty as a
moral flaw. The poor are not poor because they lack moral virtues, nor are
the wealthy granted their exalted lives because they are morally superior. In
the worldview of Marx, the distinction between the poor and the wealthy
comes about through the operation of impersonal and natural forces to be
found within the economic structure, and is essentially a rationalization of
that structure. Therefore, moral action cannot be separated from economic
action. After Marx, the day and age of simple moralizing was over. It was
not enough to condemn the poor as people lacking in the moral virtues
necessary for a better life. The time had come to deal with moral issues from
a broader perspective. The human moral condition was taken out of the
church and into the marketplace.

❖ *The Marxist Vision*

It is too easy to dismiss Marx because his predictions of the collapse of capitalistic countries did not come true in quite the manner he anticipated.
Prophets in the realm of economic and social affairs, whether Marxist or
capitalistic, have a record of miscalculations and erroneous forecasts that is
all too well known. If we condemn Marx because he was not perfect in his
forecasts, then we must condemn any other social visionary as well.

It is difficult at times to determine why American industrialists are so
anti-Marxist. Most of them, as we have suggested before, take an economic
approach to history—to the extent that they are concerned with the interpretation of history. Most of them think that money is essentially what
makes the world go round. Marx would agree. Most of them are inclined to
believe that satisfying physical needs through production, more production,

and still more production is the highest thing one can work for in life. Marx would still be inclined to agree. Where, then, is the cleavage? What is it about Marxist doctrine that is so distressing to Americans?

The answer, we believe, lies in the vision Marx offered of a world in which people will be judged by the worth of their labor, rather than by the more spurious forms of worth to be obtained through the control of wealth. A person who has inherited a million dollars from a father or mother and who has not done a lick of work since the inheritance is an object of contempt to the Marxist. Marx called such people "parasites," and this is proper invective. American capitalism, despite demurrers to the contrary, is ambivalent about work or physical labor. Work is good, yet it is something for suckers. The Marxist vision is grounded in a belief in the value of work and the worth of all forms of human labor. So it was that the Chinese sent their intellectuals into the rice paddies to find out about aching backs and muddy feet. Possibly it is this aspect of the Marxist vision that chills the soul of the American sophisticate.

It is sufficient in this brief discussion of Marx simply to note that Marx was not content to allow those who purchase labor to define the morality of labor. He argued that labor itself must establish a just morality with respect to its contributions to the community. This certainly sounds fair and reasonable enough if we subscribe to the belief that one should receive the full benefits of one's labor. It is precisely at this point, however, that we uncover a distressing problem–not only with respect to Marxist thinking, but with respect to any social philosophy or theory.

The problem lies in attempting to define what is meant by "the full benefits of one's labor." If the free market defines such benefits, then we find ourselves confronted with the anomaly that men and women who play silly games (such as swatting little balls into holes arranged around a cow pasture) make hundreds of times more than people who provide us with such essentials as our food and clothing. In this instance, it is not labor itself that determines its value, but rather its relationship to the marketplace—and this produces obvious inequities and peculiarities, the very things Marx railed against. On the other hand, if any particular class (say, the physical laboring classes) acquires the power to define such benefits, then we encounter imbalances and misunderstandings of other forms of labor, such as occurred when Chinese Marxists pulled intellectuals out of the universities and research centers and made them work in rice paddies. The vision of labor receiving a fair share of what it produces is difficult to argue against in any ethical scheme. How such justice is to be attained probably requires more than a simple proletarian revolution.

Whether this is true or not, there is no denying the impact that the Marxist vision has had on the world. It produced in our time several major national bureaucracies surprisingly free of corruption (though corruption is found in all systems). It produced a nearly puritanical morality in social and economic systems that, before being transformed by the Marxist vision, were corrupt and ineffective. We are witnessing today a historical epoch in which the forces opposed to the Marxist vision stand in somewhat the same position as those countries that stood opposed to the Protestant Reformation in the sixteenth century.

Marxism is an essential part of the studies of anyone who is going into economics, sociology, anthropology, political science, or any of the other areas of humanistic interest. Marx offers one of the finer models of how to cope with a social or economic concern. He was thorough in his examination of the facts. He was broad in his historical perspectives. He developed a theme or theory in which the historical progression of a variety of events could be systematized. These are essential features of any powerful approach to social issues. Still, there is something else in Marx's writings that gives them special vigor in this day and age of social objectivity. There is a sense of moral dedication and outrage. Marx documented that the nineteenth-century road to progress was paved with decadence, corruption, and suffering. He not only described the social illnesses of his time; he also prescribed what was needed if real progress was to be achieved. No other person in modern times has exerted as powerful an impact on the course of the world's political, social, and economic future.

Encounters with Social Thought

Looking at the Testing Movement in America
Using a Marxist Perspective

The intellectual vitality of Marxist theory is quickly revealed by the extent to which it redirects our imagination as we explore nearly any topic relevant to human social concerns. Marxists have written on virtually every aspect of the human condition, and in doing so have given us yet a different way of seeing that condition. In the following discussion, we have selected psychology, as we know it in America, and psychological tests as a topic to be viewed from a Marxist slant. Certainly, in a discussion as brief as this, we can only suggest how Marxist ideas might be used to examine such a subject. We make no claim to any kind of definitive, final, or authoritative analysis. The reader is encouraged to consider this or any other topic in which he or she might be interested from a Marxist perspective. It is only when we begin to use Marx's ideas to extend our own vision that we also begin to see why Marx was the foremost social philosopher in Western culture of the late nineteenth century.

We need to make one more comment before entering into this exercise in the use of Marxist thought. Different individuals, relying on the same theoretical perspective, will reach different conclusions concerning a given topic. There is no precise way in which social thought can be applied. This means that there is always an irreducible element of controversy in nearly any discussion of the human social scene. The following consideration of psychological testing is critical, because Marxist theory tends to be highly critical of much that goes on in modern Western industrial states. At the same time, we have also tried to indicate where Marx might have welcomed psychological testing. However, the principal goal in the following discussion is to get the reader involved and using the ideas of Marx to improve his or her own imaginative awareness of our modern, complex world.

Psychology and Individualism

The industrial age brought along with it transformations in how we look at ourselves and think about ourselves. Foremost among Western institutions that have shaped and continue to shape our view of ourselves was the establishment of a complex professional system dedicated to the scientific exploration of the human psyche. This professional system, of course, is what we now refer to as "psychology." Psychology is a broad field with a tremendous range of sentiments and beliefs among its practitioners. However, psychologists share in common a belief in rational approaches to solving human problems, and they are inclined to emphasize the individual. For example, if a person is suffering from a malady, the psychologist attempts to cure the individual.

This concentration on the individual serves several purposes. For one thing, it assigns responsibility for failure (or success) to the individual, and in so doing mutes consideration of social contexts or the greater socioeconomic structure as a problem. It tends to promote the notion that social movements are the product of great individuals—the so-called "Great Man" approach (a term grounded in the prefeminist era) in human affairs. In all of this, psychology sustains the dominant Western ideology of individualism and, indirectly, the idea that an individual's fate is whatever he or she wants to make of it. If something is wrong, it is the individual who must be examined and then "cured." Psychology sustains the American fantasy that if the individual really, really tries, nothing is impossible. Therefore, if the individual does not succeed, it follows that he or she did not really try.

From a Marxist stance, it is difficult to avoid the conclusion that psychology exists as an elaborate "cooling-out" device for those who are rejected or oppressed by the industrial system. Those who fail are counseled and given "therapy." In this act, psychology implicitly locates the conditions that led to failure within the individual, whereas it is possible that the conditions that led to failure lie elsewhere.

Psychology, in administering to the stresses and breakdowns of those who fail in a highly competitive system, also sets itself up as the proper agency for correcting ills inherent in the system itself. In other words, psychological therapy—along with other forms of welfare assistance, and palliatives—works to mute and redirect the frustrations and dissatisfactions that might otherwise lead to truly revolutionary restructurings of the system.

In addition, psychology gives itself over to an examination of qualities of the individual, with the end in mind of identifying those men and women who will efficiently serve the interests of the industrial economy. Psychological testing began at much the same point in history that quality control began. The standardization of mass production and the standardization of psychological tests appeared at much the same moment in history. Psychology has, among its various goals, the desire to establish more precisely who belongs where in the system. Actually, the problem of who belongs where is relegated primarily to the laboring classes. It is they, more than the members of powerful elites, who are subjected to myriad personality, vocational aptitude, and intelligence tests. Tests not only identify those who are fit for work; they also identify those who are not fit, and in so doing provide a further rationalization for excluding individuals from participation in the industrial community. In such instances, the individual is led to believe that it is not the fault of the system that he or she cannot be employed; it is the individual's fault.

Personnel Tests: Do You Have Talent?

Consider, for example, psychology tests of a pencil-and-paper variety, used commonly by state and federal agencies to determine who will get various civil service positions. Although there is a place for testing in any culture, and nearly all cultures employ some kind of "test" to determine who will occupy critical positions, it is characteristic of modern times that vocational tests—generally designed and administered by psychologists—are constructed and used in peculiar ways. For example, one test with which we are familiar is a pencil-and-paper test that supposedly identifies people who have special abilities as firefighters.

What is interesting about this test is that it correlates, at best, only about 2 percent of the time with actual rated performances in the field.[19] It is basically a worthless test. Yet it has been quite seriously used to tell people they cannot be considered as possible members of local firefighting units. Although it is useless as any serious kind of test of potential firefighting ability, it is quite useful as a way of making an individual feel that he or she simply lacks talent. What is especially curious about this particular firefighting test is that although it does not effectively discriminate between individuals in terms of firefighting ability, it does a much better job of discriminating between people who are good at pencil-and-paper tests and those who are not. So the poor, the improperly educated, and the naive are led to believe that they lack ability.

The IQ Test

A Marxist slant gives us a novel way of looking at something we might otherwise accept in a more conventional sense. We refer now to the idea of intelligence in modern society. Even those who are aware that intelligence tests are culturally and racially biased tend to subscribe to the more general idea that intelligence is a matter of being able to solve problems. However, intelligence has not always been viewed as we view it today. In earlier times, intelligence was not so important as other qualities of the intellect.

We can infer from medieval literature that the men and women of that age framed the problem of intelligence differently from the way we frame it today. The problems and concerns confronting the medieval citizen were not similar to the problems coming out of an industrial society. The primary force in industrial society is the engine, in one form or another, and our conception of intelligence is basically the quality of the mind that can deal with the kinds of problems engines get us into. That is to say, engines are basically logical in their structure, and we therefore come to define intelligence primarily in terms of spatial and symbolic forms of logic. Such intelligence serves the needs of a mechanical system, but it is not necessarily effective with respect to other systems.

In earlier societies, for example, the demands of the economy and the society were more direct; machines did not exist as intermediaries between human beings and nature. Death was always close. Religion was profoundly real. The major problem of the time was to retain a sense of community or a sense of membership with a larger identity. This was accomplished through the church and through military systems. Within the church and the military of any society, the primary quality sought in the individual is loyalty or faith.

Even if keeping the faith is an admirable human quality, it is not something that requires great intelligence as we define it in the present time. Indeed, a keen intelligence probably finds faith or even loyalty, on occasion, an issue to question. Quite obviously, questioning faith or loyalty imperils the community. The quality of character that the medieval mind was interested in was the character not of the intelligent or unintelligent person, as we think of intelligence today, but the character of the wise person or the fool. The opposite of foolishness is not intelligence, but wisdom. After all, one can be quite intelligent and not be wise. Wisdom, like the modern concept of intelligence, had its political aspects. For example, wisdom was usually thought of as a property of men (wise women are even more rare than wise men in medieval literature). Wisdom was also generally a property of men and women of leisure.

The Politicizing of Intelligence

In brief, the social and economic structure of a particular era is relevant to the manner in which people define intelligence and the ways in which they seek it, constrain it, and reward it. To put it more boldly, intelligence is as much a political concept as it is a psychological concept. We can appreciate the difference between modern conceptions of intelligence and older ones by noting the uniquely twentieth-century quest for artificial intelligence. Somehow it seems reasonable to talk about "artificial intelligence" when intelligence itself has been subordinated primarily to the end of serving artificial machines. However, it makes no sense at all to talk about "artificial wisdom." We accept the idea that intelligence can be artificial, and, in so doing, reveal the extent to which our understanding of intelligence is unique to our age.

Or, to consider the matter from a slightly different slant, we have intelligence tests but we do not have tests for wisdom, at least to the same extent that we have intelligence quotient (IQ) tests. Psychology, at least so far as we are aware, has never concerned itself in any serious manner with the construction of a wisdom quotient(WQ). The extent to which intelligence, as a concept, overtook the "older-fashioned" notion of wisdom can be seen by acknowledging that library holdings list about eight or nine times as many works dealing with intelligence as with wisdom. Given the needs of the modern state, we have abandoned wisdom in favor of smartness. This discussion is not passing judgment on whether we have gained or lost by such a choice. The point being made here is that a personal characteristic such as intelligence is not only a psychological matter but also a socioeconomic matter. How a society is ordered in terms of its economic infrastructure has a bearing on what will be considered psychologically significant.

Although an explicit treatment of intelligence as such, does not, to our recollection, appear in Marx's writings, it certainly was a matter of concern to Marx in an indirect way. Consider, for example, the following:

> A classical example of over-work, of hard and inappropriate labour, and of its brutalizing effects on the workman from his childhood upwards, is afforded not only by coal-mining and miners generally, but also by tile and brick making. . . . Between May and September the work lasts from 5 in the morning till 8 in the evening, and where the drying is done in the open air, it often lasts from 4 in the morning till 9 in the evening. Work from 5 in the morning till 7 in the evening is considered "reduced" and "moderate." Both boys and girls of 6 and even of 4 years of age are employed. They work for the same number of hours, often longer, than the adults. It

is impossible for a child to pass through the purgatory of a tile-field without great moral degradation . . . the low language, which they are accustomed to hear from their tenderest years, the filthy, indecent, and shameless habits, amidst which, unknowing, and half wild, they grow up, make them in later-life lawless, abandoned, dissolute.[20]

Marx noted that earlier craft or guild systems and the training of the apprentice could enhance the intellectual development of the child. By the twentieth century, however, the machine had turned things around.

In the English letter-press printing trade . . . there existed formerly a system . . . of advancing the apprentices from easy to more and more difficult work. They went through a course of teaching till they were finished printers. To be able to read and write was for every one of them a requirement of their trade. All this was changed by the printing machine. It employs . . . boys mostly from 11 to 17 years of age whose sole business is either to spread the sheets of paper under the machine, or to take from it the printed sheets. They perform this weary task, in London especially, for 14, 15, and 16 hours at a stretch, during several days in the week, and frequently for 36 hours, with only 2 hours' rest for meals and sleep. A great part of them cannot read, and they are, as a rule, utter savages and very extraordinary creatures. To qualify them for the work which they have to do, they require no intellectual training; there is little room in it for skill, and less for judgment. . . . As soon as they get too old for such child's work, that is about 17 at the latest, they are discharged from the printing establishments. They become the recruits of crime.[21]

Marx also stated a little later:

The children and young persons, therefore, in all such cases may justifiably claim from the legislature, as a natural right, that an exemption should be secured to them, from what destroys prematurely their physical strength, and lowers them in the scale of intellectual and moral beings.[22]

These passages make it quite obvious that Marx was concerned with the intellectual as well as the physical well-being not only of children who were oppressed by the factory system, but of adults as well. *Das Kapital* first appeared in 1867; the Binet-Simon intelligence test did not appear until nearly forty years later (1904–1905, roughly a year or so after the first heavier-than-air flight by the Wright brothers). It is difficult to believe that Marx would not strongly have endorsed intelligence testing in the early years of the century. The intelligence test, first of all, could have provided more specific information with regard to the extent to which child labor was intellectually stultifying, as Marx claimed. Second, it could have been used to identify young people of talent. Third, it could have been used to demonstrate Marx's conviction that decent working environments could bring about a positive change in the intellectual quality of people.

The Eugenics Movement

The intelligence test, however, was not used in this fashion. Virtually from its inception, the intelligence test became the centerpiece of a struggle between those who argued that people who make up the failures in life are genetically inferior and those such as Marx who argued that they are the consequence of an oppressive and exploitive economic system. Intelligence became a political issue and, like any other political issue, became sloganized. Perhaps the most bizarre attempt to sloganize intelligence came out of the claim of psychologists in the middle of the twentieth century that intelligence was whatever intelligence tests measured.

The consequences of such a definition, if taken seriously, are loaded with profound political consequences. Indeed, by the middle of the twentieth century, social critics were using intelligence in a fashion revealing not only its political implications, but the more profound Marxian possibility that intelligence was now a device for promoting class distinctions. We have already noted that in medieval times wisdom, if not intelligence, was more likely to be associated with men of leisure (either the nobility or the priesthood) than with the peasantry. The peasantry were more likely to be mocked than listened to as voices of either wisdom or intelligence. In the twentieth century, intelligence became associated with the industrial elite. This is nowhere better illustrated than in the writings of followers of the eugenics (from *eu* = "good," *genes* = "genes"—or "the good genes") movement. The following quotes are taken from a work popular in the middle of the twentieth century. It offers a fine example of a writer concerned over the differences in birthrates between members of the lower classes and members of the upper classes, and the implications of this for the intelligence levels of the greater society. In this author's view, because the lower classes are less intelligent and have larger families, they are creating a situation in which the average level of intelligence of the country as a whole is declining.

> In the United States, England, and every Western country, misplaced and badly distributed human fertility is leeching away the inborn qualities of tomorrow's children. This biological "erosion" is insidious in its action: No barren, gullied hillsides meet the eye, but in the foreseeable end such erosion of the biological quality of the people may, after no great lapse of time, result in disaster.
>
> In England, a Royal Commission of experts in sociology and population had been studying this part of the fertility problem. Its 1949 report concluded that the average intelligence quotient of the British people was declining about 2 points every generation. The same pattern exists in the United States, where the experts consider a similar decline to be a "moral certainty." If this trend continues for less than a century, England and America will be well on the way to becoming nations of near half-wits.[23]

This source is worth quoting a little further, for the author makes his case graphically. Arguing that the less intelligent people of the world are reproducing more rapidly than the intelligent people, he describes the 1937 wedding of impoverished and ignorant little nine-year-old Eunice Winstead of Sneedville, Tennessee, to a man named Charles Johns. In 1950, a reporter who covered the marriage returned to visit Eunice. Now twenty-two years old, Eunice was the mother of four children with the prospect of a great number more. The author then continues:

> The story of Eunice and Charles illustrates a strange paradox in our modern urban-industrial society—the ill-fed, ill-clothed, ill-housed, and ill-educated parents of our depressed rural and urban areas are producing an increasing proportion of tomorrow's citizens. This differential in births is at the center of the genetic crisis of our time.[24]

The intelligence test, rather than clarifying the problems Marx saw as the darker side of the Industrial Revolution and modern capitalistic practice, only led to an intensification of the controversy. In its most viciously sloganized form, it appears as a question asked by those who believe in a correlation between wealth and intelligence: "If you're so smart, why ain't you rich?" Implicit in the question, of course, is the argument that if you are not rich, or at least a member of an elite social class, you probably are not smart. If you were smart, you would be wealthy. In sum, according to this mentality, poverty is the direct consequence of stupidity.

At the present time, the controversy continues to rage. Psychiatry and psychology are too effective as social control agencies to be left alone by men and women of power. The Marxist commentary on Western psychology is blunted somewhat by the observation that socialist countries have their own ways of using and abusing modern psychological theories and ideas. Still, Marxism is a powerful social philosophy. When we take it on an intellectual journey, we always return with something worth giving serious thought to. Certainly Marxist theory does not deserve much of the unthinking condemnation it receives in popular literature and the media. Before preparing this material, we were informed by teachers in colleges throughout the country that students are "afraid" of Marx and that we should keep this in mind. Marx should not be feared as an ogre or evil demon; Marxism is one of the more humane of modern social philosophies. The only thing to fear in reading Marx or any other social theorist, is that one might be forced to think about matters one did not have to bother with before. One does not need to be a Marxist to appreciate the questions that Marxism can raise.

Putting Social Thought to Work

1. The controversies and conflicts that now spread through the world because of Karl Marx are legion. No writer in modern times ever came so
   close to the heart of major social issues and expressed them in a way
   that divided people so forcefully into one camp or another. The issues
   are relatively simple and clear-cut. One is concerned with the distribution of wealth. There are four ways in which wealth can be distributed: (1) to each according to need; (2) to each according to want; (3)
   to each according to what is earned; (4) to each according to what can
   be taken (by whatever means). People typically appear to subscribe to
   the idea that people should get what they can. It is a Marxian position.
   Social injustice constitutes in its most pernicious form, the exploitation
   of those who work by those who have the power to exploit them. What
   is a proper basis for the distribution of wealth? Is the American system
   of distributing wealth democratic, fair, and just? How is it that someone
   who picks vegetables and serves the community gets little income,
   whereas one who serves no useful purpose (such as a champion golfer)
   may earn millions?

2. Another issue arises out of the fact that Marx focused attention on the
   class structure as no other writer before him was able to do. Instead of
   idealizing the members of the upper classes, Marx described them as
   parasites who lived in luxury only because they stole from the working
   classes that which belonged to the working classes. Much upper-class
   wealth is inherited and therefore is unearned. If you believe people
   should be granted only what they earn, how do you deal with the
   problem of inheritance? This is no simple or light question. American
   democratic ideals sprang, in part, from the injustices that derived from
   the feudal system in which power was inherited. In America, money
   is power, and to inherit money and the power associated with it is to
   participate in a social and economic system that is closer to feudalism
   than to democracy. On the other hand, the denial of inheritance does
   not seem reasonable either. How do we deal with the problem of inherited wealth and power?

3. Marx dealt with the problem of labor—the exploitation of labor, the
   value of labor, the idealization of labor. It remains a problem for us
   today. At first, the distinction between leisure and labor appears to be
   an easy one. Further thinking about the matter reveals that defining
   the nature and character of work is really rather difficult. For example,
   is work simply any activity at which one makes a living? If so, then
   people would have to be called workers who engage in little more
   exertion than clipping the coupons on their stocks and bonds. Is a professional boxer really a worker? What kind of conception of work did
   Marx offer the world? (We are reminded in this discussion, of a little

girl who asked a young graduate student, "Do you work? Or are you going to school?") What is the American attitude toward work?

4. Marx is commonly thought of as a "materialist." That is, he believed that people are basically influenced by how they deal with the problems of the material world. At the same time, we are aware today that people also seek material goods for their "symbolic" or "status" value. What does it mean to be a materialist? In what ways are capitalistic ideologists and Marxists similar in thought? Where do they differ?

Endnotes

1. Thomas Robert Malthus, *An Essay on the Principle of Population: Or a View of Its Past and Present Effects on Human Happiness*, 7th ed. (London: Reeves & Turner, 1872; originally published, 1798). Seven editions, each enlarging and refining the original essay, attest to the concern Malthus gave his argument and the care he took to meet the criticisms leveled against him.

2. For a literate and sensitive description of the new "global slums" and the misery of their inhabitants, see Frantz Fanon, *The Wretched of the Earth*, translated from the French by Constance Farington (New York: Grove Press, 1965).

3. The major works of Karl Marx include the following: *The German Ideology*, parts 1 and 3, with Friedrich Engels; introduction by R. Pascal (New York: International, 1939; originally written, 1845–1846); *The Poverty of Philosophy*, with an introduction by Friedrich Engels (New York: Washington Square Press, 1964; originally written, 1848); *The Eighteenth Brumaire of Louis Bonaparte* (New York: International, 1964; originally written, 1852); *A Contribution to the Critique of Political Economy*, translated by N. I. Stone (Chicago: Kerr, 1904; originally written, 1859); *Das Kapital: A Critique of Political Economy* (New York: International, 1967; originally written, 1867–1879).

4. See Marvin Harris, *Cultural Materialism: The Struggle for a Science of Culture* (New York: Random House, 1979).

5. The humanistic psychologist Abraham Maslow developed a hierarchy of needs with the suggestion that "higher" needs cannot be fulfilled until others are met. See Abraham H. Maslow, *Personality and Motivation*, 2d ed. (New York: Harper & Row, 1970).

6. Marx, *A Contribution to the Critique of Political Economy*, p. 11.

7. Originally published in London in 1848, in German only, *The Communist Manifesto* was the platform of the Communist League, a workers' association and secret society. The document was drawn up by Marx and Engels, who were commissioned to prepare a program for the league. The first English translation was made by Helen Macfarlane and was published in London in 1850 by G. J. Harney.

8. Charles Beard, *America Faces the Future* (New York: Books for Libraries, 1932); Charles and Mary Beard, *America in Mid-Passage* (New York: Macmillan, 1939).

9. An interesting case in point is the popular bandit who, like Robin Hood, redresses excesses of the state by robbing from the rich and giving to the poor. The subject is not without interest to sociologists and is discussed by Eric J. Hobsbawm in *Primitive Rebels* (New York: Crowell, 1973), pp. 262–265.

10. Anyone interested in the nature and character of great wealth should read Ferdinand Lundberg's *The Rich and Super-Rich* (New York: Grosset & Dunlap, 1968).

11. There is still much reason to dispute whether or not we are continuing to move in such a direction. Lundberg notes in *The Rich and Super-Rich*, for example, that the relative distribution of wealth in the United States and India is the same. And, of course, at a global level, we are all familiar with the data showing that America, with 6 percent of the world's population, consumes over 40 percent of the world's available energy sources. It is ironic to watch the world's most powerful people groan over the prospect that they may someday lose out to others in the race for consumption, when losing would simply mean the achievement of parity in gluttony.

12. The term was borrowed from the ideas of Hegel, a German philosopher who saw historical change coming about as a result of each cultural epoch creating its own antithetical forces in a constant "dialectical" exchange. See Georg W. R. Hegel, *Encyclopedia of the Philosophical Sciences* (New York: Macmillan, 1967; originally written, 1817).

13. Even Weber, a profound critic of Marx, found the dialectic an implicit, if not explicit, model for his study of the paradoxes of Puritanism and capitalism. He could not help noting the ironies to be found in the extent to which ascetic Puritanism brought about the sensate excesses of capitalistic economies.

14. Marx, *Das Kapital*.

15. Ibid., p. 259.

16. The terminology here is vague. Later in his discussion of the working day, Marx made clear, by implication, what constitutes a "normal" working day by providing astonishingly detailed observations on the extent to which the working day in industrial Europe was, by any reasonable consideration, abnormal.

17. Marx is sometimes considered to have advocated violence as a proletarian virtue. The issue, however, is more profound than that. Violence or revolution is unavoidable, for the simple reason that there is absolutely no other device for resolving the confrontation arising out of the rights of *both* the working classes and the bourgeoisie. Revolution is an unavoidable historical necessity. It is a logically reasonable event.

18. Marx, *Das Kapital*, pp. 280–281.

19. The specific test being referred to here is the Fire Fighter B-1 (M) test. Validation studies (rather interesting validations they are, too) of this test can be obtained from the Selection Consulting Center, 455 Capital Mall, Suite 250, Sacramento, California 95814.

20. Marx, *Das Kapital*, pp. 463–464.

21. Ibid. pp. 484–485.

22. Ibid., p. 489.

23. Robert C. Cook, *Human Fertility: The Modern Dilemma* (New York: William Sloane Associates, 1951), p. 6.

24. Ibid., p. 233.

Sexuality and Social Force

Social Thought and the Contribution of Sigmund Freud

❖

❖ A New Philosophy of Suffering

The intellectual history of those who live within a Western European heritage is saturated with grim and bloody images. Foremost among these, dominating the thought of humanity, is the agonized figure of Christ hanging from the cross, His face tormented by the anguish of solitary pain. This image personifies for us the clash between good and evil, purity and sin. It also helps perpetuate a conception of humanity that has been influential down to the present time and that even highly liberated modern thinkers draw on for inspiration and insight. This conception, in its essence, sees people as creatures caught between the forces of good and evil, purity and sin. Our lives are ultimately subject to the judgment that we lived as sinners or saints, or, in more modern terms, as "losers" or "winners." This judgmental tradition in Western culture is one of its significant qualities. Not only do we judge others; we also conduct ourselves in ways that will, we hope, produce judgments from others that we find gratifying. We judge ourselves, at times, as critically and as harshly as we are often disposed to judge others.

Judgments, of course, mean that we must make distinctions. Distinctions, in turn, rest on conceptions of what constitutes a preferred pattern of action. Moreover, the distinction between what is preferred and what is not preferred must involve an implicit (or explicit) conflict or struggle between the available alternatives. For example, it would be silly to admire people for having a pulse rate of seventy or for having five fingers on their right hands. We do not generally need to struggle to have five fingers on one hand; they come for just about every one of us as standard equipment.

However, there are evaluations that people dedicate their lives to attaining. In these quests, we encounter dramatic and agonizing human efforts. Indeed, as we review the innumerable contrasts between those judged great and the rest of us, a common theme is the theme of suffering. Heroes and heroines must suffer and, in the conduct of their adventures, risk even greater suffering. To live a life in which one passes from cradle to grave enjoying hedonistic delights while suffering no trials or tribulations is to risk, at least in this society, acquiring a contemptible reputation. It is to risk being judged worthless.

Redemption through suffering is a pervasive idea to us. There is, of course, the possibility of suffering and still not achieving redemption. However, the idea of not suffering and yet being allowed redemption is, even in our modern materialistic culture, not a readily accepted idea. The dominant theme in all of this is that people are confronted with conflict throughout their lives. Whether we succeed in overcoming our difficulties is perhaps a matter of chance and fortune. However, it is obvious from this perspective that we must suffer, and it is not surprising that the sufferings visited on many people become intolerable. They are crushed and destroyed by the struggles thrust upon them.

The theme of suffering in America is, however, one balanced by the daily fare of hedonistic commercials and advertisements which promise the consumer heaven on earth and salvation from the ordinary torments of life. It is certainly true that our literature, journalism, dramatic presentations, and art dwell on the theme of suffering. At the same time, we have found that when students are asked whether it is possible to accomplish something great without having to suffer, they generally reply that it is. In one class, twenty-eight students out of thirty said that it was possible to achieve greatness without suffering. Interestingly enough, the two exceptions were students who came from a Japanese-American background.

Freudian theory rests on the idea of conflict and inevitable suffering. In this respect, it is in harmony with the Christian ideology of the broader culture. The unique contribution of Freud, however, was to suggest that conflict and suffering are the natural consequences of human biological nature and the problems that arise when one attempts to transform the stuff of biology into a social being. The result, Freud suggested, is a complex set of conflicts and consequent forms of guilt and anxiety that penetrate deeply into human character. People knew long before Freud that suffering and conflict with external forces were part of life. After Freud, they became aware that each individual was a battleground, so to speak, wherein a continuous *internal* struggle was waged between the demands of the body and the demands of society. What made Freud's contribution unique was his claim that the individual is generally not aware of the conflict in any clearly conscious manner. Much of the struggle takes place at an unconscious level.

❖ The Freudian Heritage

The Freudian conception of the psyche took hold in the early twentieth century and quickly became one of the most influential perspectives on human activities of our time. The Freudian argument is significant in two respects. First, it leans on the premise that there is an unavoidable conflict between individual people and the societies they create. (Later, we shall see that this is overly simple. Freud did not consider society to be the exclusively repressive agent in human affairs. He argued in his later works that several aspects of human physiology make frustration and discontent a consequence of the act of living, no matter how we organize our lives—take aging, for example.) According to Freud, then, conflict, suffering, agony, repression, frustration, and the aggressive response are universal features of human life.

In the second place, the Freudian perspective is grounded in observations coming out of Freud's medical and clinical practice. Freud's early investigations into hysteria were investigations of the actions of people who, one way or another, were wracked by the problems of living. The Freudian view, therefore, offers a highly dramatized and possibly exaggerated awareness of the extent to which conflict is a part of our lives.

There was certainly nothing new in Freud's observation that human beings can be crushed by the difficulties of day-to-day living. People had known this for centuries. It was in the elaboration of this theme that Freud brought about his achievement. It was Freud who promoted the discovery of the extent to which conflict not only takes place at the surface (in such actions as physical combat, argumentation, and economic struggle), but is also going on within deeper, unexplored facets of the personality. Conflict is unconscious as well as conscious. The Freudian heritage brought with it revolutionary implications. For one thing, it suggested that what we think of as rational conduct at one level may be the consequence of unconscious motivations of an irrational nature. If nothing else, Freud made everyone aware of the extent to which our social and personal lives are more deceptive than we can begin to suspect.

What was there, in the final summing up, that made the Freudian conception of human actions so appealing? To answer this question, we must turn to an examination of Freud's work and evaluate it in terms of the sentiments and ideas it so effectively challenged.

❖ *The Person in Three Parts*

Freud was born of Jewish parents in Freiburg, Moravia, in 1856. He chose medicine as his profession and graduated from the University of Vienna at the age of twenty-five. Before he took up psychology, his writings were devoted to investigations of nervous diseases. As his work in psychoanalysis proceeded, Freud became interested in the use of hypnosis in the treatment of hysteria. He served as a professor of neuropathology at the University of Vienna from 1902 to 1938. The Nazis' rise to power in Germany in the 1930s seriously threatened Freud's life and career. He left Germany for London in 1938 but lived only one more year, dying of cancer in 1939. During his highly productive and radically innovative intellectual life, Freud created a model of human actions that, like Darwinism, took people away from spiritual forces and saw them instead as products of natural forces. Freudian theory was not especially popular with religious leaders.[1]

We have already suggested that the Freudian model of humanity rests on a premise of conflict between the individual and the community of which he or she is a part. In developing this conception, Freud appears to have transformed Judeo-Christian mythology into a configuration more in keeping with the naturalistic philosophies of modern times. The Christian myth views people as creatures born in sin and engaged in a struggle to achieve a state of grace. To be in a state of grace is to be judged favorably by the most important of all judges, God. The judging agent, in this instance, is a spiritual entity removed from any direct communication with people. Sin is relevant insofar as it condemns one to rejection by God.

The whole idea, when taken seriously, is frightening enough in itself. One cannot be certain that one is acceptable to God. Moreover, people are informed that the path to God is hard. To achieve acceptance by God means, according to Christian doctrine, a denial of the gross appetites coming from one's flesh and from one's carnal nature. The extremes to which this doctrine was carried are not always recognized by modern men and women. Here, for example, is a brief comment about church leaders of the third century A.D.:

> All the Church Fathers, meanwhile, agreed on one point: half-abstention was only half-emancipation from the evil. The truly pious man must abstain from all sexual intercourse; only so could he achieve inward spiritual peace. This lofty goal could not be reached without sacrifice; thus Origen, one of the greatest and most original thinkers of the Alexandrine School, chose to give mankind an example by emasculating himself. . . . He who would free himself from sin must first purify the spirit, then the body would follow. The best means was to take a vow of chastity.[2]

The interesting thing about this philosophy is the extent to which it has appealed to millions of men and women, who, with surprisingly few exceptions, never questioned its repressive nature. The goliard poets of the twelfth century might be an exception. Another notable deviation is the sixteenth-century writer Rabelais, whose works, even in this supposedly liberated age, offer some of the most sensible advice and best humor Western literature has to offer. Rabelais argued that people are both carnal and spiritual, and that they risk crippling themselves if they deny either facet of their character. Freud also argued for such a balance of forces, and saw in that balance the essence of the healthy person and the strong ego.

After Freud, repression of the individual, viewed as a negative act, became a central intellectual interest. At the same time, Freud's scheme suggests that it is impossible to obtain the advantages offered by communal living without having to pay the price of living a repressed life. Freudian psychology certainly does not suggest that happiness can be attained by totally removing the repressive censors of the community. Such a drastic measure may liberate the individual, but at the price of creating a monster. On the other hand, the total incorporation of the individual into the state or the community can also create a generation of monsters. There is, from a Freudian point of view, no happy resolution to the problem of repression.

The Freudian scheme is simple in its barest outlines. Despite similarities in the conception of people as embattled creatures, the Freudian model is a profound shift away from earlier ideas about the nature of people. Where the Christian model looks on us as creatures of choice, the Freudian model denies us choice. It is a conception in which each and every action, no matter how trivial or apparently accidental, is shaped by innumerable causal influences. Choice is an illusion, and accidents are never accidental. They always make sense, according to Freud, when viewed within the context of their occurrence. This is the rationale behind what is commonly referred to as the "Freudian slip." In such a case, a person says or does something that seems to be a slip or error. Further examination reveals, however, that the error is meaningful.

The popularity of Freudian psycholanalysis has diminished in recent years so that the following anecdote seems more characteristic of the current attitudes toward the influence of the Freudian interpretation of the world. An urbane psychoanalyst remarked that if he goes to a party and says he is an analyst, people respond with great interest because they think he is a financial analyst. When he explains that he is a Freudian psychoanalyst they just turn away, and mutter, "Oh, that."

Another feature of Freudian thought separating it from earlier conceptions and setting it in conflict with them was the development of the idea that conscious and unconscious forces interact within the individual. Unconscious impulses give rise to conscious actions in ways the person may never suspect or comprehend. Earlier views emphasized rational and conscious levels of action. Again, it is important to see the extent to which a causal approach to human actions forced Freud to this conclusion. Freud argued that if something happens, there must be a cause for it. No matter how peculiar a pattern of activity may be, it is not a consequence of choice, but, instead, a pattern caused by a given set of events. Since people are capable of retaining the memory of events that took place much earlier in their lives, it made sense to conclude that such early events can influence current actions.

Still another central feature of Freudian thought is the idea that character and personality are pretty much established by the time a person reaches early childhood. Unlike the two claims described above, this one did not conflict with earlier religious orthodoxy, which was also inclined to see character determined relatively early in life. However, Freud went far beyond the elemental notion that if a child is trained in a given religious philosophy early in life, it will remain powerful through the rest of the individual's life. Freud claimed that we all go through a similar pattern of early life experiences within the family—particularly with respect to our relationship with our parents and that these experiences create a uniquely human form of impasse between physical desires and communal constraints. He called this experience the "Oedipus complex," and we shall discuss this provocative and uniquely twentieth-century notion further on.

One of the best-known features of Freudian thought is his tripartite division of the person into the "id," the "ego," and the "superego." This imagery of the person in three parts is similar to Christian imagery. The id is the devil, the superego is the saintly or angelic conscience, and the ego is everyman and everywoman struggling for salvation (which, if it ever comes, is achieved in all certainty after death). In this division, the central forces are located within the id and the superego. The *id* (Latin for "it") is the "animal impulse," or the various biological drives, urges, needs, instincts, or other physiologically determined impulses to act that are a part of the genetic inheritance of the individual. The id is significant in several respects. It can be presumed that, within limits, all people are born with a relatively common set of such impulses. Today this is, among sophisticated people at least, a commonly accepted idea.

If we look at the id for a moment as representing the asocial, egocentric force within us, and if we consider it, in a sense, bad, then we must assume that Freudian thought shares with Christian theology the idea that all people are born with sinful inclinations. However, whereas Christian theology offers a hope for redemption, Freudian psychoanalysis claims that we can never rid ourselves of the directives coming from the id. There is no redemption. There is no freedom from the constant urging of the id to engage in asocial actions. Rather, if we are to be acceptable to the rest of society, we must find ways to "sublimate" such desires and inclinations, transform the raw material of physiological impulse into socially valued forms of action.

At this point, the logic of Freudian thought leads to a conclusion that places us forever in a state of conflict. The transformation of physiologically grounded impulses into socially acceptable actions requires us to control or "repress" the pleasure-seeking demands of the id. The Freudian model thus places us in an inescapable bind. If we are to be individuals—if we are to gratify ourselves as physical beings—we must deny our communal commitments to a great degree. If, on the other hand, we are to be acceptable to the community, we must deny the deeply compelling and demanding urges grounded in our biologically established human nature.

It should be mentioned that Freud was aware of the peculiarities of this apparently simple argument and observation. Although we are generally inclined to accept this vision of ourselves, it contains several drawbacks. Foremost among these is the question of how it could happen that we develop communities that do not represent our "natural" character and are, in many ways, antithetical to that character. How could any community develop to the point where it possesses a force greater than the biological reality of human nature? The problem was sufficiently demanding to force Freud to pay attention to it in several major essays,[3] one of which we shall consider in detail later in this chapter.

The force within the person representing the imperatives of the community—the internal agent limiting and constraining the impulses of the id—is the *superego* and it consists of the acquired ethical and moral standards of the community. The superego is what we ordinarily refer to as the conscience.[4] It is in the superego that the sociological significance of Freudian thought appears. The superego is a product of the community and its concerns. With the incorporation of the superego into the self, the individual becomes, at all times, subject to the directives of the community. Even in isolation, the community is represented, as it were, within the individual. The superego transforms the individual into a social being responding to the demands of the community as well as to the demands of the id.

Freudian thought inspires more questions than it is able to answer. Nonetheless, the questions themselves offer a form of understanding. For example, communities characteristically demand leadership. Leadership requires relatively close conformity to the demands of the community, that is, a well-developed and effective superego. However, a highly developed superego tends to promote inhibited, rigid, and anxious responses. Is it possible, then, that leaders possess a unique type of personality that supports a repressive mentality? Several interesting efforts to demonstrate the validity of this idea have appeared in recent literature. Such work attempts to probe the character of leaders from Martin Luther to Adolf Hitler. It is difficult to resist speculating that perhaps the overkill effort of Richard Nixon's supporters to sabotage the Democratic party in the 1972 presidential elections is a confirmation of Freud's observations.

The last of the three major elements of the individual is the ego. The *ego* is the part of us that experiences reality and integrates the conflicting demands of the superego and the id. Unlike the id, the ego manifests itself in growth. The superego and the ego develop with the acquisition of moral knowledge. The ego is a realist. It must adapt to the pleasure desires of the id, and it must also be concerned with the moral censorship of the superego. A person with a strong ego is one who is able to accomplish the best compromise between the conflicting demands of the id and the superego. To give in to the id is to indulge in infantile and immature actions. To be totally at the mercy of the superego is to be rigid and repressive. Between these opposed demands, the ego struggles to retain a balance. Failure to attain a reasonable balance produces, of course, an unbalanced individual.

❖ *The Oedipus Complex*

The more elemental concepts of Freudian psychoanalysis do not in themselves reveal the rich possibilities that this system of thought offers for interpreting human activities. It is commonly known that Freudian theory is not generally supported by empirical research and that great portions of it are probably beyond any kind of truth test. Other Freudian ideas, such as the notion that women suffer from a deep unconscious envy of the penis, have now been generally discredited. Granting all of this, it is a testimonial to the strength of Freud's observations and ideas to find that the concepts of psychoanalytic theory still exert a strong influence among those who concern themselves with the problem of understanding human actions—including psychologists, sociologists, anthropologists, political scientists, artists, novelists, and philosophers. Freudian ideas are still popular today among French intellectuals, who rely on these concepts to interpret such diverse matters as cinema and the modern prison.

One reason for the continued popularity of the Freudian mode of thinking about human activities comes out of the unusual possibilities that suggest themselves after one masters an understanding of the major concepts. It is as though Freud created seven or eight basic notes that, in various blendings, produce a nearly infinite set of possible combinations and alternatives. Moreover, once one has a grasp of the basic concepts, the temptation to run off variations of one's own is nearly irresistible. This is what is meant by "cocktail party psychoanalysis." There is a facile quality to Freudian interpretations that must be guarded against. Freudian thought sometimes seems too easy; within the works of Freud, however, there is a logic that is effectively coherent. Nothing, we believe, better illustrates the logic of Freudian thought than the well-known psychoanalytic conception of the Oedipus complex.

The *Oedipus complex* arises out of the logic of the relationships among instinct, opportunities for gratification, the nature of the family and fear of the father. We have noted already that the instinctive nature of the person, located within the impulses of the id, is amoral (neither moral nor immoral). The id seeks gratification and pleasure and is not especially concerned with whether these accomplishments come about in a manner that is socially acceptable. It is the superego that imposes a moral sense on the quest for gratification.

As the young male child begins to mature and experience sexual desire, he naturally turns toward the person nearest him who might be a possible source of gratification. This person is usually his mother. Note, again, the logical simplicity of this idea. If the id seeks gratification and is not concerned with social niceties, then efficiency, immediacy, and the heritage of already established pleasurable experiences received at the hands of the mother would make the mother attractive in a primary way. The mother becomes a logical choice for the young boy. In a similar way, the young girl finds the father an attractive person as she begins to mature sexually. The term *Electra complex* is used to designate the case where the female child is attracted to her father.

The desirability of the parents introduces, of course, the possibility of incestuous sexual relations, and this is morally intolerable. The censoring functions of the superego militate, in part, against the fulfillment of the boy's desire to possess the mother sexually. There are even more ominous features to the logic of the Oedipus complex. Not only do the moral standards of the community stand against the young man in his desire to make love with his mother, but he also finds himself wanting to challenge the established and almost godlike power of his father. The father shares the marital bed with the mother, while the son is excluded. To attempt to intrude into this domain would be to risk the wrath of the father, who possesses the power to castrate the son.

To make matters more complicated, the id, being an amoral force, does not react to such frustrating situations with a mannerly sense of resignation. The inclination of the id, when frustrated in its desires, is to seek to destroy that which stands between it and gratification. In this situation, the father is the barrier to gratification. The response of the id is to seek to destroy the father. Murdering the father, of course, is as repugnant to the superego as the idea of having incestuous relations with the mother. The logic of family relations, when viewed from a Freudian perspective, produces a remarkably messy emotional can of worms.

This, then, is the situation into which the Oedipus complex brings the young child. For the boy, it means desiring the mother, being frustrated by the father, and then wishing to kill the father. For the girl, it is desiring the father, being frustrated by the mother, and then wishing for the mother's death. The logic of the pattern of relations is so compelling that Freud was inclined to see the Oedipus and Electra complexes as universal, something all people in all cultures experience. Recent studies indicate that this is evidently not the case, although the Oedipal pattern is probably more common than critics of Freud are willing to grant.[5]

This "family romance" is the original setting, or initial testing ground, for the individual's response to innumerable conflicts that will henceforth be part and parcel of his or her active social life. It is in the Oedipal moment that we each come of age. The agony of a totally forbidden but nonetheless compelling desire is made apparent. How we manage to resolve this first major encounter with the greater forces of the id and the superego will shape our future destiny. If we remain fixed in the love for the opposite parent and cannot redirect the desire, then we may become relatively inflexible in our social life.

A number of consequences are possible, according to psychoanalytic theory, when the Oedipus complex is inadequately resolved. It can be the source of sexual fears; it can lead to highly compulsive actions in which the individual attempts to atone for having such base desires; it can help account for people who reject marriage entirely. According to this interpretation, such people have never been able to find anyone who can truly compete with the mother or father as a person worthy of love.

Two further comments should be made about the Oedipus complex before we move into more sociologically relevant features of Freud's theory. The resolution of Oedipal stresses is promoted by two factors. The first involves the boy's identification with his father, who is a social role model. As the relationship between the father and the son is secured through common masculine social interests, the boy is drawn away from his mother. The second resolving factor is the boy's fear of his father's authority, which could lead to punitive retaliation. The boy is thus drawn toward his father by both the positive attraction of the masculine social interests that the father offers and by the fear of the father's authority, which the boy dares not antagonize. The attraction toward the father permits a breaking away from the desire for the mother and, eventually, the freedom to find women outside the incestuous bed.

We have considered the problem of resolving the Oedipal dilemma. Now we will discuss the domain wherein much of this conflict is experienced. This domain, the realm of the "unconscious," is a truly unique territory Freud brought before the world. The Oedipus complex, to a great degree, occurs in ways not made directly available to conscious thought. Individuals, Freud suggests, are influenced by unconscious forces that affect their waking, knowing, and conscious activities. Psychoanalysis deals with the problem of finding ways to ascertain the things people do not themselves know. The quest for knowledge of the nature of the unconscious made Freudian thought seem, to more conservative scientists, perfectly impossible. The unconscious, according to this point of view, remains beyond empirical observation and therefore is not a proper subject for scientific investigation. However, to others it is an effort that must be undertaken because the reality of the unconscious cannot be easily denied—and science is concerned with investigating anything that happens in nature.

❖ The Unconscious

The concept of the *unconscious* put the new and struggling efforts to achieve a science of human beings into a quandary. If we grant the existence of the unconscious, then the methodological problem is to find ways of gaining access to it. At the same tune, the unconscious, by definition, is not readily accessible to our awareness; it is an elusive part of ourselves. It is intriguing by the very fact that it is inaccessible. On the other hand, if we deny the concept of the unconscious and try to deal with human actions in terms of what is consciously known, we run the risk of being superficial and of violating a concept that makes too much good sense to be ignored. This was, in part, the impact of Freudianism: It opened the question of how one ascertains what people are, in fact, intending when they do something.

Even at the dawn of time, it must have been apparent that what people say and what they are up to can be two quite different matters. Politics, love, poker playing, and salesmanship are only a few of the human activities involving duplicity at conscious levels. If there is duplicity at the level of conscious action, then how much more involved does the situation become when it includes the possibility of unconscious desires and fantasies?

Freud made people self-conscious in a new way. Before Freud, people believed that human beings struggle to achieve a variety of conditions they consider to be good and worthwhile. After Freud, any quest had to be reexamined in the fight of both its conscious and its unconscious possibilities. Consider, for example, the crime of murder carried out by two young and unusually brilliant students at the University of Chicago during the 1920s. The two were caught, convicted, and sent to prison for their crime. Although the killers were motivated at a conscious level by the desire to show their superiority over everyone else, they seem to have been motivated at a different level by a desire to be apprehended and punished. They did this by leaving a trail detectives found astonishingly easy to follow.[6]

The significance of this feature of Freud's thought cannot be too heavily underscored. Before Freud, the task of ascertaining why people do the things they do seemed to be relatively easy. From a theological point of view, people behave badly because they are driven by demons. From an economic point of view, people are driven by a desire to possess the good things of life. From a political perspective, people are driven by a desire for power. Freud muddied the waters. Human motivations, after Freud, became an impossibly complicated problem.

Possibly it was Freud's greatest insight and argument to suggest that not only are other people's motivations difficult for us to ascertain from outside, but even we ourselves cannot, on our own, come up with a clear picture of why we act as we do. For example, consider people who work late at night, apparently driven by a desire to succeed in business. Their motivation appears clear and evident, both to those who know them and to themselves. Nevertheless, Freud, as we said, muddied the waters forever. We are now aware that any number of possibilities may exist and that these must be examined—psychoanalyzed—if we want to find a reasonable answer. It may be that such persons live with a repressed but dreadful hatred of their parents. They may, in turn, unconsciously direct this hatred toward their spouses, whom they unconsciously would like to murder. They therefore spend a lot of time at work, thereby avoiding their families and evading their complex, intense, unconscious, and horrific desires and motives.

Freud made it evident that we are not as aware of ourselves as we might like to think. To obtain deeper self-awareness, it is necessary to rely on the services of an expert—a psychoanalyst—who may be able, if the lengthy process of examination goes correctly, to uncover what we "really" are up to when we do something. It was as devastating a notion to the rational Victorian mind as Darwin's evolutionary ideas had been. Much is made of the shockingly sexual nature of Freudian thought. The deeper shock was the discovery that individuals may not be the masters of their fates and the captains of their souls. On the contrary, we have little personal understanding of the forces within ourselves or in others. Such understanding, if it is to be found at all, can come only from the extensive probings of psychoanalysis.

❖ *The Superego*

The idea of unconscious forces poses serious methodological problems for the social sciences. (One problem, which is certainly worthy of consideration but which we cannot go into here, is the question of the unconscious motivations of those who press toward a neat, tidy, and "systematic" science of human beings. What kind of authoritarianism might be lurking in the hearts of these people? Freud actually forced a reexamination of the motives of behavioral scientists themselves!) If the unconscious has an influence over the affairs of people, and if it is lost or remote from the rational and ordinary understanding we have of the world, then how can the unconscious be approached? Freud argued that one way to find out about the nature of the unconscious is to examine it when it manages somehow to slip by the controls or censoring activities of the superego. When the superego is, so to speak, asleep at the switch, the fantasies and desires that give form to the unconscious may reveal themselves. During such moments, the id can break into overt expression. This, again, is the so-called Freudian slip. One might, for example, write the word "sex " when one intended to write the word "six." An unconscious desire has possibly gained expression during a moment when the superego is not paying attention.

A second form of betrayal of the unconscious reveals itself in the serious neurotic and psychotic activities of people who are nearly destroyed by conflicts between the demands of the id and the superego. The unraveling of such conflicts is, of course, part of psychoanalytic therapy. One aspect of Freudian theory features the idea that becoming aware of unconscious impulses and gaining a clearer understanding of them can help resolve the tensions the underlying conflict brings about.

A third approach to the unconscious is through the analysis of dreams. During the sleeping and dreaming state, the superego is less effective than during the waking hours, and the unconscious can speak with less likelihood of being censored. Thus the content of dreams offers an opportunity to examine the character of the unconscious. But dreams, of course, cannot be observed directly. They must be described in terms of the conscious state, and recalled during consciousness; thus the superego has an opportunity to impose censorship once again. Trying to fathom the character of the unconscious by means of conscious recall is something like trying to find out about corruption in government by employing a governmental investigation committee. The threat of the committee leads to a tendency on the part of those who indulged in corruption to hide their activities all the more carefully. Nonetheless, a committee can hope to get partial information, and psychoanalysis relies on dreams and their interpretation as at least one available means (albeit a crude one) for probing into the unconscious.

Freudian analysis opened up new ways of looking at old problems. It created nothing less than a way of going beyond the apparently rational acts of men and women. Ancient humanistic concerns could now be approached in a distinctively modern fashion. Among the issues psychoanalysis has considered are war and crime, madness, the relationship between men and women, growing up, our need for machines, and the rise of civilization. There really are few areas in which Freudian analysis has not, at one time or another, intervened and left its mark. The modern stamp Freudian analysis gives to these old issues involves a marked lack of moralizing, an extremely deterministic premise, a tendency to see all people as having essentially the same instinctual nature, and a conception of conscience and moral action as products of human rather than divine intervention. At the same time, as the opening of this chapter suggests, the Freudian model leans heavily on a Christian vision of people, which finds them embattled and struggling to deal with their ''base'' nature.

We have just said that Freudian thought does not moralize. This comment should be tempered slightly. There is a morality to Freudian thought that leans toward a kind of enlightened nineteenth-century domesticity—if one can have such a thing. But this morality is attained only after one comes to grips with and accepts the fact that morality is not good in and of itself Nor is one's animal nature necessarily bad. Freudian thought moved modern society far down the road toward a position not so much amoral as critical of any morality presuming to be of worth simply because it is rooted in tradition.

It is when Freudian philosophy moves beyond the level of individual emotional disturbances into an examination of social issues that it becomes relevant to sociological concerns. There is no possible way in which a discussion as brief as this can consider all the contributions of Freudian thought. Instead, we shall now consider an engaging intellectual problem having to do with modern life and how Freud responded to the problem.[7]

❖ *Civilization and Its Discontents*

In 1930, Freud published a work entitled *Das Unbehagen in der Kultur (Civilization and Its Discontents)*. He originally intended to use the term *Unglück* rather than *Unbehagen*. *Unglück* means "unhappiness." *Unbehagen* is more difficult to translate into English; it is close in its meaning to the French *malaise*. The title implies that there is dissatisfaction in the finest of human creations—civilization. However, if this is so (and there is much current as well as past evidence to suggest that people find their civilizations a source of considerable frustration), then how can one say that civilization came out of human desire?

A simple conception of the rise of civilization would be that it emerged to provide people with greater protection, more freedom, and a degree of security against the onslaughts of nature. But if civilization makes us miserable, then why bother with it? Indeed, recent social movements within the United States and other so-called "advanced" countries are in the direction of moving away from the entrapments of civilized living. The question, then, is this: How could civilization arise out of the needs and character of people and yet, at the same time, not enhance or improve their chances for happiness? A commonsense approach to civilization would see it as leading to an upward-spiraling trend in human happiness. The fact that civilization retains a great degree of discontent suggests a disparity between people's sociological and psychological natures. This disparity forced Freud, later in his life, into a penetrating consideration of the relationship between society and the individual.

Freud began by taking up the nature of happiness. He saw happiness as a universal human concern, but he considered happiness to be more difficult to attain than unhappiness. Unhappiness is something we cannot avoid. Freud listed three major sources of unhappiness or misery. The first is found in the elemental physiological limitations of the body, which is subject to decay and dissolution with the passage of time, regardless of how we struggle to dodge our fate. The second is found in natural catastrophes of various kinds, which, again, are difficult to avoid. The third and—said Freud—perhaps most unbearable of all is the unhappiness laid upon us by other human beings.

Unhappiness cannot be avoided. By what means, then, can people hope to attain happiness? What constitutes the greatest happiness a person can experience? The quest for happiness involves both positive and negative approaches. In the negative approach, one attempts to evade the sources of pain; in the positive approach, one seeks to enhance the extent to which one is able to experience pleasure. Freud turned his attention to this latter form of the quest for happiness and made the following observation:

> What we call happiness in the strictest sense comes from the (preferably sudden) satisfaction of needs which have been dammed up to a high degree, and it is from its nature only possible as an episodic phenomenon. When any situation that is desired by the pleasure principle is prolonged, it only produces a feeling of mild contentment. We are so made that we can derive intense enjoyment only from a contrast and very little from a state of things. Thus our possibilities of happiness are already restricted by our constitution.[8]

This statement is significant in that it points to a particular characteristic of Freudian thought—its inclination to turn toward people's physiological nature to explain their actions. In this brief comment, Freud tells us that the possibilities of happiness are already restricted by our biological nature. Then, when we add the frustrations imposed by communal living, it is a wonder that people are not more unhappy than they are.

The Freudian picture of humanity is one of a general state of wretchedness. Freud and Henry David Thoreau would agree that the mass of men and women lead lives of quiet desperation. Not only is happiness attainable only in brief and episodic moments, but the fulfilling of instinctual needs—one form of happiness—can be a threat to communal order. Civilization came about as a result of a precarious balance of payoffs. Freud, like too many present-day social writers, reveals an inclination to romanticize primitive people. We can see this in his summary of how civilization came into being, even though it brought still more unhappiness with it.

> If civilization imposes such great sacrifices not only on man's sexuality but on his aggressivity, we can understand better why it is hard for him to be happy in that civilization. In fact, primitive man was better off in knowing no restrictions of instinct. To counterbalance this, his prospects of enjoying this happiness for any length of time were very slender. *Civilized man has exchanged a portion of his possibilities of happiness for a portion of security.*[9]

It is a questionable response to an engaging problem. The shakiness of the response suggests some of the problems with Freud's approach to human activities. Is civilized humanity actually more repressed? Do primitive people—at least as we know them—live in "free" and instinctually fulfilling circumstances? Is the fulfilling of instinct actually the locus of happiness? Can people sometimes be highly gratified and happy with themselves, even as they deny themselves physiological forms of gratification? There is, for example, a surprisingly happy and exultant quality in the diaries of Japanese *kamikaze* pilots who were waiting to go out on suicidal missions in World War II. It would assuredly seem that such total denial of the self would produce great unhappiness.

We have raised these questions because more recent forms of social theory, particularly those developed by George Herbert Mead and, somewhat later, by Erving Goffman, take a different approach to the interpretation of human activities. We find that the logic of Freudian analysis is not quite so tight as his more devoted followers see it. In one sense, this is unfortunate. It would be nice, after all, to have a definitive statement that would be binding in its understanding. On the other hand, it is good to know that there are possible ways out of the dilemmas Freud kept putting us in.

Freud himself was not quite so dogmatic as many of his disciples were. He opened a new set of approaches to the study of human eccentricities, neuroses, and various forms of madness. He placed people in a natural universe in which their bodies and their instincts, in conflict with the powerful demands of the greater community, were viewed as the cause of behavioral problems. The older religious notions of sin, divine intervention, wickedness coming from the proddings of the devil, and other "unnatural" explanations were brushed aside. Freud also claimed that people are destined, even at best, to live lives in a state of uneasy and delicate balance between the growling demands of the id and the imperious censorship of the superego. As we have said earlier, it is a dramatic notion—that people are destined to live out their days in conflict, and that the mind is a locus for battle. It is a lively, romantic, and exciting interpretation of the human condition.

Although those who consider Freud the final answer to everything are probably fewer in number today than in the 1940s and 1950s, his work still has a large following. Freud was well aware of the limitation of his ideas. We pick up this sentiment in the closing sentence of *Civilization and Its Discontents*. Freud was aware, as he wrote this essay, that people had created vast engines of destruction and, given the human instinct toward aggressiveness, were likely to use them to destroy the earth. Perhaps, he argued, the forces of love and the natural urge to live would move into the picture and struggle against the darker forces of aggression, hate, and destruction. Freud then closed his essay with an admission of the fallibility of all intellect: "But who can foresee with what success and with what result?"[10]

❖ *Psychoanalyzing a Nation*

The Freudian perspective draws on such terms as "hysteria," "neurosis," "id," "psychopathic problems," "sexuality," "lust," "unconscious," "repression," "transference," "sublimation," "defense mechanisms," and a host of other terms now associated with mental disturbances. Freudian theory, however, sought more than simply to cure mental distress. Freud wanted nothing less than to offer a means of analyzing the psyche. The late nineteenth century was an age of analysis. It made sense to attempt to analyze the psyche along with everything else. Freud referred to his work, rather presumptuously, as "psychoanalysis"—daring to claim that even the spirit is subject to analytical investigation. The essence of psychoanalysis, as Freud saw it, is to bring into view the spirit of the individual by investigating the forces that struggle within the person and threaten to damage the ego or the self.

The analyst, listening to a patient caught up in a stream of conscious recollections of the past or talking about dreams, is looking for revelations of experience that permit the analyst to see through the present facade or "persona," which the patient offers as the real self. The drama of psychoanalysis comes out of unsuspected revelations obtained by deep probings into the memory, forcing it to abandon its deceptions until, eventually, the forbidden thought comes forth—the real spirit shows itself. The analysis is then complete.

If nothing else, the compulsive nature of psychoanalysis, the constant probing, is a goad to the imagination. Analysis, when properly carried out, goes on for years and years. The analyst can never be certain that the final revelation has been made. Regardless of whether or not a "cure" is achieved, psychoanalysis always offers those involved, the patient and the analyst, a dramatic encounter. Psychoanalysis, in a way, is a kind of detective mystery in which the analyst, as the detective, works along with the patient to find the real self that has been hidden from the patient's view.

Now presume, for the moment, that there are neurotic and compulsive aspects of the national psyche. What insights might be generated by drawing on the Freudian imagination as a perspective for looking at our collective selves? To put it another way, if we know something about Freud, then what might we come to see about the American people of which we were perhaps not previously aware? It is a brash question, obviously. We know that the psychoanalytic probing of just one person can take twenty years. It can be a lifetime endeavor. Each fifty-minute encounter in the analyst's office adds to the growing detail of a single memory—a single life. When we seek to interpret the lives of several hundred million people, we draw the Freudian perspective quite thin. Perhaps it is a measure of the power of the Freudian perspective that it continues to offer fascinating possibilities about the human spirit even when drawn this thin. It is no more possible to investigate the total psyche of a nation than it is to investigate that of a single individual. Yet, if we focus on a particular segment of that psyche, psychoanalysis does offer at least the opportunity for broadening our imagination with respect to why we do the things we do.

Encounters with Social Thought

Travel as an American Compulsion

As an exercise in social thought, let us select for our topic a most evident situation—the American love for traveling. Americans do get around! Just examining the pages of a Sunday *New York Times* travel section makes the extent to which Americans are dedicated to leisure travel apparent. Domestic travel alone for Americans, amounts to trillions of miles. When one adds to this the extensive amount of international travel, we begin to realize just how much Americans get around. We travel by plane, by cruise ships, by train, but most of all we travel by automobile. Most frequently, when Americans set forth on vacations they go by car. Some travel specialists estimate that the average distance

2. Richard Lewinsohn, *A History of Sexual Customs* (New York: Harper & Row, 1959), p. 99.

3. This issue is the central concern of *Civilization and Its Discontents* and is the theme, in great part, of the mythical turmoil described in *Totem and Taboo*.

4. Freudian thought emphasized the conflict between the id and the superego. The process whereby the superego is acquired was of interest to Freud, but he never really examined it in depth. Other writers (notably George Herbert Mead) were led to conclude, as they looked into the matter more profoundly, that perhaps the idea of conflict was overemphasized by Freud. From Mead's perspective, individuals in their social character are reflected in the demands of the community. From this position, individuals and the society of which they are a part are merely different manifestations of the same thing.

5. For a scholarly treatment of this issue, see William N. Stephens, *Oedipus Complex: Cross-Cultural Evidence* (New York: Free Press, 1962).

6. For an interesting novelistic treatment of this true story, see Meyer Levin, *Compulsion* (New York: Simon & Schuster, 1956).

7. We do not subscribe, in general, to a Freudian approach to human activities. However, we believe it is foolish not to respect the tremendous opening of awareness—the forced expansion of possibilities—that Freud brought to the investigation of human conduct. For a highly sophisticated (and sympathetic) critique of Freud, see H. D. Duncan, *Communication and the Social Order* (New York: Bedminster Press, 1962), pp. 3–17.

8. Freud, *Civilization and Its Discontents*, pp. 23–24.

9. Ibid., p. 62. Italics are Freud's.

10. Ibid., p. 92.

11. *Totem and Taboo*, p. 117, cf. fn.

Chapter 6

Symbolic Interactionism and the Work of George Herbert Mead

❖

❖ The Problem of the Individual and Society

Social theories have a tendency to get entangled in the problem of the primacy of the individual over society or society over the individual. At first the question of this relationship seems like an idle form of speculation—an empty argument similar in character to the medieval riddle concerning how many angels can dance on the head of a pin. Yet it is not in the least an idle question. The proper nature of the relationship between the individual and society (or the state, culture, or community) still constitutes one of the more exasperating and contentious of all humanistic concerns.

It is the ideological fracture line for great masses of people who have turned against each other, at least in part, because of the stand they took on this issue. There are those who believe that society should reflect the nature and character of the particular men and women who make it up; society is, according to this view, properly subordinated to the individual. On the other side are those who believe that individuals must reflect the nature and character of the society of which they are a part; from this perspective, the person is properly subordinated to the society or state.

Ayn Rand, for example, does not equivocate in the resolution of this issue. For her the individual is paramount, and the greatest person is the one who is able to force his or her will upon the state. On the other hand, until recently at least, academic anthropology tended to give strong emphasis to the argument that the individual is an almost helpless agent of the state or "culture." A quite radical form of this thinking appears in the writings of Leslie White, who sees the individual as a relatively passive conductor of culture (somewhat like a wire conducting an electric force), no matter how great or unique the person might appear to be. Geniuses, from White's point of view, are only better conductors of the cultural force.[1]

One manifestation of this debate appears in the beliefs of racists. Racism advocates the idea that society or culture is a product of the biological and psychological nature of those who make up the society. From this perspective, society is subordinate to the individuals composing it. Superior individuals make superior societies. It is a naive approach to the complexities of the relationship existing between human beings, as individuals, and the communities in which they live.

Another form of the society-versus-the-individual issue appears in the interest many people take in the matter of whether a person should be a conformist or a nonconformist. To be a conformist, of course, is to give in to the demands of the state. It means burying one's own identity within the corporate identity of thousands of others who speak the same language, wear the same clothes, share the same style of haircut, live in the same kind of house, drive the same kind of automobile to work, and eat the same kind of dinner from the same kind of table when they come home at the same time in the evening to the same kind of family. The dismal portrayal of the conformist, now so popular in Western literature, does not need to be stressed here. We are all familiar with it.

The American tradition of conformity bashing is peculiar, in a way. Conformity is characteristic of all human cultures. In America, one way of conforming is to mock the conformist. This suggests the ironic impasse, of course, of having a conformistic conception of the nature of nonconformity: Part of being a conformist in Western society, particularly America, is to appear to be a nonconformist.

If being a conformist is a dismal moral fate, then the fate of the nonconformist or deviant is hardly any better. True deviants are those persons identified by other people as being sufficiently individualistic to attract attention, concern, notoriety and the threat of (or imposition of) constraint. If deviants continue to assert themselves, they are subjected to constraining sanctions. One way to define deviance is to argue that it is conduct that leads to such sanctions.

This is not a technical definition of *deviance*, a difficult term to pin down when examined closely. We are excluding here unusual but accepted persons such as state governors or best-selling authors. They are in a statistical minority and, in this sense, deviant, but they are generally highly conformistic. We should also mention that the number of devices society is capable of employing to promote conformity to established standards is considerable. They range from the use of violence to the modification of belief systems. They are generally effective enough to induce high degrees of standardization among people. (See, for example, Peter L. Berger's discussion of social control, described in Chapter 13.)

The assertion of self is, by definition, an act against society. Even relatively minor forms of self-assertion, such as bargaining with store clerks, are beyond the capacities of the typical American. Harold Garfinkel, of the University of California at Los Angeles, had his students attempt to bargain for items in stores. It was common for students to reply that they experienced difficulty in telling a clerk they would offer less for an item than its established price. Some students found it impossible. Those who were able to bargain, however, discovered that it became easier with practice. Some eventually concluded, after gaining several surprising bargains by doing their homework for the course, that they would never buy any item priced over ten or twenty dollars without first offering a lower bid.[2]

True forms of individualistic conduct exact a great price on the person who is willing to engage in such assertion. Even outwardly acceptable actions, such as exercising one's right to remain unmarried, will evoke sanctioning activity and negative labeling by those who look on marriage as a proper form of living. In a society that extols marriage, trying to remain single for any great length of time can be a modest adventure in individualism.

At the moral level, then, the problem of the relationship between individuals and the state is a profound one, centering on the extent to which individuals, by losing their identity through conformity, have in effect sold their personal souls for a mess of collective pottage. To conform or not to conform is a daily matter calling for personal judgment. At the same time, it is a question that becomes as abstract, complicated, and impossible of precise resolution as that medieval riddle of the angels dancing on the head of a pin we referred to at the beginning.

This brief consideration of the problems contained within the alternatives offered by conformity and nonconformity highlights moral aspects of the problem of the relationship between the individual and society. That is to say, *should* one be a conformist or nonconformist? But there is another way of dealing with this issue.

Instead of asking whether the individual *should* conform to the demands of the state or the state *should* conform to the demands of the individual, we can ask this question: To what extent does a person in fact conform, and to what extent is that person, under the best of circumstances, able to express his or her individuality? This shift in the character of the question moves the problem from the moral realm to the more empirical realm of observation.

"a feeling of moral obligation or duty." It is easy to dismiss an abstraction such as "social conscience" with the attitude that it properly belongs in theological discussions and is not especially "real."

So it is essential at the outset of a consideration of Mead's thought to keep constantly in mind an awareness of the fact that the constraints imposed by conscience are able to surpass even biological urges and physical demands in their forcefulness. However one responds to Freudian theory, it is difficult to deny that what Freud referred to as the "superego" is commonly capable of suppressing the animal impulses of the "id."

Thus we have the interesting situation in which an abstract condition, namely social conscience, arising out of the social training of the child is able to coerce and frustrate more "primitive" or more "real" biologically grounded impulses. Once we recognize this, it is reasonable—indeed, it is absolutely necessary—to wonder about the source of the coercive power of belief, where belief exists as a form of symbolic meaning.

The first step in beginning to comprehend the coercive nature of symbols is to recognize that symbols can, in fact, construct a reality of their own. This contention was one of the central thrusts of Mead's argument. Mead did not have the advantage of being able to refer to research that later demonstrated, in dramatic ways, the extent to which human perception can be influenced by symbols. Following Mead, researchers such as Muzafer Sherif and Solomon Asch provided several clear demonstrations of the capacity of language to influence perception and thereby "create," as it were, a unique reality. Having noted this, it will help to explicate Mead's argument if we make a brief digression and quickly sketch in the general character of the work of Sherif and Asch.[6]

All Sherif did was have people sit in totally darkened rooms and observe a stationary pinpoint of light placed in front of them. People, under such circumstances, see the light as moving in an erratic and random manner. This is referred to as the "autokinetic" or "self-movement" effect. Sherif, however, told his subjects that they would see the light move in a straight horizontal line, and that they were to inform him of the extent of the movement. So instructed, the subjects did in fact see the light move in a straight horizontal line, drifting slowly back and forth. The subjects then orally informed the experimenter how far they saw the light move.

Sherif found that when people who saw the light move large distances were placed in communication with those who saw it move small distances, and each group communicated its perceptions to the other, the result was a modification of perceptions in such a way as to approach a common mean. That is, those who saw it move large distances reduced the distance when told by others it was not moving as far, and those who saw it move small distances increased their perceived distance of movement. It is particularly important to comprehend that perceptions actually changed. People who participated in the demonstration saw actual increases or decreases in the distance the pinpoint of light apparently moved.

Sherif, interestingly enough, did not comment on the extent to which his own suggestion of apparent horizontal motion was a coercive symbolic construction of perception. Some researchers found that subjects who were told that the light would move in a circular manner, and that they were to estimate the radius of the circle, saw the light move in a circle. Incidentally, it is easy to demonstrate this in a classroom. All that is necessary is a room that can be *totally* darkened. A flashlight with a small tinfoil cover allowing only a point of light to appear can serve as a light source.

There is one important aspect of this study that must be mentioned. Such high susceptibility to suggestion takes place when the situation confronting a person is without any apparent external structure. Such situations are sometimes referred to as "unstructured" settings. Asch was able to demonstrate that even in structured settings there are ways of convincing individuals to deny the evidence of their own eyes. Asch placed subjects in the company of people who were told to disagree with the subjects about the length of two sticks. In such situations, the subjects tended to agree eventually with the majority and say that the shorter stick was longer.

From the work of Sherif and Asch, we can formulate a conservatively stated principle offering a profound basis for the more elaborate theories and ideas of Mead. The principle is this: *In unstructured settings, the introduction of symbolic statements can order perception so that the symbolic presentation is perceived as a real event.*

This proposition requires some comment. It implies that what we think of as "merely" symbols are, in fact, an integral part of what we think of as reality. Virtually any real event a person encounters will be given some kind of symbolic interpretation, and almost any kind of symbolic construction will have implications for how people respond to what we generally think of as reality.

Consider, for example, something as real and as concrete as a mountain. Depending on the kinds of symbolic environments from which a person comes, a mountain can be seen as a romantic wonder—a manifestation of the majesty of nature. A mountain might also be viewed, as the Alps were at one time, as a kind of imperfection in nature, a jagged mess of rocks. Or mountains might be seen by a geologist as repositories of mineral wealth.

In other words, reality responds to the ways in which we define it. The point we wish to emphasize is that the definitions have real consequences. Physical reality, then, is somewhat subject to symbolic modification. Where there are no external constraints on our perception, symbolic modification can become the total reality. A person literally responds to the symbolic definition of the situation and acts accordingly.

Examples of this are common enough. Studies show that people are much more likely to give assistance to someone in trouble who is well dressed than to someone who is not. People respond to the symbolic meaning of attire. The "reality" of the character of the person beneath the clothes is not directly apparent. It does not have an overt or easily perceived "structure."

Character is, then, established in part through the symbolic means of clothing or dress. A "good" person in "bad" clothes will immediately be perceived as "bad." A "bad" person in "good" clothes will immediately be perceived as "good."

This is not to say that one cannot have altered perceptions as a result of developing longer-term relationships. This phenomenon of changing one's opinion about someone else is something we typically experience. It can be an intense experience at times. It is intense because what we thought was "real" at an earlier time is eventually perceived as not having been "real" at all. A person we once admired is seen later to be despicable. A person we once despised we come to see as being admirable. Usually it is the same person throughout the period in which we undergo our "change of heart." Our perception is influenced by the way we come to modify our symbolic impressions of the other person.

We are all vulnerable to this aspect of symbols. When we confront a stranger, we are faced with the task of discovering what this person "really" is. But the reality does not exist in any physical form. It is rather obvious, then, that the quest for "true" identity involves symbolic exchanges, and that the identity will be grounded in some kind of convincing story. We find out what a person is as we are told stories about his or her character. Such stories become a serious form of reality, as many a martyr has found out. Continuing with this line of thinking leads to the suggestion that literature and storytelling are essential acts for the creation of human character and that human character is, ultimately, grounded in the "fictional realities" within which we live.

To come back to Mead, we are now ready to move into a consideration of the social nature of self. We have seen that when individuals are confronted with an "unstructured" setting or event, they are vulnerable to symbolic forms of suggestion. Moreover, these suggestions have real effects on perception. It is axiomatic to Mead's thought (and the thought of orthodox social scientists in Western culture) that at birth an individual is not provided with any inborn self-concept or socially structured self-awareness. This is something the person must, in large part, learn. Mead accepted this notion, but pushed the issue further by raising the question of how the learning takes place. What is the process which results in self-conceptions, which come to be so profoundly learned and accepted by most of us?

The beginning moment for the development of self and society comes with the acquisition of symbols, permitting the person to identify himself or herself as an event that can be separated from the rest of the world and referred to as an object much like any other. It appears to be the case that all human cultures go to the trouble to identify individuals as individuals: People are given names and other forms of self-referent terms.

This raises the empirically interesting question of whether there are cultures in which people do not have well-defined self-referent terms. If so, then it would be a weakening of the Meadian position. We do not know of such a social or cultural system. Along with class structures, the communally given identity of the individual seems to be a cultural universal.

In our symbol system, we use self-referent terms such as "I," "me," "mine," "myself," and our personally identifying names. In the use of these terms, we are able to achieve the social bond—the force that binds the individual and the community together. Curiously enough, self-referent terms cannot be used without bringing up some aspect of a communal concern.

This is virtually a tautologous statement. The late Manford Kuhn of the State University of Iowa developed a "twenty-statements test" in which people were asked to give twenty responses to the question, "Who am I?" Categorizing responses to this question enabled Kuhn to probe the ways in which people modify their conceptions of themselves as the character of their relations with others changes. He found that people ordinarily refer to themselves in terms of social statuses of one kind or another. However, he also reported that people who have been socially "clobbered" or "put down" tend to change their responses to the "Who am I?" question in a way that makes greater use of "mystical" concepts.[7]

We have said that the use of self-referent terms commonly involves some aspect of the community. This is obvious in the case where a person relies on a social identity in the use of a self-referent term (for example, when someone, in response to the question "Who are you?" says, "I am a Catholic" or "I am married" or "I am a student" or some similarly obvious conjoining of self-referent terms with communal status systems). Unless there is a self-referent term awareness of one's own individuality, this form of conjoining of the person and society cannot occur.

We are able to interact with the community by virtue of the fact that we have at least two primary sets of symbols permitting the interaction to occur. We have, on the one hand, self-referent terms, and, on the other, terms for various communal statuses. This, in part, is what symbolic interaction is about. Society and the person are generated together in those moments when people develop conceptions of themselves by virtue of symbolic interactions with others.

Other forms of the relationship between self-referent terms and communal concerns can be more remote and subtle, but the pure expression of self, independent of communal relations, appears to be impossible. Self is always connected symbolically with others, and in this sense it is always associated with society.

The concept of self is acquired with the acquisition of language. Modern symbolic interactionists are inclined to agree with Mead that self-conception is not inherent at birth. The acquisition of self-concepts comes through a process now referred to as "socialization." The most significant feature of the process of socialization is the development of a particular set of conceptions about the self. One of Mead's better-known formulations was his discussion of the stages of development of self-awareness.

❖ *Symbolic Interaction*

Although symbols depend on people for their existence, they also display a surprising amount of autonomy. Symbols interact with each other and, as we are all aware, can take on a kind of life of their own. Anyone who has ever been the subject of a news story in the papers or on television gains a stronger understanding of this. How a news story might define you and what you know yourself to be are generally two quite different things.

There are rules that define how symbols are to be related to each other. These rules are commonly referred to as "syntax" and "grammar." A fair notion of how symbols can interact outside the rules of syntax, however, can be obtained by simply associating several in a random manner. In the following example, we have taken six symbols, drawn from a dictionary by using a table of random numbers. Here they are:

cosh, unbuckle, nonconformist, canker, Dow Jones, up

The only peculiar word is *cosh*, a British slang term meaning "a blackjack" or "to use a blackjack on someone." The point we are interested in here is that, even though they have been randomly drawn, there are little sequences among these random terms that make a kind of sense—for example, "Dow Jones up," or "nonconformist canker." If we throw in some articles and an occasional conjunction or preposition, we can string these random terms together in a more elaborate manner:

Unbuckle the nonconformist with the canker if Dow Jones up.

By using only a few operational terms, we can put the six terms together in a fairly meaningful way:

The unbuckled cankerous nonconformist was coshed because the Dow Jones was up.

It reads like something a surrealist poet might write. However, we are not interested in meaning as much as we are in the elementary fact that symbols are capable of interacting with each other simply as symbols. Obviously, if such wordplay is possible with six purely randomly drawn words from a large dictionary, an astonishing variety of symbolic creations can be obtained by drawing on larger symbolic sets. All we need is a few rules for playing with symbols, and we are ready to go. However, even if we play with symbols merely by placing them next to each other, we can still get creative effects.

A different form of the point we are trying to make appears in the old puzzle about whether a million monkeys typing random sequences for a million years would manage to type Shakespeare's *Hamlet*. Probably not. However, they would type a large number of sequences of some length— perhaps a page or two—which would, in themselves, be interesting. The ability of symbols to interact, in a sense, among themselves is one of the major arguments in Mead's philosophy. If we are the agents through which symbols are expressed, and if symbols possess the property of being able to interact with each other as vigorously as we have suggested, then the symbolic character of people has virtually infinite possible variations and permutations.

We can now make the point we are trying to make by turning to the self-referent symbols "I," "my," "me," "mine," personal names, "self," and so on. *Strictly as symbols*, such terms can interact with other symbols in a purely symbolic interaction. We can, for example, take the phrase "I am _____" and place any of a tremendous variety of symbols in the blank.

This creative power of symbols brings into being an entirely new class of creature—one that acquires its nature through its symbolic definitions. Since these are capable of astonishing variety, an astonishing variety of human social types can be generated. Tigers are pretty much tigers, and horses are pretty much horses. People, however, are not pretty much people unless we ignore their social identities. People can be presidents, failures, Americans, sluts, mystics, Zulus, cads, poets, heroines, cheats, dreamers, blacksmiths, classy, foul, scum, rich, Ph.D.s, neurotics, and an infinite variety of these labels. This can happen only because the self, *as symbol*, is capable of interacting with other symbols.

Now, it is generally evident that people are not allowed to place just any old kind of qualifying symbol next to their self-referent terms except in fantasy. If we are poor, for example, we are not allowed to say we are rich. If we do not have medical degrees, we are not allowed to say we are physicians. Of course, one can cheat; however, there is the risk of paying a penalty for this. Obviously, there is a socially established set of rules that limits the free interaction between symbols and self-referent terms.

These rules work well enough, though just how they work is not well understood. Meadian theory suggests that the individual is especially vulnerable to symbolic manipulations of self-identity, and this is commonly the case. We tend to become what we are told we are. Young men brought up as lords in the feudal period commonly thought of themselves as lords and acted as lords. Those brought up as peasants thought of themselves as peasants and acted as peasants.

However, we are not vulnerable to all possible forms of self-definition. A Caucasian American is not likely, for example, to accept the argument that he or she is actually Chinese. (An interesting aspect of all of this is so-called "New Age" thinking, in which an individual attaches self-identity to previous incarnations. By this device, it is possible to be anything and everything—a Stone Age hunter, a six-legged green-haired seal on the planet Uglik, or whatever one might fancy. New Age thinking, from this perspective, is nothing less than an indirect challenge to the socially established rules determining how we are to define ourselves.)

Although we cannot pursue the problem in any great depth, social control over self-referent terms is maintained, at least in part, through the process of designating (again symbolically) people who are given the right to define you for yourself. In the severest form of this process, such a person is the judge who has the right to determine whether "innocent" or "guilty" is to be placed in the blank "I am _____." In other forms, it is the teacher who determines whether you can say "I am a good student." It is the boss who determines whether you can claim you are a good worker. Self-determination is less self-determinant than we are probably inclined to think. This is one of the central messages of Mead's philosophy, and probably one of the reasons he remains a popular theorist in academic sociology.

For most people, probably, language and symbols are simply devices through which communication takes place. In the hands of a philosopher and thinker of the stature of George Herbert Mead, language is much, much more. It is the source of social structure. It is the element required for the creation of human social systems. It is the agent through which the intense bonding, so to speak, of the individual with society takes place. It is the means whereby human communal systems are assured that the individuals who constitute the "cells" of communities will do what they are supposed to do to assure the continuity of the system.

Whereas common sense tells us that communities exist to sustain the individual, Meadian philosophy forces us to consider the equally interesting alternative argument—that individuals exist to sustain the community. This brings us back to the individual-versus-the-state argument with which this chapter began.

❖ Stages in the Development of Self-Awareness

The acquisition of self-awareness is, paradoxically enough, tied in with the extent to which individuals come to be aware of the complexity of human social interactions taking place around them. Until this occurs, we are separated from others and, by virtue of that separation, not able to comprehend the meaning of ourselves as social beings. The development of a conception of self, then, is essentially a matter of the growth of social sensitivity. It is a matter of coming to understand the community.

However, a good understanding of what Mead is talking about requires that the student not just see these "stages" of development of the self as a simple progression of sophistication in the person as he or she moves from infancy to maturity. It is a concise formulation of the intimacy of the bond between the individual and the community. It is a statement that reveals the extent to which both are dependent on each other. Self-consciousness, from Mead's point of view, is, strangely enough, a matter of community consciousness.

To have a self, one must at the same time have a knowledge of the moral order of the community. In order for the community to exist, the individuals within it must be possessed of a sense of their individuality and the relationship of that individuality to the community. We are aware of ourselves through our communal experiences, and our societies are able to exist in large part because we experience a strong sense of our social identities.

Mead's process of self-development can be divided into three broad stages:

1. *Preparatory stage.*[8] The preparatory stage is a period extending from infancy up to the point where children are able to begin dealing with themselves from the perspective of others. The essential feature of this stage is imitative action, in which children reveal a capacity to mimic others who are engaged in real role performances. A good example of what is being referred to here takes place when a child who happens to see his or her parent reading a newspaper picks up part of it and starts "reading" it too. The only thing giving the child's performance away is that the paper is upside down. Such mimicry or aping of adults or older children prepares the child for a fuller social life as an adult.

2. *Play stage.* In the play stage, children begin to reveal a capacity for seeing themselves from the perspective of someone else. This is an important development and is associated with "mind" and the development of self-awareness. In this stage, children literally "play" with social roles of a great variety. They are able to construct and formulate roles of one kind or another. They are able to enact various roles in a general way, and, even more interesting, they are able to play by themselves as social beings. In such play they assume different roles and then relate one role to another.

   A child is a sort of one-person band at this point. We should add that if children are one-person bands at this stage of development, they become intricate and elaborate one-person orchestras by the time they are adults. When we refer to children as "one-person bands," we mean they are able to play out a scene against themselves. This might occur, for example, when little Johnny, playing alone, pretends to steal a cookie. He might then assume the role of mother and admonish himself, and he might stand in the corner until, as his mother, he permits himself to go play once more. Then he might enact the role of "father" and, as the father, suggest to the mother that he be allowed to go play. In this little "drama," the child is a band with three instruments.

   The ability of young children to look at themselves through the eyes of others in a sustained and involved way places them on the threshold of being human. They are nearing the point where they can begin to function as integral members of the community. They acquire a sense of their own individuality and worth (or lack of worth) even as they become laced into a larger social unit. Self and society are different sides of the same coin.

The significant feature of the play stage is the involvement of the children with a variety of social roles. They are not merely little Caroline playing astronauts and Martians, little Roger playing with his Transformer, and so on. One minute the child may be playing a teacher, another minute a firefighter, another minute a grocery clerk, another minute an explorer, and so on. Children put on and take off roles as though the roles were elaborate symbolic wardrobes of possibilities. The roles might not be systematically related to one another, but children develop an awareness of their character through play. Such play occurs alongside the development of the symbols enabling the children to acquire a sense of the nature of the roles.

3. *Game stage*. The currently popular metaphor of "life as a game" shows up in the writings of Mead. However, whereas the present-day ordinary use of this notion is moderately pejorative (as, for instance, in the phrase, "Don't play games with me, you so-and-so"), Mead viewed games as an integral part of the process of socialization. They are particularly significant for children as a device for locating their sense of self within a systematic ordering of roles.

Children must come to view themselves in terms of their location within a network of roles, and they must perceive themselves not simply in terms of how they are related to some other single person, but in terms of how they are related to large numbers of other people. Moreover, these other people are related to each other in complex ways, and the form of their relationship will affect the child's own significance. It is quite an achievement. The game offers one of the simpler forms of entry into this system of relationships.

Keep in mind that role and status networks are, in themselves, quite complicated and abstract matters. In modern social systems, they are sufficiently complicated to call for the employment of a new group of specialists whose task is to attempt to understand them better. These specialists are called "sociologists." Every child born into this society must gain at least sufficient awareness of the system to be able to work and live within it. Games promote this awareness. Mead's arguments suggest that children who have difficulty in games will have difficulty in locating themselves in the community of adults in later life.

In the game situation, a new feature is added to the abilities of the child to relate symbolically with others, for it is in this stage that the child acquires a sense of what Mead referred to as the "generalized other." Mead developed his argument by using as an example the game of baseball. Consider, for a moment, the actions of the pitcher on the mound. A casual consideration of his action makes it seem as though the pitcher and the batter are locked in a duel and the pitcher's actions are a simple response to the hitting habits of the man at the plate. From a Meadian perspective, however, the situation is more involved, less physical, and more symbolic than the ordinary fan in the stands is likely to appreciate.

When we see the pitcher as a person who is simply responding to the problem of the batter confronting him, we tend to think of him as involved with one other person.[9] Mead observed that what seems more reasonable is to understand that the pitcher is actually relating to a large number of people at any one time. An interesting case in point is when a runner gets to first base. The pitcher obviously relates to both the batter at the plate and the runner on first. But Mead sees the pitcher as more highly involved than this. Not only is the pitcher necessarily relating to the runner at first and the batter who stands before him; he must also relate to the catcher, the infield, the outfield, the manager, the fans in the stands, the press, the coaches, the umpires, members of his family, and others.

Mead termed this broader association with others the "generalized other." The generalized other, achieved through the imaginative symbolic act of relating one's self to innumerable other people, becomes the incorporation of the community within the individual. It is, in a sense, the source of social conscience. Children encounter it and learn it through play experiences in which they are related to others who are themselves related to each other. The whole process depends on interaction and the ability to elaborate and expand interaction by means of symbols.

❖ Signs and Symbols

When people interact in terms of symbols, they are engaging in an activity that is quite unique. We must be constantly wary of thinking that we can understand human symbolic actions by referring to the behavior of nonsymbolic creatures. Such creatures are able to interact in terms of signs but not symbols. People interact in terms of both signs and symbols. Mead distinguished between signs and symbols by suggesting that signs always elicit a given response. Symbols, on the other hand, do not elicit a particular response, but must instead be interpreted by those engaged in a symbolic exchange.

Mead was inclined to be critical of purely behavioristic psychologists, such as John B. Watson, who wanted to ignore the trickier aspects of language—a feature of behaviorism that continues down to the present time. Behaviorism, Mead argued, must include a consideration of the nature of symbolic action if it is to have any value for the further development of the understanding of human social conduct. Behaviorists are all too willing to bring over into the human realm proofs for arguments that have as their sole support findings obtained from non-symbol-using rats or other laboratory animals.

One of Mead's more popular observations concerns the character of interaction between two fighting dogs. In such a moment, the animals may circle each other while making threatening gestures. Each dog is responding to the other in terms of an immediate stimulus, and the stimulus elicits relatively fixed responses. When the stimulus is withdrawn, the behavior is modified. In such instances, the organism is responding to the stimulus as a sign (or signal) to respond.

So it is with animals that, while the stimulus sign is before the animal, it responds in a particular fashion. When the stimulus for fighting is present, the animal reacts with a fighting response. However, when the stimulus sign is withdrawn, the animal immediately turns to something else. It is not the same with human beings. The urge to continue fighting can remain strong even though the enemy is nowhere in sight. The enemy is retained, so to speak, through symbolic devices. The animal responds only in terms of direct reference; humans can respond through indirect reference. It is a difference that definitely makes a difference when thinking about human beings and the other creatures of this planet.

A chimpanzee, for example, when in the presence of another chimpanzee in distress, will behave with evident signs of fear or distress of its own. However, as soon as it is removed from the sight of the suffering comrade, the chimpanzee will immediately resume normal activity. There is evidence suggesting that the human capacity to suffer over the misfortunes of another for any length of time (after the person is out of view) is a function of our capacity to translate the person's condition into a symbolic presence, which then is able to stand for the reality of the other person's suffering. Empathy, in other words, rests on a symbolic base.[10] With signs, then, the response is relatively fixed. When, for example, a lion roars in peace and contentment upon awakening from a little nap after a big meal, other animals may run away in fear, even though the roar has no threatening meaning behind it. The roar is a sign that produces a given response.

With symbols, an added element is called into play—the necessity of shared meanings. This aspect of symbolic action, to the degree that we consider it significant, implies that human social conduct will always be, to some considerable extent, immune to exact analysis. If there is a sharing of symbolic content, then interaction is relatively ordered or easy. Where symbolic content is not shared, then interaction is considerably inhibited, although it can continue at "lower" levels.

Anyone who tries to associate with a person who does not speak the same language discovers how difficult a social relationship can be. This is an elementary kind of observation. At the same time, it is an important one because it is so basic and because it is so easy for people to confuse signs and symbols. The use of symbols presumes the existence of a social and cultural system—a network of values, meanings, interests, concerns, and labelings that are wrapped up in the elaborate form a language can, in itself, take. The use of signs does not require a social and cultural system: Ants and bees use signs, but they do not live in cultures in the human sense of the term.

❖ *Symbols, Reality, and History*

One problem that the symbolic interactionists keep encountering is the argument that symbols are not "real." This argument, at its broadest level, contends that the human social order and individual consciousness are located in something less ephemeral and more tangible than symbols. This leads, in turn, to a quest for the "real" locus or foundation of human social order.

One approach is to look for this locus in kin systems and the bonds of sexuality. Another is to seek it in economic relations and the necessity of labor and exchange. Still another approach uses the argument that communities arise out of the survival needs of people—the community is essentially a defensive structure. These efforts try to locate the real foundations of the human community in the family or the marketplace or the military. They share a tendency to reject symbols as a basis for community. Symbols are something that came after human societies were established. They remain, somehow, insignificant when pitted against the more fundamental forces of sex, labor, and conflict.

Mead, of course, was not unaware of the significance of such matters as sexual bonding, the power of the marketplace, or the demands of defense. According to Mead, however, these are not forces that in and of themselves account for the elaborate and continuous forms human communities can give to these activities. An important word here is "continuous." In order for continuity to exist within human communities, the community must have some kind of history.

History, however, is an almost bizarre accomplishment. It transforms into a "real" and present condition something that occurred in the past, and therefore no longer exists and is not "real." By producing and sustaining histories, symbols are able to retain pasts. Mead considered this ability of symbols to be especially important for the formation of communities. In a sense, history offers the community a mirror in which it can view its collective self. Just as the concept of self is significant for the individual and provides the means whereby the person and the community are conjoined, histories enable entire communities to develop a sense of identity or self.

From a Meadian point of view, time and symbols are integral features of each other. Without symbols, people would not be able to experience time. Symbols provide us with a past and a future that can be discussed in the present moment. Other animals respond to time in terms of physiological mechanisms that enable them to adjust to seasonal changes and the need to procreate. They probably lack, however, any elaborate conception of their past or concern for the distant future. Through language we are given a communal history, or, to use an equivalent term, something anthropologists call "culture." Through language we are also given a personal history, or what social psychologists call "personality."

People are unique in that they possess a sense of self. They are also unique in that they possess a sense of history. No other creature on the face of this earth is concerned with its own history. All other animals are "locked," as it were, in the present. The past contains little meaning, if any. The future is poorly comprehended.

For human beings, how they perceive the future has profound implications on how they will respond to the present. How they construct the past, or what they think of as their history, also has profound implications on how they enact their lives in the present moment. But the future and the past can only exist in symbolic constructions.

Symbols, then, are at the bottom of what it means to be a human being. They offer us a means for examining ourselves, and in the process we acquire self-awareness. With self-awareness comes consciousness and the ability to reflect on our worth or sense of worth, which influences our ability to relate with others and is therefore a social factor as well as a personal factor. Symbols also give us a sense of history. We become aware of our own past and the past we share with others. We can also construct imagined futures to which we respond in the present.

In the works of a subtle philosopher like Mead, the symbol becomes a form of reality with implications that far transcend common and ordinary notions of what it is to be a symbol-using creature. Language does more than simply transmit culture; it is more than a "tool" early people developed to solve their material problems. Language is the agent through which people become aware of themselves even as they become more aware of their physical surroundings. As they do so, they are able to form the most elaborate and unusual social and cultural systems on the face of the earth.

Encounters with Social Thought

Self-Image and Self-Concept in Today's Changing Society

The topic selected as an illustration of how Mead's social thought can be applied to a particular issue is a focus on how our conception of ourselves is so deeply influenced by our socialization in the early years of life and enculturation into the ways of the group in which we are reared. This is a topic of concern to nearly everyone—if popular magazines and trendy sociological and psychological commentaries on self-perception and "knowing who one is" are any indication.

In the following discussion, the theoretical theme, symbolic interactionism, that guides our interpretation of modern-day success in one's schooling and academic career, work or professional career, and marital relations, is made explicit. In common discussions, particularly in popular journalism, theory remains implicit—leading to the impression that there is no theory. That, of course, is a false impression. In any consideration of any social issue, theory is always involved.

It is rather obvious that sexual identity is an important aspect of any individual conception of self. Mead's ideas are given support by the fact that we are not able to identify ourselves as men or women, boys or girls, until we are informed that we are one sex or the other. In those instances where boys are brought up as girls by doting mothers, the shock of self-identity takes place when the children encounter other people who express a different awareness of the children's sexuality. These children are then faced with the problem of resolving contrary definitions of a particular dimension of their self-conception.

For human beings, sexuality is a complex resolution of physiological, psychological, and sociological elements. Few aspects of our lives come closer to our concerns with self. Certainly our sexuality and our relationships with same-sex and opposite-sex people are inextricably interlaced with symbolic elements.

Consider, for example, a device commonly used by gay rights lecturers. The lecturer (the cases we have observed involved male lecturers), standing before an audience of men and women, looks at the people before him and then says, "You are all aware of the old adage that it takes one to know one. Well, in the gay community this is true. If you are a homosexual, you can immediately recognize another homosexual just by looking at him. In fact, I can point to a number of homosexuals in this room this very minute."

The effect of this statement is electrifying. The men in the room are alarmed. Who will be pointed out? Now, if sexual identity were a definite matter, those who were not homosexual would not need to be concerned. They could be assured, through self-knowledge, that they would not be pointed out by the lecturer. Few men, evidently, possess such certain self-knowledge. The moment the lecturer states his intent, they panic.

It still makes a case for Mead's contention if a man in the audience is concerned about being pointed to, because, even though he may possess certain self-knowledge with respect to his sexuality, he still may not like being labeled a homosexual publicly and erroneously—especially by someone who claims special abilities with regard to such identifications. The label, in and of itself, possesses powers. Here is a situation in which a word has a powerful influence on the way in which one's self is defined.

This illustration is even more interesting because it points to the elementary fact that how one's self is labeled is not completely under a person's control. If the lecturer stares at you and the audience begins to follow his stare as he says, "You, I can tell, are one of us," what do you do? Suddenly you find that you are forced to recognize that your sexual character has a symbolic side. You remain the same physically, but the symbolic context within which you are operating is altered.

Actually, in the several instances where we have witnessed gay rights lecturers using this stage device, no lecturer ever went on to identify anyone specifically. Instead, each one simply stated that if we experience a sense of panic over the possibility of being pointed to, it might mean that our heterosexual identity is more precarious than we previously suspected.

It is for this reason that the psychiatric concept of latent homosexuality is so traumatizing. It can be leveled against anyone. What, after all, can such a concept possibly mean? With respect to latent qualities, we can be nearly anything—latent geniuses, latent fools, latent bums, latent athletes, latent artists, latent successes, latent failures, latent shoemakers, latent bakers, latent candlestick makers. Note, in this example, that nothing changes or changed in the lives of the men in the audience of the gay rights lecturer—only a symbolic change occurred. Symbolic change, however, can be enough.

The Significance of Childhood Play in the Development of Self-Image

Echoing the theme detailed previously in this chapter on Mead's interest in childhood play and its importance in the process of self-development, we can examine early childhood activities and games in the preschool, kindergarten and early elementary grades with a new significance for symbolic meanings. The reader will recall that Mead outlined three stages in the development of the self as expressed in play and childhood games. These stages are: the preparatory stage, the play stage, and the game stage. Mead noted that throughout these three stages the child has an opportunity to examine adult roles and situations in the much less threatening atmosphere of the classroom, playground, home setting or backyard. From the Meadian preparatory stage where solitary and parallel play patterns are characteristic of the two- to three-year-old, the child emerges into the "play" stage at about four years of age. From this time to about seven years of age children usually engage in forms of play characterized by the imitation of adult occupations and pastimes. More specifically, these are labeled by early childhood educators, teachers, and researchers as play in the housekeeping corner, the "doll house," the "Wendy house," the homemaking area. This type of play can be extremely gender stereotyped and rigidly circumscribed by the control of teachers, parents, and other adults who insist that only the girls can play with dolls, while only the boys must play with trucks, cars, and building blocks. Additional forms of adult-imitative play are displayed in activities where children recreate stores or banks (most recently with automatic teller machines, as well) or simulate shopping at the supermarket, or playing "school" where roles of the teacher, pupils, and school administrator are emulated.

Children's play and games have been chronicled, researched and analyzed from a biological, ecological, psychological, sociological, and anthropological viewpoint to amass an extensive literature on the subject. Well-known and beloved childhood singing games such as "Farmer in the Dell," "Luby Loo," "Ring Around the Rosy," "In and Out the Window" have been described, analyzed, and categorized as dramatizations or pantomimes consistently centering around a main character with a chorus or group response. These singing games usually feature a mother, or a witch or some other main character who gives the group directions on an action or choice to be made. In the traditional singing games cited above the child can take on the role of the parent or the teacher telling, or sometimes showing, the other children just what to do. There arises social power that brings excitement and pleasure when one controls a group of others and can elicit a specific response from them. The child suddenly has a mastery over his or her peers and the social surroundings when playing these traditional children's games. The rules must be strictly adhered to. One must pick a "farmer" first in the "Farmer and the Dell," a wife, second, then the dog, the cat, and so on. If one attempts to change the order and pick a cat right after the farmer is chosen, a chorus of objections greets the innovator, especially in a kindergarten or first-grade class.

Here we have described behavior on the part of four, five, or six-year-olds that is indicative of the potency of Mead's symbolic interaction theories using the crucial nature of play and games in childhood socialization. As we pointed out earlier in this chapter, Mead, in his seminal book *Mind, Self and Society,* utilized the play and games of very young children to explicate his theory of the dual nature of the self and society. He argued that what goes on in child-play is at one with child-life. Children, Mead believed, were continually being bombarded by all those who in some sense controlled them and on whom they depended. And this is how all of us learn to internalize the rules, mores, attitudes, and values of the society in which we live.

Putting Social Thought to Work

1. It is characteristic of Americans that they are contemptuous of conformism while, at the same time, highly prone to conform. College students, for example, pride themselves on their individuality while dressing alike, eating alike, and generally subscribing to the same habits and tastes. To what extent are we free to express ourselves? If our society provides us with a highly individualistic self-concept, are

we being individualistic when we assert ourselves, or are we conforming to a social norm? Is the self a psychologistic or a sociologistic quality? That is to say, does it come from the person or the community (or some combination of the two)?

2. To what extent are physical qualities of people granted symbolic significance? For example, sexuality among humans is both a physiological and a symbolic quality. We even have languages that, at least until recently, were uniquely masculine or feminine in nature. A man, for example, would be considered effeminate if overheard saying something such as "Isn't that simply a precious and adorable little straw hat Chuck is wearing?" He would be using feminine symbols in a masculine context. We have other physical characteristics than sexuality that are symbolically transformed. Identify three physical qualities common to people, and then reveal the ways in which these qualities take on special significance through how they are symbolically labeled.

3. We are capable of logical thought by virtue of the fact that we can create logical symbols. Symbols enable us to be logical. At the same time, it is obvious that people do not always act in logical ways. Is it possible that there are types of symbols that prevent us from being perfectly logical in our lives? To what extent do symbols introduce a kind of "messiness" in our affairs and in our conceptions of our selves? Is our sense of self a "logical" matter, or is it something else? If it is something else, what does this say about the dream of attaining more "rational" forms of social order?

4. One of the most interesting of modern fictional characters is Mr. Spock, the cool and knowledgeable first officer in the television and movie series *Star Trek*. Spock is constantly talking about being "logical." In what ways must he deny his own philosophy of the "logical" life?

5. How much of the social interaction in which you participate each day involves symbolic interaction? How much of it is grounded in purely physiological concerns? Symbols do not have real properties, as do physical objects. For that reason, this culture tends to ignore symbols as a part of what influences and gives shape to our lives and our institutions. What evidence, of a solid variety, can be offered in support of Meadian theories? What evidence would appear to make Mead's ideas less tenable?

6. What single word or phrase in your life has made you unusually happy? What single word or phrase in your life has made you unusually miserable? Is it possible to be made sick by a word? Why is it that when some people offer you praise, you are delighted; yet, when others say the same thing, you see it as manipulative or even deprecative?

7. Jean-Paul Sartre once observed, somewhat in line with Mead's arguments, that young men commonly "find themselves" or acquire a sense of self by becoming involved with highly authoritarian social organizations (football teams, the Marines, street gangs, and so on). For Sartre, this was something of a paradox. Do you agree that authoritarian social systems often provide a heightened sense of self? What is the appeal of authoritarian systems? Why do young people often find social organizations that grant them great independence and freedom intolerable? What evidence can you find to support or contradict these observations?

8. What kind of self-concept does this culture promote as a general "culture type"?

9. We commonly describe ourselves as Republicans, Democrats, Catholics, doctors, wives, husbands, and so on. That is, we describe ourselves in terms of social roles or group memberships. What clues might this offer as to why people are commonly resistant to changing their political, religious, or social beliefs?

10. The social insects form elaborate communities through physiologically instinctive devices. Humans form their communities through symbolic devices. What are the relative strengths and weaknesses of each device, strictly with respect to forming large, effective, efficient, and long-lasting communities?

Endnotes

1. See, for example, Ayn Rand's *Atlas Shrugged* (New York: Random House, 1957) and *For the New Intellectual* (New York: Random House, 1961), or any of her other works. In contrast, see Leslie White, *The Science of Culture* (New York: Farrar, Straus, 1949); *Leslie A. White: Ethnological Essays*, edited by B. Dillingham and R. L. Carneiro (Albuquerque: University of New Mexico Press, 1987).

2. See Harold Garfinkel, *Studies in Ethnomethodology* (Englewood Cliffs, NJ: Prentice-Hall, 1967).

3. See the brief note on this in *Psychology Today*, June 1968, p. 76.

4. The major writings of George Herbert Mead are as follows: *The Philosophy of the Present* (La Salle, IL: Open Court, 1932); *Mind, Self and Society* (Chicago: University of Chicago Press, 1934); and *Philosophy of the Act* (Chicago: University of Chicago Press, 1938).

5. See Bernard N. Meltzer, "Mead's Social Psychology," in Jerome G. Manis and Bernard N. Meltzer, eds., *Symbolic Interaction*, 2d ed. (Boston: Allyn & Bacon, 1972), pp. 4–22.

6. See Solomon Asch, *Social Psychology* (Englewood Cliffs, NJ: Prentice-Hall, 1952). Also, see Muzafer Sherif, *Psychology of Social Norms* (New York: Harper & Row, 1936).

7. See Manford Kuhn and Thomas McPartland, "An Empirical Investigation of Self-Attitude," *American Sociological Review* 19 (February 1954), 68–76.

8. We are using Meltzer's description of the first stage, which is, as he points out,

only implicitly developed in Mead's books. See Meltzer, "Mead's Social Psychology," p. 8.

9. We are relegating to a footnote the still popular "looking-glass self" formulation of Charles Horton Cooley. This concept is often mentioned in introductions to social psychology and is similar to Mead's ideas. However, it is much simpler and somewhat misleading in its simplicity. The "looking-glass self" suggests that people see themselves in terms of others by (1) imagining how they appear to others, (2) imagining how others judge their appearance, and (3) responding accordingly. Cooley's statement has the strong virtue of emphasizing that a person's conception of self involves both imagination and some kind of relationship with other people. It has a tendency, however, to leave students with the belief that the self is located in encounters with specific other individuals, taken one at a time. Mead's point of view suggests a capacity on the part of individuals to locate themselves within a system of other persons at any point in time. In other words, people respond to a community of others and, ultimately, to the community itself as they experience it, hear and read about it, and imagine it. See Charles Horton Cooley, *Human Nature and the Social Order* (New York: Scribners, 1922).

10. See A. R. Lindesmith and A. L. Strauss, *Social Psychology*, 4th ed. (Hinsdale, IL: Dryden Press, 1974).

Chapter 7

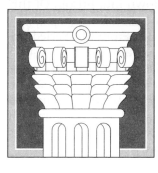

The Social Thought of Pitirim A. Sorokin

❖

together, ar
integration,
and which
live and pul
area one kii
in another
the course
changed in

Sorokin ap
profoundly aff
Such definitio
variety of beh
okin saw it, th
think of that v
real reality is

A very di
beled as Idea
Captain Ahab

"Hark ye
pasteboard
there, son
features fi
the mask!
wall? To r
there's na
outrageou
thing is cl
principal,
murmure

The othe
which is imr
believe in oi

❖ **Ideati**

To locate re
of what Soi
locate realit
of perceptic
cepts of Ide
Sorokin wa
Ideational a
various ess
his case cle
Dynamics:

❖ A Controversial Sociologist

Professor Pitirim Sorokin stands as one of the most prolific and controversial of modern sociological writers. Few sociologists have been referred to with such a diversity of terms as "Old Testament prophet,"[1] "severe and sarcastic,"[2] "renowned,"[3] "bullheaded,"[4] "moderate,"[5] "unexcelled powers of penetration,"[6] and "philosophic."[7] Friendly or unfriendly, the readers and critics of the works of Sorokin[8] are forced to recognize the exceptional energy, imaginativeness, and involvement of the man who wrote them. Two colleagues paid Sorokin a tribute which, we believe, aptly sums up the quality and extent of his work. "We can, in fact, imagine that the sociologist of the future may well complain, much as a frustrated successor to Plato once did, 'Whenever I go anywhere in my attempts, I meet Sorokin coming back.' "[9]

Sorokin's life career spanned nearly two-thirds of the twentieth century. It was a career marked by adventure, controversy, astounding scholarly productivity, and laudatory recognition from professional societies and the

general
the Bol
experie
the Cza
perienc

He
ever, r
arrived
contint
in thre
would

❖   *S*

The ric
and tr
made
tions (
his fou
ics.¹³ I
patter
the re
too va
cized
civiliz
intrig
"yarr

S
of an
sense
cultu
duct
scien
each
ketpl
tices
cultu
relat
brin;

the same literary and art forms were employed all over Europe, or even the same legends of Charlemagne, Alexander, and King Arthur; Latin was the Universal language of educated men. There were no strict nationalities, no fixed boundaries, no armed frontiers, no passports. Merchants, students, minstrels, buffoons, pilgrims, pedlars, friars, masons, scribes, pardoners, cheap-jacks—all wandered freely from place to place, to give the medieval scene everywhere the same gaudy variety.[23]

Finally, the ethical commandments of an Ideational culture emanate from God or some other supersensory source. The point Sorokin was concerned with here was that the locus of the Ideational ethical system comes from a point outside this world. It is, to use a term of Max Weber's, "other-worldly."

In contrast to the Ideational ethical system, that of the Sensate culture reflects a radically different set of premises concerning reality and people's relationship to that reality. First of all, Sensate ethics are concerned with moral conduct geared to promote human happiness, comfort, and pleasure here on this earth during the person's lifetime. Compare, for example, the Ideational sexual codes of St. Paul with the Sensate sexual ethic (before the AIDS crisis) represented in a trendy magazine such as *Playboy*.

St. Paul, attempting to interpret the nature of the divine, reached the point where he was concerned with whether or not even a virgin girl commits a sin if she marries. Paul's famous statement reads, "Art thou bound unto a wife? seek not to be loosed. Art thou loosed from a wife? seek not a wife. But and if thou marry, thou hast not sinned; and if a virgin marry, she hath not sinned. Nevertheless such shall have trouble in the flesh: but I spare you."[24]

Followers of the "Playboy" set, on the other hand, once promoted an ethic of indulgence which permits the widest latitude in sexual gratification—constrained primarily by the limitation that it should not be damaging to other people. The significant thing to note in those who espouse the fullness of sexual gratification is that ethical constraint has its locus in this world rather than in some supersensory realm.

A second characteristic of a Sensate ethical system is its relativism. It is subject to changing times and it changes along with them. Some contemporary intellectuals are of the opinion that the modern world may reach the point where morality will become largely a matter of style. Today one reads and discusses the homosexual experiences of Genet and takes LSD; next month the style will be to read and discuss Ralph Waldo Emerson and drink hot chocolate. We ought to point out here that Sorokin was entirely in disagreement with such a point of view. As we shall see a little later, Sorokin argued that Sensate ethics, and Sensate culture more broadly conceived, have reached what he referred to as an "over-ripe" stage of development. The thrust of the future will be in the direction of a reestablishment of Ideational values.

Finally, Sorokin observed, Sensate ethics are patently human rules. If they serve the purpose of happiness, they are justified. A nearly perfect illustration of what Sorokin is saying appears in the writings of A. E. Taylor, who in 1899 wrote a dissertation, published in 1901, which argued that the meaning of morality is to be found in the individual and not in the absolute.

> The first law of moral action is, Know what you really want, and the second, like unto it, See that you are not misled into accepting a spurious substitute. . . . Only before you embark on the profession of a harlot, it is your duty to find out all you can about the life to which you are committing yourself, and to make sure that a career of prostitution ending in a Lock Hospital will really give you what you want. If you decide that it will . . . you are morally on the same level as the missionary who chooses to end a career of self-devotion by dying alone and untended in a leper-settlement; that the world in general does not recognize the resemblance is only another proof of the world's ample stupidity.[25]

The quotation from Taylor is all the more significant because Taylor was an assistant lecturer in Greek and Philosophy at Owens College, Manchester. It would be a trying task to find a medieval moralist who argued that an individualistic ethic could be used as the justification for becoming a prostitute as a career.

❖ Economics Under Ideationalism and Sensatism

The differences between an Ideational and Sensate system of ethics seem clear enough. What about some of the other characteristics of a sociocultural system? What about economic activities, for example? The differences between Ideational and Sensate cultures with regard to economic practices are as definite as they are with respect to ethics. Both economics and ethics, Sorokin claimed, are enmeshed in the domination of the Ideational or Sensate point of view. In an Ideational culture the attempt to amass wealth and to concentrate on wealth-for-the-sake-of-wealth is considered a sin. Wealth is subordinated to greater ends. Business and economic conduct is a tolerated necessity, not an activity meriting the exclusion of an individual's other interests. For this reason, medieval society—a highly Ideational system, according to Sorokin—punished those who sought wealth beyond what was necessary for a modest living. Moneylending for interest could and did result in expulsion, excommunication, and other severe measures.[26]

The role of wealth and the importance of the economic life are, of course, elevated considerably in the Sensate culture. Benjamin Franklin put it baldly and succinctly when he said, "Honesty is useful because it assures credit; so are punctuality, industry, frugality, and that is the reason they are virtues . . ."[27] Because it is of this world, because it can promote temporal physical pleasure, because it can augment worldly power, and because it is a visible and measurable sign of worth, wealth assumes greater importance in a Sensate culture than in an Ideational culture.

future, to his prognostication merely by assigning to a term like creativeness meanings that will back up his predictions. Yet, even as we mention this criticism, we are loath to carry it very far. Despite a lack of focus, it is better to see vaguely than not to see at all. And, though every reader will interpret the thirteen forecasts somewhat differently, it seems, at least to us, that they are more often right than wrong. Though Delphic in many places, Sorokin's probe into the future still provides a means of broadly interpreting a variety of modern events, ranging from the once flourishing subculture of communes to the noisy wasteland of current American commercial television.

❖ Fads, Foibles, and Faults

Sorokin's vast and roving scholarship is impressive. He directed it toward an understanding of broad patterns of historical change and development. As we have seen, he also directed it toward a critical examination of modern Western civilization. Sorokin, like C. Wright Mills (see Chapter 8), expressed his love for humanity by poking fun—and not too gently—at its ugliness and shapelessness. If he could not exorcise its faults, he could at least try to make others painfully aware of them. When Sorokin moved from a global examination of the entirety of humanity down to more specific and local events, his critical reflections became more pointed and devastating. Sorokin was not only concerned with humanity in general but with the specific means people have established for observing and thinking about themselves. Among these means is what we today refer to as sociology. Sorokin took a look at sociology—a field to which he devoted a long and intelligent life— and appeared to throw up his hands in horror.

Sociology, as Sorokin saw it, is overrun with any number of faults.[32] It suffers from what he called the "discoverers' complex." This consists of forgetting that others have already observed or commented on what the sociologist has observed—and often the earlier observer has done a better job. In his biography he complains, at one point, that C. Wright Mills wrote to him and said that he had used much of Sorokin's critique as a basis for his own book, *The Sociological Imagination*. Sorokin then wryly commented that nowhere in Mills's book is his effort cited. Having conveniently forgotten or overlooked that others have already covered the same terrain, the sociologist can then shout, "Eureka, we are onto something hitherto unheard of!" Sociology also suffers, said Sorokin—and he is not the first, nor will he be the last, to make this point—from involuted language and "sham-scientific slang."

Sorokin went on to examine with an extremely critical eye a variety of other fads, foibles, and faults in the repertory of the sociologist, psychologist, economist, political scientist, or anyone else he happened to come across. He picked at nearly every weakness known to exist in psychological tests, and he used pungent language in the process.[33] He referred to our present "testomania" and to the twentieth century as an age of "testocracy." The quest for quantification in the social sciences he dismissed as "quantophrenia."

Moreover, Sorokin did not hesitate to attack the very core of modern sociological belief—the idea that our knowledge of the social world should be grounded in "empirical" fact. This notion, Sorokin argued, is both faulty and senile. Intuition plays a very important role in the development of scientific understanding and we cannot limit ourselves merely to the "empirical" realm of the senses. Indeed, social behavior is, when properly understood, beyond the direct observation of the senses. Furthermore, any number of fictions—in the strongest meaning of that word—play a most important role in scientific work, whether it is in physics or in sociology. The square root of minus one or the concept of infinity defies any empirical observation,[34] yet science would be seriously inconvenienced without them. Sociologists are fooling themselves when they think they can observe directly certain units of action or role behavior.

Worse yet, for all of their emphasis on empiricism, sociologists, like the worst gossip mongers, are too often willing to go along with "hearsay" evidence. Sorokin used the definition of marital happiness set forth by one sociologist as an illustration.

> Clifford Kirkpatrick operationally defines "marital maladjustment" as "that quality in marriage which causes one close friend to classify the couple as maladjusted." Thus, if a scholar wants to give an "operational" definition of happiness or "adjustment" in marriage, all he has to do is, first, to ask a friend of the married couple whether the marriage is "adjusted" or "maladjusted"; second, without any verification, to accept this opinion as valid and scientific; and, third, to build upon it a huge statistical superstructure of measurements and predictions of success or failure in marriage.[35]

Sorokin then went on,

> One can . . . sympathize with a physician who uses a thermometer to determine his patient's temperature or a cardiograph to diagnose his heart activity, instead of adopting the much simpler and more infallible operation of just asking the patient or his friend whether the former's temperature and heart-activity are "normal" or "abnormal."[36]

These barbs, and others before them, did not endear Sorokin to members of the sociological community. Sociologists have been inclined to ignore Sorokin (which is roughly akin to trying to ignore the Eiffel Tower while visiting Paris) or to dismiss him with a casual shrug.[37] Yet Sorokin persisted, and his writings, in many places, remain viable while those of his critics have receded into obsolescence.

Sorokin's criticism of sociology is lengthy and negative, with only a brief and general suggested remedy. He recommended that integralist sociology replace the atomistic, analytic, pseudo-operationalistic, and empirical sociology of the present. As he developed his suggestion he also antagonized deeply those sociologists of today who are committed to "factual" sociology. The reason is apparent. Sorokin suggested that it was necessary to transcend the observable in order to understand the reality around us in a fuller sense.

> The integralist conception views psychosocial reality as a complex manifold in which we can distinguish at least three different aspects: sensory, rational, and supersensory-superrational. The sensory aspect is present in all psychosocial phenomena that can be perceived through our sense organs. The rational aspect is present in all the rational phenomena of the psychosocial universe: in logically and mathematically consistent systems of science, philosophy, religion, ethics, fine arts, up to the rationally motivated and executed activities of an individual or group. The supersensory-superrational aspect of psychosocial reality is manifested by the highest creative activities and created masterpieces of genius in all fields of cultural activity: by the great creative achievement of a genius-scientist, philosopher, founder of religion, great law-giver, great apostle of unselfish love, genius-writer, poet, painter, sculptor, composer, architect, and so on.[38]

What Sorokin is saying here (in terminology that lays him open to his own criticism of the sociologist's inclination for obtuse jargon) is that intuition and "spirit" are a part of the act of knowing. The present empirical psychosocial sciences have grown "tired" and "less creative." There is a need for a more daring integration of fact, reason, and intuition. Our awareness should not be subordinated to any single one of these three aspects of thought. In sum, Sorokin is saying that Sensate social science has exhausted itself as it passes into its "overripe" stage. The time has come to move back toward a more Ideational awareness of the nature of people.

Sorokin's criticism of the psychosocial sciences stands as a controversial statement, to say the least. It is written seriously, but not without humor. Sorokin indicated that he was shocked by what some of his colleagues were doing, but he was not so shocked as to divorce himself from the ranks of sociology. He depicted a situation which seemed nearly hopeless, but he never went to the extreme of claiming that it was. He grudgingly conceded that, when judged overall, the social sciences have provided people with important knowledge about themselves—but the time has come for reform. The wit and knowledge in Sorokin's critique, *Fads and Foibles in Modern Sociology*, make it useful reading for anyone about to enter the miasmic swampland of a career in the modern psychosocial sciences.

❖ *Altruistic Love*

One phase of Sorokin's career must not be overlooked as we conclude this brief introduction to his work. At the end of World War II, Sorokin turned his attention toward a subject that other social scientists were inclined to ignore—the subject of altruistic love. One of the motivating factors behind Sorokin's interest in this subject was his growing awareness that democratic government, improved educational opportunities, or increased religious dedication were not, in themselves, sufficient to halt or even to slow down present levels and trends in intranational and international violence. He wrote:

> Having completed my *Society, Culture and Personality* [first published in 1947], I began to orient myself in the vast and almost entirely unexplored field of the phenomena of altruistic, creative love. An "inventory" of the existing knowledge in this field showed that this gigantic problem had been largely neglected by modern science. While many a modern sociologist and psychologist viewed the phenomena of hatred, crime, war, and mental disorders as legitimate objects for scientific study, they quite illogically stigmatized as theological preaching or non-scientific speculation any investigation of the phenomena of love, friendship, heroic deeds, and creative genius. This patently unscientific position of many of my colleagues is merely a manifestation of the prevalent concentration on the negative, pathological, and subhuman phenomena typical of the disintegrating phase of our sensate culture.[39]

In 1948 he published *The Reconstruction of Humanity*, a book concerned with the topic of altruistic love. This, along with other works on the same subject, reveals Sorokin's most serious intellectual involvement. The results, in terms of the extent to which they met support within the greater public domain, were extremely disappointing to Sorokin—a disappointment which he covered with the statement, "the results are more modest than I might have wished."[40] It might be worthwhile to conclude our discussion of Sorokin by outlining some of his conclusions on the nature of altruistic love and creative genius, because, we believe, young people today appear to be more overtly concerned with the nature of love and the use of love than older generations seem to have been.

The Reconstruction of Humanity is an unusual work. Certainly this is true when it is viewed as the effort of a sociologist; it is also true even if we disregard this fact. *The Reconstruction of Humanity*, like most of Sorokin's efforts after 1937, contains reiterations of the main themes in *Social and Cultural Dynamics*. Sorokin criticized Sensate values and saw in them the cause of the decline of altruistic sentiments. He lashed out at everything from decadent jazz music and demoralizing movies to the loss of creative genius in the arts. Nothing, as Sorokin saw it, will bring back altruistic morality short of a complete overhaul of the elemental cultural premises upon which our society rests. To find altruism we shall have to move away from Sensate values and toward Ideational values. We shall have to return to universal moral precepts, and we shall have to not only envision these precepts but establish a state in which people live and act by them.

Sorokin made clear his position when he discussed what he considered to be the role of education in the improvement of society:

> As educational agencies the schools must establish a carefully elaborated system for developing altruism in their pupils. They must instill in them a set of universal values and norms, free from superstition and ignorance as well as from the

degrading, cynical, nihilistic, and pseudoscientific theories of our time. This task should be deemed as important as intellectual training.[41]

But how is the foundation of the culture to be modified? How can we come to find the necessary "set of universal values and norms"? If it were found, how could people be made to endorse it and live by it? How could a self-indulgent, relativistic, and atomized society become unified in common expressions of the altruistic life? This question has probably concerned every person who has given serious thought to the nature of modern humanity. Each has tried, in various ways, to answer it, and each, possibly leaving some small mark, has generally failed. Nonetheless, Sorokin suggested, it is from the models offered us by the great altruists of history that we might find some solution. So it is that Sorokin's solution to modern world problems is essentially a religious one and is cast in the form of an ill-disguised sermon. In substance, Sorokin said we must turn to the model offered by the great yogis, the Christian mystics, and the teachings of the great world religions— Buddhism, Hinduism, Christianity, Judaism.

It is surprising, as Sorokin developed his plea, to note the correspondence between his ideas and those endorsed by the former "hippie" culture and, to a lesser extent, the "beat" culture that preceded it. Sorokin wrote:

> As a preliminary condition for obtaining control of the unconscious and conscious by the superconscious and for unlocking the forces of the superconscious, they unanimously demand the liberation of a person from all forms of egoism and the development of a love for the Absolute, for all living beings, for the whole universe, in its negative aspect of not causing pain to anybody by thought, word, or deed, and in its positive aspect of unselfish service, devotion, and help to and sacrifice for others.[42]

But the problem still remains: How do we achieve a general endorsement of such altruistic sentiments? How do we help precipitate the movement away from a Sensate system toward an Ideational one? Here Sorokin's platform falters on the steps of a series of "If only . . ." phrases. For example, he wrote at one point, "If most persons would even slightly improve themselves . . . the sum total of social life would be ameliorated."[43] It is difficult to disagree with this statement, and it is also difficult to do much with it.

Sorokin's program for social change and reform has grand aspirations and a very naive and ill-developed sense of political strategy. Yet this may not be as bad or as common as it appears. Possibly Sorokin's is one of the early voices calling for a return to more religious concerns and understandings of ourselves and the mysteries in which we find ourselves enmeshed. We need to look at science, commerce, education and the other orthodoxies of our time, and concern ourselves with their excesses.

Our postmodern culture has produced a group of people, cryptic and awkward, who are attempting to express in their own purposely inarticulate way, the same criticism that Sorokin stated academically and at great length. Moreover, they are attempting to act according to the precepts of what might be called modernized altruism. This group—the critical theorists—might not be exactly what Sorokin had in mind when he called for a "well-planned modification of our culture and social institutions,"[44] but they come closer to moving us in the direction Sorokin claimed is necessary than do any other groups extant.

❖ Approaching the Twenty-First Century

Like many of the other social observers considered in this book, Sorokin was pessimistic about the future. He believed that unless humanity is able to reverse its present egoistic and Sensate trend, we shall have to resign ourselves to the inevitable end of creative culture. He saw hope, but not much. He knew where we ought to direct our ambitions, but he was, in the final analysis, unable to tell us how to acquire such direction. Sorokin, like many other social scientists, reveals to us the frustration of having knowledge and vision and, at the same time, knowing as fully as it is possible to know, the frail capacity of a single person to act on the basis of that knowledge.

The humanistic nature of Sorokin's writing and involvement is so apparent we need only underscore it slightly to bring this discussion to a close. He was a man of broad and critical knowledge. He was open in his dislike and contempt for postmodern "Sensate" culture, and he was strong in his enthusiasm for a return to more religious or "Ideational" forms of culture. His endorsement of "superconscious" approaches to the problems of life and the human social order endeared him to numerous religious groups and churches. At the same time, we should recall Durkheim's admonition that even a society of saints will have its sinners. The history of Ideational societies is also marked with grisly examples of inhumanity.

Encounters with Social Thought

Ideationalism and Sensatism in Shakespeare's Macbeth

Sorokin's dualist theory of culture and society is implicitly evident in much we read and view—in the media, in the press and in the arts. For example, the continuing rhetorical uses and interpretations of Shakespeare's monumental works reflect the themes of the Ideational and Sensate views of society. The following editorial in an issue of the *Detroit Medical News* presents one such example. The author of this editorial, titled "Macbeth's Physician," sets the background for the article by noting that the physician's brief appearance in Shakespeare's play, *Macbeth*, suffices to give the audience a portrait of the doctor in Elizabethan times.

Shakespeare depicts the doctor in his play as an individual free of bias, pomposity, cant or corruption; a man stalwart, earthy, and discrete. In other words, the physician is a person possessing characteristics of the Ideationalist culture. As the article on "Macbeth's Physician" continues we see the interplay of the Ideational versus the Sensate utilized in the interpretation of the physician's role.

> The act begins with Lady Macbeth's sleep walking scene in which she re-enacts the murders of Duncan, Banquo and Macduff's wife. Witness to this agitation are her maid-in-waiting and "A Doctor of Physic" consulted to cure her malady. In Scene III, Macbeth engages the Doctor in a short, intense exchange. These two episodes, taking less than ten minutes in a play of three hours, provide medical commentary that tomes cannot equal.
>
> To illustrate on confidentiality: the physician is privy to Lady Macbeth's confessions: "Who would have thought the old man had so much blood in him . . . The Thane of Fife had wife; where is she now?"
>
> Even then, the medical privilege to information carried an equal responsibility. The physician now aware of Lady Macbeth's deeds, addresses the servant: "We know what we should not." He instructs her to keep Lady Macbeth's words private as if ignorant of it. He later restates the point: "I think, but shall not speak." The physician says: "I will set down what comes from her to satisfy my remembrance the more strongly." Well might we envy him; he documents his appointments not to fend off lawyers or to prove his case to insurance carriers, but to provide a basis for further thought.
>
> On the limits of medicine: As Lady Macbeth leaves, the doctor addresses the audiences: "This disease is beyond my practice. . . . More needs she the divine than the physician." He continues with "God, God forgive us all." He notes the anguish of Lady Macbeth and regrets his inability to help one in such distress.
>
> In Scene III, the doctor meets with King Macbeth. The King, attempting to place responsibility for Lady Macbeth's state upon the doctor, begins the dialogue with: "How does your patient doctor?" The doctor clarifies her problem in a breath: "She is not so sick as troubled." Macbeth ignores the message and admonishes the doctor to "find the antidote" that will "cleanse" her; the King goes on, promising the doctor great fame if treatment succeeds. The physician is not taken in and says succinctly: "The patient must minister to herself."[45]

In his portrayal of Macbeth and the doctor, Shakespeare, the great dramatist, pits the sensate character of Macbeth against the Ideational role carried out by the physician. The physician shows respect as he listens to the maid-in-waiting, a person of lowly station; to Lady Macbeth he shows loyalty and concern. Even though he knows he cannot cure her, he feels it is his duty to minister to her. Toward Macbeth, though the king, the doctor gives scarcely disguised contempt, being careful not to reveal his real opinions since he knows that the royal hand grips a bloody sword. The author of this article on Macbeth's physician concludes with the following: "Inform the ethicists that they may leave their lecterns, request the pious to end their homilies and tell the critics to quit their carping ways. Shakespeare states what doctors were and are: all else is rhetoric and redundancy."[46] Here is the demonstration of Sorokin's theories of Ideational morality—imperative, everlasting, and unchangeable through the centuries.

Putting Social Thought to Work

1. Sorokin's thinking is based on the belief that cultures must choose between two basic ways of viewing the world: One of these is the Sensate view, in which one is expected to trust only one's senses. The other is the Ideational view, in which one seeks to "go behind" what is perceived by the senses. Sorokin, of course, believed that our times are dominated by a Sensate mentality. But is this so? Science, which is often thought of as being completely Sensate, is quite Ideational at times. Science teaches us about worlds that are far beyond our immediate senses. Much of our knowledge of "black holes," for example, does not come from direct observation but is, instead, "theoretical." Does science appear to be reaching a state of exhaustion of Sensate values?

2. Most controversial in Sorokin's thought is the idea of cyclical changes in culture throughout history. Sorokin is one of the last cyclical thinkers. At present there appears to be little likelihood that Western civilization will become less Sensate than it already is. What would have to happen to bring about Sorokin's belief that within the next century or two we will begin a turn toward a more Ideational form of culture?

3. Sorokin was concerned with the problem of altruism. Americans, generally, seem to be excessively interested in altruism and, in a more profound way, with the problem of love. What are the differences between a Sensate approach to love and an Ideational one? How have Sensate values influenced marriage, the family, and friendship? For example, this is a society in which friends are looked on as functional associates. When they no longer function to assist one in one's career, they should be dropped. Some corporations, today, are beginning to see that the executive who has to get a divorce may be more valuable to the company than one who insists on keeping his family intact. The former is probably getting a divorce because he works too much and gives his loyalty to the company rather than to his family.

4. Sensate values influence how we tend to evaluate people insofar as we attach much importance to "impressions." What evidence is there that Americans are nearly pathologically involved in the problem of their "looks"? Where did the idea of "beautiful" people come from? How

beautiful are beautiful people? What constitutes an American's conception of "beautiful"?

Endnotes

1. David R. Mace says, "The book [Sorokin's *The American Sex Revolution*] does, indeed, convey the atmosphere of grave concern and urgent warning that we find in the writings of some of the Old Testament prophets." See *Pitirim A. Sorokin in Review*, edited by Philip J. Allen (Durham, NC: Duke University Press, 1963), p. 141.
2. Alexandre Vexliard in *Pitirim A. Sorokin in Review*, p. 179.
3. Lucio Mendieta y NuFiez in *Pitirim A. Sorokin in Review*, p. 319.
4. Sorokin cited some of his critics as claiming him to be idiosyncratic, bullheaded, and deviationist. See *Pitirim A. Sorokin in Review*, p. 35.
5. Arnold J. Toynbee in *Pitirim A. Sorokin in Review*, p. 73.
6. Othmar F. Anderie in *Pitirim A. Sorokin in Review*, p. 121.
7. Joseph B. Ford in *Pitirim A. Sorokin in Review*, p. 39.
8. An incomplete listing of Sorokin's works covers ten pages of printed material. We cannot list the nearly forty books and several hundred editorials and essays he has published. Among his more important works we can mention *Leaves from a Russian Diary* (New York: Dutton, 1924); *Sociology of Revolution* (Philadelphia: Lippincott, 1925); *Social Mobility* (New York: Harper Brothers, 1927); *Contemporary Sociological Theories* (New York: Harper Brothers, 1928); *A Systematic Source Book in Rural Sociology*, with C. C. Zimmerman and C. J. Galpin, 3 vols. (Minneapolis: University of Minnesota Press, 1930–1932); *Social and Cultural Dynamics*, 4 vols. (New York: American Book, 1937–1941); *Crisis of Our Age* (New York: Dutton, 1941); *Man and Society in Calamity* (New York: Dutton, 1942); *Sociocultural Causality, Space, Time* (Durham, NC: Duke University Press, 1943); *Russia and the United States* (New York: Dutton, 1944); *Society, Culture and Personality* (New York: Harper & Row, 1947); *The Reconstruction of Humanity* (Boston: Beacon, 1948); *Altruistic Love: A Study of American Good Neighbors and Christian Saint*s (Boston: Beacon, 1950); *Social Philosophies of an Age of Crisis* (Boston: Beacon, 1950); *S. 0. S.: The Meaning of Our Crisis* (Boston: Beacon, 1951); *The Ways and Power of Love* (Boston: Beacon, 1954); *Fads and Foibles in Modern Sociology and Related Sciences* (Chicago: Regnery, 1956); *The American Sex Revolution* (Boston: Sargent, 1957); *A Long Journey: An Autobiography* (New Haven, CT: College & University Press, 1963). This is only a partial listing. The more complete list from which this partial listing was taken can be found in *Pitirim A. Sorokin in Review*, pp. 497–506. Even this partial listing makes one aware that to read the entire works of Sorokin would, in itself, constitute quite a sociological education.
9. Matilda White Riley and Mary E. Moore in *Pitirim A. Sorokin in Review*, p. 224.
10. Sorokin, *A Long Journey*, p. 11.
11. Ibid., p. 142.
12. Ibid., p. 171.
13. It is recommended that the student read *The Crisis of Our Age* before turning to the four-volume work.
14. In the conclusion of his autobiography, Sorokin says, "Therefore I scarcely have reason to complain of being 'a forgotten man' or a 'has-been scholar.' If anything,

the world seems to be paying my 'yarns' attention far beyond their merit." See *A Long Journey*, p. 319.

15. Margaret Mead attends to this matter at some length (see Chapter 9).

16. Ruth Benedict, *Patterns of Culture* (Boston: Houghton Mifflin, 1934). Sorokin cites Benedict but disagrees with some of her conclusions.

17. Sorokin, *Social and Cultural Dynamics*, vol. 1, p. 3.

18. From Herman Melville, "Moby Dick or The Whale." in *Works of Herman Melville* (New York: Crown, 1987) p. 283.

19. Sorokin, *Social and Cultural Dynamics*, vol. 2, p. vii.

20. Ibid., vol. 1, pp. 97–99. The comparison presented here is a highly modified and very abbreviated version of the one presented by Sorokin. Sorokin included in his discussion a cultural mentality type that is between the Ideational and the Sensate. He called this an "Idealistic" system. We have, in the interests of brevity, omitted this middle category.

21. The phrasing here is essentially that of F. J. Foakes Jackson, who is cited by Sorokin in *Social and Cultural Dynamics*, vol. 2, p. 495.

22. Ibid.

23. From Herbert Muller, *The Uses of the Past: Profiles of Former Societies* (New York: Oxford University Press, 1953), p. 239.

24. See 1 Corinthians 7.

25. Quoted in Homer Smith, *Man and His Gods* (Boston: Little, Brown, 1953), p. 423.

26. Sorokin, *Social and Cultural Dynamics*, vol. 2, p. 501.

27. Ibid., p. 506.

28. This Sensate art form has its ultimate current expression in the advertising appeals for contemporary films and pornographic videos.

29. Sorokin, *Social and Cultural Dynamics*, vol. 1, pp. 499–501.

30. Ibid., p. 505.

31. Sorokin, *Social and Cultural Dynamics*, rev. and abr. (Boston: Porter Sargent, 1957), pp. 699–701. The list presented here is a slightly reworded version of Sorokin's list.

32. He lays out these faults in *Fads and Foibles in Modern Sociology and Related Sciences*.

33. A later criticism of psychological testing, which is more comprehensive and deals specifically and only with the problem of testing, is Martin L. Gross, *The Brain Watchers* (New York: Random House, 1962) and was published four years after Sorokin's.

34. For a very engaging discussion of the purely fictional qualities of a concept like *infinity*, read *Mathematics and the Imagination* by James Newman and Edward Kasner (New York: Simon & Schuster, 1940). Visualize, if you will, a quantity which, when divided by two, provides itself. That is infinity.

35. Sorokin, *Fads and Foibles in Modern Sociology and Related Sciences*, p. 37.

36. Ibid., p. 38.

37. Cowell made the following comment concerning the response of the sociological community to Sorokin: "It has already been recorded that there was no discussion of Sorokin's views in the *Sociological Review*." *Pitirim A. Sorokin in Review*, p. 284.

38. Sorokin, *Fads and Foibles in Modern Sociology and Related Sciences*, p. 316.

39. Sorokin, *A Long Journey*, p. 277.

40. Ibid., p. 292.

41. Sorokin, *The Reconstruction of Humanity*, p. 153.

42. Ibid., p. 224.
43. Ibid., p. 233.
44. Ibid., p. 234.
45. Joseph J. Weiss, M.D. "Macbeth's Physician," *Detroit Medical News*, December 1990, p. 6.
46. Ibid., p. 6.

Chapter 8

C. Wright Mills
Born: 1916 · Died: 1962

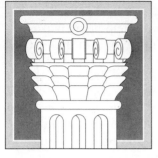

The Sociologist in Anger

The Views of C. Wright Mills

❖

❖ Introduction

Sociologists commonly follow either of two separate paths during their professional lives. The first path moves toward a sense of detachment from social affairs. Greater sophistication with respect to social knowledge and the comfortable jobs that can be obtained from such sophisticated knowledge elevate people until they are looking down on the world, at which point they seem to lose any strong sense of involvement with it. In this instance, the acquisition of social sophistication produces the feeling that this is the best of all possible worlds. Or, if it is not, then certainly it is a world so big and so massively organized that there is not much anyone can do about it.

The second path—one that many a sociologist has traveled—leads to personal anger and a sense of frustration. The more one becomes aware of human irrationality and self-deception, and the more one becomes aware of the extent to which people could spare themselves much of the suffering they have endured, the more it seems necessary to lash out at human folly. This second pathway is, in an age of rational detachment, professionally unbecoming. It means, to use nonacademic terms, that one has blown one's professional cool. But for the sociologist who cannot help being personally dismayed by what he or she learns about people, it might only mean a greater emotional commitment to all of humanity than to the small segment of it that forms the professional community of sociologists.

To choose one path or the other establishes how one will express whatever power one possesses as an intellectual. As C. Wright Mills saw it, the first path means the abdication of responsibility. It leads to either the cult of alienation or the fetish of objectivity. It promotes the sentiment that the social scientist has the right to analyze but not the power to criticize. The social scientist becomes an observer of the passing scene, but not emotionally and morally caught up in it. The academic researcher who remains in this camp can only describe what is happening, but cannot suggest that there is anything especially wrong or good in the actions being described. This, the first path, remains the orthodox position for academic social research and theory.

C. Wright Mills went down the second pathway. His work began with several relatively objective and empirical studies. Gradually, toward the end of his career,[1] his writing became more vehement and took on the character of moral sermonizing. He became famous as a young man with a ''cool'' examination of the white-collar worker. He closed his career with violent denunciations of the clergy,[2] American culture, and the historical drift toward war. The more heated his accusations became, the less he was tolerated by academic social scientists. Even so, he earned the attention of students and humanistic intellectuals who were looking for people with enough sociological sophistication to give them new critical perspectives. C. Wright Mills did just that.

Mills's career was brief. His first essay was published when he was twenty-three.[3] His work ended twenty-three years later, when he died from a coronary condition. During the last years, a friend visiting Mills told him candidly that he looked terrible. Mills replied, ''Yes, I know. But, God, how I have lived.''[4] Perhaps it was this zest for living as well as his social criticism that made Mills the idol of young liberal intellectuals of the 1950s.

❖ *The Question of Power*

Though social change is so rapid today that social commentary becomes dated as quickly as the news, Mills's observations retain much of their original relevance. There is a good reason for this. Mills was concerned with one aspect of society that never loses its significance: the question of power. His work remained centered on power—the nature of power, the distribution of power, the uses and abuses of power, the person of power, the power of organizations, the myths of power, the evolution of power, the irrationality of power, and the means of observing and comprehending power in the vastness of modern society.

In his writings, Mills concentrated particularly on power elites within business. He was concerned with both the business executive and the labor leader. He was interested in the political influence of business and labor, and he examined the extent to which business elites are tied in with military and governmental elites. The observation that the leaders of various sectors of the society are rubbing elbows with each other is not, as one British reviewer of Mills's work put it, very shocking. It has been going on for years in all civilized countries. But this criticism misses the point.

It was not the relationship between the elites per se that was the motivation behind Mills's effort. He was interested in the relationship because of its historical and political significance in a nation that subscribes to an ideology of democracy and to the concept of separation of powers among the various parts of the system. The most notable of these "separations," of course, is the constitutionally authorized guarantee of separation of church and state—a separation that Americans have never achieved with complete comfort and satisfaction. For example, despite a Supreme Court ruling to the contrary, many schools throughout the country, with the tacit support of state and local authorities, still have silent prayers in class. The same authorities reveal a certain hypocrisy in wondering at times why "other" people are lawless. But the American system, in its ideal form, also seeks to hold military authority in a position subordinate to and somewhat independent of civilian governmental authority. A similar relationship is supposed to exist between government and business.

The conservative ideal, of course, is to keep government out of business. The position with respect to keeping business out of government is less clear. As John Kenneth Galbraith has often observed, however, existing tax structures, transportation regulations, antitrust laws, the need for governmentally supervised inspection procedures, and the like have led to a situation where the distinction between private and public industry is becoming increasingly hard to establish.

Mills was vehement in his argument that American military, industrial, and political leadership is integrated. It works together to form what he referred to as a "power elite." The merging of powers at the highest level is cause for concern, according to Mills, because it can lead to a disengagement of leadership from the problems of the people that leadership is supposed to represent.

In other words, the growth of a power elite in America is contradictory to the democratic principles upon which the nation is supposed to conduct its affairs. What concerned Mills most of all was that an emerging power elite would, in protecting its interest, lose sight of the greater interests of the people. The "realities" confronting the elite would be those that dominate the industrial-military mentality. The result would be a continuing drift toward war. Long before the Johnson and Nixon administrations became caught up in such a drift, Mills was labeling the attitude of American leadership as one approaching catastrophic madness; he referred to it as "crackpot realism."

American leadership is drifting, Mills claimed, from a democratic separation of powers toward concentration of power in the hands of a strong, but informally related, elite. This elite is inclined to accept simple notions of what constitute the economic and military realities of the present world. Mills became increasingly critical as he searched for more and more evidence to support his beliefs.

We wish to point to three features of his writing at this point. First, Mills was rhetorical as well as scholarly. His writing was engaging to large numbers of people because he was not afraid to lean on common language. Instead of using elaborate psychiatric or academic terms, he used terms such as "crackpot realism." Second, Mills believed he had evidence that American leadership is becoming more and more an ingrown elite. This claim led to a lot of discussion and research among American social scientists. The present attitude toward Mills's argument is that power in America is not as centralized and concentrated as Mills claimed. Still, Mills raised the issue in a sufficiently demanding manner to lead to a careful reconsideration of what was and is, in fact, taking place in American halls of power. Third, Mills was a social critic who lived through the period when America had revealed its military power most fully—culminating in the staggering display of weaponry that heralded the close of World War II.

America's military and economic power is great, and it is all the more imperative that such power not be allowed to come into the hands of people who lack the sense and sensibility to employ it properly. At the same time, Mills felt that even the most reasonable people, when placed in positions of power, are subject to the corruptions of power. This makes it vital, then, that the checks that have been placed on the unhampered centralization of power in America be sustained.

An important point is that Mills was not concerned with attacking the personalities of people in power—a simplistic approach to power that remains popular down to the present time. Mills was worried that the structural checks on the centralization of power were weakening. If those features of the American political structure that restrain the concentration of power are weakened, the result will be a growing centralization of power. Centralization of power can, in itself, produce the blindness and madness that can lead the world into a drift toward the ultimate catastrophe.

It is important, then, in grasping Mills's conception of power, to know that he located power (much as Weber did) within an institutional context. In order to have power, one must, as it were, be able to tap the power of something greater than oneself The "something greater" consists of the collective power of an institution. This is practically tautological; yet, in a society that goes so far as to celebrate the individuality of the person of power, it is a necessary corrective. Mills said:

If we took the one hundred most powerful men in America, the one hundred wealthiest, and the one hundred most celebrated away from the institutional positions they now occupy, away from their resources of men and women and money, away from the media of mass communication that are now focused upon them—then they would be powerless and poor and uncelebrated. For power is not of a man. Wealth does not center in the person of the wealthy. Celebrity is not inherent in any personality. To be celebrated, to be wealthy, to have power requires access to major institutions, for the institutional positions men occupy determine in large part their chances to have and to hold these valued experiences.[5]

People of power must be understood, then, to derive their power from an institutional base. This means, very broadly, that the exercise of power cannot be simply the exercise of individual eccentricity, but must, to a considerable extent, run parallel with the "grain" of power that characterizes the institutional source. This is obvious in the case of political and church leaders, where adherence to the policies of the system is a *sine qua non* of an individual's ascendancy in the hierarchy. The study of power, then, becomes the study of institutions, the power relations between institutions, and the people who represent the expressions of those institutions.

Although Mills claimed that power has its locus within supporting institutions, he still was concerned with the fact that it is individuals who make decisions and are responsible for the consequences. Mills was torn on the one hand by an analytic perspective that properly located the individual within the broader system, and on the other by a humanistic sensitivity that made him critical of any apparent inability on the part of powerful individuals to assert their autonomy.

❖ The Power Elite

In *The Power Elite*, Mills made explicit his belief that the American doctrine of balance of power or "checks and balances" is an ideal showing less vigor today than it did in the past. Particularly significant in this respect has been the recent ascension to power of the military in American life. In the nineteenth century, the American military establishment was relatively weak, subordinate to civilian authority, and even respectful of civilian values and ways of life. Today, primarily because of the growth of military technology— a truly devastating technology with implications that cause civilian politicians to shy away from decisions involving its use—the military elite is acquiring greater authority in nonmilitary contexts. If the military has acquired a greater voice in American affairs than has previously been the case, it has not been because the military man has aggressively sought political power. It has been, instead, because of civilian political default.[6] Mills viewed this state of affairs with open dismay.

> Once war was considered the business of soldiers, international relations the concern of diplomats. But now that war has become seemingly total and seemingly

permanent, the free sport of kings has become the forced and internecine business of people, and diplomatic codes of honor between nations have collapsed. Peace is no longer serious; only war is serious. Every man and every nation is either friend or foe, and the idea of enmity becomes mechanical, massive and without genuine passion. When virtually all negotiation aimed at peaceful agreement is likely to be seen as "appeasement," if not treason, the active role of the diplomat becomes meaningless; for diplomacy becomes merely a prelude to war or an interlude between wars, and in such a context the diplomat is replaced by the warlord.[7]

Although Mills viewed the ascendancy of the military in modern America with a sense of dismay, he did not limit his concern to those in the military. If there is a military ascendancy—and Mills openly and vehemently believed this to be the case—then it extends beyond the confines of our military institutions. It is more than simply the rising power of a military clique. The various institutions of our society have, through the rise of modern technology, the practices of big business, and the irresponsibilities of American politics, found a military posture socially expedient. It is expedient with regard to our international image; it is expedient with regard to internal control or management.[8]

"Internal control or management" means, essentially, handling a large and amorphous mass of people who take on the character of a market. The mass market exists not only with respect to the sale of Mustangs and motorcycles, but also with respect to the "sale" of opinions. Thus the people became a "media market."[9]

This media market, this mass of people, stands passively at the bottom of American society. Just above it is an increasingly ineffective and fragmented middle level of professional people, politicians, educators, and intellectuals who are alienated from the lower levels and not a part of the power elite. At the top stands an increasingly unified and coordinated elite of power. This, as Mills saw it, is the trend in American social structure. It is a trend that, as he put it, is moving a considerable distance along the road to the mass society. At the end of that road there is totalitarianism, as in Nazi Germany or in Communist Russia. Mills believed that we are not yet at that end; but we can see that many aspects of the public life of our times are more the features of a mass society than of a community of publics.[10]

The impact of *The Power Elite*, then, comes not from the observation that the "high and mighty" share clubs and secrets, profits and power. The impact comes from Mills's insistence that this is an increasing trend in America. Moreover, this is a trend that violates the liberal democratic traditions of the society.

❖ The White-Collar Worker

The Power Elite, when viewed from the vantage point of the present, seems like a natural development in Mills's thinking. Five years earlier, Mills published *White Collar: The American Middle Classes* and gave Americans a not very flattering look at themselves. Most significantly, Mills saw the middle stratum of American society as people who have gained economic security and material advantages and have lost just about everything else. Above all, they had lost any sense of personal power or the sensible use of power. If *The Power Elite* is a discussion of the locus of power in America, *White Collar* is a discussion of those Americans who, like Sinclair Lewis's Babbitt, are losers and really never know it—they are the unwittingly passive voice in American politics. They suffer from the illusion of having power, while in fact they have none. Mills made this very explicit from the beginning:

> The white-collar people slipped quietly into modern society. Whatever common interests they have do not lead to unity; whatever future they have will not be of their own making. If they aspire at all, it is to a middle course, at a time when no middle course is available, and hence to an illusory course in an imaginary society. Internally, they are split, fragmented; externally, they are dependent on larger forces. Even if they gained the will to act, their actions, being unorganized, would be less a movement than a tangle of unconnected contests. As a group, they do not threaten anyone; as individuals, they do not practice an independent way of life.[11]

It is extremely difficult—indeed impossible—to ascribe a unitary character to that segment of American society that refers to itself as "white-collar." The training of such people can vary from a few days to twenty or more years. Income of white-collar workers can vary from minimum wage levels to high six- or seven-figure salaries. White-collar workers can be occupied with work that is physically exhausting—as is much sales work in department stores—or work that places modest demands on mind and body. White-collar workers can be aggressive salespeople or retiring laboratory technicians. They can operate within a system that nearly guarantees the opportunity to rise to higher levels, or they can be caught in a cul-de-sac. Their work can be clean, or it can involve an element of dirtiness—as is the case with medical technicians who examine specimens of excrement.

Yet, despite this tremendous variety of social character, the term "white-collar" has a special significance for American culture. Migrants to this country saw white-collar employment as a hope for their children, if not for themselves. It was an ambition worthy of self-deprivation and toil. The most vulgar form of the American dream has been to strike it rich—to win the lottery or to inherit an astounding fortune from a distant relative. The realistic American dream has been to find a good white-collar job—to work, if necessary, but to work "respectably." It was the aspiration of people who sought to disengage themselves from their peasant status; it was the collective impetus of people who were being subjected to the pressures of urbanization. City life was better than country life, and, within the city, white-collar status was better than blue-collar status. To understand the white-collar class, then, requires a comprehension of the quest for prestige in America. It requires, as Mills put it, an examination of the "status panic."

In traditionalistic societies, prestige claims are relatively easily recognized, and persons making the claims are likely to have them honored. In our society, the situation is more anomic. People cannot be certain that their claims for prestige will be honored, and, if they are, they cannot always be certain that the claims are being honored for the proper reason. Although it is not all the way there yet, America is moving in the direction of becoming a society where:

> All the controlling devices by which the volume and type of deference might be directed are out of joint or simply do not exist. So the prestige system is no system, but a maze of misunderstanding, of sudden frustration and sudden indulgence, and the individual, as his self-esteem fluctuates, is under strain and full of anxiety.[12]

The status panic, the drive for prestige, is a central (though not all-encompassing) characteristic of the white-collar worker. Some white-collar workers experience less panic than others. Even so, concern with status is probably more characteristic of white-collar workers than of blue-collar workers. Mills observed that the blue-collar workers' greater concern with the immediate necessities of living—a fair day's pay for a fair day's work—made them easier to organize in the labor movement. White-collar workers have had a tendency to feel that such organization is degrading, because it results in an association with the tactics of blue-collar workers. For example, college professors, until recently at least, have been very sympathetic with the labor movement in the United States. This sympathy, however, has been restricted pretty much to intellectual support. The academic world has been resistant to unionization for itself.

It is this feature of the prestige quest among white-collar elements that Mills found especially intriguing. Prestige, or the lack thereof, does not particularly come from the value or lack of value of the work performed. Instead, to a great extent, it comes from the real or imagined associations of white-collar workers. They obtain their prestige from the capacity to identify with some source that does, in fact, have recognition. The mechanic in the shop may be making a good income and performing miracles in the way of taking apart and putting together complex machinery. The minimum wage, fresh-out-of-business-college word processor in the front office may, however, feel that this is the more prestigious work. The reason is apparent: It is easier to associate oneself with the management when one is working in the front office. The prestige of the white-collar worker is often a borrowed prestige.

In surveying the status panic, Mills looked to the future and reached a grim conclusion. One of the features offering greater status to white-collar workers has been the fact that often their work identifies them as people of superior education. By virtue of being a bank clerk, one can be more readily associated with people of some education than would be the case if one were a gas station attendant. At the same time, in the driving surge for better positions, national educational levels have been rising; as they have been rising, the educational demands of most white-collar positions have, according to Mills, been falling.

> As the general educational level rises, the level of education required or advisable for many white-collar jobs falls. In the early 'twenties, personnel men said: "I think it has become a principle with the majority of our progressive offices that they will not take into the office any person or candidate who has not had the benefit of at least a high-school education." But soon they began to say that too much education was not advisable for many white-collar jobs.[13]

If this is so, then the disparity between the reality and the ideal—the hope education offers and the actuality it brings—may produce profound disillusionment. At best, said Mills, it opens the white-collar worker to a precarious psychological life.

The white-collar mentality, combined with the vastness of the white-collar element in American society, makes it a key to the understanding of American character. For this reason, Mills devoted much effort to an attempt to fathom the nature of this class of Americans. His conclusions written in 1956 give us insights on the contemporary job scene of today. In sum, Mills said the following:

1. White-collar workers are being squeezed economically and in terms of real power by the unionized blue-collar wage-earning workers.
2. White-collar status claims are becoming more precarious and unrealistic.
3. The threat of growing discontent and frustration among white-collar workers is enhanced by the flood of educated young people coming into the labor market and the increasing simplification of routinized clerical work.
4. The lack of political identity among white-collar workers makes them a politically malleable group for the power elite.
5. The traditional signs of success will be increasingly evaluated in an ambivalent or confused fashion: Is it worth it to fight one's way to the top?

Of these possibilities, the political malleability of the white-collar class and the psychological strains of what Mills termed the status panic may produce a strain toward authoritarianism—the quest for clearly delineated status in a nation-state geared to attain goals of simplistic and readily determined worth.

If there is a strain toward authoritarianism in America today, then one form it might be readily expected to take would be an acceptance of military regimentation. Thus, Mills's concern in *The Power Elite* was a logical extension of observations made during the preparation of *White Collar*. His interest in the power elite further increased his concern that America is indeed moving in the direction of a capitulation to the simplicity and formality of military regulation and military thought. This capitulation, he felt, is pressing the world ever closer to World War III.

❖ The Causes of World War III

In *The Causes of World War III*, Mills repeated the central ideas of his earlier works. He noted again the ineffectiveness of the white-collar element, and he commented on the solidarity of the power elite. But in this work he was more concerned with the implications of these observations: What do they suggest with respect to possibilities for the future? The possibilities that seemed clearest to Mills were those leading toward war. Moreover, the historical possibilities were leading us toward war of a new kind—one that promoted efficiency and impersonality in much the same manner in which a large industry promotes impersonal and efficient production. Long before the Vietnam War forced greater consideration of moral issues and split the nation into "doves" and "hawks," Mills was saying:

> In the expanded world of mechanically vivified communication the individual becomes the spectator of everything but the human witness of nothing. Having no plain targets of revolt, men feel no moral springs of revolt. The cold manner enters their souls and they are made private and blasé. In virtually all realms of life, facts now outrun sensibility. Emptied of their human meanings, these facts are readily got used to. In official man there is no more human shock; in his unofficial follower there is little sense of moral issue. Within the unopposed supremacy of impersonal calculated technique, there is no human place to draw the line and give the emphatic no.
>
> This lack of response I am trying to sum up by the phrase "moral insensibility," and I am suggesting that the level of moral sensibility, as part of public and of private life, has sunk out of sight. It is not the number of victims or the degree of cruelty that is distinctive; it is the fact that the acts committed and the acts that nobody protests are split from the consciousness of men in an uncanny, even a schizophrenic, manner. The atrocities of our time are done by men as "functions" of social machinery—men possessed by an abstracted view that hides from them the human beings who are their victims and, as well, their own humanity. They are inhuman acts because they are impersonal. They are not sadistic but merely businesslike; they are not aggressive but merely efficient; they are not emotional at all but technically clean-cut.[14]

The driving energy that employs moral insensibility and uses it in the working out of our fate comes primarily from our conceptions of the realities of our circumstances. If, for example, we are walking past a graveyard on a dark and eerie evening, and we begin to walk faster and faster and then break into a run, the driving energy that impels us comes from our conception of the "reality" of the situation. If we believe we are in a dangerous setting, then we react accordingly—regardless of the "realities" surrounding us. Those in power, like umpires at a baseball game, must give their conceptions of the complex interplay between nations, the *imprimatur* of realism.

They must refer to themselves as realists and as leaders who see the situation realistically.

A seat of power is no place for idealistic indulgences. So it is, then, that from the offices of the high and mighty come supposedly hardheaded and realistic appraisals of world tensions. But just as an individual walking past a graveyard can be unrealistic in his or her appraisal, so can those in power collectively become deceived, while at the same time patting each other on the back for their "realism." This, said Mills, might better be termed "crackpot realism."

❖ *Crackpot Realism*

Among the features of crackpot realism that define world realities today are the following salient elements:[15]

1. The prevailing belief is that war, rather than peace, is the natural character of people and nations; therefore, it is only realistic to assume as belligerent and as potentially destructive a posture as it is possible to assume.

2. It is only realistic to assume that the "other side" is as anxious to see us fail as we are to see them fail. National paranoia, suspicion, and ill will are universal, permanent, and part of the primitive and unalterable nature of humanity.

3. It is simpler and more realistic to prepare for war than to prepare for peace. The problems of preparing for peace are more complicated and abstract than those involved in the preparation for war. It is, therefore, more realistic to solve human problems by resorting to military coercion.

4. Since war is natural, suspicion and ill will are universal, and a military posture is the simplest solution, then it follows that our military leaders are the most qualified to cope with the complexities of the modern world situation. It is only realistic to give over to the war lords the control of enlarged and centralized means of violence. To be realistic is to give the generals free rein in the conduct of war.

5. It is, if the preceding "realities" are reasonable, only a matter of being realistic for politicians to encourage the growth of a military bureaucracy, rather than the building of a civilian civil service of real integrity.

6. For businesses, given the preceding set of realities, it is only hardheaded business realism to take advantage of the situation. This means the exploitation of circumstances in which there is profit in the manufacture of the means of violence and profit in the use of government-supported research that comes from the quest for ever-greater sources of destructive power.

7. It is also realistic and simple—indeed, it is a cliché—to recognize that

the economy is supported by the war effort, whether the effort, is sustained in a shooting war or a cold war.

8. The very simplicity and "reality" of the situation have led to a circumstance whereby the different political parties have accepted a common definition of the world situation. The consequence is a political climate in which there is no real choice. It is realistic to have a political directorate composed of former generals and former corporation officials, whose world appraisals share so much in common.

9. The massive hold of this "reality" has been overwhelming, both for the general public and for members of the leading intellectual, scientific, and religious circles. For the general public, the "realistic" response is that of moral insensibility. For the intellectuals and scientists, the "realistic" response has been to echo and endorse the confused reality of officialdom. The intellectual's greatest moral failure has been an incapacity to propose alternatives and to be tenacious in the support of alternatives.

10. Crackpot realism replaces the goal of an anxiously held and frustratingly established state of peace and balance of power with the idea of "winning." One is never told what is won. It is sufficient simply to seek to win. To desire to win, even without knowing what it is that one is to win, is more "realistic" and sensible than to abdicate the concept of winning.

11. The general product of crackpot realism is a slow movement toward World War III. The individual consequences of such "realism" are, generally speaking, beneficial. People are rewarded for endorsing these conceptions of the world situation—they benefit individually. But the collective and historical thrust of these opportunistic views of world reality will be toward total military engagement.

And so, in the name of realism, people behave unrealistically. It was a view that Mills could see only as absurd.

If the view of world realities as seen by those in power today (whether in Beijing, Washington, or Tokyo) is appropriately termed crackpot realism, then what does it mean, given present world conditions, to think in a manner that can be called "hardheaded realism?" We must recognize, perhaps above all else, that war alone is the greatest enemy confronting humanity today. We must come to see world reality in terms other than those imposed by a military metaphysic. Industry must be used as a means of coping with world problems, rather than as a means of buoying further the consumptive egos of those countries which have achieved industrialization. Finally, using Mills's phrasing, "The world encounter of coexisting political economies must be conducted in cultural, political, and economic terms."[16]

We must, as individuals, never lose our commitment to humanity. We must not allow ourselves, individually, to represent the broader trend of moral insensibility. Mills expressed this preachment eloquently:

What scientist can claim to be part of the legacy of science and yet remain a hired technician of the military machine? What man of God can claim to partake of the Holy Spirit, to know the life of Jesus, to grasp the meaning of that Sunday phrase "the brotherhood of man"—and yet sanction the insensibility, the immorality, the spiritual irresponsibility of the Caesars of our time? What Western scholar can claim to be part of the big discourse of reason and yet retreat to formal trivialities and exact nonsense, in a world in which reason and freedom are being held in contempt, being smashed, being allowed to fade out of the human condition?[17]

An academic sociologist might shake a finger at Mills and chastise him not for his eloquence but for his presumption—and eloquence often flows from presumption. After all, can we reasonably conclude that reason and freedom are being held in contempt? How can we be sure? How does one measure reason and freedom? How rapidly are they fading out? Are things really as bad as Mills said they are? Was Mills crying out against injustices and human circumstances that came more from his own fears and anxieties than from the world itself? Certainly the strong possibility of this would seem to be sufficient to incline us to ignore Mills when we settle down to the task of creating a serious sociology.

Mills would reply, we believe, somewhat as a meteorologist might: In predicting storms, it is better to say that one is coming when in fact it might not be. The other kind of error is more disastrous. We leave ourselves defenseless when we conclude that a storm is not on the way, even as it bears down on us.

If Mills erred, he erred on the side he believed to be morally more defensible. Sociologists are involved in the system they are writing about and attempting to fathom. Mills saw the sociologist as a person morally obligated to provide social knowledge that is significant. Because society is essentially a moral order, as Durkheim had already noted, this means that significant social knowledge must be morally significant. The sociologist must attempt by writing as well as by observation to prevent people from falling into patterns of belief and action that appear catastrophic from a sociological perspective.

Mills functioned as a critic of the greater society and, as a critic, expressed great concern over the role of the intellectual. More specifically, he was concerned with the duties and character of the social scientist. He was quite unappreciative of sociologists who tease at trivialities in a pseudoscientific mumbo-jumbo jargon. His irritation with the work of some of his colleagues appeared in nearly all his works. However, it was elaborated and expressed most fully in *The Sociological Imagination*.

❖ *The Sociological Imagination*

Like Mills's other works, *The Sociological Imagination* reveals a man exasperated by the discrepancy between the potential value of a human effort and its actual value or attainment. If Mills lambasted some features of sociology, it was because he felt they deserved criticism. Sociology is too important to be ignored, and it is not beyond the need for some reforms. As Mills saw it, intellectuals stand as one of the constraints against the abuse of power—but only for so long as they retain their sense, sensibility, and tenacity.

The importance of sociological thought comes out of the fact that it is not something limited to professors of sociology or courses in modern society on the campuses of American colleges. Instead, it is an exercise that all people today must attempt with more or less success. For Mills, the difference between effective and ineffective sociological thought rests upon the use of imagination. This would not seem especially radical, were it not for the fact that Mills's assertion appeared as a reaction against the sociology of the 1930s and 1940s, which argued, in effect, that worthwhile sociological thinking comes mostly from facts. Theory is supportive, but its main task is to lead to further facts. The product of this kind of sociology, said Mills, is factual in a sense, but lacking imagination. More importantly, in the quest for factual information, it often bypasses problems that are more centrally significant. Speaking of studies of voting behavior—an area of interest that lends itself to empirical or factual examinations of opinion—Mills said:

> It must be interesting to political scientists to examine a full-scale study of voting which contains no reference to the party machinery for "getting out the vote," or indeed to any political institutions. Yet that is what happens in *The People's Choice*, a duly accredited and celebrated study of the 1940 election in Erie County, Ohio. From this book we learn that rich, rural, and Protestant persons tend to vote Republican; people of opposite type incline toward the Democrats, and so on. But we learn little about the dynamics of American politics.[18]

There is the suggestion in Mills's criticism of what he refers to as "abstracted empiricism" that sociological research is guided more by the requirements of administrative concern than by intellectual concern. The "scientific method" relied on by the contemporary empirical sociologist is actually more an administrative method than a scientific one. Certainly, Mills suggested, it is more an administrative method than an *intellectual* one. The results of an opinion survey or a political preference poll can be of inestimable value to an official running for office. At the same time, they have relatively restricted scientific value. Because administrative concerns are virtually infinite and can penetrate into the most trivial aspects of organization, the kinds of research that can come out of an administrative interest will be infinitely varied and range from that which has some possible promise as an intellectual interest to that which will have none whatsoever.

The narrow concern with "factual science" that attracts many sociologists today, said Mills, has produced a constrained view of humanity. It is a view that, incidentally, would be in keeping with an "administrative view" of humanity. That is, abstracted empiricism fits nicely into a research program geared toward the more effective control of human beings. Indeed, orthodox sociologists such as George Lundberg have specifically stated that the goal of science—and they include sociology here—is to achieve prediction and control. With respect to human behavior, this means controlling the lives and actions of people, and this concern is the paramount concern of the administrator.

The field of demography offers us an example of research that has great administrative value. Administrators cannot function effectively without reliable census information concerning the communities and states within which their organizations operate. At the same time, the scientific character of demography suffers from a peculiar constraint: There is only so much one can do with census data. Usually academic or scientific considerations of census data prove to be elaborate exercises in the use of statistical devices. So severe is the problem with respect to population studies that some of the finest demographers and human ecologists in the country have seriously dealt with the issue of whether or not there is such a thing as population theory and what theory means in the field of population studies. That is to say, they are concerned with the problem of whether demography is intellectually engaged. Mills would have argued that demography is preponderantly the accumulation of facts for the purpose of facilitating administrative or political decisions. There is support for this contention in the fact that population studies received their initial impetus from political and military concerns. The development of census data in the United States came originally from the need for population data to determine the distribution of representation in Congress.

It is elementary but necessary to remember that sociological writing, like any other type of writing, is concerned with convincing others. Convincing others involves at least two rudimentary and important considerations. First of all, we need to convince others that what we have to say is significant and worth the effort of their review. Second, we must convince others that what we are saying is valid. The empiricist has concluded that the only form of validity is that established through fact, and, moreover, that validity provided through fact is more important than any other consideration in the communication process. The result, Mills wryly observed, is thin.

But there is more to it than that. It is not so much that the empirical sociologist has become bogged down with statistics; this in itself is not a completely hopeless situation. A person living under a haystack of facts and figures might reasonably be expected to dig out to a point where he or she could see clearly the outlines of what previously had only been a dark and suffocating pressure. The serious problem, as Mills viewed it, is that empiricists, even as they suffocate, think that building haystacks is the best of all possible lives. But perhaps this figure of speech goes too far. Mills put it this way:

What has happened in the methodological inhibition is that men have become stuck, not so much in the empirical intake, as in what are essentially epistemological problems of method. Since many of these men, especially the young, do not know very much about epistemology, they tend to be quite dogmatic about the one set of canons that dominate them.[19]

But if facts are not enough—if the empiricism of modern sociological research is producing inconsequential and "thin" results—then what is one to do? Mills set forth his own conception of how a social scientist should undertake such work. He endeavored to convey a sense of what it means to be an intellectual who concentrates on the social nature of human beings and seeks that which is significant. (It is worth a parenthetical comment here to observe that Mills recognized that one can make a significant statement that is not necessarily factually valid. For example, the philosopher Karl Jaspers, in an essay on the nature of totalitarianism, comments that totalitarianism cannot be destroyed from within; it must be destroyed from without.[20] It is difficult to assess whether historical records will back up such a statement. The statement is nonetheless significant when we wish to consider the nature of the completely autocratic state. Jaspers is correct in a logical or definitional sense, though he might be subjected to criticism from an empiricist.)

Mills was critical of textbooks used in sociological courses. In his criticism, he indicated the direction he thought contemporary sociology should take. Sociological texts suffer from being overly concerned with settled conceptions, and they tend to ignore new ideas. The textbook provides the student with old ideas supported by new facts. New ideas might endanger the number of adoptions of the text.

Mills illustrated his point with a consideration of the concept of "cultural lag." This concept, popular in sociological thought down to the present time, has achieved an almost venerable position in the lexicon of sociological terms. The concept of cultural lag claims, essentially, that there are two aspects of culture. One aspect is the immaterial, consisting of ideas, sentiments, beliefs, values, interests, meanings, and other facets of a subjective or mental character. The other aspect consists of the material features of the culture, such as tools, artifacts, equipment, hardware, produce, chemicals, and other directly observable and "touchable" features. The concept of cultural lag then goes on to suggest that the development of the immaterial aspects of culture lags behind the development of the material aspects of culture. We have a twentieth-century technology, for example, embedded in a moral, religious, and legal system that its roots in a Mediterranean pastoral society of three thousand years ago. We have the atomic bomb and, at the same time, a conception of warfare and conduct between nations that is more in keeping with the ideas held by Napoleon.

It is not so much that the concept of cultural lag is "bad" as that the sociologist tends to use it in an uncritical, unexamined, and unimaginative way. All too commonly, the notion of cultural lag is used as simpleminded "scientific" justification for a progressive ideology whose contention is that the problems of the present lie in the moral inadequacies of the past. The concept of cultural lag enables us to make value judgments about where we ought to go and what ought to lead our movement—namely, technological advancement and physical science—while at the same time disguising the fact that we have been making value judgments.

But it is not the naive hypocrisy of the sociologist who thinks in this fashion that bothered Mills the most. Certainly it is inconsistent to claim to be making objective statements about the social order that are, by their very nature, moral judgments. However, as Mills viewed it, this is not the most serious fault of sociology. The most serious faults are the lack of imagination and the dullness of thought that characterize much sociological work. There is, said Mills, quite a difference between the way the sociologist uses an idea like cultural lag and the way a thinker of the magnitude of Thorstein Veblen uses the same idea.

> In contrast to many sociologists' use of "lag," Thorstein Veblen's phrase "lag, lead and friction" led him to a structural analysis of "industry versus business." He asked: where does "the lag" pinch? And he attempted to reveal how the trained incapacity of businessmen acting in accordance with entrepreneurial canons resulted in an efficient sabotage of production and productivity. He was also somewhat aware of the role of profit-making within a system of private ownership, and he did not especially care for the "unworkman-like results." But the great point is that he revealed the structural mechanics of "the lag." Many social scientists, however, use the politically washed-out notion of "cultural lag," which has lost any such specific and structural anchorage: they have generalized the idea in order to apply it to everything, always in a fragmenting manner.[21]

But what, in more specific terms, did Mills have to suggest? How, if all of this is so, is the sociologist to break away from the "washed-out" usage of social concepts and ideas? In answer, Mills provided some guidelines that he believed could lead toward a greater sense of intellectual craftsmanship.[22]

❖ *Guidelines for Intellectual Craftsmanship*

First of all, a good scholar or intellectual does not split work from life. Both are part of a seriously accepted unity. Life experience can be used in one's work, and the fruits of one's work can be used to enrich life. The sociologist must not bureaucratize work and conclude that it is a nine-to-five business, to be abandoned with a sense of relief when the whistle blows in the late afternoon.

Second, a good scholar must keep a file. This file is a compendium of personal, professional, and intellectual experiences. Such a file promotes organization, the preservation of experience, and the discipline of writing.

Third, a good intellectual engages in continual review of thoughts and experiences. One does not write for the moment; one does not wait until the pressures of professional advancement call for writing up a request for governmental or foundation funds, and then sit down and think up a "project."

Fourth, a good intellectual may find a truly bad book as intellectually stimulating and conducive to thinking and effort as a good book. Whether one is reading a good book or a bad one, it must be an intense experience and one that has relevance for the file. But, at the same time, reading is a matter of balance; one should know when to read and when not to. To soak up too much literature is to risk being drowned by it.

Fifth, in the development of a system of notes, it is a good idea to lay out (at least in a sketchy manner) designs for research that would be relevant to interests stimulated by reading or by other experiences. In the course of this, there is a constant rearranging of ideas and approaches. It is in the exercise of rearrangements that imagination is stimulated.

Sixth, there must be an attitude of playfulness toward phrases, words, and ideas. Along with this attitude must go a fierce drive to make sense out of the world.

Seventh, the imagination is stimulated by assuming a willingness to view the world from the perspective of others. It is stimulating to the imagination of the sociologist to wonder how, for example, a political scientist, a historian, or a biologist might think about the topic under investigation.

Eighth, one should not be afraid, in the preliminary stages of a speculation, to think in terms of imaginative extremes.

Ninth, one should not hesitate to express ideas in language as simple and as direct as one can make it. Ideas are affected by the manner of their expression. An imagination encased in deadening language will be a deadened imagination.

In this manner, C. Wright Mills left behind a statement of his concern and his mode of living with those concerns. His attempt to delineate the way to a brighter "sociological imagination" was, in a more serious sense than perhaps some of his colleagues would accept, an attempt to correct the excesses of an unimaginative empirical methodology.

Yet Mills was excessive in the other extreme. He seemed too involved. He was too much a part of the times. He was too clever in his writing. He showed too much interest in the well-turned phrase and possibly too little in the well-tuned fact.[23] If so, Mills was aware that this was his personal choice. Social thought, to Mills, was a matter of individual commitment, and it involved a sense of responsibility. The greater the commitment, the greater the responsibility. To Mills, social thought was the stuff of life. To live intensely was to think and to work intensely. Life, work, and thought were inseparable. This was what Mills meant when he said, a year or so before his death, "God, how I have lived." It was a fitting commentary on his work.

Encounters with Social Thought

C. Wright Mills and the Entertainment Industry

C. Wright Mills was more effective as a social critic than as a social theorist. This distinction is significant. A social critic of the stature of Mills takes on the task of holding a nation to its promises and judging whether or not those promises are being kept. A theorist, in turn, is not concerned with judging a society, but instead with understanding it as it is. When a theorist comes up with an explanatory principle, it generally can be applied across a broad array of topics and issues. An obvious reason for the popularity of Freudian thought, for example, is that it can be applied to anything and everything as an interpretive scheme. Indeed, one of the limitations of Freudian theory is that it is all too easy to give an object or an action a Freudian coloring.

In the following section of this chapter, we shall try to show, through illustration, the difference between applying the ideas of a writer who is basically a critic and applying the ideas and concepts of those who write as theorists. It is perhaps not easy to see at first that the work of a theorist is more broadly and effectively applicable than that of a critic. (Reading criticism, because it commonly exhorts and urges the reader, is more fun than reading theory, which usually does not.) Some hint of the difference between the two approaches to social issues can be had by recognizing that although all critics lean on one theory or another, theories are, in themselves, not critical. Theories, simply as theories, are primarily concerned with explanation and the simplification of complex issues, not criticism. They walk more along the first path mentioned in the beginning of this chapter.

Marxism provides a fine example of the point we are trying to make here. Marx was obviously a powerful critic of his times. He was also a major theorist. He sought an explanation of the dehumanization of people that he observed in industrial Europe. As a theorist, he argued objectively and coolly that the owners of factories and farms must rely on cheap labor or be forced out of business by those who have fewer scruples. The consequences of this, however, were repugnant to Marx as a critic of what he saw. As a theorist, Marx was surprisingly objective; as a critic, he was scathing.

Mills contributed little new in the way of theory. Instead, he drew heavily from the theories of his time. He was influenced strongly by Marx, Weber, Durkheim, and Veblen. It was his ability to make use of these theories in a critical manner that led to his recognition as the foremost American social critic of the 1950s. In applying Mills's thoughts to our own present times, then, we must understand the critical stance taken by Mills.

We have elected to discuss the entertainment industry, with special emphasis on television, as an encounter with social thought, the social thought of C. Wright Mills. Mills's approach, as a critic, to American culture and social institutions rested primarily on a foundation of moral questioning. A good place to start would seem to be with the questions Mills raised in his major works.

Mills was concerned with power, but the central question undergirding all of his work was whether power in the United States is a matter of democratic practice, or resides within elite groups that are removed from democratic restraints. Is America governed through a representative government, or is democracy, as we practice it, less democratic than we are led to believe? Are we a peaceful nation, as our political rhetoric assures us, or a military nation of a belligerent nature? Do we respect labor and honesty, or, instead, are we a nation driven by status panics and the pretense of accomplishment? Are we a nation obsessed by trivia rather than a deeper concern with human issues?

If we are to apply our understanding of the works of Mills to any matter of interest to us, we must address that topic from a critical stance. Although Mills drew on the theories and ideas of writers such as Karl Marx and Thorstein Veblen, his major concern was to probe the extent to which there are disparities between national promise and national accomplishment. A good place to begin, then, might be with a broad consideration of the disparity between the promise of entertainment and what it has become.

The Entertainment Industry and the Mass Manipulation of Power

Within a surprisingly brief period in human history, entertainment has moved from being a privileged, peripheral, and occasional matter in the day-to-day lives of working men and women to an ordinary, central, and constant matter. Whereas a common person of even a century ago might have considered it unusual to attend the theater as much as once a month, modern people observe theatrical performances—movies, television, stage plays, and so on—as daily events. In the United States, television viewing is considered the right of everyone; even men and women in prison have a right to watch TV.

The variety of offerings available to anyone with access to a television set or money for a movie ticket is staggering. People who live in or near large American cities (and that includes by far the greater percentage of the total population) can choose, during any week, among five or six hundred films being shown, along with hundreds of other programs. Films, in the form of videocassettes, are now as widely available as books once were. Private film showings, once the entertainment of privileged and wealthy men and women, are now the privilege of anyone.

The entertainment industry can no longer be dismissed as a trivial institution whose sole function is a matter of providing simple amusements to work-weary people. Sociologists, from the beginning of the century until the late 1960s, looked on the arts generally and entertainment specifically as institutions given over to recreational concerns—mere amusement without depth or any particularly significant influence. Having, at least so it seemed, no serious intent, these institutions were not to be taken seriously. Now they must be taken seriously. Therefore, what they are doing—whatever their intent might be—calls for careful reexamination.

Entertainment is not easy to define. By the "entertainment industry," we mean the loosely assembled complex of men and women who work together in a variety of organizations to produce and then distribute professionalized performances to publics, which, one way or another, pay to observe these performances. This definition enables us to bypass, in this discussion, any consideration of the informal entertainments that have, down through history, been common to all human communities. Whereas informal folk entertainment is universal and, in the form of play, probably as old as humankind itself, the "entertainment industry" is relatively new.

In entertainment's highly professionalized, bureaucratized current form, it is reasonable to say that nothing like it has ever been part of any previous human cultural system. The entertainment industry, in many ways, is a new institutional complex within modern societies. It is not the same as the arts, nor is it the same as folk entertainments, though it has connections with both these older forms. What is especially novel about the entertainment industry is the extent to which it permeates the daily life of everyone.

The introduction of radio and television as technologies has further enhanced the democratic distribution of information that came with the invention of print. The technologies are democratic in the extent to which they reach people; few are too poor to afford access to television. The difference between the wealthy and the poor with respect to these technologies is possibly that the rich have more, bigger, and better sets, while the poor must make do with less—but they are equal in terms of access.

This in itself is a major shift in social relationships. Professional entertainment of a highly skilled nature was primarily the privileged right of those who possessed great wealth. Indeed, part of being a peasant was a matter of being removed from the refinements offered by professional entertainments. Until the advent of the printing press, large segments of civilized nations lived as illiterates. They were illiterates with respect to literature, and they were further lacking in exposure to the higher arts and the sophisticated presentations of professional entertainers.

Radio, film, and television, unlike books, have had a broader impact insofar as they do not require special training. Three-year-old children can watch television with the same fascination as adults. Whereas books insist on literacy, television insists on nothing. Books, even for a period after the invention of the press, remained a privileged source of information available principally to men and women of learning— priests, poets, and scholars. So it is that literature is taught today as a special discipline. We still refer to scholars and intellectuals as men and women "of letters." We have no similar term for those well versed in the media arts, nor are we likely to have one in the future. If so, it tells us something about the extent to which the media arts are removed from elitism. They are the democratic art form *par excellence.*

The general relationship between entertainment and class structure has been characterized by two significant features. First of all, elite forms of entertainment defined elite memberships. Access to the finest in music or drama or the arts also meant access to the more elevated ranks of the society. The higher entertainments were a sign of "class." So were the common entertainments, which signified lower-class identifications.

A second feature of the higher entertainments, until the middle of the nineteenth century, was that those involved with such entertainment catered to elites as a special group. As a consequence, "serious" music was restricted to that which was played before elite audiences. Some of this tradition still remains, though it has been badly battered by the times. In 1950, for example, one could still encounter musical purists who exuded supreme contempt for, let us say, the blues guitar of a folk singer such as Josh White. Now folk music stands alongside so-called "classical" music. Whether you like Mississippi John Hurt or John Williams or Bo Diddley is regarded as a matter of personal taste rather than as an indication of your status.

John F. Kennedy was the first really powerful figure in American politics to use, in a calculated way, the power of the entertainment industry as an adjunct to his political career. In the famous debate with Richard Nixon on television during the 1960 presidential campaign, he was canny enough to get the background set painted a light color. He then wore a dark suit for the debate, and Nixon, not aware of the situation, wore a light suit. Nixon got "lost" in the background, while Kennedy appeared strong and in bold relief. Since Kennedy's time, television—and all that the term "television" implies—cannot be ignored by anyone in quest of power.

Much attention has been given to the role television plays in the making of presidents and the creation of political "images." (One only needs to mention the name of Ross Perot in this instance.) Television, of course, is there not only when aspiring candidates are trudging the campaign trail seeking party nominations; it is there after the president is elected (as Bill Clinton's press corps are quick to comment). It is a constant and intense force. Television does more than "make" presidents. It sustains or attacks them in office. It has the power to expose or withhold information and scandal. It is a creative agent within the political arena. Like American politics, it relies on public popularity for its strength.

Rather than looking on television as an adjunct of power—an image maker and news breaker—television must now be seen as a major power bloc within American society. It is not structurally a part of the political system, and yet it is not separate from it. The leading public figures on television, particularly newscasters and anchors, do not administer policies, enact legislation, balance large federal budgets, oversee taxation, and so forth. At the same time, it is obvious that they influence public perceptions.

If television is a power within modern American politics, and it obviously is, then the serious question within a democracy is this: Who controls television? In the broadest sense, television is controlled by business interests of one kind or another. Television thrives through selling its time to the highest bidder. It is a business, and it is controlled by business (for example, Ted Turner's rise to fame with TNT). It caters to large audiences in order to enhance its appeal to those who are interested in its services, not because it is interested in the audience per se. The consequence, with respect to entertainment, has been a variety of entertainments designed not to influence change for the better, but to gratify whatever sentiments are currently in vogue.

With respect to political dialogue, much the same pattern has been set in place. Political figures are "imaged" to have broad popular appeal. The consequence, increasingly over the years, is a parade of political candidates who look more and more alike. The differences between one candidate and another are much like those between one situation comedy and another. With respect to entertainment, it seems that we are faced with an infinitude of choice when, in reality, the media's need to lean on "formula" plots and situations means we can select only between one mediocre offering and another. With respect to political campaigns, the situation is the same. The media, dominated by the demands of commerce and the interests of big business, are democratic only in the sense that they broadcast to large publics. The public is, indeed, given what it wants—the ratings see to that. However, the media rarely deal with what the public needs. To enter this domain is to enter the domain of controversy, and this is one area that is assiduously avoided by the masters of American media programming. So far as the media are concerned, what the public needs is determined by what the advertisers say it needs.

If the domain of controversy is avoided with respect to entertainment programming, it is also assiduously avoided with respect to political programming. Yet controversy is at the heart of democratic procedures. Without controversy, there is no democratic process. The media, in diverse ways, operate to muffle controversy. First of all, there is the control of the media by business interests. To the extent that controversy might affect sales of a product, the controversy will be bypassed in favor of something more innocuous. Second, there is control of the media by small public factions, resulting in large effects from relatively small forces. In its desire not to alienate any potential viewing audience, the media must not affront anyone in any fashion. Therefore, issues that might be of general interest to the population as a whole but are offensive to a small segment of that population are likely to be swept under the rug. A current case in point might be the present relationship between the people of Japan and the United States. By no means is this an easy relationship. Yet it is rarely discussed with openness within the popular media, for obvious reasons: It could be easily seen as offensive and threatening to Japanese Americans.

The upshot of this dynamic for American democracy is a move away from choice and from profound and serious discussions of extremely controversial matters—all elements of the democratic process—in favor of a pervasive blandness. It is a matter of the bland leading the bland. It is obvious in our entertainment. It is becoming increasingly obvious in our politics.

Putting Social Thought to Work

1. Americans have a certain reputation for being idealists. People from other countries thought it was strange that we should be so upset over the discovery of criminal activity in the Nixon administration. The question of idealism is a part of Mills's concerns. Mills believed that as a nation is progressively freed from the pressing demands of hunger, privation, and vulnerability, it is increasingly called upon to put into effect the higher ideals of a civilized society. Mills argued that as we are freed from the harsh realities of existence, it becomes more possible to be idealistic. At the same time, there is a strong pragmatic streak in American culture that distrusts idealism. What constitutes "realistic" thinking today? Is Mills correct in suggesting that we must either become more idealistic or die?

2. Mills, like many other intellectuals of the 1950s, was deeply concerned with the issue of authoritarian rule. Mills feared, above all, that there might be a tendency toward authoritarianism in America. People in a

"panic" to establish status might seek some system in which worth would be well defined and delineated. Mills warned of the possibility that the white-collar element might accept a more repressive social structure to resolve the stresses of uncertainty. What evidence is there for such a development in modern America? What argument can be made that American society is suffering, not from an increasing authoritarianism, but from a crisis of the weakening of authority?

3. Mills spent extensive energy and work during his shortened, but illustrious career as a sociologist describing the "white-collar worker." How characteristic of white-collar workers today, as we enter the twenty-first century, is Mills's characterization of their situation? Are white-collar workers actually being squeezed economically? By blue-collar workers? By a flood of highly educated people in the labor market? By the growing numbers of women (sometimes termed pink-collar workers) and new waves of refugees entering the American labor market? Is the myth of the security for the "company man" about to be exploded at the close of the twentieth century?

4. How insightful was Mills in predicting the causes of World War III? How has the end of the Cold War, the break-up of the Soviet Union, the Unification of Germany, and the great unrest in the Arabic Gulf states and the Middle East affected implications for the causes of World War III? Could worldwide realities be so influenced by "crackpot realism" now, at the end of the twentieth century, as Mills believed they could be during the 1950s and 1960s?

5. Among Mills's major contributions to social thought and social scientific writing were his delineation of the *Guidelines for Intellectual Craftsmanship*. Reread these guidelines in the this chapter and consider how you could utilize and implement them in your academic work, research, and writing.

Endnotes

1. A comprehensive listing of the works of C. Wright Mills appears in *Power, Politics and People: The Collected Essays of C. Wright Mills*, edited by Irving Louis Horowitz (New York: Oxford University Press, 1963), pp. 614–641. This list also includes various reviews and essays that have taken the work of Mills as their subject. It will suffice to mention here some of the more important or better-known of Mills's works: *The New Men of Power: America's Labor Leaders*, with the assistance of Helen Schneider (New York: Harcourt, 1948); *White Collar: The American Middle Classes* (New York: Oxford University Press, 1951); *The Power Elite* (New York: Oxford University Press, 1956); *The Causes of World War III* (New York: Simon & Schuster, 1958); *The Sociological Imagination* (New York: Oxford University Press, 1959); *Listen Yankee: The Revolution in Cuba* (New York: McGraw-Hill, 1960).

2. Both *The Causes of World War III* and *Listen Yankee* illustrate the "preachiness" of Mills. Mills himself referred to his work as "preachings." See Horowitz (ed.), *Power, Politics and People*, p. 2.

3. C. Wright Mills, "Language, Logic, and Culture," *American Sociological Review* 4 (October 1939), 670–680.

4. This anecdote comes from a conversation with William Bruce Cameron, Professor Emeritus of Sociology, University of South Florida.

5. Mills, *The Power Elite*, pp. 10–11.

6. Ibid., p. 205.

7. Ibid., p. 206.

8. An exclusive concentration on this point is seen in Fred J. Cooke, *The Warfare State* (New York: Macmillan, 1962). A better treatment of the economic factors involved in the ascendancy of the military in America can be found in Seymour Melman, *Our Depleted Society* (New York: Dell, 1965).

9. Mills, *The Power Elite*, p. 304.

10. Ibid.

11. Mills, *White Collar*, p. ix. Political leaders we have talked with are well aware that today the masses no longer consist of the disgruntled poor. They consist of the more or less disgruntled middle-income elements.

12. Ibid., p. 240.

13. Ibid., p. 247.

14. Mills, *The Causes of World War III*, pp. 78–79.

15. This list of the features of crackpot realism is a highly modified version of one appearing in *The Causes of World War III*, Chapter 13, pp. 81–89.

16. Mills, *The Causes of World War III*, p. 98.

17. Ibid., p.125.

18. Mills, *The Sociological Imagination*, pp. 52–60. Mills was critical of both narrow factual scientism and grand theory. The former gets lost in trivialities, and the latter gets lost in its wordplay. Because of space limitations, we have emphasized Mills's critique of empiricism.

19. Ibid., p. 74.

20. Karl Jaspers, "The Fight Against Totalitarianism," in *The Dilemma of Organizational Society*, edited by Hendrik M. Ruitenbeek (New York: Dutton, 1963), p. 6.

21. Mills, *The Sociological Imagination*, pp. 89–90.

22. Ibid., pp. 195–226. In a lengthy appendix, Mills set forth a number of sensible suggestions concerning intellectual craftsmanship. The list presented here is a modified summary of Mills's comments.

23. Mills was candid. At one point he said, "Now I do not like to do empirical work if I can possibly avoid it. . . . It is a great deal of trouble" (*The Sociological Imagination*, p. 205). Mills was suggesting, however, that all other avenues of exploration should be exhausted before the empirical one is taken up.

Chapter 9

Cultural Revelations

The Work of Margaret Mead

❖

❖ Introduction

The age of great artistic and scientific heroes and heroines is dead. Only a few decades ago, the leading modern figures in virtually any of the arts and the sciences were household names. We all knew of composers such as Igor Stravinsky, Maurice Ravel, or Claude Debussy. We read the poems of T. S. Eliot and Robert Frost. We knew of Albert Einstein and Linus Pauling, even if we knew little of their ideas. Psychologists such as Abraham Maslow and Rollo May were talked about in coffeehouses as well as in lecture halls. Sociologists such as David Riesman and C. Wright Mills were cult figures. In this recent but now dead era of celebrated artists and thinkers, one of the best-known was an anthropologist whose works, by the middle of the 1940s, were familiar to anyone who read the newspapers or bought an occasional magazine. We refer to the anthropologist Margaret Mead.

Margaret Mead was a giant among giants not because she was an innovative thinker. The major ideas and theories upon which she relied were already well developed in her field. Margaret Mead was a celebrated writer among celebrated writers because she, more than anyone else in her time, knew how to make use of ideas. She wrote on the human condition across the entire sweep of human cultures in the twentieth century. She was a celebrated figure because, like most celebrated figures, she was at the center of life and at the center of pressing human concerns. She gave life to anthropology and made it a household interest.

Our last memory of Margaret Mead comes from a recorded televised interview with her that appeared on a public television program. She was within a few months of dying. Her conversation was animated, and she talked knowingly of human issues ranging from the oppression of women to the problems of war. Here was no brooding soul turned inward by the thoughts of impending death. Here was a woman who gave the last moments of her life as energetically, as intelligently, and as openly as she had given the early years of her life. It was only at the end of the program that she revealed, for a second, her attitude toward life and work and death. After her talk she rose and then began to walk backward slowly, into the shadowy and dark recesses of the stage setting, still facing the camera. She smiled a charming smile, waved her cane, and said, "Goodbye, goodbye, goodbye"—knowing it was the final goodbye as she stepped into the darkness. It was an act, but it was a wonderful act. It summed up the way she lived, wrote, and felt about people.

We no longer have intellectual heroes and heroines. Sociologists, when asked who the greatest sociologist is today, usually do not have a ready answer—though the answer came easily enough just a few decades ago. It is the same with other fields. However, even in this day of quickly forgotten figures, Margaret Mead's name is still recognized by men and women who might not be able to name even one other major figure in American anthropology or social science.

❖ The Concept of Culture

It is one thing to define a term and quite something else to comprehend in a deeper way what the concept implies. Students commonly can define terms and concepts for examinations in an adequate fashion, and then, when asked to use the terms to explore a particular problem, fail. Memorizing the definition of a concept is relatively easy. The hard part comes in grasping its deeper implications. This is certainly the case with one of the most significant concepts to come out of modern social philosophy and social theory—the concept of "culture." Here, most definitely, is a term that is simple enough in its definition and yet almost impossible to grasp in the fullness of its meaning.

At the simplest level, culture is everything learned and shared by people. Culture is not simply a knowledge of the arts or the social graces; it is much more. It includes the profane as well as the sublime, the secular as well as the sacred. What we learn from others and what we share with them is the basis of our humanity. We learn and we share the language we use for communication—language is a part of culture. We learn and we share the attitudes that affect our actions toward others—these attitudes are part of culture. We learn and we share certain conceptions about how we should behave as males or females—sex roles are part of culture. We learn and we share various ideas about the nature of God—religious beliefs are part of culture. And so we could continue. But this is prosaic stuff. All we have said so far is that we learn many things, and much of what we learn we hold in common with others who share and transmit their cultural backgrounds. What is so profound about this?

The profundity of the concept comes from the extent to which it can be applied to innumerable realms of human conduct. To the extent that we can do this, we are able to ascertain that people are ruled not only by biological or physiological demands, but also by different ways of perceiving the world; and these modes of viewing the world are shaped by cultural background. Culture, as a concept, leads us toward a recognition of two things about people. First, it forces us to see that although individuals may be quite similar in physical form, they vary tremendously in their cultural forms. Second, it forces us to recognize the myriad ways in which we are, so to speak, personally "invaded" or "penetrated" by the cultures in which we mature. All too often, what we believe to be "instinct" or simple "human nature" proves to be a matter of cultural indoctrination.

Various illustrations come to mind. For example, as we have noted earlier in this book, a physiologist once referred to love as nothing more than DNA calling out to itself. This is a physiologist's approach to love and sex, and there is no denying that love and sex have a biological basis. The physiologist is right. It is a matter of DNA calling out to itself. However, DNA is not immune to cultural forces. A student of culture is aware that for culture-bound creatures like ourselves, love is considerably more. Culture can prescribe whether or not a person is more likely to fall in love with someone who is fat or thin, is taller or shorter, has blond hair or dark hair. Culture can determine whether people will fall in love at all. It can affect the extent to which people are aggressive or passive in making love. It can influence the extent to which people are aware or unaware of their sexual natures. At some times and in some cultures, the calling out of DNA has been met by attempts at self-castration. In a word, a comprehension of the nature of culture extends our understanding of the degree to which we are more than chemistry or physiology, or a set of biological drives or animal instincts.

The concept of culture is similar, in at least one respect, to a physical concept like gravity. Both culture and gravity gain their value from the degree to which they are found to operate in the universes they deal with.

Neither culture nor gravity is especially useful or valuable as an explanatory concept in individual cases. If, for example, we say that a ball fell to the floor because of gravity, we have not really said much. After all, how do we know gravity exists? We know it exists because the ball fell to the floor. So when we say that something fell because of gravity, we are only saying it fell because it fell; in other words, we have engaged in circular argument or a tautology. The significance of the concept of gravity comes from the fact that gravity is now known to reach out beyond the trees from which nuts fall, above the mountain heights, and farther yet—continuing *forever* into the outermost reaches of the physical universe.

The significance of the concept of culture acquires much of its significance through its extensions, just as gravity acquires its significance through its sweep into the infinite limits of the universe. As we begin to comprehend the cultural nature of people, we begin to see—in ever more subtle rangings—the intrusion of cultural influences. Emotions that may have their chemical origins in DNA will have the style and form of their expression dictated by culture. A brief observation provides a quick introduction to the pervasiveness of culture. One aspect of our cultural training—what we have learned and shared as a part of cultural experience—is the acquisition of a language. The dictionary that we rely on as we write this material contains over 260,000 entries. It is a crude measure of the variety and scope of the English language. We draw from this stockpile of words what we need. To what extent, as individuals, do we add to the stockpile from which we draw? It is a rare individual who adds even a single term of the general language. Culture gives us much—language, ideas, beliefs, moral understandings, tools, knowledge, art, and literature. We each make small individual contributions in return. But the ratio of an individual contribution to the cultural contribution is extremely low. Even if we manage to add a new term to the dictionary, the ratio is only 1:260,000—and we must remember that only an extremely few people each year get to add a new word.

The concept of culture does not find a receptive audience in a nation and a time when individualism is at its zenith. We pride ourselves on our individualism. That this age should be the age of individualism is something of a paradox, for never in human history have people been less individualistic. That is to say, never in history have people been more dependent on each other for virtually every step they take. It is impossible, for example, to determine how many people we depend on to get through an ordinary day. The bed from which we rise in the morning is the product of at least several hundred workers, ranging from those who designed and shaped the springs of the mattress to those who wove and sewed the material used for the sheets and pillowcases. So it is with each other item of the morning's routine—the toothbrush, the clothes, the breakfast items and the appliances on which they were cooked, the electricity on which we rely for the alarm to wake us to go to work, and so on. We depend, daily, on millions of other men and women working in concert. This is yet another facet of culture. We live within a culture. If the culture dies, we might manage to survive somehow. But the odds are against it.

❖ How an Anthropologist Views Culture

In modern times, we have acquired so much cultural baggage that the problem of determining what is significant and what is not has become a central task of the intellectual. One kind of intellectual especially qualified to perform this service is the anthropologist; after all, an examination of culture, either primitive or modern, is the primary concern of the anthropologist. The anthropologist, more than the sociologist, is aware of the range of cultures—from the simple, so-called "primitive" systems to the modern, more elaborate, and more complex so-called "civilized" systems. The sociologist concentrates on modern systems, the anthropologist on earlier systems. The anthropologist forces us to recognize our cultural patterns by contrasting them with patterns found in smaller or earlier cultural forms.

That we are more aware of ourselves through our awareness of other cultures is a consequence of the work of anthropologists of the stature of Margaret Mead. Mead's most famous work is certainly her study of adolescent girls in Samoa during the 1920s at the inception of her career in anthropology. In her autobiography, *Blackberry Winter*, she wrote:

> When I sailed for Samoa, I realized only very vaguely what a commitment to field work and writing about field work meant. My decision to become an anthropologist was based in part on my belief that a scientist, even one who had no great and special gift, such as a great artist must have, could make a useful contribution to knowledge. Even in remote parts of the world ways of life about which nothing was known were vanishing before the onslaught of modern civilization. The work of recording these unknown ways of life had to be done now—NOW—or they would be lost forever.[1]

Mead was just twenty-three years old when she set out for Samoa and her first attempt at studying another culture. In the initial weeks, she worked hard to become conversant with the language. On one of the Samoan islands, T'au, she was provided a home with an American medical officer, within the environs of a village and in easy reach of her subjects. For the rest of that year on the small Samoan island, Mead moved and lived among the people and especially was able to observe the life of adolescent girls.

From Samoa, she returned to the United States to take up the post of assistant curator that had been offered her at the American Museum of Natural History. It was here that she wrote the report that later was published as her first book, *Coming of Age in Samoa*. No other anthropologist had written such a book before about an exotic culture; it read like a novel, not like a scientific tome. Moreover, until Mead went to Samoa and wrote about young girls, focusing on their lives, their thoughts, their habits, and their folkways, children and women had largely been ignored by anthropologists. Although she chose never to study Samoan culture again, the themes of this study—the rearing of children, the shaping of personality, and the central role of women in society—came to be the themes that inspired Mead's studies for the rest of her career.

Margaret Mead said:

> Before I started out for Samoa I was warned that the terms in which others had written about the culture were anything but fresh and uncontaminated. The recorded grammar was contaminated by the ideas of Indo-European grammar and the descriptions of local chiefs by European notions about rank and status. I knew I would have to thread my way through this maze of partial understandings and partial distortions. In addition, I had been given the task of studying a new problem, one on which no work had been done and for which I had no guidelines.[2]

Coming of Age in Samoa was a tradition-breaker. It appeared in 1928 and quickly became a best-seller inside and outside of anthropology. The book thrust Mead into prominence in the United States at a time when people were already caught up in a growing revolt against Victorian attitudes about child rearing and sexuality. What was particularly astonishing, however, for readers of the time, was the revelation that adolescence is not a fixed pattern. The young women and young men of Samoa did not, Mead observed, experience adolescence as we do. Rather than thinking of adolescence as a purely biological determined aspect of the maturation process, people were now aware that it was more complex. Adolescence was a matter of cultural as well as a biological aging.

❖ The Work of an Anthropologist

During the 1930s and into the beginning of the 1940s, before the outbreak of World War II, Mead continued her studies of childhood and child rearing in other exotic and "primitive" cultures of the Pacific—the Manus of New Guinea and the Balinese. She now had partners—Leo Fortune, her second husband, with whom she studied the Manus, and later Gregory Bateson, her third and last husband, who made trips with her to Bali and back to New Guinea.

In working with the Manus people, she chose to study the mental processes of children and pioneered the use of psychological tests to examine the thinking of her subjects. This is detailed in the book *Growing Up in New Guinea*. Margaret Mead's fame grew in the United States following World War II. One of her most important and most strongly felt issues was the women's movement. She was recorded as remarking, "I've never been an imitation man. I've done things in my work only a woman can do. I've studied and observed children in areas where no man would be tolerated."[3]

Only a few years before her death, she wrote:

> Today, the discussions that bring women together from every level of technical development all over the world reveal what women—and the world—have lost.

Increasingly centralized, industrialized planning and production steadily reduce women to choosing between the role of housekeeper with mild supplementary activities—in the performance of which she is unprotected and ill paid in the marketplace—or that of educated but subordinate and unmarried competitor in all the other spheres of life.[4]

She then went on to note that the current questioning of the status of women is part of the whole process of questioning a social order that no longer meets the newly aroused hopes of the people who live within it. The voices of women are combining with voices all over the world against a modern worldwide system of political and economic exploitation of the land, the sea, and the air, and the endangered populations that depend upon them. Mead saw a new strength in women's empowerment. When women speak and exert their influence and power, Mead asserted that not only women gain, but society gains too.

Where once half of the best minds were consumed in the performance of small domestic tasks, society can now draw on them. Where women's experiences— inevitably different from men's because women all had mothers with whom they could identify—have been fenced off from contributing to the high-level planning of the world, they can now be used in the attack on such problems as chaotic abuse of food, resources, human settlement and the total environment. When women are once more able to participate in decisions and are free to be persons as well as parents, they should be able to contribute basic understandings that are presently lacking in the world. These basic new understandings include the fact that food is meant to be used to feed human beings, not to serve as a weapon or commodity; that towns were meant for generations to live in together, not only as barracks or bedrooms; that education can be used to make life meaningful; that we do live in a world community that is here but is unrecognized, in all its interdependence and need for shared responsibility.[5]

❖ Margaret Mead on North American Society

In the concluding chapters of her first book, *Coming of Age in Samoa*, Mead related her experiences in various cultures and societies to the problems and the conditions in contemporary American society. Mead tried this tactic out first through her lectures and personal appearances after returning from the South Seas. When it proved successful, it set the pattern for later studies and field research. For example, in her study of Samoa and other cultures of the South Pacific, Mead began to recognize that adolescence is not characteristically a period of stress and strain for individuals, as it has been considered by most authorities in the Western world. She posited that cultural conditioning is what makes adolescence a difficult period for American teenagers; she pointed to the extended period of puberty, the intricate rituals of dating and going steady, and questions of permissiveness in sexual mores.

Margaret Mead was one of the founders of the culture and personality studies within anthropology and as a joint study between anthropology and psychology. In a movement begun during the 1940s at the Institute of Human Relations at Yale University by Geoffrey Gorer, this interest was taken up by Gregory Bateson and Margaret Mead. The basis of these studies, now termed "national character studies," was the contention that culture shapes behavior and that cultural traits can be attributed to groups of people even as large as the nation-state. In her writings and in a well-known film made for the National Film Board of Canada, titled *Four Families*,[6] Mead projected the idea of national character beginning in the first year of life and stemming from the child-rearing practices through which the child is socialized and learns to become a member of the society. In the film, which Mead created and in which she "starred," four families were featured—each with mother, father, an infant, and older children. The families were from India, France, Japan, and Canada, all living in a rural setting.

Four Families was just one vehicle that gave Mead an opportunity to demonstrate cultural traits of national character to American audiences. (The term "American" here applies to North Americans in general, not just residents of the United States.) She noted that with the French family, the love of food and "play around the mouth" was very obvious; mystical gestures and special rituals were used to keep the baby safe in the Indian family, indicative of Indian heritage; in Japan, children were given beautifully carved and exquisitely rendered toys to play with, creating an early exposure to artistic beauty; and in Canada, the baby was put to sleep in her crib with the bottle propped by her mouth and the music box playing a lullaby, so she could contemplate her independence and ability to go to sleep in the dark and alone.

Margaret Mead wrote extensively about the attributes and peculiarities of Americans. For example, she contended that because Americans are upwardly mobile, often changing geographic and socioeconomic situations, in contrast to older, more settled, and more rigidly class-structured societies, they have a longing and need to find specific roots. Therefore Americans attach much more importance to their "home towns" than do citizens of other nations. Mead describes how one American will meet another traveling abroad, and as soon as they establish that they both grew up in the same town, they become close friends for the remainder of the journey. Or Mead notes that this may possibly explain the American penchant for joining clubs, groups, and associations, so that membership in an organization somehow fills a gap in one's life. For Mead, Americans display national character traits of being extremely independent and extroverted, while masking an inner longing for deep roots and a family lineage. In addition, she believed that Americans are overly success-oriented. This is demonstrated, in part, by the urgency parents feel to have their children do better in their careers than they have done, both financially and socially.

Mead always made sure in her writings and in her lectures and speeches to emphasize that it was not just one single custom, event, experience, or example that afforded social scientists the claim of imputing a "national character" to a people. Rather, it is necessary to consider the whole complex of traits, cultural conditioning, social mores, values, and attitudes that combine to create the attributes of the American, or, any other nation-state's specific "character."

❖ Margaret Mead and the Worldwide Culture

The legacy of Margaret Mead as an outstanding social analyst and critic, however, is to be found in her contributions to the development of a global culture and a worldwide view of humanity. She wrote:

> We have the means of reaching all of earth's diverse peoples and we have the concepts that make it possible for us to understand them, and they now share in a world-wide, technologically propagated culture, within which they are able to listen as well as to talk to us.[7]

Mead pointed out that today we have available to us for the first time on the "spaceship Earth" examples of the ways people have lived at every period over the last fifty thousand years.

> At the time that a New Guinea native looks at a pile of yams and pronounces them "a lot" because he cannot count them, teams at Cape Kennedy calculate the precise second when an Apollo mission must change its course if it is to orbit around the moon. In Japan, sons in the thirteenth generation of potters who make a special ceremonial pot are still forbidden to touch a potter's wheel or work on other forms of pottery. In some places old women search for herbs and mutter spells to relieve the fear of pregnant girls, while elsewhere research laboratories outline the stages in reproductivity that must each be explored for better contraceptives. Armies of twenty savage men go into the field to take one more victim from a people they have fought for five hundred years, and international assemblies soberly assay the vast destructiveness of nuclear weapons. Some fifty thousand years of our history lie spread out before us, accessible, for this brief moment in time, to our simultaneous inspection.[8]

Beginning with the book *Continuities in Cultural Evolution* and culminating in a series of lectures for the American Museum of Natural History, published in a volume titled *Culture and Commitment*, Mead set forth her theory about cultural learning and the evolution of humanity and human culture on the planet. She stated that it was her goal to explore existing cultures of different degrees of complexity, all existing at the present time (in the post–World War II era) but exhibiting essential differences, discontinuities, that distinguished them as primitive, historic, or contemporary. She emphasized that in the presentation of this paradigm of cultural development or continuities, she would deal with cultures that had been observed and recorded among contemporary living primitive peoples, and eschew all examples from historical data. "I shall draw only on studies of contemporary cultures 'in vivo,'" she wrote.[9] Mead then set out to describe three major types of cultures. She labeled them as follows:

1. Postfigurative cultures, or cultures of the past
2. Cofigurative cultures, or cultures of the present
3. Prefigurative cultures, or cultures of the future

She began her discussion by stating that all three types of cultures are a reflection of the period in which we currently are living.

The postfigurative culture is characterized as one in which change is so slow and imperceptible that grandparents cannot conceive of any other future for their grandchildren than that of one like their own lives. Postfigurative cultures are ones in which elders cannot conceive of change and so can only convey to their descendants a sense of unchanging continuity, asserted Mead. Postfigurative culture depends upon the actual presence of three generations. So this type of culture is peculiarly generational. Its continuity comes from the expectations of the old and its imprint of those expectations upon the young: "It depends upon the adults being able to see the parents who reared them as they rear their children in the way they themselves were reared."[10]

Mead gave these examples of postfigurative culture: In 1925, after a hundred years of contact with modern cultures, Samoans talked continually about Samoa and Samoan custom, rebuking small children as Samoan children, combining their remembered Polynesian identity and their sense of contrast between themselves and the colonizing foreigners. In the 1940s, in Venezuela, within a few miles of the city of Maracaibo, Indians still hunted with bows and arrows but cooked their food in aluminum pots stolen from Europeans with whom they had never communicated in any way.

Mead went on to say that the diverse peoples of the Pacific whom she had studied for forty years illustrate postfigurative cultures very well. Focusing on the Arapesh, she noted that there is no past for them except the past that has been embodied in the old, and in a younger form in their children and their children's children. Change is so completely assimilated that differences between earlier and later acquired customs vanished in the understanding and expectations of the people. Mead described Arapesh culture thus:

> As the Arapesh child was fed, held, bathed, and ornamented, myriad inexplicit and inarticulate learnings were conveyed to it by the hands that held it, the cadences of lullaby and dirge. Within the village and between villages, as the child was carried over and later walked on expected paths, the slightest disturbance of the surface was an event to be registered in the walking feet. When a new house was built, the response of each person who passed it registered for the carried child that there was something new here, something that had not been here a few days before and yet was in no way startling or surprising.[11]

This, then, is Mead's theory of cultural continuities and discontinuities in postfigurative cultures, cultures with well-known forebearers. Today, she noted, we have before us examples of people who represent successive phases in the history of humankind from hunting and gathering societies to the present. Our modern technologies give us the means to study and record the actions of these people for later analysis. We can even put a camera in their hands to record and help us see what we, by virtue of our upbringing, cannot ascertain or know to record and document. After a millennium of postfigurative and then cofigurative cultures, Mead asserted, we have arrived at a new stage in the evolution of human cultures.

Taking up the "cofigurative" culture, Mead characterized it as one in which the prevailing model for members of the society is the actions of their contemporaries. Why should a society change from a postfigurative to a co-figurative type of culture? Explaining the change, Mead said that cofigura-tion has its beginning in a break in the postfigurative system. Such a break may come about in many ways. She listed the following possibilities:

> through a catastrophe in which a whole population, but particularly the old who were essential to leadership, is decimated;

> as the result of the development of new forms of technology in which the old are not expert;

> following migration to a new land where the elders are, and always will be, regarded as immigrants and strangers;

> in the aftermath of a conquest in which subject populations are required to learn the language and the ways of the conqueror;

> as a result of religious conversion, when adult converts try to bring up children to embody new ideals they themselves never experienced as children and adolescents;

> as a purposeful step in a revolution that establishes itself through the introduction of new and different life styles for the young.[12]

The forces that contributed to the change from postfiguration to cofig-uration were set in motion by modernization and the aggressive colonization of developed nations of the world during the close of the nineteenth and into the early twentieth century. Searching for material resources, for their ever-expanding production of goods and later services, the industrialized, technologized nations of the world—Britain, France, Germany, and the United States—expanded around the globe, annexing, subjugating, and con-trolling the natural and human resources of other countries and groups of people.

So, Mead pointed out, the situation in which cofiguration occurs is one in which the experience of the younger generation is radically different from that of their parents, grandparents, and other older members of their im-mediate community. And, she stressed, the transition to a new way of life in which new skills and modes of behavior must be acquired appears to be much easier when there are not grandparents present who remember the past, shape the experience of the growing child, and reinforce all the unverbalized values of the old culture. "The past once represented by living people becomes shadowy and easier to abandon and to falsify in retrospect."[13]

Mead drew examples and cases of cofiguration from her extensive fieldwork among many cultures and traditions. She wrote that the mere condition of rapid change can produce cofiguration in countries such as India, Pakistan, and the new nations of Africa. Here children become the authorities on the new ways, and parents lose their power to judge and control. Similarly, when non-English-speaking immigrants to America had to give up their own language and specific culture, parents had no control over the new learning or formal education of their children, as they did in the countries from which they came. "They had to entrust their children to the schools and accept their children's interpretation of what was 'correct' American behavior."[14] Noting the power of peers, Mead went on to note that children had for guidance only the precepts of their teachers and the examples of their age-mates.

The immigrants rapidly learned to change traditional and long-standing customs in their newly adopted culture, said Mead. With characteristic humor, she described the staid European fathers of daughters who in the "old country" looked for promising sons-in-law; in America, however, it became fashionable for upwardly mobile young men to look for the daughters of wealthy fathers as marriage partners.

Mead theorized that rapid change brought about extreme discrepancies in some countries where postfigurative and cofigurative systems existed side by side. Yet there were always adults who knew more and had more experience than any of the young people in that country or culture. But what has happened today?

> [S]uddenly, because all the peoples of the world are part of one electronically based, intercommunicating network, young people everywhere share a kind of experience that none of the elders ever have had or will have. Conversely, the older generation will never see repeated in the lives of young people their own unprecedented experience of sequentially emerging change. This break between generations is wholly new; it is planetary and universal. Today's children have grown up in a world their elders never knew, but few adults knew that this would be so. Those who did know it were the forerunners of the *prefigurative* cultures of the cultures in which the prefigured is the unknown.[15]

Thus, Mead set forth the third stage of her theory of cultural continuities—prefigurative culture, a totally new conception of living, in which adults learn from their children. Because change has occurred so rapidly within one person's lifetime, the older generations can no longer teach the young. Specifically, Mead pointed to the entrance of all humanity into the nuclear era. In the past, no matter how terrible the war, humankind did survive. But, today, a nuclear conflagration means there will be no survivors, no humanity. However, Mead contended, we still continue to think that a war fought with more lethal weapons would just be a worse war. We still do not grasp the implications of scientific weapons of extinction. She emphasized that in having moved into a present for which none of us is prepared by our understanding of the past, our interpretations of ongoing experience or our expectations about the future are clouded. We have left behind our familiar worlds to live in a new age under conditions that are different from any we have ever known, but our thinking still binds us to the past.

With the unbridled optimism that characterized Margaret Mead all her life, she challenged the younger generation to lash out against the controls to which they are subjected. She told the young that they have never known a time when war did not threaten the annihilation of humankind; that they realize there is continuing pollution of the air, the water, and the sod; that it soon will be impossible to feed an indefinitely expanding world population; that we must find a feasible and humane means of population control; and that racism is untenable. In short, the young must now insist on some form of world order or our planet is doomed.

Mead summed up her theory of cultural continuities as follows:

> For I believe we are on the verge of developing a new kind of culture, one that is as much a departure in style from cofigurative cultures, as the institutionalization of cofiguration in orderly—and disorderly—change was a departure from the postfigurative style. I call this new style *prefigurative*, because in this new culture it will be the child—and not the parent and grandparent—that represents what is to come. Instead of the erect, white-haired elder who, in postfigurative cultures, stood for the past and the future in all their grandeur and continuity, the unborn child, already conceived but still in the womb, must become the symbol of what life will be like.[16]

In his thorough and highly readable biography of Margaret Mead, Robert Cassidy concludes with the observation that Mead's most important contribution as a social thinker of the twentieth century was her ability to assimilate information from a wide range of fields, process the facts, create a whole new viewpoint, and then communicate her findings in plain English to the American public.[17] And she will always be remembered for her optimism. Her colleagues, friends, and family are quick to respond at the mention of her name that Mead believed human beings were capable of ridding the world of hunger, spreading the benefits of technology to developing nations, and achieving world peace. Margaret Mead stands as a social thinker, a prophetess, and America's unforgettable anthropological grandmother.

❖ *The Concept of Culture: A Reprise*

The concept of culture is abstract, and cultural forces themselves are extremely vast, powerful, and subtle. Yet, despite this, the anthropologist does not lose sight of the fact that the matter of culture is essentially a matter of what we do to ourselves. For, after all, culture is simply what generations of people have passed on to those who follow. Culture is the hand of the dead on the shoulder of the living. It may be a very powerful hand, but it is still human and still fallible.

As we have written elsewhere, humanity has reached the point where it is confronted with the ultimate cultural dilemma, the problem of world-wide nuclear destruction. We can continue the quest for technological "fixes," or we can work toward the end of promoting new forms of social awareness. As Margaret Mead has urged us, we should work toward attaining a world order in which social conflicts can be handled by less than ultimate forms of threat and counterthreat. Now, we have no choice in the matter. All societies must work to solve these social conflicts or witness the end of human cultures as we have known them. Certainly, the very least we can do is put our minds to the problem.

Encounters with Social Thought

Religion and Cultural Continuities

The work of Margaret Mead is some of the most appropriate to develop for our encounters with social thought. Mead was not primarily a theorist. As noted at the outset of this chapter, her contribution consisted of taking established ideas and applying them in new contexts. The concept of culture, for example, was well developed by the time Mead began her work. Mead examined a different culture, found further exemplifications of the forces of culture in the adolescent activities of Samoan children, and then turned her attention to her own culture. Mead is an example of the applied social thinker *par excellence*. She revealed the power of anthropological concepts and their relevance to the personal and immediate lives of the general public.

Second, Mead was as much concerned with rectifying the injustices and follies of the human scene as she was with analyzing them—more so, perhaps. Still, the same comment can be made about Marx, and Marxian theory is certainly more powerful as theory than anything we find in the writings of Mead. In Marx, however, the development of theory was never dominated by the anger that Marx felt over the injustices he witnessed. In Mead's work, theory is displaced by an emphasis on cultural description and comparison. There is certainly nothing wrong with this. It does, however, reveal the difference between theoretically useful work and that which is more applied in nature.

Third, Mead eventually drifted into social commentary that at times was little more than a kind of benign advice to the bewildered. She spent her energies on magazine columns in which her work was on a par with that of a skilled journalist. In this capacity, she was working as an applied anthropologist. One is tempted to compare her with Dr. Ruth Westheimer (television and radio's "Dr. Ruth") in this regard. Both women represent a high degree of training and knowledge that is directed toward helping people more than it is toward the task of developing new ways of understanding.

However, the same concepts that Margaret Mead drew on for applied inspiration can be used by anyone else. Mead's basic conceptual foundation was the idea of culture. In the following application of her ideas, we shall draw on the concept of culture and her delineation of cultural continuties into the postfigurative, the cofigurative, and the prefigurative. The subject we have selected to examine is religion. We have selected this not because it is obviously relevant to the concept of culture, but because it is the realm of human concern that is possibly most tormented by the transitions modern cultures are passing through. It is also an interesting topic because young people today, the agents of the prefigurative culture, are turning back to religion as a postfigurative cultural form. Moreover, the most highly prefigurative cultures we know of—modern revolutionary socialist states such as Russia and China—find that this holdover from the most primal forms of postfigurative cultures is not easily supplanted by a materialistic-technocratic mentality.

How might Mead respond to this? First of all, we might expect her to point out that religion is, in the most general sense, a cultural phenomenon. This has been demonstrated so thoroughly that we hardly need press the matter further here. There are cultures in which God does not exist in the form of any kind of supreme being. In such cultures the idea of God is much closer to our notion of "luck." There are cultures with gods, but the gods have no direct interest in the moral activities of the people. There are cultures in which the relationship between people and their gods are more companionable than adulatory, such as we find in our religion. There are cultures in which the gods are numerous and cultures in which the gods are few. In our culture we like to think of ourselves as monotheistic when, in fact, we list two major deities (God and Satan) and then a host of minor ones (saints, archangels, demons, etc.).

The gods vary in number, temperament, concerns, and talents according to human culture. Religion varies with culture. The most devout Christian, if born in another culture, would be devoted to another religious view. We know of no child brought up exclusively in a French environment who has spoken any language other than French, despite occasional sensational tales of people speaking foreign languages while in trances. Likewise, no child brought up in an exclusively Muslim religious environment is going to have even the faintest notion of

Christian ideology. It is, given the nature of human life, a purely logical matter.

We begin, then, with the elementary observation that religion is cultural. This is disturbing to orthodox religious beliefs and traditions. After all, the fountainhead of religious orthodoxy is the idea that one's religion sprang, more or less full-blown, from the spirit of God Himself, not from cultural histories. (The philosopher Baruch Spinoza was excommunicated for arguing that religious ideas are basically historically and culturally determined.) Because each religion, at least as we commonly know modern religions, makes claims to being God's way, it separately asserts its total validity. The one thing that all religions seem to share is the belief on the part of each one that it is *the* true religion. Yet the evidence and the logic are simply overwhelming and obvious: This cannot be true. If religions vary, and each claims to be the true religion, then at most only one can be correct. If each claims to be the voice of God, then God must be speaking with a forked tongue. Given the anthropological evidence and the simple logic of the matter, we are led to the more reasonable conclusion that religion is a human creation and that it is relative to the culture it happens to serve.

If it is cultural, and if Mead's conception of cultural change is correct, then we might expect to see a transformation in religion—along with other elements of the culture—from a postfigurative form to a cofigurative and then a prefigurative form. This implies that, for one thing, religion will increasingly be guided not by elders, but by those who are on the cutting edge of cultural progression—the young people. Religious institutions, at one time under the total dominance of the elderly, will find themselves undergoing a transition toward less certain control.

In postfigurative cultures, change is slow, and children live as their grandparents did and their grandparents before them. Religion, in modern societies, attempts to retain some of the qualities of the postfigurative culture. Orthodox and conservative forms of religion exist as subcultures within a broader cultural context. The Hasidic Jews, the Amish, cloistered Catholics, and fundamentalists of all religions endorse religious doctrines that have a long cultural history. The grandchildren, as Mead might put it, look and act much like the grandparents.

The cofigurative culture is one in which the elders no longer dominate the transition or passing of the culture through the generations. The prevailing model for members of the culture is whatever their contemporaries are doing. The past loses its significance, and the present becomes a dominant concern. Nothing sums up the cofigurative culture better than the phrase "the now generation." Whereas ancestor worship—or, at least, a sanctification of and respect for the dead—characterizes the postfigurative culture, the dead become increasingly irrelevant in the cofigurative culture. Religious doctrine and ritual, which in the postfigurative culture are directed toward retaining continuity with the past, become more oriented toward dealing with concerns of the present.

A cofigurative religious development might, then, be expected to endorse prevailing fads and fancies rather than reject them. Psychological counseling; the use of rock-and-roll instead of traditional forms of liturgical music; the use of contemporary slang, slogans, and language in ritual; and so forth would be characteristic of a cofigurative form. The child, instead of being kept with the parents in the confines of a pew while listening to a sermon, might be sent instead to the church's child care center to be with peers. The church, in the cofigurative form, would tend more and more to separate age groups and even occupational groups in an attempt to encourage peer relationships.

Even church architecture, if Mead is correct, should respond to the demands of cofigurative cultural forms. In the postfigurative church, the architecture is either extremely simple or, if ornate, is ornate in a manner that conforms to the traditional configuration of a church. In Christian Europe, of course, this tradition has emphasized awe-inspiring towers supported by flying buttresses, stained-glass windows, high ceilings, solid stone construction, and so forth. Solid and traditional architecture serves the purpose of providing buildings that can be readily identified as places of worship. Moreover, such buildings have a continuity. They remain standing over the centuries, generation after generation, as reminders of the glories of the past as well as the present. As such structures age, their grandeur increases and their powers are enhanced. They become the very same places in which one's great-great-great grandparents worshiped or were married or were laid to rest.

Cofigurative church architecture can be so "trendy," so much a part of the "now generation," that it is at times difficult to tell whether a church represents a place of prayer or a drive-in bank. The cofigurative church building, if nothing else, moves away from the severely established traditional form in the quest for more "modern" or current structures. The consequence has been the appearance in the cities of the United States and Europe of churches that fit into the urban environment much as any other building does. They are notable not by their imposing presence, but by their lack of it. Within an industrial area, the church may occupy an old factory building or a new building that looks much like an old factory. Within a commercial district, a church may be located in a former bank building or in a new building that looks much like a bank. The church, in the cofigurative culture, has to deal with the problem of being different but not too different.

In the extreme form of prefigurative religious practice, the idea is to execute ritual in as precise a manner, as closely to the way it had always been executed, as possible. We understand, for example, that the rain dances of the Indians of the southwestern United States require extremely close attention to detail on the part of those participating. Costumes, expressions, gestures, and the content of the ritual are controlled to be as exactly like previous enactments of the ritual as possible. In the cofigurative religious practice of ritual, that which offends, tires, bores, or confuses the younger participants becomes a matter of concern. Eventually, it becomes something to be changed. If Latin is incomprehensible, then Latin is archaic, irrelevant, and beside the point. It is not part of the "now generation" and accordingly it can be dismissed. If the Gregorian chant is not in keeping with the more sensate forms of popular music, then the choir can add a guitarist and perhaps a drummer. Ritual becomes flexible. More to the point, it becomes a way of relating not to the past generations but to the present generation.

In sum, whereas postfigurative religion is relevant in itself and seeks to be "timeless," cofigurative religion becomes more concerned with the problem of being relevant and, as a consequence, becomes locked into the present. The purity of tradition is sacrificed to the ideologies of the moment. We find numerous illustrations of this in the practice of religion in the United States at the present time. Perhaps the most extreme exemplification has been the transformation of the celebration of Christ's birth by those of Christian faith. We hardly need elaborate on the extent to which Christmas has become a depressing indulgence in commercialism. There are other examples, however. "Christian" seminars that seek to blend commercial interests with Christian dogma are a nice case in point of religion taking on a cofigurative cast. Although the Bible tells us it is easier for a camel to pass through the eye of a needle than for a rich man to enter the kingdom of heaven, modern evangelists do not hesitate to suggest that Christ enjoins us to enjoy great wealth. The mind-boggling wrenching of the spirit that can come from such contradictions results from cultural traditions that are in conflict. Mead, rather than launch an attack against the "hypocrisy" or the personalities of the new ministers, would suggest that we examine the cultural contexts within which they are working.

The prefigurative form is uniquely modern. It is more an anticipation than a reality. Yet it is based on Mead's astute observations of what has been going on in the world. The prefigurative form essentially turns the postfigurative form on its head. Whereas in the postfigurative form continuity is a primary concern and the elders are in charge, in the prefigurative form change is the primary concern and young people are in charge.

Possibly Mead was responding, as she thought of the prefigurative form, to the times in which she lived her later years. *Culture and Commitment*, where these ideas are most fully elaborated, was published in 1970. The 1960s, in America, were a time in which we talked not only about the "now generation," but also about the "generation gap." It did appear in the 1960s that the elders had lost their grip. It was a time when anyone over the age of thirty could not be trusted. Elders were not only not respected; they were not trusted. At best they were objects of contempt, and at worst objects of thinly disguised hatred. The story is told of an elderly couple on a street corner in New York who were told by a group of college students to "go home and die." Mead was certainly influenced by the tenor of the times. It was a far departure from the postfigurative cultures in which she had lived and worked.

A notion of what prefigurative religion might be like can be obtained from the age of *Jesus Christ Superstar*. In the 1960s (and it remains a common practice), the notion of writing one's own wedding vows became popular. Marriages took place in a great variety of settings and forms. The bride could be found wearing anything from Day-Glo body paints to a jumpsuit. The groom might be wearing anything from overalls to a Wild Bill Hickok outfit. Rings might or might not be exchanged. Above all, the ceremony was in the hands of the participants rather than tradition. It could be ad-libbed on the spot. It was "free" in form. No two were necessarily alike. In extreme cases, a couple might decide to marry themselves by their own means. Drugs might or might not be a part of the ceremony.

More interesting, a ceremony did not have to adhere to any orthodox religious point of view. A single ceremony might incorporate readings from Christian, Jewish, Islamic, Buddhist, and Vedic sources. Religious purity was not only rejected with respect to ritualistic exactitude, but was rejected in content as well.

There has not been sufficient time for a prefigurative religious architecture to develop, but if the 1960s are any indication, such architectural forms would have to be as eclectic and diverse as the wedding ceremonies that characterized that period. In the 1960s the trend seemed to favor no architecture at all. Ceremonies were celebrated in the wild. People were married under the trees and in the fields. Where the people were when the spirit stirred them to think of God and cosmic matters was good enough in itself. No special "house of God" is necessary. This, however, might change.

One new development that was just on the threshold of making its presence known when Margaret Mead died was the modern desktop personal computer. The ways in which this device has been incorporated into religious institutions lends some credence to the cultural classification scheme that Mead gives us. Postfigurative religious forms would be inclined to reject the computer. Older people characteristically find the computer threatening and not especially necessary. We would expect to find extremely orthodox groups shying away from the computer. Again, we think of the Amish (who shy away from any kind of modern invention), Hasidic Jews, and cloistered Catholics. The cofigurative religious forms incorporate the computer, but not in any innovatively religious fashion. For example, television evangelists and modernized religious organizations use the computer to keep track of members, deal with financial problems, and print out mailing lists. The prefigurative religious groups, however, will turn to the computer for innovative religious purposes. One envisions, in this regard, the possibility of vast, global religious networks communicating messages and graphics that move religion totally away from the idea that it is a dogmatic set of sacred texts, unchallengeable, to a vital religious culture that undergoes constant change.

On this note, we shall close this excursion into the realm of social thought using Margaret Mead's concept of cultural continuities. The purpose of theory is to enhance our speculative powers. In the material above, we have indulged in several speculations concerning the future of religion in America, as we might think about it after reading Mead. Our speculations are meant to encourage the reader to indulge in further speculations—either about religion or about some other topic of concern. Speculation, however, should never be confused with reality. The speculations that Mead stimulates are, we think, interesting in themselves. However, until we spend a great deal of time investigating the matter further—getting evidence, engaging in critical argument and discussion—we should keep in mind that we have only engaged in the first step toward seeing further than we have seen before. It is an important first step, but it is not sufficient by itself to stand as truth.

Putting Social Thought to Work

1. Drawing on her experiences and studies in societies throughout the world, Margaret Mead speculated that there is a distinct and growing generation gap—not only in developed, highly technological nations such as the United States, Britain, and the Soviet Union, but also in developing nations, such as those of the Pacific Rim. She believed that youths the world over are caught up in the same electronically produced, intercommunicating network that has enculturated them into a universal culture their parents have never known and could never know. Further, this new generation faces a future shaped by nuclear energy and weapons, satellites, computers, rapid worldwide transport, rampant population growth, the disintegration of metropolitan areas, and the steady destruction of the environment. Do you agree with Mead that we have an unprecedented, global generation gap today? Do you think the youth of today can succeed in solving the problems of the quality of life?

2. Mead believed that once the fact of a deep, new, unprecedented, worldwide generation gap had been firmly acknowledged by both the young and the old, communication could be reestablished and a dialogue

across the generations could take place. Moreover, she was of the opinion that such a dialogue would work toward a solution of modern global troubles. Do you agree? Do you think the generation gap has narrowed in recent years or is growing wider? What kinds of evidence do you rely on to support your opinion?

3. Mead's concentration on the generation gap stemmed from her deep concern over education, particularly American education. She characterized education in America as the entwining of three main themes or heritages: the little red schoolhouse, where a democratic, stable, deeply rooted American tradition held sway; the academy, where a privileged, upper-class elite was educated; and the city school, where the children of the waves of immigrants were "Americanized." From your school experience, does this image of American education hold true? What type of school did you attend? Did your elementary and secondary school education serve to widen the generation gap or reduce it? What events have occurred in American education since Mead analyzed our schools that might further support her contention or weaken it? What impacts have global forces had upon schooling in America? What role do you see for schooling in America for the future and its effect on the generation gap?

4. Influenced by her belief in a national character, Mead wrote that each society practices child rearing in a distinct and characteristic way: Russian parents nurture children in a rough-and-tumble, strong, and individualistic manner; British parents look on themselves as gardeners who need to cultivate the natural development of the child; and the French see the child as growing up like a tree that needs pruning. From your experience of growing up in your family, do you think there is a distinctive child-rearing tradition characteristic of Americans? If so, how would you describe it? If you have children or plan to have children, is it your intention to raise them in specific ways to shape them as Americans? As world citizens? As citizens of a region or specific town or city?

5. Mead endorsed the idea of "women's liberation." What do you think led her to this way of thinking? What might there be about the training of an anthropologist or social scientist that would promote greater "liberalization" of ideas and traditions? Do you think this is good or bad? Why?

6. Do you think American society will gain when women are able to participate fully at every level in the complexities of contemporary life? Which aspects of our culture do you believe are most open to change and liberation? Which aspects are most closed? What does this tell you about the nature of human social systems?

7. Mead spent her life popularizing the idea that culture or social forces dictate much of what we are. This idea stands in opposition to the idea

that we are what our "genes" make us or what our psychological or individual nature makes us. Modern thinkers are beginning to see that social and psychological qualities are capable of interacting and mimicking each other. With respect to human sexuality, to what extent do you think cultural forces play a role in determining what a "woman" is? What a "man" is? Provide illustrations to back up your contentions.

Endnotes

1. Margaret Mead, *Blackberry Winter: My Earlier Years* (New York: Morrow, 1972), p. 137. Margaret Mead's writings are wide ranging and extensive. Some of her best-known works are: *Coming of Age in Samoa: A Psychological Study of Primitive Youth for Western Civilization* (New York: Morrow, 1928); *Growing Up in New Guinea: A Comparative Study of Primitive Education* (New York: Morrow, 1930); *Sex and Temperament in Three Primitive Societies* (New York: Morrow, 1937); *Cooperation and Competition Among Primitive People* (Editor) (New York: McGraw-Hill, 1937); *Balinese Character: A Photographic Analysis* (with Gregory Bateson) (New York: New York Academy of Sciences, 1942); *And Keep Your Powder Dry: An Anthropologist Looks at America* (New York: Morrow, 1942); *Male and Female: A Study of Sexes in a Changing World;* (New York: Morrow, 1949); *Soviet Attitudes Toward Authority* (New York: McGraw-Hill, 1954); *The School in American Culture* (Cambridge, MA: Harvard University Press, 1951); *Cultural Patterns and Technical Change: A Manual Prepared by the World Federation for Mental Health* (Editor) (Paris: UNESCO, 1953); *Childhood in Contemporary Cultures* (Editor, with Martha Wolfenstein) (Chicago: University of Chicago Press, 1955); and *New Lives for Old: Cultural Transformation—Manus, 1928–1953* (New York: Morrow, 1956).
2. *New Lives for Old*, p. 144.
3. Robert Cassidy, *Margaret Mead: A Voice for the Century* (New York: Universe Books, 1982), p. 14.
4. Margaret Mead, "Needed: Full Partnership for Women," *Saturday Review*, June 14, 1975, p. 130.
5. Ibid., p. 131.
6. Margaret Mead (producer), *Four Families* (film for the National Film Board of Canada) (New York: McGraw-Hill, distributor, 1959).
7. Margaret Mead, *Culture and Commitment: A Study of the Generation Gap* (Garden City, NY: Natural History Press/Doubleday, 1970), p. xvi.
8. Ibid.
9. Ibid., p. xxvi.
10. Ibid., p. 5.
11. Ibid., p. 7.
12. Ibid., p. 33.
13. Ibid., p. 44.
14. Ibid., p. 56.
15. Ibid., p. 64.
16. Ibid., p. 88.
17. Cassidy, *Margaret Mead*, p. 332.

Abundance, Leisure, and Loneliness

Observations on Society from David Riesman

❖

❖ Sociologists and Their Commentaries on Society

Some sociologists, like the gifted ones presented in this text, take it upon themselves to produce major dissertations on the evolution and the change occurring in the social order of their own society, as well as in other cultures. The readers of this book have been introduced to social thinkers of this caliber—for example, in the chapters on Sorokin, C. Wright Mills, and Margaret Mead. Sorokin's grand theory saw cultural patterns changing from the Ideational to the Sensate; Mills was consumed with the identification of the power elite; while Margaret Mead delineated three types of cultures—the postfigurative, the cofigurative, and the prefigurative. We now describe the work of another major social thinker of the twentieth century, David

225

society but becoming downright dangerous—a luxury only more primitive social systems can afford—is hinted at by Norbert Wiener. Speaking of war games, he says, "It has been said that in every war, the good generals fight the last war, the bad ones the war before the last. That is, the rules of the war game never catch up with the facts of the real situation." In the context here, Wiener is pointing out that the traditionalist in war is the one who stands the greatest chance of losing. Ominously enough, he adds, "Moreover, remember that in the game of atomic warfare, there are no experts." The course of social movement today is one which provides less and less traditional basis for decision making.[3]

The tradition-directed person possesses a social character uncritically accepting of tradition and resistant to innovation. The major problems of the society are resolved by the willingness of the individual to rely on tradition. Tradition provides a place for the individual in society, and the individual responds by tenaciously endorsing tradition. In contrast to other societies, traditional societies incorporate all their members. No one is "surplus."

> Indeed, the individual in some primitive societies is far more appreciated and respected than in some sectors of modern society. For the individual in a society dependent on tradition-direction has a well-defined functional relationship to other members of the group. If he is not killed off, he "belongs"—he is not "surplus," as the modern unemployed are surplus, nor is he expendable as the unskilled are expendable in modern society. But by very virtue of his "belonging," life goals that are *his* in terms of conscious choice appear to shape his destiny only to a very limited extent, just as only to a limited extent is there any concept of progress for the group.[4]

A small and relatively stable society may be able to maintain itself almost exclusively in terms of traditional definitions of roles and interpersonal behavior. Then, for reasons not well understood today, such societies may undergo a number of small but cumulative changes that tend to destroy the effectiveness of tradition as a basis of organization. (Relate these ideas to the movement from the postfigurative to cofigurative culture in Chapter 9 on Margaret Mead.) With a decline in the effectiveness of tradition, the society enters a transitional stage of development and, during this stage, relies on a different form of social character—that of "inner-direction." Riesman puts it this way:

> In western history the society that emerged with the Renaissance and Reformation and that is only now vanishing serves to illustrate the type of society in which inner-direction is the principal mode of securing conformity. Such a society is characterized by increased personal mobility, by a rapid accumulation of capital (teamed with devastating technological shifts), and by an almost constant expansion: intensive expansion in exploration, colonization, and imperialism. The greater choices this society gives—and the greater initiatives it demands in order to cope with its novel problems—are handled by character types who can manage to live socially without strict and self-evident tradition-direction. These are the inner-directed types.[5]

The inner-directed person is provided with the ambition to seek out generalized social goals. This may require novel solutions to problems that a traditionalistic approach would not have been able to resolve, or that, more likely, would not even have occurred. Inner-directed individuals are not completely lacking in a tradition-directed society; but—and this is Riesman's point—they will be more typical of a society that has need of them. They are more likely to be aberrant or unique in other forms of society. Inner-directed people appear when a society is in process of expansion.

After the expansive movements of a society have been completed, a new problem arises. During the expansive phase, the problem is to cope with novel situations and to pursue doggedly the task of exploiting a hostile environment; once this has been achieved, the problem then becomes one of making peace with success. A period of entrenchment ensues. The land, the resources, the markets, the colonies have been successfully exploited. But the process of exploitation, of developing these resources, brings into being powerful agents of control; the most significant of these is the large-scale organizational system. Whereas people previously found themselves locked in dubious battle with nature, now they find themselves confronted with bureaucracies. The problem is to adjust to others around them. Social adaptability rather than inner moral strength becomes a leading characteristic of the successful type in this new stage of social development.

Some people fear that Riesman is opposed to inner moral strength and that he is justifying more callow forms of opportunistic conformity. This would be unfair. Riesman is trying, as realistically as possible, to evaluate the impact of modern forms of social organization on character, and he concludes that, for the most part, a common character of the hardheaded inner-directed type would prove extremely disruptive. Ayn Rand's plea for a return to older individualistic values is not so much right or wrong as it is unrealistic. A few people of the character of the hero of *The Fountainhead* can be absorbed by this society. But such willfulness would prove intolerable in great numbers. Riesman, incidentally, views Rand's work as a caricature of inner-directed values. In any event, we cannot avow the rightness or wrongness of strong moral character. We can, however, consider the possibility of its disruptive effects if practiced on a large scale in a society where the central problem confronting people is that of making their peace with other people.[6]

Because relations with other people become crucial and because the individual is sensitive to the demands of others, Riesman calls a person having this form of social character "other-directed." He defines the other-directed person and society in the following way:

> Under these newer [other-directed] patterns the peer group (the group of one's associates of the same age and class) becomes much more important to the child, while the parents make him feel guilty not so much about violation of inner standards as about failure to be popular or otherwise to manage his relations with these other children. . . . What is common to all the other-directed people is that their contemporaries are the source of direction for the individual—either

those known to him or those with whom he is indirectly acquainted, through friends and through the mass media. . . . This mode of keeping in touch with others permits a close behavior conformity, not through drill in behavior itself, as in the tradition-directed character, but rather through an exceptional sensitivity to the actions and wishes of others.[7]

This tripartite typification of societies and social character, relatively simple and straightforward, proves to have astonishing success in making sense out of a tremendous variety of social events, ranging from changes in child-rearing practices to the problems of personnel management in modern industry. As we shall see, practices taking place in one sector of society are not always as removed from those taking place in another as it might first appear. Indeed, the hallmark of an outstanding social scientist is the capacity to reveal commonalities in events that have, in the past, seemed perfectly disparate. John Kenneth Galbraith expresses this point better in his description of Marx as a social scientist. He refers to the breathtaking grandeur of Marx's achievement as an exercise in social theory. "No one before, or for that matter since, had taken so many strands of human behavior and woven them together—social classes, economic behavior, the nature of the state, imperalism, and war were all here and on a great fresco which ran from deep in the past to far into the future."[8]

If vast changes in the social structure can be summarized in terms of pervasive effects on social character, then we should be able to find these effects at work in almost any setting. We should be able to see shifts from tradition- to inner- to other-direction at work in the army, the school, the practice of medicine, the practice of law, the treatment of criminals, the practice of business, leisure pursuits, literature, government, religion, and any other part of the social order. One social activity that occupies much of Riesman's thinking is education, and he turns toward a consideration of the tradition-, inner-, and other-directed school.

❖ Schooling in Different Societies

In the tradition-directed society, children are likely to have little encounter with schooling. The traditions they come to rely on are acquired through intimate observation and involvement with adults and peers. For example, Navajo children whose parents belong to the Native American Church, a peyote-using religion, are taken to all-night peyote sessions and allowed to watch and participate to whatever extent they can. When they become sleepy, they are allowed to fall asleep. The children are allowed to experiment with peyote at any time they wish—regardless of age. Reliance on tradition does not necessarily mean a stultified life-form for the tradition-oriented person. Part of the peyote ritual consists of singing hymns. These hymns are traditional, but they can be varied to a considerable degree within this limitation. We were informed by a colleague that he once learned to sing a peyote hymn from a Navajo Indian with whom he collaborated during a "dig" in the American Southwest. In turn, the Navajo learned the hymn from the generator of his automobile as he was driving home one evening.[9]

In the inner-directed society, the problems of education are more complicated. Children must be infused with general goals that they are willing to pursue even though they may exact a cost in terms of indifference and hostility on the part of others. The governess in Victorian England helped promote such a character. The relationship of the governess to the head of the household was such as to provide the child with a very realistic training in the disparities of power. A child reared under such conditions was less likely to be awed by the authority of his or her teachers. As Riesman puts it:

> When he goes off to boarding school or college he is likely to remain unimpressed by his teachers—like the upper class mother who told the school headmaster: "I don't see why the masters can't get along with Johnny; all the other servants do." Such a child is not going to be interested in allowing his teachers to counsel him in his peer-group relations or emotional life.[10]

The character of schooling in the inner-directed society can be summed up as follows: The task of the teacher is to train children in matters of decorum and intellectual subjects. The approach is impersonal. The sexes are segregated. The emphasis is on learning a curriculum, and whether or not one enjoys it is really beside the point. Standards are unequivocal—they are immutable. They cannot be challenged nor can they be seen in a relative manner—they apply to all. They are not held to be more appropriate for some students than for others. Thus, children are ranked in terms of their ability to conform to the standards, and the security they achieve from knowing where they stand in terms of these standards is balanced by the fact that little mercy is shown them by taking into account any psychological or social handicaps under which they might be straining.

George Orwell, describing his experiences at Crossgates, nicely underscores Riesman's main point:

> That was the pattern of school life—a continuous triumph of the strong over the weak. Virtue consisted in winning: it consisted in being bigger, stronger, handsomer, richer, more popular, more elegant, more unscrupulous than other people—in dominating them, bullying them, making them suffer pain, making them look foolish, getting the better of them in every way. Life was hierarchical and whatever happened was right. There were the strong, who deserved to win and always did win, and there were the weak, who deserved to lose and always did lose, everlastingly.
>
> I did not question the prevailing standards, because so far as I could see there were no others. How could the rich, the strong, the elegant, the fashionable, the powerful, be in the wrong? It was their world, and the rules they made for it must be the right ones.[11]

But times and social character have changed—and these changes can be seen dramatically within the context of the school. Riesman describes schooling in an age of other-direction: Children go to school at earlier ages, and the two- to five-year-old schoolchildren come to associate school more with playing and with games than with forbidding adults and dreary subjects. Physical arrangements are altered. The sexes may be mixed, and alphabetic placement of students may give way to sociometric forms of seating—children sit not where they are told to sit but where they find their friends. Concern is focused increasingly on problems of group relations and decreasingly on problems of production. The teacher conveys to the children that what matters is not their industry or learning as such but their adjustment to the group, their (carefully stylized and limited) initiative and leadership.[12] In the other-directed school there is a deemphasis on the content of learning and an emphasis on democratization of social relationships. What a child learns is not too important—so long as he or she learns it in a way that shows a capacity to get along with others. Children are readied for their place in a society that is moving increasingly from a dedication to morality to a promotion of morale.

The value of Riesman's inner- and other-directed classification of social character is, as we mentioned before, that it has the capacity to bring together a great variety of social threads and show them to be part of a common cloth. We have, at this point, briefly examined differences between schooling in the inner-directed and other-directed society.

❖ Literature and Entertainment in Different Societies

Let us turn from education to Riesman's comments on literary movements and entertainment and their relation to ideals of success. As we go from a period of inner-direction to one of other-direction:

> We can trace an edifying sequence that runs from the success biography of the Samuel Smiles or the Horatio Alger sort to the contemporary books and periodicals that deal with peace of mind. The earlier books were directly concerned with social and economic advance, dealt with as achievable by the virtues of thrift, hard work, and so on. . . .
>
> From then on, inspiration literature becomes less and less exclusively concerned with social and economic mobility. Dale Carnegie's *How to Win Friends and Influence People*, written in 1937, recommends self-manipulative exercises for the sake not only of business success but of such vaguer, non-work goals as popularity.[13]

This reference to Carnegie is pertinent because *How to Win Friends and Influence People*, perhaps more than any other written work, illustrates what Riesman is saying. It is worth spending a few moments to look further at this extraordinary book.

What Carnegie does, as a self-help expert and as many imitators who followed him also attempt to do, is to lay down a set of rules or suggestions for transforming the individual into an other-directed person. Carnegie boasts:

> The rules we have set down here are not mere theories or guess work. They work like magic. . . .
>
> To illustrate: Last season a man with 314 employees [applied these rules]. For years he had driven and criticized and condemned his employees without stint or discretion. Kindness, words of appreciation, and encouragement were alien to his lips. After studying the principles discussed in this book, this employer sharply altered his philosophy of life. . . . Three hundred and fourteen enemies have been turned into three hundred and fourteen friends. As he proudly said . . . "When I used to walk through my establishment, no one greeted me. My employees actually looked the other way when they saw me approaching. But now they are all my friends and even the janitor calls me by my first name."[14]

It is difficult to imagine an earlier, inner-directed employer being concerned with getting someone to call him by his first name. He might, to the contrary, have found the whole idea worse than an affront; it would have made things messy. We encounter a similar thing happening in Dickens's *A Christmas Carol*, but the effect is achieved through the power of Christmas. We are not as inclined to see the victory over the inner-directed person in *A Christmas Carol* in the same way we see the victory over the inner-directed person in a work like Carnegie's. Yet Scrooge, before his transformation into a "nice guy," was a man who drove himself as hard as he drove his employees. If he was grim toward them, he was equally, if not more, grim toward himself. We tend to react negatively toward the Scrooge-like character that makes up a greater portion of the inner-directed person. For this reason it is enigmatic that students seem to romanticize the inner-directed person—finding in that kind of individual a moral quality they believe is lacking in the other-directed person.

It is possible that the other-directed person, at least as that individual appears in Carnegie's writing, loses a great deal of individuality in the attempt to be delicately and sensitively responsive to the needs of others. Consider the implications, for example, of the following observation by Carnegie:

> I go fishing up in Maine every summer. Personally I am very fond of strawberries and cream, but I find that for some strange reason fish prefer worms. So when I go fishing, I don't think about what I want. I think about what they want. I don't bait the hook with strawberries and cream. Rather, I dangle a worm or a grasshopper in front of the fish and say: "Wouldn't you like to have that?"[15]

One sacrifices one's taste for "strawberries and cream" in order to gain access to the other person's preference for worms. Such a procedure, it seems, would strip both individuals of the vigor of their own characters and identities. Evidently, in this scheme of things, the extent to which this would greatly facilitate social exchanges would make it worth the cost.

It is instructive to note further, in Carnegie's bible for the other-directed person, that he often dehumanizes his subject by making use of figures of speech that reduce humans to animals. He does it in the above quotation by talking about dangling "worms" in front of "fish." He does it again in the following suggestion:

> Many of the sweetest memories of my childhood cluster around a little yellow-haired dog with a stub tail. "Tippy" never read a book on psychology. He didn't need to. . . . He had a perfect technique for making people like him. . . .
>   Do you want to make friends? Then take a tip from Tippy. Be friendly. Forget yourself. Think of others.[16]

Or consider the following: "That is why dogs make such a hit. They are so glad to see us that they almost jump out of their skins. So, naturally, we are glad to see them."[17]

Finally, we should consider one last quotation from Carnegie. Here we come to possibly the ultimate reduction of the worth of the individual. While reading this quotation keep in mind that the individual is being subordinated to the greater goal of making him or her socially viable. It is supremely ironic that this book, which in our estimation is perhaps the most deviously anti-individualistic work ever written, has been magnanimously endorsed by the more conservative business elements in American culture—a group that likes to believe it stands behind the cause of individualism. Carnegie says:

> We ought to be modest, for neither you nor I amount to much. Both of us will pass on and be completely forgotten a century from now. Life is too short to bore other people with talk of our petty accomplishments. Let's encourage them to talk instead. Come to think about it, you haven't much to brag about anyhow. Do you know what keeps you from becoming an idiot? Not much. Only a nickel's worth of iodine in your thyroid glands. If a physician were to open the thyroid gland in your neck and take out a little iodine, you would become an idiot. A little iodine that can be bought at a corner drugstore for five cents is all that stands between you and an institution for the mentally ill. A nickel's worth of iodine! That isn't much to be boasting about, is it?[18]

This is one of the most peculiar pieces of humanistic reasoning in Western literature. The individual is evaluated in terms of chemical makeup and its current price on the market. After being reduced to physical nature, one is then, not surprisingly, found to be worth nothing! In his eagerness to create a friendly, outgoing, socially sensitive, other-directed kind of person, Carnegie loses sight almost completely of the broader implications of his arguments and his imagery. What an astounding assertion! A human being is worth a nickel . . . one must be modest . . . one's accomplishments are petty . . . encourage the other person to talk . . . be responsive . . . avoid argument . . . watch what the other is doing so you will know how to match his or her performance . . . do not assert yourself.

In Carnegie's book we have a direct, if crude, delineation of the personal qualities of the other-directed person. Though Carnegie unwittingly makes the other-directed type of character look bad, it is not necessarily true that such a character is bad. The friendly, sociable, other-directed kind of person can be and is socially valuable. Carnegie was only gauche enough to make the social and individual costs of other-directed morality glaringly apparent. Riesman is aware of the problem. At the beginning of the revised version of *The Lonely Crowd,* he comments on the preferences of students for the inner-directed type. He goes on to point to the sensitivity and adaptiveness of the other-directed person—qualities that can be and are virtues. Each social type has virtues as well as vices.

The literature of the other-directed society achieves an extreme form in the works of Dale Carnegie. But the other-directed theme appears diffusely throughout a great variety of novels, stories, movies, and dramas. The gangster, for example, is mentioned by Riesman as a case in point. The gangster is a tragic hero despite, rather than because of, his violation of the rules of the law-abiding community. If he is successful, he isolates himself not only from society at large but from his own gang as well. Success forces him into a cul-de-sac where he must wait, alone and frightened, for the miserable finish to his career.[19]

Riesman's approach to individuals, society, history, human character, and action is thematic. Like a composer, he takes a simple but expressive theme and then proceeds to create a series of variations. Eventually we are overwhelmed by the potential contained within what, at first, seemed to be no more than a minor melody. This, incidentally, seems to be characteristic of many of the works on individuals and society that have gained great popularity in recent years.

Any number of examples come to mind. Arnold Toynbee's "challenge and response" theme was applied to the historical development of all of civilization. Pitirim Sorokin utilized the theme that cultures go through cycles of intense religious experience and then degenerate into "sensate" forms of experience, from which they return to the religious state. Ruth Benedict used a simple dichotomous theme of Dionysian and Apollonian ways of living to bring together a variety of behaviors. Freud took the elementary theme of conflict between human animal nature and the demands of society and worked it into one of the most fully orchestrated and developed variations on a theme in the literature of psychology. Marshall McCluhan hit upon a responsive theme with the simple idea that the medium of a message is of as much importance as the message itself. A similar theme, developed in a slightly different way, is Goffman's elementary observation that how one says something is as important as what one says. In each case, the simplicity of the theme is shocking. The theme often boils down to a cliché or bit of folk wisdom that everyone has known for centuries. After all, the men in Caesar's armies probably joked about the relationship between sexual deprivation and nervous conditions several thousand years before Freud came along. The difference, of course, between the soldiers' superficial grasp of a truth and that of a perceptive intellectual is in the capacity to see that truth in thousands of different settings and applications—recognizing those where it has a validity and those where it does not. In this respect, when someone says that psychology or, more often, sociology, is an elaboration of the obvious, they are many times quite correct. The point is, the process of elaboration is often worth the effort. Proper elaboration of the obvious can lead—and almost invariably does lead—to the not so obvious. If this is disputed, look to the humble origins of modern mathematics and physical science.

Riesman takes the rather simple theme, then, of three types of people: tradition-directed, inner-directed, and other-directed. This theme is applied to various settings, ranging from sexual behavior to the realm of political action, and, seemingly, it brings together what otherwise would remain greatly disparate areas of social behavior. But what is the final movement? Where do the variations lead? In music, despite pretensions to the contrary, it is not proper to ask such a question. A string quartet, after all, is a string quartet. It really is not supposed to lead us anywhere—it begins and ends with itself. However, people can and do ask more of the social scientist. It is not sufficient for science or the humanities to begin and end with themselves—though some scientists and humanists would insist that this is exactly what they should do. There is always some pressure to bring thought around to application—to orient science, whether physical or social, to some kind of utility. Does Riesman have utility? Or is his work like a symphony by Mahler, something that induces a mood, something that depends on the artistic or humanistic sensitivity of the person responding to his work?

❖ The Adjusted, the Anomic, and the Autonomous

In the final passages of *The Lonely Crowd*, Riesman provides his readers with what amounts to a set of program notes on how to interpret and respond to what he has had to say in the earlier segments of the work. The notes lean, interestingly enough, on another tripartite classification of people—the adjusted, the anomic, and the autonomous. The adjusted are those who conform to, and at the same time make their peace with, the demands of their culture—whether it is tradition-, inner-, or other-directed. The anomic are those who are, in some serious way, shattered or broken by the culture; they are those who cannot, for whatever reason, meet the demands of the culture; they are lost in their culture. The autonomous are those who neither become lost to the demands of the culture nor are broken by them. They live within the culture, but they retain a strong and assertive sense of self. It is the autonomous type, the most difficult and yet the most engaging of the three, that receives most of Riesman's attention.

The attainment of autonomy for the tradition-directed person is extremely difficult, if not impossible. Riesman tells the story of the Lebanese farmers who for centuries suffered from invasions by Arab horsemen; it never occurred to the farmers to become horsemen, and it never occurred to the horsemen to become farmers. Through the centuries they remained locked in a pattern which had an almost animalistic inevitability about it. Then Riesman makes his point:

> If Arabs could imagine becoming cultivators, and vice versa, it would not necessarily follow that the symbiotic ecology of the two main groups would change. These tradition-directed types might still go on doing what they realized they need not do. Nevertheless, once people become aware, with the rise of inner-direction, that they as individuals with a private destiny are not tied to any given ecological pattern, something radically new happens in personal and social history. Then people can envisage adapting themselves not only within the narrow confines of the animal kingdom but within the wide range of alternative possibilities illustrated—but no more than illustrated—by human experience to date. Perhaps this is the most important meaning of the ever renewed discovery of the oneness of mankind as a species: that all human experience becomes relevant.[20]

Relevant to what? Relevant to our own autonomy would be the reply. The practical consequence of social knowledge is that it provides the individual with the capacity to empathize with others and thereby gain two very broad but powerful extensions of choice. One can, for example, empathize to the point where one becomes the other in actuality. A person might gain sufficient understanding of the life of an executive to enable him or her to rise to that status—or decide not to take on that role. The second consequence of empathic knowledge is the extent to which it can promote manipulation. If one does not elect to become an executive on the basis of this knowledge, one may, nonetheless, find such knowledge helpful when it comes to managing those whose task it is to manage.

The fate of autonomy is different in inner- and other-directed societies. Riesman speculates that the attainment of autonomy—the maintenance of individuality in the midst of social control—is probably easier to achieve in an inner-directed society than in modern other-directed forms of society, though it is not easy to attain in any society. Society has a way of either inducing one to adjust to its demands or breaking one, leaving the person in an anomic condition in the process.

In the inner-directed society a person's place in the social order was relatively definite, and the boundaries of custom were sufficiently clear to enable the autonomous person to define the enemies, define the causes, assert the self as a unique force. It is no longer so simple. In an age of other-direction, individuals seeking autonomy are confronted not only with the problem of determining who is, in fact, the enemy to serve as the background for the portrayal of self; they are also confronted with the problem of their own motivations. There always exists the possibility, in an age of social and psychological enlightenment, that the other person is not really the enemy after all but only a projection of some despised element of one's self.

In an age of inner-direction, autonomous people could assert themselves against the tastes and insensitivities of the middle class. Today such an enemy is both difficult to find and, at the same time, too much on the defensive when discovered. In part, this is why the quest for autonomy within Bohemia is probably more deceptive today than in the past. Bohemian conduct is simply too matter-of-fact to allow us to view it as a manifestation of autonomy. There are exceptions, but for many others it may be a different matter. As Riesman expresses it, ''Young people today can find, in the wide variety of people and places of metropolitan life, a peer-group, conformity to which costs little in the way of search for principle.''[21]

The only road to autonomy, if this is a valued goal—and Riesman makes it apparent that it ought to be—is, paradoxically enough, through further self-consciousness. It is paradoxical because it has been self-consciousness that has made the acquisition of autonomy more difficult.

> This heightened self-consciousness, above all else, constitutes the insignia of the autonomous in an era dependent on other-direction. For, as the inner-directed man is more self-conscious than his tradition-directed predecessor and as the other-directed man is more self-conscious still, the autonomous man growing up under conditions that encourage self-consciousness can disentangle himself from the adjusted others only by a further move toward even greater self-consciousness. His autonomy depends not upon the ease with which he may deny or disguise his emotions but, on the contrary, upon the success of his effort to recognize and respect his own feelings, his own potentialities, his own limitations. This is . . . the problem of self-consciousness itself, an achievement of a higher order of abstraction.[22]

The consciousness of self, the ability to provide an identity for one's self in the midst of pressures to dissolve into the tastes and sensitivities (or insensitivities) of the other-directed society, is the only way, as Riesman sees it, one can achieve autonomy.

Riesman's contribution, in the final pages of this still powerful and relevant book, is not only to bring together in a meaningful way the many practices of society—probing them with the concepts of inner- and other-direction. More important, Riesman tries to retain a sense of social values and relate his thought to such values. He is not radical in the selection of new values. He is quite conservative when he chooses freedom and autonomy and the dignity of the individual as his primary values. But he is radical in his comprehension of what is involved in the quest for such values and in his analysis of the relationship between the individual and society and the bearing of that relationship on the development of individual worth.

Small wonder, then, that Riesman has proved popular among many humanists and social scientists. He has shown, perhaps better than any other writer living today, the promise that modern social science holds for deepening further our comprehension of age-old humanistic concerns.

Encounters with Social Thought

Some Comments on the Other-directed Universe of Academe

The fable that follows reflects David Riesman's deep concerns for the fate and the future of higher education and his message to American society about inner- and other-directedness. This story of academe begins in the early 1970s and takes place in the environs of a sociology department. As characteristic of most social science departments in those years, all the members of the department were, of course, males. Women at that time could be secretaries or graduate students, or wives or mistresses—but not fellow academics, especially in sociology departments. This, too, was a time in university faculty offices when no one dared to suggest that smoking—cigarettes, cigars or pipes—be curbed. No one even envisaged a nonsmoking classroom area, building, offices, or meeting rooms. This was an era before the ready access of personal computers, word processors or sophisticated statistical software programs. Hand counting or adding machines were employed by departmental secretaries or occasionally a struggling graduate student to meet the assigned tasks when measurements were required for reports or forms.

    This academic narrative commences. . . .

THE FISCHBEIN INDEX: AN ACADEMIC TALE

Hensley arrived, as he always did, about ten minutes early. By the time the others started coming into the room, he had finished one sandwich and was taking another out of its plastic baggie. The smell of bananas floated from the brown paper bag that sat, rumpled and spotted, next to his briefcase. He watched casually as the other men came into the room. It was Hensley's belief that the way a man walked into a room gave away secrets about his character. (At the same time, Hensley also considered himself to be above irrationality and superstition.)

    Hensley knew, for example, how Hartung would come in. He would be smiling and slightly stiff, as though somewhere in his background there was a metallic grandfather. Hartung was small and in his early fifties. He was impeccable in his manners and clothing. He was the only person Hensley had ever met who never seemed to commit any kind of *faux pas*. Hartung never stumbled when he came through the doorway. (Hensley was impressed by how often the more ineffectual members of the department revealed themselves with awkward movements.) Hartung was properly proper. He did not eat his lunch during the meetings and Hensley could not determine whether this was because Hartung was dieting or because he did not care to be seen carrying a little brown bag to work. It was certainly the latter. Hensley noticed that when Hartung pulled his chair back to sit down, there was never a scraping sound.

Morse came in behind Hartung. Morse was still not a full professor despite thirteen years of service to the department. Morse was beginning to affect a stoop. He was tall and ungainly. He had narrow shoulders and a ponderous, sagging stomach. When he came through the door he looked up, as if the ceiling might come down on him. He smiled at everybody, but no one, with the exception of Hensley, appeared to notice. He carried an oversized brown bag which he emptied on to the table. The room was taking on a strong odor of coffee, bananas, and cigarette smoke.

Six other members of the department came in. Hensley put his sandwich down. He was anticipating that Fischbein would be the last to come, if he came at all. Hensley was right. Fischbein was ten minutes late. Harley Gummer, the chairman, had already started the meeting.

It was an interstitial period for Hensley. So far, no one had brought up any issues that touched his personal interests. He used the time to review the strengths and weaknesses of his colleagues. Most complex and possibly threatening was the character of Fischbein. Fischbein had been hired the previous year. He was a good teacher. At least the students spoke well of him and there had been no complaints. Fischbein had written an article for one of the best journals in the field and it had just been published. Hensley still had a copy of it lying, unread, on his desk. Fischbein had been apologetic when he gave the reprint to Hensley. Hensley had not published anything for three years. His last writing effort was a mimeographed report on the use of audiovisual devices by members of the department.

Hensley could hear Hartung speaking. Hartung always enunciated clearly. Each word seemed to be given special attention. Hartung intoned:

"The promotion and tenure committee of the department still finds itself debating how we ought to go about the matter of evaluating the work of the members of this department. We have tried, of course, to take into account teaching and research. But you know the problem. We still cannot determine what weight to give to different activities. Should we, for example, give greater weight to research? To teaching? What about service to the community and the school? It is an old thing."

He flapped his hands ever so slightly and Hensley thought, for just a second, that Hartung might display a sign of frustration. Hartung looked around the room and went on.

"Even if we knew how to weigh these activities, we still have the problem of establishing what constitutes good research and good teaching. Should a man who does bad research be elevated above a man who does an excellent job in the classroom? Is a poor journal article—and there are enough of them around—somehow better than a superb classroom lecture?"

Hensley was certain that Hartung, underneath, was feeling slightly uncomfortable. On the surface, however, there was no betrayal of such feelings.

There was a pause. The air conditioner was making an aggravating noise. People slouched in their chairs. For the older members of the faculty the question was not only familiar, it was dull. It was not only dull, it was not especially relevant. The matter of promotions and tenure was necessarily complicated and subtle. It could not and should not be routinized. It was a many-splendored-thing. It was something that generated talk, worry, and a bit of hustling. Promotion and tenure should have an element of uncertainty about it. It made the university and the department more like the real world. Who wanted to make it tidy? At the same time, everyone knows that it was necessary to make noises that revealed a commitment to the demands of bureaucratic rationality.

These discussions were a ritualistic purging. They acknowledged the possibility of a pure and professional morality. At the same time, the discussions invariably went in the direction of granting a deeply regretted awareness of "realities." Somehow, the discussion always stopped at the point when it was forced to talk about reality. Hensley looked on it as some kind of minor paradoxical performance. The department met to tell itself that it had a profound understanding of what was "good" while, at the same time, it publicly confessed that the "good" could not be attained. At this point in the ritual there was usually a settling down and a great deal of rustling of paper bags and some sporadic coughing.

Hensley, during Hartung's comments, had been watching Fischbein. Fischbein had not appeared to be paying much attention. As Hartung finished, Hensley saw Fischbein raise his fist, in slow motion, and bring it toward his chin. Had the action been speeded, Fischbein would have slugged himself. No one else saw the gesture. Fischbein turned toward Hartung and began to speak. He was almost drowned out by the hum and rattle of the air conditioner. Hensley became attentive. Fischbein spoke:

> "We are all familiar with the problem and we all know, if we want to be honest about it, that nothing much can be done that has not already been done. Nothing. So, perhaps the thing to do is change the problem around a little. It cannot be solved in its present form. Maybe we can change it into a form where it can be solved. This is one of the most elementary canons of scientific procedure, gentlemen."

Hensley, without quite knowing why, was already beginning to feel irritated. Fischbein, with his low voice and carefully strung together sentences, had taken on an unctuous quality. Before continuing with his argument, Fischbein took out a small fingernail file and began working on the fingers of his left hand. Fischbein continued:

> "What *really* determines the 'worth' of a faculty member? He put quotation marks around 'worth' as he spoke it. For dramatic effect he repeated the question and Hensley squirmed. What *really* constitutes the 'worth' of a faculty member? How do we, in fact, respond to each other in terms of respect, deference, or a sense of professional value? I submit that we do it much like the member of any other community does it. We have a system of stratification and ranking that is our very *raison d'être*. It is a most arbitrary sort of thing, actually. How do we ascertain our standing in an arbitrary and uncertain prestige system? Again, let me suggest that we do it the way everyone else does. You have status if you are associated in some way or fashion with others who have it."

Hensley found himself listening. Fischbein was talking slowly and without effort. It was hard for Hensley to tell whether Fischbein was amusing himself or being serious. The pose with the fingernail file was close to insulting. At the same time, it appeared to work. Everybody was attentive. Fischbein continued.

"We defer to those who somehow have 'tapped' into the deference system. If, for example, we had a member of this department who was a close friend of the President of the United States but was, otherwise, just an ordinary and modestly competent professional, he would probably have an 'aura' that would sustain him for a while at a rather high level in the deference system. There is no hypocrisy in this. Such a man would have considerable potential value. We all recognize and understand this kind of thing. I would submit further that anyone who is going to be of value to an academic department must maintain, in some form or other, relationships with people whose potential value to the department is generally understood. That is, to some extent we have to be political. Right, huh?"

The simplicity of it was interesting in itself. Hensley knew that Fischbein was verging on the morbid and the threatening. However, he had sustained such a simple style of argument that it was difficult to interrupt. To the contrary, so far there was enough agreement and acceptance to produce a feeling of slight boredom and several members of the department were showing signs of distraction. Hensley stayed with it. He had the feeling this was just a preliminary warm up. Fischbein was leading toward something more interesting as he proceeded:

"I would wager, gentlemen, that the pay scale and other signs of status and worth in this department are directly related to the extent to which a faculty member is capable of demonstrating extensive relationships with people of status and prestige in the profession and, more broadly, maintaining relationships with people of status in the country—regardless of how that status was attained. All we have to do, if we want to routinize this business, is make use of some of the current devices that exist for measuring human relationships and getting some kind of ranking system for status. It should be simple enough. *All we need is a status index.* If indexes are good enough for science—and we do subscribe to scientific procedures, don't we?—they should be good enough for the department. We are all scientists. We should practice what we preach."

Fischbein was coming close to being nasty. Hensley was aware that every one of the members of the department spent much time telling students that society should be approached from the perspectives of science. Hensley was also cynical enough to think that there was probably no one in the department who seriously and personally cared about the implications of such a view. It seemed, to Hensley, that Fischbein was about to put the ideological commitments of the department to some kind of test.

The department believed in, almost worshipped, indexes. Seminars were taught in which the most elaborate varieties of indexes were developed and discussed. They were the foundations of methodology—and one should, above all else, be methodical. But, were there places where the methodology was not appropriate? Hensley had the feeling that Fischbein was putting on a little demonstration. If it failed, it would be revealing. If it succeeded, that would also be revealing. This was another of the "simple canons" of good scientific procedure. Fischbein went on.

"Yes, an index. A status index. If my earlier premise is correct—that we are of value to the extent we are able to maintain relations with others of value—then, it seems to me, we can get at this in a simple way. All we have to do is set up a measure of the extent to which each of us is associated with or is, somehow, close to people of prestige or value. To simplify the process, I suggest we limit ourselves to those who are considered to be of value within our particular discipline.''

The rustling of bags stopped. Hensley watched as Hartung began stuffing his pipe. Morse appeared to be engaged in the effort of establishing an appropriate expression for the occasion. Two of the younger faculty members were slouched low in their chairs. They were dogmatic in their understanding of the world. They were not perplexed by anything—or, at least, they gave that impression.

Hensley found them easy to deal with. If they liked the turn that Fischbein's argument was taking, they would say little or nothing. If they did not like it, then they would come on strong with a forceful denunciation that would be nested within a complex string of theoretical references and conclude with a vigorous claim that they were only working toward the end of making certain that the injustices of the world were not allowed to become greater. Fischbein was saying,

"My proposal is in keeping with the current methodological procedures acceptable to each of us in our studies of similar problems in other communities. All I am suggesting is that we approach the problem, as it appears within the department, with the same rationality we display when we come upon the problem in other areas. Sauce for the goose and that sort of thing. So, I believe the matter can be resolved with three or four easy steps. The final operation can be carried out by an untrained person after a brief period of instruction.

The first thing to do is identify people of prestige and high status within our field. This can be done simply enough. We can go through the directory of the National Association and compile a list of, let us say, the five hundred most influential and prestigious workers in our field. I would suspect that most fields do not have more than a few hundred. The nice thing about prestige is that it is so limited. This makes our task all the easier. In fact, various professional *Who's Who* listings take care of about 90 percent of the job.

After we have the list, each person in the department, each of us, will be asked to give some kind of ranking to these people. We should be able to come up with a rough ranking. We could give any person on the list a number from, perhaps, one to five. Or, we could divide the five hundred into the top hundred, the second hundred, etc. The bottom hundred would be given a value of one, the next a value of two and so on until the people in the top hundred would have a value of five.

After this has been done, we are ready to establish the worth of the members of this department. We could assign the secretaries of the department the task of making a note, each day, of the source from which a faculty member receives mail. If I were to receive a letter from, let us say, Robert M. . . , recognized by all of us as the dean of American intellectual effort in our field, then I would get five points.

You can see the general nature of what I am getting at. All the secretaries would have to do is keep score and, at the end of the year, we could add up the points and we would have a well delineated and measurably established statement of worth. It would be quantitative and it would be realistic.''

The room was quiet. The air conditioner cut off just as Fischbein closed his speech. One of the members of the department snorted and folded his lunch bag and tossed it across the table toward the wastebasket. He missed. Hartung laughed in a way that Hensley decided revealed both irritation and amusement. Enough time had been wasted. There were serious matters to be attended to. Hartung leaned toward Fischbein. "I have heard that your students think you are funny, Fischbein. Now I think I know why. There is no way such an index would work. It would be exploited immediately. . . . "

Fischbein interrupted with more seriousness in his voice than the others had expected. He said:

"The question is not whether it would or would not be exploited. The existing procedures are also exploited. That is why we are having this discussion. The question is whether it would be exploited as readily as we exploit the existing system. A person who writes one banal paper and it is published in four or five slightly modified forms—claiming, then, to have several publications where he actually only has one—has engaged in exploitation of the prevailing system. I sincerely doubt that a status index could be exploited as easily."

Hartung put down his pipe. Fischbein had not done the right thing. He was supposed to have resigned from further support of his ridiculous proposal and he was not doing it. Hensley knew that Hartung had little alternative. He could cut Fischbein off, which he did not want to do just yet; or, he could continue to argue against what had to be a bad joke. Hartung was pinned. The only thing, then, was to come up with a counter of some kind and hope that it would suffice to shut up Fischbein and provide a space during which the affairs of the department could be shunted around to something more significant.

Hartung scratched his nose with a slow gesture which, to Hensley, gave subliminal indications of contempt. He said:

"Fischbein, be reasonable. We can't engage in a snooping examination of each person's mail. It would be a gross invasion of privacy. Surely you aren't recommending such an absurd thing. If we don't examine their mail, how can we tell what sort of value to place on a letter that a man receives? It might be perfectly innocuous or even negative. What, for example, would prevent any one of us from constructing some kind of 'survey' of the leaders that would result in a response from all five hundred of the people in the list. This would balloon things out of all proportion."

Fischbein put down his fingernail file and pulled his chair closer to the table. He spoke slowly:

"Well, at least it would be something. Such a survey, if it brought about a response from the leaders of our field, would be good in and of itself. I doubt, however, that anyone here would attempt such a thing. It would be too obvious and, unless it were done well, would probably backfire on the person who tried it. Done well, it could enhance a person's status and worth and, ultimately, the prestige of the department. I would be in favor of it.

However, if this still seems to be a violation of the spirit of measuring a faculty member's value to the department, it could be handled by a simple sampling procedure. That is to say, certain weeks of the semester could be randomly set aside as periods during which the status value of the mail received by the faculty would be measured. So, returns coming in from a survey could be bypassed. It certainly would make such an effort to gain status a more risky matter."

Hartung had allowed his jaw to drop ever so slightly. He pointed his pipe stem toward the ceiling. "This is really getting to be absurd. Do you intend to go on with this farcical proposition?" Fischbein smiled and said:

"You started it. Is this any more farcical than any of a number of other procedures we have used? It is grounded on a solid premise, that is to say, a man's worth is determined by the extent to which he is able to associate with and relate to those people who have established in some tangible manner their own worth. No one has challenged that premise as yet. If we accept it, then all we have to do is measure such associations. A simple approach is to evaluate the extent of communications that take place between any individual and others who are generally accepted as worthy. The most available communication system we have at hand is correspondence. This can be counted. You all believe in counting. So, the problem is solved with simplicity and reason.

I most seriously set this proposition before the department as a matter on which a decision should be reached. I would like to say this, however, before putting the question to a vote. If we are not to be a bunch of hypocrites, we should take indexes as seriously for ourselves as we take them for others. Would this procedure suffer from any greater weaknesses than the system we now think we use—if we use any system at all? If it is rationally superior, and that can be established only by careful argument and by demonstration, we have no choice. We will have to try it."

Hensley was watching Hartung. Hartung was choking without giving any visible sign of it. Hartung spoke, "I . . . can't believe . . . that . . . you are serious." Fischbein responded:

"What do I have to do to convince you? Why not give the issue over to a committee? The department can then wait for the committee's report. I believe, in any event, that the matter should be discussed further and not simply dismissed in some casual way."

That meeting took place in 1973. It has been nearly a decade since the department, to its surprise, found itself saddled with the Fischbein Index. The committee wrestled with the issue for six months before coming back with a number of modifications and refinements that led to accepting the index.

In 1973, the department was an out-of-the-way academic outpost. It bothered no one and it certainly was not bothered by anyone. The Fischbein Index changed that. We are now the fifth most powerful department in the country and there is every reason to believe the department will come to dominate the field within the next ten years. Two of our faculty have international reputations and there is not a single person within the department who lacks at least some national recognition.

Fischbein received an offer from a larger school and left two years after we voted in the index. Hartung hit upon the device of writing a series of volumes on the lives of the twelve most eminent writers in the field. It led to Hartung carrying on a constant and eventually quite lively correspondence with some extremely well-known people. He became one of the most sought out people at regional and national meetings. He was constantly traveling about the country. The publication of his rather small book was hailed as a landmark in reviews that appeared in the best of journals.

Morse was never able to handle the situation. He never received communications from anyone. This, along with his inability to demonstrate any other signs of value to the department led to his eventual isolation. He left the department about five years after Fischbein left.

Young people coming into the department were informed about the index. It led to the better ones carefully retaining the connections they had established in graduate school. We now have a stable of young assistant professors who are probably better known and more powerful as a group than any other such collection in the country. They will be the ones who, in the next decade, will come to be the true leaders of the discipline.

I found myself drawn into the index and handled the problem by working my way into the more important committees of the National Association and by getting an editorship in one of the professional journals. I usually do not come up to Hartung's quite high ratings at the end of the year, but I am invariably a comfortable seventh or eighth. People have come to respect the name of Hensley.

Ironically, the success of the index has created a problem. Two of the twenty most prestigious members of the discipline are now in this department. Our correspondence with each other is beginning to distort the Fischbein Index. We shall have to discuss the problem at our next departmental meeting. . . .

As David Riesman reminds us in his aptly titled book, *Abundance for What?*, "typologies (and indexes) are scaffoldings, good for a single building only, and need to be scrapped when the movements of history and of thought present us with different problems and different ways of perceiving problems."

Putting Social Thought to Work

1. Whether we are trying to understand physical nature or the social systems of human beings we run into a common problem. Nature and society manifest themselves in numerous and complex ways. If we are to have any kind of understanding, we must select from the complex reality before us features that appear to be especially significant and that manifest themselves within the greater complexity. Any society is nearly infinitely complex in the variety of possibilities it offers for interpretation. How do we go about selecting what we are going to focus on as key features of the society? This is no small issue. Many of our modern social controversies derive from precisely this problem. Should we concentrate on the activities of the wealthy? the intellectuals? the

workers? the young? the old? Where do we turn to bring together the myriad goings-on of human communal life? What are the implications of selecting any particular theme over any other?

2. David Riesman attempted to account for major historical changes in American character by the concepts of inner-directed and other-directed people. Is other-directedness a reasonable interpretation of modern character and institutions?

3. What are some other ways in which one might explain changes that have taken place in the institutions of American society? For example, would it be more correct to argue that America has gone from an agricultural-rural society to a technological-urban one?

4. Riesman's well-known book, *The Lonely Crowd*, caused a considerable stir when it was published in 1961. What does the great public interest in works such as this indicate about society?

5. Readers of Riesman often find themselves sympathizing with the older, inner-directed type as characterizing a person of strength and fortitude. The other-directed type is less attractive, appearing to be a weaker character. How do you account for this—presuming that it is true? Is the inner-directed type essentially "masculine" and is the other-directed type "feminine"?

6. Do Riesman's concepts offer some clues for further understanding and interpretation of the feminist movement in America today?

7. At one point Riesman notes that the individual has a worth in traditional societies that he does not necessarily have in modern societies. That is, concepts such as surplus labor (surplus people) are not as prominent in primitive societies. This suggests a change in the value assigned to the individual in modern societies. We claim to value the individual while, at the same time, calling large numbers of individuals "surplus." What is the American attitude toward the individual? How do you think such attitudes developed? Are we as interested in the welfare of the individual as we claim to be? In what ways can an individualistic social morality work against the individual?

Endnotes

1. Riesman's major works are *Faces in the Crowd: Individual Studies in Character and Politics*, in collaboration with Nathan Glazer (New Haven, CT: Yale University Press, 1952); *Individualism Reconsidered* (New York: Free Press, 1954); *Constraint and Variety in American Education* (Lincoln, NE: University of Nebraska Press, 1958); *Thorstein Veblen: A Critical Interpretation* (New York: Scribner, 1960); *The Lonely Crowd: A Study in the Changing American Character*, with Nathan Glazer and Reuel Denney, abr. ed. with new foreword (New Haven, CT: Yale University Press, 1961); *Abundance for What?* (Garden City, NY: Doubleday, 1964, and reissued in 1993 by Transaction Books); *The Academic Revolution*, with Christopher Jencks (Garden City, N.Y.: Doubleday, 1968); *The Perpetual Dream: Reform and*

Experiment in American Colleges, with Gerald Grant (Chicago: University of Chicago Press, 1976), and *Choosing a College President: Opportunities and Constraints*, with Judith B. McLaughlin (Princeton, NJ: Princeton University Press, 1990).

2. Riesman, *The Lonely Crowd*, p. xxix. Reaction to Riesman's work was so enthusiastically favorable that it led to the distinction of a cover story in *Time* magazine (September 27, 1954).
3. Norbert Wiener, *God and Golem, Inc.* (Cambridge, MA: MIT Press, 1964), pp. 60, 85.
4. Riesman, *The Lonely Crowd*, pp. 11–12.
5. Ibid., p, 14.
6. Ayn Rand, *The Fountainhead* (Indianapolis, IN: Bobbs-Merrill, 1968).
7. Riesman, *The Lonely Crowd*, pp. 21–22.
8. John Kenneth Galbraith, *The Affluent Society* [New York: New American Library, Mentor Books, 1958], p. 63. Originally published by Houghton Mifflin (Boston, 1958).
9. We are indebted to Professor Omer C. Stewart of the University of Colorado for this illustration.
10. Riesman, *The Lonely Crowd*, p. 56.
11. Few accounts more dramatically reveal how education practices have changed than reading Orwell's description of his experiences as a boy in attendance at Crossgates. See George Orwell, "Such, Such Were the Joys," in *A Collection of Essays by George Orwell* (Garden City, NY: Doubleday Anchor Books, 1954), pp. 9–55. The quotation cited here appears on pages 43–44.
12. Riesman, *The Lonely Crowd*, p. 63.
13. Riesman, *The Lonely Crowd*, pp. 149–150.
14. Dale Carnegie, *How to Win Friends and Influence People* (New York: Simon and Schuster, 1937), p. 22. This book, published in 1937, is still selling. Few books provide a more blunt and open insight into the American ideal.
15. Carnegie, *How to Win Friends and Influence People*, p. 56.
16. Ibid., p. 83.
17. Ibid., p. 97.
18. Ibid., p. 205.
19. Riesman, *The Lonely Crowd*, p. 155. Riesman refers here to Robert Warshow's article, "The Gangster as Tragic Hero," which appeared in *The Partisan Review* XV (February 1948), 240–244.
20. Riesman, *The Lonely Crowd*, p. 246.
21. Ibid., p. 258.
22. Ibid., p. 259.

Chapter 11

The Unanticipated Consequences of Human Actions

The Functional Analysis of Robert K. Merton

❖

❖ Introduction

American sociology, up to the time of World War II, engaged in an indirect idealization of the American family farm and the small, semirural American community. For American sociologists of that era, the problem confronting humankind was largely how to regain a rural paradise lost. Sociological studies took the form of elaborate comparisons between rural and urban modes of living. The rural mode somehow usually appeared as the better way of life.

This naive and pastorally romantic sociology gave way before more analytic forms of social theory and research which sought to identify and then relate the most fundamental, and therefore the most abstract, conditions of society. This approach to sociology is not especially concerned with such specific social problems as rural-urban contrasts in divorce rates or crime. It turns, instead, to a consideration of what is meant by a social system. What are the properties of any and all human social systems? How are the elements within a human community interrelated to form a structure? How do the parts, and the manner of their relationship, bear upon the performance of the entire system? What are the functions and dysfunctions of the different parts? What are the consequences of a given structure for the people who move within it?

❖ *The Structural and Functional Approach*

Sociologists taking this approach to the study of human social organization call themselves "structural and functional" sociologists. By the end of World War II, structural and functional analysis was extremely active. In 1949, the publication of *Social Theory and Social Structure* placed Robert K. Merton at the forefront of those who advocated structural and functional approaches to the study of society.[1]

There is an important caveat to enter here before going on. The structural and functional analyst presents the appearance of being a scientist analytically examining the parts of society in much the same manner as a biologist examines the functioning of the organs of a dog or monkey. Merton even relies on such examples to help define what he means by function. However, unlike biologists, sociologists *never* have an opportunity to observe the whole of society. They work, instead, with the idea or concept of a society.

The term "function" refers to the extent to which a particular part or process of a social system contributes to the maintenance of that system or to some designated section of that system. It is necessary, if we are going to gain a clearer conception of Merton's use of this term, to note that "function" does not mean the same thing as "purpose" or "motivation." It means, instead, the extent to which a given activity does in fact promote or, in the case of a dysfunction, interfere with the maintenance of a system. As Merton puts it, "Social function, refers to observable objective consequences, and not to subjective dispositions (aims, motives, purposes)."[2]

This distinction is subtle, and it calls for clarification through an illustration. It is one thing, for example, to speculate on the aims, motivations, and purposes underlying advertising in modern America, and another to see it from a functional perspective. If we ask an advertising person to tell us the aims or purposes of the profession, he or she might mention several things. Advertising seeks to make Americans aware of the wealth of goods and services American industry has the capacity to provide. Advertisers are motivated to sell their clients' products. Advertising seeks to upgrade the consumer tastes of people. Advertising keeps alive the American dream of happiness through possessions. The list can be extended.

A functional analysis promotes a different way of looking at advertising. What does advertising in fact do? Furthermore, what are the unintended consequences of what it does for the greater society? Compare the following functional evaluation of advertising with the motivational evaluation given above.

It is well known that one thing advertising does is to pretend to make significant differences out of what are known to be virtually identical products. It has been factually established, for example, that the typical consumer cannot tell one brand of cigarettes from another when blindfolded. Typical beer drinkers cannot distinguish between one brand and another. By creating differences where none in fact exist, advertising serves the function of enabling a variety of cigarette manufacturers, brewers, and other companies to survive where there is no utilitarian basis for their survival. Thus, a functional analyst would claim that one of the functions of advertising is to maintain a form of industrial and commercial pluralism.

❖ *Manifest Functions and Latent Functions*

Merton makes a distinction between two forms of social function. One of these he refers to as "manifest function" and the other as "latent function." *Manifest functions* are objective consequences (for an individual, group, or social or cultural system) that contribute to its adjustment *and were so intended*. *Latent functions* are consequences that contribute to adjustment but *were not so intended*.

The manifest-latent distinction is a valuable one; it makes clear the nature of sociological investigation as perhaps few other distinctions do. Manifest functions are essentially "official" explanations of a given action. Latent functions are the unrecognized or "hidden" functions of an action. Socially patterned motives and purposes are essential concepts for understanding the interaction between social structures and individual behavior.

An example of latent function used by Merton is the Hopi Indian rain ceremony. The manifest function—the intended use of the ceremony—is to bring rain. At the same time, it is obvious that these ceremonies do not bring rain. Even the Hopi, over the long generations, must have observed that there was little connection between annual levels of rainfall and the conduct of the rain ceremonies.

Yet the ceremonies persist. The Hopi have retained the ceremony regardless of its bearing on actual rainfall levels. The reason, Merton informs us, is that the ceremony performs other functions for Hopi society than merely bringing rain. To examine only the manifest functions of a ceremony, a tradition, a social group, or a particular role, is to examine it at a superficial level. The beginnings of sociological understanding are found in a consideration of the latent functions. Referring to the Hopi rain ceremonies, Merton goes on to say,

> With the concept of latent function, we continue our inquiry, examining the consequences of the ceremony not for the rain gods or for meteorological

phenomena, but for the groups which conduct the ceremony. And here it may be found, as many observers indicate, that the ceremonial does indeed have functions—but functions which are non-purposed or latent.

Ceremonials may fulfill the latent function of reinforcing the group identity by providing a periodic occasion on which the scattered members of a group assemble to engage in a common activity. . . . Such ceremonials are a means by which collective expression is afforded the sentiments which . . . are found to be a basic source of group unity. Through the systematic application of the concept of latent function, therefore, *apparently* irrational behavior may *at times* be found to be positively functional for the group.[3]

When a latent function is important, though the manifest function is not being met, there is a tendency to rationalize social action. Thus, when a rain ceremony does not produce rain, it is not considered the fault of the ceremony. Instead, the fault is likely to be found in the incompetent performance of one of the participants. In this manner, it is possible to show a perfect relationship between the ritual and its intended effect.

It becomes apparent, with further thought, that the concept of latent function has the qualities of an after-the-fact rationalization or excuse for the world as it is. The functional analyst appears to be saying, "Well, if something exists in the social order, there must be a good reason for it—otherwise it would not exist. Therefore, let us think long and hard on the matter, and sooner or later the reason for its existence will come to us."

Are latent functions an apology for the status quo? We have found ourselves running into much the same problem in connection with Durkheim's discussion of crime (see Chapter 2). After all, when Durkheim said that crime is necessary to any society, he provided crime with a latent function. With the example of the Hopi, the structural and functional sociologist is explaining the persistence of superstitious rain dances as functional features of the social order. Merton, aware of this disturbing feature of structural and functional thought, has tried to get around it by introducing yet another idea—the idea of dysfunctions.

❖ *The Dysfunctional Process*

Dysfunctional events lessen the effective equilibrium of a social system. Dysfunctional aspects of a society imply strain or stress or tension. A society tries to constrain dysfunctional elements somewhat as an organism might constrain a bacterial or viral infection. If the dysfunctional forces are too great, the social order is overwhelmed, disorganized, and possibly destroyed.[4]

One of the clearest examples we know of a dysfunctional feature in a social system was the Catharist heresy in Europe in the twelfth century. The Cathars were of the opinion that affairs of the flesh were damning to the spirit. As a consequence, they concluded that the ideal relationship between a man and a woman is one of brother and sister. They advocated brother-sister relationships in marriage. So extreme were their views that they would eat no food that they considered the product of a sexual union. They would not, therefore, eat eggs, milk, meat, or cheese.

They married, but, ideally, they did not consummate their marriages sexually. Feudal leaders in provinces where such heretical views existed recognized fully the implications of this point of view: It meant, if followed through, an attrition of population. Had the Cathars been completely successful, the consequence would have been the loss, in a generation or two, of the total society—perhaps a painless loss, but a certain one. Despite their peaceful and gentle nature, the Cathars were too threatening. They were destroyed. Their elimination from society was unusually thorough. The only evidence we have of their existence is of an indirect nature, consisting for the most part of allusions to the Cathars in church records.

The next example, illustrating the possible dysfunctional use of prisoners as slaves in ancient Rome, is an engaging one.

> Lead poisoning, according to Dr. Gilfillan, killed off most of the Roman ruling class and damaged the brains of Commodus, Nero, and all those other mad emperors. Such poisoning became common, he points out, about 150 B.C., after the wealthy Romans began to use Greek prisoners of war as their household servants. These slaves brought with them the Greek custom of using lead-lined pots for cooking, especially for warming wine and for concentrating honey and grape syrup, the sweeteners most popular at that time. . . . Writing in the *Journal of Occupational Medicine*, Dr. Gilfillan notes that fashionable Roman matrons began to drink wine at about the same time they acquired Greek cooks; and that they soon began to show the classic symptoms of lead poisoning—sterility, miscarriages, and heavy child mortality. Their surviving children often suffered permanent mental impairment. As a consequence, he estimates, the aristocracy lost about three-quarters of its members in each generation.

Gilfillan goes on to report that meanwhile the common people were spared—because they cooked in earthenware pots, and couldn't afford to drink much wine. Moreover, they did not use the lead water pipes and lead-based cosmetics which the wealthier classes enjoyed. The result, Dr. Gilfillan argues, was a systematic extinction of the ablest people in the Roman world.[5]

Let us suggest one more illustration of a dysfunctional process that has evolved over the past forty years with the desegregation and integration of American public schools. Political and educational leaders believed that the desegregation of elementary and secondary schools would lead to equal opportunities in education for all children. They fought for and conscientiously worked to pass laws to achieve educational equity. When laws were passed mandating the integration of public schools, these leaders conceived of busing black students from segregated schools within a school district to integrate them with the white children in that district. Yet, what has arisen in the decades since the Supreme Court decision in the *Brown* versus *Topeka Board of Education* case in 1954? Busing children to desegregate schools has triggered "white flight" from the major city school districts to the suburbs, creating a resegregation of schools into even more viciously segregated inner-city school districts of mainly poor children of color and outer-area metropolitan schools districts of mainly white, more affluent students. (See Jonathan Kozol's documentary and prize-winning volume, *Savage Inequalities: Children In America's Schools*, New York: Crown Publishers, 1991.) These deleterious conditions demonstrate quite clearly how the dysfunctional process occurs over time. Further busing for integration of students in the American public schools and the resultant white flight from urban areas becomes a classic example of another of Robert K. Merton's contributions to social thought—that of the unintended, or as Merton labels the phenomenon, *unanticipated consequences of social actions*. Later in this chapter we will return to this concept; but first we want to press on to elucidate the uses of the structural and functional analysis.

❖ *Values of Functional Analysis*

The point of these illustrations of the dysfunctional process is that functional analysis orients thought toward the social consequences—intended and unintended—of a particular action. Merton maintains that functional analysis has the following virtues.

First of all, it inhibits the tendency to dismiss a seemingly irrational social event with the casual observation that it is merely superstition, foolishness, or craziness. For example, instead of ignoring astrology as nonsense or idiocy, functional analysts would be inclined to ask what it does. Why does it exist? What function does it serve? Why is astrology, or something similar, a part of virtually all known human communities? How does astrology relate to the other elements in the system?

Second, the concepts of manifest and latent function provide sociologists with a means of probing into features of social action that are more theoretically valuable. The sociologist can, for example, study the effects of a federal government bond campaign to determine its effectiveness. At the manifest level, we consider its purpose as that of stirring up patriotic fervor to get people to invest their money in public projects or, in times of major wars, to help finance the warfare. Such an investigation is of primary value to administrators and others interested in producing an effective propaganda campaign. The latent consequences of the campaign carries us further into the matter. In the 1940s Merton investigated the appeals used by the singer Kate Smith during a war bond campaign during World War II. One of the latent consequences of the campaign was to stifle expressions of objections about official policy.

Third, a functional approach to social action has ethical and moral implications. Essentially, such an approach brings a more sophisticated awareness to the moral issues involved in a particular situation. Merton puts it this way:

> The introduction of the concept of latent function in social research leads to conclusions which show that "social life is not as simple as it first seems." For

as long as people confine themselves to *certain* consequences (e.g., manifest consequences), it is comparatively simple for them to pass moral judgments upon the practice or belief in question. Moral evaluations, generally based on these manifest consequences, tend to be polarized in terms of black or white. But the perception of further (latent) consequences often complicates the picture.[6]

Thus, to return to an earlier illustration, the desegregation and integration of schoolchildren is an obvious moral good at the manifest level. However, at the latent level, we see how over time the movement for school desegregation has caused severe societal problems and inequities, possibly exacerbating the very inequalities the original measures were intended to ameliorate.

A fourth value of structural and functional analysis, somewhat similar in nature to the last-mentioned value, is that it replaces naive moral judgment with sociological analysis. Merton illustrates his meaning, in this instance, with a reference to political "machines." Traditionally, the political machine in America has been viewed simply as an evil. It is a source of graft, it is corrupt, and it is a perversion of democratic processes. The political boss buys votes instead of earning them through public service. The political machine protects criminal elements rather than exorcising them. The machine gives public jobs and offices to loyal members of the organization, rather than to the people best fitted to the task. So the criticisms continue. A functional analyst, however, argues that their existence over relatively long periods of time suggests that political machines serve social ends abdicated by other, morally approved organizations. Merton says:

> Examined for a moment apart from any moral considerations, the political apparatus operated by the Boss is effectively designed to perform [various] functions with a minimum of inefficiency. Holding the strings of diverse governmental divisions, bureaus and agencies in his competent hands, the Boss rationalizes the relations between public and private business. He serves as the business community's ambassador in the otherwise alien (and sometimes unfriendly) realm of government. And, in strict business-like terms, he is well paid for his economic services to his respectable business clients.[7]

This statement should not be read as an apologia for bossism and the political machine system of municipal or local government. Merton continues:

> To adapt a functional outlook is to provide not an apology for the political machine but a more solid basis for modifying or eliminating the machine, *providing* specific structural arrangements are introduced either for eliminating [certain] demands of the business community or, if that is the objective, of satisfying these demands through alternative means.[8]

If we wish, then, to operate either as relatively detached social analysts or as social and political activists, a structural and functional point of view is necessary. It inhibits a tendency toward naive moralizing about social issues, and it places any given social action within the greater context of the total social structure.

❖ *The Nature of Deviant Actions*

Among the contributions to social thought by Merton, perhaps the best known and most generally applied has been his consideration of the nature of deviant actions. Rather than view such actions as the product of abnormal personalities, Merton is concerned with the extent to which it might, at least in considerable part, be a result of the structural nature of society itself.

It might seem that Merton's theoretical position, first introduced in the 1930s, was obvious and one that had become a labored cliché. However, Merton is concerned with more than merely stating a truism on the order of statements that delinquents or social derelicts are the sorry products of the society that spawned them. He is, instead, interested in specifying the *process* whereby deviant action is generated within a social structure.

Deviant actions present a critical problem to those who accept a socio-logical perspective. The problem is this: On the one hand, the sociologist is aware that society and culture have an almost crushing capacity to induce conformity on the part of the individual. On the other hand, innovation and deviation do exist. The directives of the culture can be challenged or modi-fied. How can deviation occur within a system that has so much power to prevent it? Merton deals with this problem in the following manner, using American culture as the basis for his observations.

To begin with, he has developed the reasonable argument that American culture places great emphasis on the value of individual attainment of suc-cess. At the same time, and this is quite significant, there is relatively less emphasis on the means of achieving success. Institutional means for attaining success—the legitimate pathways to money, fame, or power—are not given any special emphasis or consideration. However, Merton points out that in order for deviant behavior to remain a useful concept rather than merely a moralizing phrase, we must distinguish two major kinds. The first can be called "nonconforming behavior" and the second labeled "aberrant behav-ior." Both types are forms of deviant actions that differ systematically in their makeup and in their social consequences. He clarifies:

> Nonconformers announce their dissent publically: they challenge the legitimacy of the rejected norms and aim to change them, lay claim to legitimacy by drawing upon the society's ultimate values rather than its particular rules and, sometimes breaking the rules of institutional process (as in cases of dedicated civil disobe-dience) seek to change the social structure to provide actual equality of oppor-tunity rather than allow its mere appearance to be mistaken for the real thing. A frequent response to principled deviant behavior of this sort has less critical, conforming members of society sometimes acknowledging, however reluctantly, that such rule-breaking represents moral behavior of a high order. In contrast, aberrants try to hide their violations of social norms even if they regard the norms they violate as legitimate. Rather than working to institute new norms and laying claim to legitimacy of their behavior, they seek only to escape the sanctions that go with violating norms. As a result, their rule-breaking is socially defined simply as an effort to satisfy their personal interests in normatively unacceptable ways.[9]

Merton is concerned with the problem of how people adapt to society and the ways in which the structural features of society affect the form such adaptations take. His approach to this problem strips social structure down to two elemental conditions that hold for any society. He does this by making a distinction between societally established goals and societal means provided for achieving those goals.

Before continuing, we should notice that on the surface, the distinction between goals and means seems simple and clear; in practice, it is not. Let us take a concern that is constantly central to student life as an example, that is: "What is my grade in this course?" Grades may be viewed simultaneously as a means and an end for the college student. At one level, they are a means of getting through school and getting into a profession. At the same time, they may be a goal for which the student must struggle.

This demurrer is important. However, a goals-means approach to social affairs is common. If we accept the distinction between goals and means, then Merton's scheme provides a new way of looking at things. How a person will respond to goals and means depends on how *the society* sustains them. If, for example, a community strongly encourages the attainment of certain goals while, at the same time, it provides little guidance with respect to the means for obtaining those goals, then deviant actions become more frequent. If means are emphasized over goal attainment, then people act differently—becoming ritualistic in their concerns. Merton has developed a typology to summarize the five forms of adaptation that are possible (see Table 11-1).[10]

The nature of these alternative modes of adaptation can be illustrated by a brief examination of goals and means in institutions of learning. One of the legitimately supported goals of educational systems is the grade-point average. To simplify things, we shall look on grades as a socially sustained goal and ignore the fact that they are also a means to broader goals. The institutionalized means for achieving grades are study, hard work, and taking tests and examinations.

At institutions where goals and means are strongly supported by the system, the common response of students is in the conformistic mode. An example, perhaps, might be the way in which goals and means are regulated in military academies. The institution itself emphasizes grades and also pays

Table 11-1   Modes of Individual Adaptation

Modes of Cultural Adaptation	Institutionalized	
	Goals	Means
I. Conformity	+	+
II. Innovation	+	−
III. Ritualism	−	+
IV. Retreatism	−	−
V. Rebellion	±	±

close attention to the fairness of the competitive process. Deviation from institutionally prescribed forms of conduct leads to severe penalties or dismissal from the academy.

In circumstances where grades are strongly emphasized and means are not as carefully regulated, innovation is more likely to occur. A possible example of this is the situation in which modern college athletes find themselves. They must make grades, and, at the same time, there are pressures to protect them from academic dismissal. A variety of innovative devices assuring the college athlete relatively safe passage through the system have been devised as a consequence. (This is a sociological stance, insofar as it suggests that corruption of the individual is a matter of corruption of the community.)

The ritualistic mode of adaptation is better seen by looking not at grades, but at learning itself. Schools are constantly criticized for emphasizing how learning takes place (the means) over *what* is to be learned (the goal). In this circumstance, what counts is that people show up for class, sit still during class presentations, make no disturbances, turn assignments in on time, and otherwise remain attentive to the proper means of conduct, while learning itself is not emphasized. A school principal in Chicago was recently rebuked severely by parents for failing a third of an entire grade school because the students could not read. The parents forced the principal to reinstate the students. This is school as ritual.

The professor who reads from yellowed notes the obsolescent ideas of another era is a ritualist. The students who come to class and then write letters during class time are ritualists. The school administrator who demands signatures on loyalty oaths—regardless of more concrete manifestations of loyalty—is a ritualist. In all these instances, we have people placing emphasis on the means of attaining an end, to the detriment of attaining the goal itself.

It is difficult to exemplify a case in which both educational goals and means are given little or no support. Usually, this occurs in other institutional complexes associated with education. For example, the spoof film *Animal House* portrays a fraternity in which grades and the means for attaining grades are a matter of scorn and contempt. The important point to grasp in this is that it is the group or community within which the pattern of emphasis on goals and means is established. Where both goals and means are rejected, the consequent pattern of action on the part of members of the community is a retreatist pattern.

A situation where there is a mixed response, with the community being ambivalent about education (either the means or the goals), might be that of inner-city schools and members of the poor families of the community itself. There is, on the one hand, a recognition of the value of education, and, on the other, an awareness that education is not immediately relevant to the problems confronting an inner-city dweller. In such community contexts, people take an adaptive pattern characterized, according to Merton, by rebelliousness. They want education, but they want to change the goals of education and the means whereby it is attained. There is a great deal of argument over the "relevance" of education.

By making these distinctions, Merton has attempted to establish more than a simple typology of different forms of individual action. His primary emphasis is directed toward locating conditions within the *community* that increase the likelihood of conformism, innovation, retreatism, or ritualism. For example, Merton is not concerned with the psychological characteristics of cheaters (an innovative approach to grades). Instead, Merton asserts that in communities where social goals are highly valued and the means for obtaining the goals are not as highly valued, the likelihood of innovation is increased.

Criminal conduct, another form of innovative action, is likely in a society that places great emphasis on individual success, wealth, and power, and that at the same time does not emphasize the value of the legitimate means for obtaining these goals. Merton points out that such a situation exists in the United States.

It is necessary, if we are to grasp the significance of Merton's conceptions, to recognize the extent to which he gives culturally established, collectively held value priorities a place in the interpretation of individual conduct. A culture that, for example, values cleverness over the dignity of work will be likely to find itself peopled with clever loafers. The source of the condition is, however, within the manner in which the culture establishes the balance between means and goals—not in the individual.

❖ *The Sociology of Science*

One of Merton's strong interests is a consideration of the sociology of knowledge and, more specifically, what has become known as the sociology of science. The emergence of science—the development of science as a massive and powerful institution—poses a variety of sociologically valuable questions.

Science is not, certainly, a simple response to the demands of a growing and expanding population. It is not a simple product of intelligence. It appears, rather, to be a way of viewing the world that emerged from culturally established attitudes conducive to its development. Moreover, Merton points out that modern science in the West was an outgrowth of worldviews contained in early Protestantism. Weber saw capitalism as coming from Protestantism; Merton sees science as yet another contribution of the Protestant ethic.

Merton summarizes the character of his argument with the following statement:

> It is the thesis of this study that the Puritan ethic, as an ideal—typical expression of the value—attitudes basic to ascetic Protestantism generally, so canalized the interests of seventeenth-century Englishmen as to constitute one important *element* in the enhanced cultivation of science. The deep-rooted religious *interests*

of the day demanded in their forceful implications the systematic, rational, and empirical study of Nature for the glorification of God in His works and for the control of the corrupt world.[11]

Merton isolated several facets of Puritan thought and practice, and concluded that scientists of the seventeenth century were functioning as innovators. Although they still held to the ethical, moral, and spiritual goals of Protestant-Christian doctrine, they were engaged in a modification of the means whereby such goals were to be attained. Specifically, they were in the process of turning to nature itself rather than to theological inspiration or speculation as a means of attaining Puritan goals.

Foremost among these goals was the endeavor to serve and glorify God. If Puritanism instilled in people the desire to glorify God, and if Puritanism had a bearing on the development of early science, then seventeenth-century scientists would evaluate their work in terms of the extent to which it worked toward the greater glorification of God. This, claims Merton, is what did in fact happen. Seventeenth-century scientists not only dedicated their works to the greater glory of God, but saw the true ends of science to be the glorification of the Creator.

> In his last will and testament, Boyle echoes the same attitude, petitioning the Fellows of the Society in this wise: "Wishing them also a happy success in their laudable attempts, to discover the true Nature of the Works of God; and praying that they and all other Searchers into Physical Truths, may cordially refer their Attainments to the Glory of the Great Author of Nature, and to the Comfort of Mankind." John Wilks proclaimed the experimental study of Nature to be a most effective means of begetting in men a veneration for God. Francis Willoughby was prevailed upon to publish his works—which he had deemed unworthy of publication—only when Ray insisted that it was a means of glorifying God. Ray's *Wisdom of God* . . . is a panegyric of those who glorify Him by studying His works.[12]

The Puritan ethic was also strongly utilitarian; that is, it emphasized human welfare. Early scientists were as eager to indicate the social merit and worth of their studies as they were to dedicate them to God's glory. Moreover, scientific studies promoted discipline, work, and serious rather than idle thoughts—all Puritan values.

There is, then, a congruence between the basic tenets of Puritan thought and those of early scientists. We are thereby confronted with the irony, if this interpretation of the origins of science carries any validity, of observing a religious ethic bringing into being (or at least serving as the midwife of) an ideology that, in its extreme forms, has generated religion's most serious opposition and intellectual challenge.

Puritan values provided the sanction for science. Scientists could feel justified in the belief that their work was meaningful, not only to themselves but also in a much greater context: Science was an entry into the works of God. There was a greater end to scientific formulations than the mere statement of empirical regularities.

The fact that Protestant thought emphasized individualism, rationality, utilitarianism, and empiricism might have had only a fortuitous relationship to the development of science. Merton has suggested that a significant test would be to determine whether or not Protestants, in the early days of scientific discovery, were more often found within the ranks of scientists than we would expect on the basis of their representation in the total population. To determine this, Merton has investigated the membership of the Royal Society, an "invisible college" of scientists, in its early formative years. He comments:

> [O]f the ten men who constituted the "invisible college," in 1645, only one, Scarbough, was clearly non-Puritan. About two of the others there is some uncertainty, through Merret had a Puritan training. The others were all definitely Puritan. Moreover, among the original list of members of the Society of 1663, forty-two of the sixty-eight concerning whom information about their religious orientation is available were clearly Puritan. Considering that the Puritans constituted a relatively small minority in the English population, the fact that they constituted sixty-two per cent of the initial membership of the Society becomes even more striking.[13]

This disproportionate representation of Protestants within the ranks of science occurs, as well, in present times. Merton cites the observations of Knapp and Goodrich to the effect that several Protestant denominations are proportionately several hundred times more strongly represented among lists of meritorious American scientists than we would expect on the basis of their representation within the general population.[14]

One of the latent functions of the Puritan form of Protestantism in the seventeenth century, then, was to set the stage for the development of rational and empirical science. Merton summarizes his argument by making four principal observations:

First, the relationships between emerging science and religion were indirect and certainly unintended.

Second, science, once the ideological orientation necessary for it was set, acquired a degree of functional autonomy—a character of its own, which eventually would lead to the point where science would appear to be completely removed from religious modes of thought.

Third, the process of institutional modification of thoughtways and the development of new institutional forms may be so subtle as to occur below the threshold of awareness of those involved in it.

Fourth, the dramatic conflict between science and religion—particularly in the nineteenth century—possibly obscures the more significant relationship that exists between the two.[15]

Merton is aware that his study follows in the path of Max Weber. Weber was concerned with the influence of Protestant thought on the development of capitalism. Weber also suggested, in a sketchy manner, that Protestantism had a similar influence on the development of science. However, Merton elaborates what Weber left implicit.

❖ *The Unanticipated Consequences of Social Actions*

Early in his career with the publication of his first monograph in 1938 titled "Science, Technology and Society in Seventeenth Century England," Merton became fascinated with the idea of the unanticipated consequences of social action. In a retrospective article some fifty-one years later, this creative social thinker writes of his enduring interest in the idea of unanticipated, unintended and unrecognized consequences and its links to the oft-cited, overused, now popularized sociological concept of the self-fulfilling prophesy.[16]

The conception of unanticipated consequences formed one of the resonant underlying themes of Merton's work. Out of Puritan religion, unexpectedly and without design, came science. From propaganda campaigns designed to solicit money came unanticipated and subtle constraints on democratic political ideology. From fears of loss of freedom came repressive measures to assure that liberty will be preserved. It is this feature of human social conduct that requires, if people are to make the best social use of their reason, a constant and subtle examination of the functional and dysfunctional aspects of any social action. To evaluate a policy only in terms of its apparent or official objectives is to see considerably less than half of what is taking place.

This amazing and superb social thinker asks us to consider how the phenomenon of unintended and unanticipated consequences comes about. How are we to think about its recurrence in every domain of society, culture, and civilization? For a half century now, Robert K. Merton has posed these questions to his students, his colleagues, and the worldwide readership of his works. Now at the close of the twentieth century we recognize that over his auspicious career and throughout his writings he has reiterated the importance and interrelations of the sociological concepts of latent functions; dysfunctions; the self-defeating or self-fulling prophecy; and the unanticipated, unintended or unrecognized consequences of human social actions.

Encounters with Social Thought

Functional Analysis and the Drug Problem in America

To illustrate the uses of the structural and functional analysis, along with the major sociological concepts detailed in this chapter, we have selected the issue of modern drug use in the United States. Few topics so quickly demonstrate the difference between a functional analysis of human activities and other fashionable or popularized explications.

Conventional explanations of drug use have several notable characteristics:

1. They tend to focus on the individual as the source of the problem.
2. They commonly are strongly moralistic in tone.
3. When they do happen to be institutional in orientation, they focus on a single institution for blame: The family, schools, or urban lifestyles, for example, are singled out for particular attention.
4. A great deal of literature on the drug issue views it as a kind of medical problem in which the drug user is seen as the victim of an "illness."
5. Drug use is looked on as "abnormal," and the drug user is thought of as suffering from a kind of moral or character defect.
6. Drug use is seen as something to be controlled primarily through appeals directed to the public and through law enforcement.
7. Drug use, as a problem, is commonly restricted to a consideration of illegally distributed drugs, as opposed to those distributed through the medical system.
8. Drug use is commonly defined in such a manner as to exclude some drugs while including others. The most obvious manifestation of this is the inclination to exclude alcohol from consideration while including marijuana or amphetamines.
9. The drug problem is viewed as a consequence of criminal mentalities to be fought as a "war against crime."

In sum, popular explanations to what we shall call, throughout the rest of this section, "the drug problem" are simplistic, psychologistic, and legalistic. They are commonly more concerned with finding a scapegoat to blame than with reasoned analysis. A structural and functional approach that includes attention to dysfunctions and to unanticipated consequences to the problem leads to a different realm of understanding. The structural and functional analysis manifests the following differences:

1. It tends to locate the individual within the social structure and hence calls for a consideration of the entire social structure for insight into why drug use is so prevalent.
2. It does not moralize about the problem. If drugs are a part of modern American life, there must be a reason for it. Drugs serve a function; they satisfy a demand coming from within the society or community itself. There are, after all, societies in which drugs are rarely used and others in which they are extremely popular. What accounts for the differences between *societies*?
3. The functional analysis does not isolate a particular institution for special blame or criticism. It argues that all institutions

interact with each other in support of the total system. Therefore, a systemic analysis is required, rather than an institutionally specific one.

4. The functional approach, rather than seeing drugs as an "illness," raises the question of whether or not they are part of the ongoing operations of the social system as a whole. If they work against the functioning of the system, then they are dysfunctional. If they sustain the system, they are functional. Whether drugs damage or sustain the socioeconomic system as a whole is not at all an easy question to answer. Certainly the instantaneous removal of what is touted as a $100 billion "industry" would have serious and unanticipated consequences for the system as a whole.

5. Whereas popular conceptions of drug use tend to view it as an abnormal or peripheral activity, a functional analysis forces us to accept the possibility that drug use is far from an abnormal condition in American culture. Few people in America are not drug users of some kind. Alcohol is popular, along with tranquilizers, stimulants of various kinds, painkillers, diet controls, nicotine, caffeine, sleeping pills, and a host of other drugs. Are there unrecognized and unintended consequences that result from the use or abuse of the substances listed?

6. Structural and functional analysis raises a disturbing question with respect to control. Since it turns to the entire community or social system as its center of concern, the implications for control are severe: If you wish to control the drug problem, you must deal with the entire system. Since people are not disposed to alter entire communal structures, there is probably little possibility of any real control having any kind of effect—short of a major sociocultural revolution or crisis.

It is immediately obvious that structural and functional analysis does not go down the same intellectual road as popular thought. It is a point of view that generates a powerful vision with respect to what is actually going on, while at the same time indicating the structural obstacles to serious reform. If this observation is correct, it suggests that apparently easy solutions to social problems are more a product of ignorance than of knowledge. The more we know about the human social condition, the more difficult are the problems it poses.

The Potential of a Structural and Functional Analysis
The basic approach to the drug problem implied in a structural and functional consideration of the issue can be seen in the kinds of questions such a perspective raises: How does the drug culture fit into the total social structure as an element of the larger system? What kind of

social structure would incorporate a strong drug culture as an element within itself? What does the drug culture "do" in terms of the rest of the system? What unanticipated consequences of the recognition of a societal drug problem might arise?

As we gain a sense of what this functional analysis is asking of us, we begin to see that the so-called "drug culture" fits into a larger pattern. No single institution is responsible for it. Instead, the complex interactions among all of the elements of the culture make the existence of a drug culture more understandable as a reasonable consequence of everything else that is going on. To clarify this, we shall lightly sketch in the characteristics of several large-scale institutional forces within modern American society—with particular emphasis given to how these institutions are, in themselves, structured in such a way as to enhance drug use. When the combined influence of all of these structures is taken into account as a macrostructure, one wonders not why Americans use so many drugs, but why the current situation is no worse than it is.

Economic Institutions

The American economy is dedicated to consumption and the idea that progress is realized through material comfort. Moreover, material comfort should be immediate. The economy exists to make people happy. American advertising, an important institution within the overall complex, contains within it an implicit philosophy of sybaritic hedonism. At another level, the American economy is a stressful one. The American worker is subjected to stresses that come from routinized work, the constant possibility of layoffs, continual changes in production systems that call for reeducation of the worker or worker obsolescence, the demands of production lines, movement from place to place, social mobility, and so forth. Dealing with stress is now a common concern. One acceptable form of dealing with stress is to rely on stress-reducing drugs. Such drugs are dispensed to a broad array of cases, ranging from instances of hyperactivity in children to high-level executives coping with the stress of possible bankruptcy or revelations of nefarious financial manipulations.

Another major element in the American economy is the multibillion-dollar legitimate drug industry. American companies thrive or falter in terms of profits and losses. That which augments productive and *consumptive* efficiency enhances the survival chances of a company within a competitive system. It therefore is incumbent on the American drug industry to "push" its products—and push them it does. Americans are encouraged to use drugs to solve every kind of problem, from drying up hemorrhoidal tissues to curing cancer. The American drug industry, by the nature of its product and the nature of how things are produced and distributed in America, must find markets for its products. Like any other economic enterprise, the drug industry is driven to expand its markets as fully as possible. It is therefore called on to create new drugs that will have a popular appeal and to encourage the broader use of drugs that have established markets. These activities could be viewed as the unanticipated consequences that promote drug use and drug abuse in America.

The Political System

To provide another striking example: the American political system historically experienced a singular encounter with drug use. It lost. The American approach to drugs has, ever since, been more tentative. The manufacture, transportation, or sale of alcoholic liquors was prohibited by law as a result of the ratification in 1919 of the Eighteenth Amendment to the Constitution. In 1920 the Volstead Act, which enforced the Eighteenth Amendment, went into effect, and the era of Prohibition was launched. Its life was short. In 1933 the Eighteenth Amendment was repealed, after a decade of the most flagrant and widespread disobedience of American federal law that had been seen up to that point. The lessons learned from the era of Prohibition still linger.

One lesson that was learned was that the political system does not have the ability to marshal effective force to uphold unpopular laws: Millions of Americans daily and quite openly flaunted the Eighteenth Amendment. Another lesson was that any political attempt to constrain a popular activity immediately generates powerful black-market systems that circumvent political restrictions. Informal systems are at work within any society to compensate for *perceived* inequities in the formal system. One other lesson learned from the Prohibition years was that social problems cannot be solved simply by legislating them out of existence.

The American political system is designed to appeal to popular sentiments. Its structure is democratic and its rhetoric is populist. It offers, ideologically, freedom and the right to pursue happiness. It encourages privacy. Given simply these qualities, we can begin to see that the political system in America is not powerfully coercive in and of itself. So it is, in present times, that powerful people in America turn to appeals and slogans as a way of trying to curb drug use.

The American political system does not, of course, encourage drug use in any explicit or overt manner. At the same time, it is not a powerful system with respect to controlling the problem. Perhaps the proper term is that it is a political system that is "congenial" to drug use. While political rhetoric condemns drug use, the political structure is essentially an ineffectual one.

Or, to consider the matter from still another perspective, we might ask ourselves this: What kind of political structure would the members of a drug ring "design" if they could create a political system congenial to their interests? They would want one that would elevate the price of certain drugs by enhancing the risk involved in the distribution of such items. At the same time, it would be one that would back away from a show of authoritarian strength or the use of an effective, massively powerful enforcement system. They would also want a system that was hesitant to censor expressions of freedom and privacy. All of these are characteristics of the present American political system.

Social Service Agencies

There now exists within American society a complex of agencies working with the victims of drug abuse. These agencies vary greatly in character—ranging from volunteer groups working within limited budgets, to elaborate hospitals staffed by well-paid professionals who provide therapy for troubled millionaire athletes, movie stars, and alcoholic politicians. These agencies, given the problems they have to deal with, do good work. At the same time, they are a structural element of the society and the economy.

Once a social agency comes into existence, it tends to look after its survival needs as an ongoing entity. The agency, in other words, acquires its own unique interests. Psychiatry, for example, in order to continue as a professional field, needs a steady supply of psychotics, neurotics, and others who feel the need for psychiatric care. Alcoholic treatment centers need alcoholics. Treatment agencies do not necessarily create the demand for the services they supply, but they are not especially interested in diminishing it, either.

The consequence, unrecognized or unintended, is a therapeutic philosophy in which emphasis is directed toward cure rather than any systematic attempt at prevention. An emphasis on curing the victim rather than trying to prevent the victimization in the first place leads to a general belief that if you get ill or addicted, someone will save you. The seriousness of addiction is tempered by the promise of a cure if things get too far out of hand.

Religious Institutions

The role played by religion in Western drug use is complex, and we can only sketch in a few suggestions. They are intended more as a point of origin for further discussion than as conclusions. There is, throughout Western religious thought, constant reference to the ecstasy of the deeper forms of religious experience. This ecstasy is sought in various ways: It can be induced through temple chanting, the overwhelming architecture of the great cathedrals, religious music ranging from gospel singing and Gregorian chants to Handel's *Messiah*, fasting, sexual repression, meditation, speaking in tongues, and other forms.

The ecstatic or Dionysian quest is characteristic of Western culture, and it permeates our institutions—religion is no exception. Although Western religions pursue ecstasy in the form of union with God, they also place severe restrictions on how this union can be consummated. In Merton's terms, the goal is well defined and institutionally sustained. At the same time, not all of the means that might possibly be used to attain the ecstatic state are legitimate. Western religion, in its more severe forms, bans the use of any kind of drug. The Mormons, for example, include coffee drinking as a violation of their tenets.

Merton argues that where the pressure to reach a socially defined goal is great, while at the same time the means for attaining the goal are less well defined or uncertain, the likely consequence is nonconformist or deviant activity. What makes the role played by religion in Western drug use so complex is that religion is embedded within other institutional systems and these other systems tend to reinforce the quest for ecstasy, while at the same time undermining the traditional, ritualistically defined means for achieving the goal. The consequence is a large number of people willing to experiment with the possibility of finding the godhead through the ingestion of an organic or inorganic chemical agent. Why go to church if a pill will do the job more sensationally?

During the 1960s, when more exotic and nontraditional drugs became a matter of common discussion, one of the rationales underlying their use was the argument that they offered people a "religious experience." Mescaline, "magic mushrooms," LSD, and other drugs were commonly described as agents capable of inducing a sense of the infinite; the perfect unity and harmony of the cosmos; a sense of divinity, love, peace, and serenity; and so forth. Drugs were talked about then, and are still talked about, as an avenue to "cosmic" revelations. It is one thing to say that drugs make people drunk, dizzy, confused, irrational, incoherent, disoriented, forgetful, stupid, and incomprehensible—and something else to say that they offer "cosmic" revelations.

Sociologists have long been aware of the fact that alcoholism rates have been lower in the Jewish community than in the Christian community. The prevailing interpretation of this finding is that alcohol is ritualistically incorporated into Jewish life and controlled much as other dietary matters are controlled. Christian practices do not include alcohol or other drugs in a controlled fashion—even the Eucharist is commonly celebrated in many Protestant churches by substituting unfermented grape juice for the wine that symbolizes the blood of Christ.

We live, then, within a social system whose central religious ideology is one that provides a metaphysical motive for drug use, while at the same time relegating drugs to the underworld. The result is a culture in which individuals are bedeviled by the appeal of drugs as a source of ecstatic experience, while at the same time having little instruction or guidance in how they are controlled.

Law Enforcement Institutions

Even as this is being written, there is much talk once again in the newspapers and on television about getting tough with drug dealers, foreign countries that smuggle drugs into the United States, and drug users. One journalist has advocated that drug users should be pilloried mercilessly before the public as living examples of what happens if people take drugs. The rhetoric is powerful, but it is expressed without much evident thought about the structural implications of such a policy.

Law enforcement is a delicate matter in a nation that subscribes to strong beliefs in freedom, liberty, individualism, and privacy. Where the law itself sustains such values, the police are placed in the odd position of having to sustain a way of life that is antithetical to police activity. That is to say, police work is much more efficient, simple, and effective when it does not have to worry about freedom, individualism, liberty, and privacy. At the same time, the American public is fearful of the police. We do not want the police to have too much power or authority. A truly effective police system has authoritarian overtones, and authoritarianism is anathema to the American spirit. So it is that the American police official is placed in a bind—a kind of "damned if you do and damned if you don't" situation. If the police are ineffectual, they are condemned. If they are unusually effectual, they are also likely to be condemned.

There is little doubt that the police could stop drug use in the United States in a relatively short period. However, in order to do so, they would have to be given powers they are not now permitted to exercise. To bring drug use to a halt through the employment of police powers would require a police system that could assure a low probability of success on the part of anyone who either attempted to distribute or use illegal drugs in any manner. This would require police surveillance of such intensity as to bring all members of the society under close and constant scrutiny. However, to accomplish this would mean ending the American dream in favor of a police state. If, on the other hand, we continue to support freedom and privacy as basic American values, then the police can make arrests and bring before public scrutiny an occasional miscreant, but the probability of being apprehended remains low enough to assure most individuals that they will not be caught.

It is not the severity of punishment that acts as a primary deterrent with respect to criminal action. It is the probability of being detected and apprehended that is the primary deterrent. In a nation in which individuals can become "lost" within the massive structures that make up a modern city or the remote areas that make up the hinterlands, to increase the probability of any criminal action's being punished requires massive funding and support.

America, in a sense, has made a choice between two evils. It can opt for a powerful, certain, effective, and highly efficient police force, or a citizenry that is relatively free to indulge itself in popular criminal activities. We appear to have accepted the notion that, at the very least, petty crime is the price we pay for freedom. There is, however, considerable controversy over the choice, and it is one we try to renegotiate every few years.

The Class Structure

We now have a more complete awareness of what a structural and functional analysis means when it is brought to bear on a given social issue. We have considered economic, political, medical, religious, and law enforcement institutions as elements in the puzzle. Each in a way has qualities that, though not openly promoting drug use, at the same time are not antagonistic to it. As a complex of interacting systems, they appear to be quite congenial to the development of what can be called a drug culture.

We shall add one more element in an attempt to reveal the implications of a structural and functional analysis. Drugs are social in character; their use does not occur in a social vacuum. A nice example of this came to our attention during a stay in South America. Excellent native rums were available at absurdly low prices in the local markets. Nonetheless, Americans staying in the area preferred high-priced Scotch. Scotch is a status drug for Americans; rum is not. Scotch is traditional; rum is not.

Drugs reflect class interests and class traditions. Like other aspects of human communal life, drugs are used to sustain as well as to reflect class structures. In industrial England, at the height of the Industrial Revolution, gin was plentiful and extremely cheap. Its use as a numbing agent in industrial areas where life was brutish, painful, short, and almost worthless became scandalously prevalent, and "Gin Row" became a place where the human detritus of the cities drowned their despair in cheap drugs.

There is a "dynamic" in human social class structures that has a place for drugs in several ways. Drugs can be used as a distinctive privilege. They can also be employed as a diversionary device, distracting attention and energy from other activities, such as political organization and resistance.

The basic point from a structural and functional perspective, however, is that drugs can be functional within a social class context. Drugs can be used to control, distract, and pacify groups that might, otherwise organize in terms of class interests. We are all familiar with the Marxist argument that religion is the opiate of the masses, though large numbers might disagree. It is more difficult to argue against the claim that opiates are the opiate of the masses.

A Concluding Comment

The structural and functional approach has then been applied to the issue of drug use in America in an effort to exemplify how a particular strategy in social thought can be used and the general conclusions it suggests. Even though we have considered only several structures in current social systems, it quickly becomes evident that any attempt to deal with social problems is also an attempt to deal with the society as a whole. If we remove a particular feature from the system, the removal has consequences for the entire society. Merton states it this way:

> [I]t is argued that the interdependence of social structure makes for ramified unforeseen consequences. Thus, precisely because a particular action is not carried out in a psychological or social vacuum, its effects will ramify into other spheres of value and interest. It is the composites of aggregated and socially patterned actions that generate various kinds of unanticipated consequences for individuals, groups, society, culture and civilizations.[17]

We must ask this question, then: If it were possible to remove the drug culture from American society, what might take its place? What would happen? Would American society be radically transformed? Would it be better? Would it be worse? A structural and functional analysis gives us a framework in which to examine these questions as well as contemplate what unanticipated consequences might arise.

Putting Social Thought to Work

1. Merton has brought us a more mechanistic view of society with various elements that form a "structure." Each of the persisting elements has functions and dysfunctions and works to sustain the entire structure. Whether we agree or not with this simile, it can be used to orient us toward a variety of problems. In modern times, sports have become an entrenched element within the society. Merton leads us to consider the manifest and latent functions of such activity, as well as aspects of dysfunctions and unanticipated consequences. How do sports fit into modern societies? At the manifest level, sports appear to function as models of enterprise and equality of opportunity. At the latent level, sports may function to sustain inequality. Consider what dysfunctions or unanticipated, unintended consequences might sports, both amateur and professional, produce in American society?

2. Merton was interested in the extent to which discrepancies between institutionalized goals and institutionalized means for achieving these goals can produce deviant conduct. What are some of the "goals" that this society promotes? How does this influence (socialize) young people in America to obtain these goals?

3. When we begin talking about the structural and functional features of a society, we have moved away from psychological explanations of human actions. Presuming, for the moment, that a psychological approach has been more popular among Americans, why might this be so? How do you think a structural and functional analyst would respond to an extensive psychological analysis of people's problems?

4. Toward what ends do we expect people of high intelligence to dedicate themselves to the betterment of our society and why? How do we define intelligence or the several intelligences? Are we coming to definitions of varying types of intelligence that permit us to think of eventually computerizing such qualities? How will this affect our society in the twenty-first century?

5. Find and describe more examples of the dysfunctional process that you are familiar with or that have occurred in your life. How did these occurrences affect you or the others involved? Were these examples of dysfunctions interrelated with unanticipated consequences or self-defeating prophesies?

6. Do you know any nonconformers? How would you describe their behavior? How do nonconformers differ from individuals who have aberrant social behaviors? Does this view of human behaviors affect our interpretations of deviance in American society?

7. In this chapter we demonstrated how Merton provided us with a subtle but important example of unanticipated, unintended consequences related to the origins of scientific thought in the Western world. Read about and discuss Merton's thesis on Puritanism and the rise of modern science. What implications does it have for science and technology in the twenty-first century?

8. Choose another social issue or social problem, such as the controversies around school integration and the busing of students to achieve equal opportunity in education touched upon in this chapter. Draw upon your own experiences and those of others you have known in relation to the issue. Delineate the manifest and latent functions, the dysfunctions, the unanticipated consequences surrounding the problems or issue. Have there also been self-defeating or self-fulfilling prophesies complicating the situation? Share your ideas with other students and obtain their reactions.

Endnotes

1. The following selected listing of Robert K. Merton's works will provide an indication of the extent and variety of his contributions to sociological thought: *Contemporary Social Problems: An Introduction to the Sociology of Deviant Behavior and Social Disorganization*, edited by Merton and R. A. Nisbet, 4th edition (New York: Harcourt, Brace & World, 1976); *Continuities in Social Research: Studies in the Scope*

and Method of "The American Soldier," edited by Merton and Paul F. Lazarsfeld (New York: Free Press, 1950); *The Focused Interview: A Manual of Problems and Procedures*, with Marjorie Fiske and Patricia L. Kendall (New York: Free Press, 1956); *Mass Persuasion: The Social Psychology of a War Bond Drive*, with the assistance of Marjorie Fiske and Alberta Curtis (New York: Harper Bros., 1946); *On the Shoulders of Giants: A Shandean Postscript* (New York: Free Press, 1985, 1993); *Reader in Bureaucracy*, edited by Merton and others (New York: Free Press, 1952); *Social Theory and Social Structure*, enlarged ed. (New York: Free Press, 1968); *The Student-Physician: Introductory Studies in the Sociology of Medical Education*, edited by Merton, George G. Reader, and Patricia Kendall (Cambridge, MA: Harvard University Press, 1957); *Sociology Today: Problems and Prospects*, edited by Merton, L. Broom, and L. S. Cottrell, Jr. (New York: Basic Books, 1959); *Sociological Ambivalence and Other Essays* (New York: Free Press, 1976); *Social Science Quotations*, Volume 19 of the *International Encyclopedia of the Social Sciences*, edited by Merton and David L. Sills (New York: Macmillan/The Free Press, 1990); *The Sociology of Science: An Episodic Memoir* (Carbondale, IL: Southern University Press, 1979).

2. Merton, *Social Theory and Social Structure*, p. 24.
3. Ibid., pp. 64–65. Italics Merton's.
4. It is worth noting that the idea of dysfunction has grown in importance over the decades, since Merton first delineated this concept, to become as familiar a sociological term as "manifest and latent functions."
5. John Fischer mentions this interesting theory in his article "Christmas List," *Harper's Magazine*, December 1967, pp. 16 and 18.
6. Merton, *Social Theory and Social Structure*, p. 68.
7. Ibid., pp. 75–76.
8. Ibid., p. 76.
9. Merton, "Opportunity Structure: The Emergence, Diffusion and Differentiation of a Sociological Concept, 1930–1950." Unpublished paper in preparation.
10. Ibid.
11. Ibid. Italics Merton's.
12. Ibid.
13. Ibid. (Merton cites Dean Stimson as the source of his data.)
14. Ibid.
15. Ibid.
16. Merton. "The Unanticipated Consequences and Kindred Sociological Ideas: A Personal Gloss," in *L'Opera di Robert K. Merton e la sociologia contemporanea*. Edited by C. Mongardini and S. Tabboni. (Genoa: Acig, 1989), pp. 307–329; and in "STS: Foreshadowings of an Evolving Research Program in the Sociology of Science," in *Puritanism and the Rise of Modern Science: The Merton Thesis*, edited by I. Bernard Cohen (New Brunswick, NJ: Rutgers University Press, 1990), p. 362.
17. Ibid., p. 308.

Theory and Practice

The Applied Vision of
Howard S. Becker

❖

❖ The Practical Necessity of
Theory in Human Affairs

Theory, in and of itself, without any consideration for practical applications, is an intellectually engaging activity. Indeed, it is intellectual activity *par excellence*. Theory is always an endeavor to press beyond the present appearances of reality. It is an effort to find the hidden masks that lie behind the masks we see. The greatest theorists in any field represent a synthesis of thought and observation that is the finest their field has to offer. Although there are differences from specialty to specialty in the way theorists are regarded by their colleagues, theory is important in all endeavors—from theories of horticulture and theories of athletic performance to theories of the cosmos.

The importance of theory is clearly seen in mathematics, where we can make two general observations of interest. First, mathematical theoreticians occupy a lofty status *vis-à-vis* their colleagues. Practical mathematicians are not as likely to share the same prestige as that accorded to theoretical mathematicians. Second, theoretical mathematicians do not vindicate themselves by attempting to develop practical justifications for their work. Like the pure artist (whatever we might mean by the term "pure"), the pure mathematician works in a realm beyond immediate practical applications.

We need to add that the real situation is more complicated than mathematical theorists might like to believe. After all, mathematics originated in quite ordinary and practical concerns, such as keeping track of the seasons, problems of the marketplace, and geometries of construction. Furthermore, theoreticians are not bashful about pointing out that a number of their esoteric imaginings ultimately led to startling practical applications (for example, the application of Boolean algebra to certain forms of telephone circuitry).

The situation is not greatly different in the social sciences. The most renowned figures in the field are generally thought of as social theorists— Karl Marx, Max Weber, Émile Durkheim, Talcott Parsons, Robert Merton, Pitirim Sorokin, and Georg Simmel, to name only a few. However, unlike the theories of the natural scientist or the mathematician, the theories of social scientists come close to the heart of our deepest concerns. The social theorist probes into the character of our institutions, our values, our folkways and mores, our ideals, and our beliefs concerning which people we think we should look up to and which we should look down upon.

The distinction between what a mathematical theorist does and what a social theorist does is so great that we are inclined to believe separate terms should be used to describe the nature of their accomplishments. But tradition has granted these diverse activities the title of "theorizing," and we shall continue in this tradition. However, when we use theory in the social sciences, we must be careful not to be misled by our terminology. After all, there is a difference between what is done in the theory of numbers and the theory of, let us say, social stratification. But this topic is beyond the present limits of our discussion.

Although the theoretician is commonly disdained by those who think of themselves as practical individuals, we would like to suggest that, at least with regard to social theories, there are almost always practical implications behind such ideas. We do not wish to spend a lot of time trying to support this contention. The argument, essentially, is based on the observation that virtually all social actions are motivated or given form by little "theories" people believe in about how they ought to act in different situations.

Racist theory, for example, has profoundly practical and critical implications for blacks in America who are trying to get a job. Evolutionary theory has practical implications for fundamentalists who are pondering the question of where to send their children to school. Theories concerning the relationship between mental illness and criminal action have practical implications for the design of systems of incarceration. And so on. Although we do not want to devote too much time in the justification of theory by pointing to its practical consequences, we nonetheless feel that the student should not casually dismiss theory because it is seen as impractical. Social theories can be as beneficial as a gentle rain during a drought and as lethal as an atomic bomb. They merit respect.

❖ *Theory and Novelty*

This chapter briefly considers several features of the work of a person who has approached practical problems with a well-developed sense of theory. The result of this effort is an unusual interpretation of human actions. The work of Howard S. Becker reveals the close working relationship between theory and practice. Before moving into a consideration of Becker's work, we need to comment on one further feature of theory (whether it is theoretical physics or social theory) that should be discussed. We are thinking now of the element of novelty or surprise, which so often adds to the significance or importance of theory and, of course, to related research.

Theory can impress us simply by its novelty. In the realm of physical theory, this is easy enough to illustrate. There is at present much popular as well as professional interest in the bizarre physical properties of black holes in space. The practical applications of such speculation are not immediately evident. This, however, does not deter us from seeking further understanding of the nature of such phenomena. Even in our sophisticated, technological, and possibly jaded and exhausted society, the sciences are able to continue to stun and provoke us with the novelty of their views. In a real sense we are, even today, still struggling to adjust ourselves to the wide-ranging implications of these modern scientific interpretations of the world around us.

Within social theory, however, we encounter difficulty with regard to the attainment of novelty or intellectual astonishment. Studying human society from the stance taken by sociologists poses particular difficulties when it comes to exciting or delighting the mind or senses. Unlike artists, sociologists are not supposed to embellish their work with hyperbole or imaginative invention. They are not supposed to make use of literary or rhetorical devices that might make their case more dramatic, entertaining, amusing, or persuasive. They are called on, instead, to use an academic prose style, which has the unfortunate effect of removing much of the joy from a presentation of even the most novel findings and arguments. Sociology is commonly offered with a sonorous heaviness, a Germanic ponderousness that we generally reserve for higher theological debate. Considering the foibles and follies of its subject matter, it is a literature strangely devoid of humor.

There are further constraints on the ability of the social sciences to offer a sense of novelty. Foremost among these is the simple fact that all people receive an intensive social training as they mature. It really makes little difference whether this training is correct or not. By the time people reach adulthood, they are generally informed, one way or another, about the society of which they are a part. It is not especially exciting, then, for people to encounter descriptions of a social world they believe they already know. Moreover, in modern society, the mass media is always ready to offer social understanding and stories of human conflict and anguish in a manner designed to attract large audiences. The ingenious understandings and interpretations of a Durkheim or Weber, a George Herbert Mead or a Kenneth Burke, are forced to compete with the more bizarre, entertaining, and novel off-the-cuff commentaries of guests on television talk shows.

So, if we make the assumption that one of the charms of either the arts or the sciences is the generation of novel understandings, we are brought to the problem of how this is to be achieved in a discipline that prosaically investigates matters people believe they already understand as well as anybody else. There are two ways to deal with this problem. The first is to generate theories and observations that strongly contradict the basic beliefs of a majority of the people. This is an adventurous road to follow. If taken too far, it leads, of course, to complete rejection of the argument. The theorist may be imaginative, but he or she will also be considered insane or, at the very least, foolish. On the other hand, if the argument is not carried far enough, one risks presenting just another banal and obvious finding.

The second, and safer, approach is to provide information about the conduct of people who are "outside" the social knowledge of the common individual. The sociologist who takes this avenue in quest of novelty allows us vicariously to be a kind of peeping Tom or sociocultural voyeur. This approach exploits existing esoteric and exotic subcultures. We are told the secrets of lives carried on outside the realms of conventional morality. A middle-class college student, for example, is given a glimpse of what it is like to be a ghetto black gang member or a person who practices the "tearoom trade."[1]

This is commonly done in the social sciences, and it is not necessarily a bad thing. Whatever might be wrong with it is a consequence of bias in the types of groups selected. Our libraries are loaded with thousands of research monographs and reports on the slums and the ghettos, the imprisoned, the indigent, the peculiar, and the injured, but only a few serious and carefully conducted studies on the inside lives of the powerful, established, and wealthy members of our society. When we get occasional objective peeks into this stratum of the social world, we learn that there is a difference between reality and what we have been led to believe. (One of the more astounding revelations of this century came out of the information contained in the taped conversations between President Nixon and his aides, which were made public as a result of the Watergate investigations. These revelations, of course, were the result of journalistic investigations into a scandal rather than systematic social-scientific research.)

The social sciences are not to be faulted for studying and reporting esoteric groups and practices, but they can be criticized for the bias displayed in who is to be studied. In a truly democratic sociology, any group's likelihood of being selected for study would be a random function of its size or significance. At present, this is not the case.

The quest for novelty through the study of esoteric human actions is common in the social sciences as a whole. Consider how anthropology handles the problem of novelty. Cultural anthropology, for example, caters to our interest in the unusual by studying and reporting the conduct of people who live in cultures remote from our own. Descriptions of the orgiastic dances of the Kwakiutl grant us a new awareness of what it is to be a human being. Within the social sciences, cultural anthropology serves much the same purpose that the reflecting telescope serves in the study of physical reality. It enables us to comprehend the great distances, as it were, involved in the range of actions and feelings of which people are capable. It serves to make us more aware of the extent to which each of us, as an individual, is subject to the historical caprices of the various times and places into which he or she is born.

Unlike cultural anthropology, sociology restricts itself largely to modern and technologically advanced societies. Much of it deals with Western culture. In sum, sociology deals with familiar realms of social conduct for the American student—those activities going on in the individual's own modern Western society. Sociology is thereby handicapped at the outset. It is plagued with the problem of bringing coals to Newcastle. It always has to run the risk of telling people much of what they think they already know. This handicap can be reduced, however, if the sociologist takes a leaf from the notebook of the cultural anthropologist and concentrates on subcultures that are relatively distant from the typical experiences of those who are likely to constitute the sociologist's audience.

❖ The Outsiders

The dual problems of practicality and novelty in social theory can achieve a kind of simultaneous resolution through making that which is novel in human social actions also that which should be of practical concern. As a consequence, we have concentrated on the insane, the criminal, the destitute, the homeless, and the dissolute people of our society—the so-called "social problems" of our times. In studying the lifeways of such people, we believe we are engaged in a study of the exotic or novel elements within our society and also concerned with work of a practical nature.

So it is, then, that sociologists have established as part of their subject matter the study of people who are looked on as "deviants" or "problems" for the greater society. From this perspective, we find some sociologists writing descriptions of the activities of people who engage in homosexual relations in public places, while others engage in studies of striptease artists.

Much can be made of the actions of those who are outside the ordinary routines of ordinary people—the criminal, the mentally ill, the divorced, the suicidal, the drug user, and the bitterly impoverished. Sociology is not above relying on a little sensationalism to maintain interest.

At the same time, there is more to the examination of exotic life-styles than simply the pursuit of sensational information. We come to the exotic life-style thinking, at first, that our interest is provoked by the difference that seems to exist between "them" and "us." Further examination brings us to an understanding even more revealing and, at first, rather disconcerting. We find that there is much "we" share in common with "them."

Howard Becker is part of a group of influential modern sociologists who did their advanced studies at the University of Chicago in the late 1940s and early 1950s.[2] These people were especially influenced by the teachings of Everett Cherrington Hughes. One of the directions Hughes gave to the study of social actions involved the investigation of various careers. Whereas the cultural anthropologist examines remote and not-so-remote cultures, Hughes got his students to investigate remote and not-so-remote careers—the career of the professional boxer, the career of the mortician, the career of the urban school teacher, and so on.

The important concept, in all of this, is the idea of "careers." At the broadest level, a career is simply a progression through a phase of life. Although we do not usually think of it as such, a child's progression through grade school is also a career progression. Becker has come to apply the concept to activities that, at first, seem far removed from being "careers." For example, he is interested in determining how people become marijuana smokers. He has concluded that it is basically a form of career. We shall comment on Becker's studies of marijuana smokers later.

Much of the novelty of the Chicago studies of careers comes from considerations of exotic or remote careers—careers of people we commonly think of as "outsiders." However, a number of the careers, such as that of the urban elementary school teacher, are rather prosaic. After all, virtually every one of us has had extended encounters with elementary school teachers. Nonetheless, it has been among the contributions of Hughes and his students to reveal novel possibilities inherent in the examination of the common daily routines of ordinary people. In the course of their work on careers, it has become more and more apparent that ordinary and deviant careers are not as dissimilar as we are generally led to believe.

As we mentioned earlier, Becker did his graduate work under Hughes; for his doctoral dissertation, he undertook an examination of the career of the public school teacher in Chicago.[3] The methods of research developed then, and the conception of lives as passing through "careers," have been interwoven into the greater part of the work Becker has undertaken in his subsequent career. His interests are quite diverse. He achieved notoriety following the publication in 1953 of a paper based on studies of marijuana smokers.[4] He then became involved in the activities of the Society for the

Study of Social Problems. With colleagues, he wrote a book based on research done in a medical school[5] and another based on research (carried out at the University of Kansas) into the careers of undergraduates as they progress through an academic setting.[6]

He has been prolific as a writer for professional journals and as an editor. Whether he is examining the secretive and coltish actions of drug users or the mundane activities of students hustling for a grade in an English "lit" course, one pervasive quality characterizes Becker's work: It is grounded in the constant application of intelligent and theoretically sophisticated observation. Becker's work offers us an opportunity to consider at length the difficulties we come up against when we undertake the study of what we refer to as "social problems" or of people looked on as social "deviants." Becker's approach to deviance is sufficiently general for us to improve our understanding of both deviant and nondeviant forms of social action. That is, what Becker has to say about deviants applies to nondeviants as well. The processes that generate classes of people who acquire the label "deviant" are much the same processes that generate classes of people who are labeled "normal."

Our emphasis, then, is on the idea of "process," or, to use another term, the "career" of the normal or the nonnormal person. Becker is interested in the ways in which people who are probably biologically or mentally typical can be led into actions causing them to be given the label of "deviant." The central thrust of such theorizing is to claim that deviant activity is not the product of a deviant personality. Or, at least, this perspective argues that if the personality is a product of social relationships with others, then the entire process must be examined.

❖ Statistical and Medical Definitions of Deviance

To gain an idea of the extent to which Becker's thinking is different, it is worthwhile to review, briefly, a few of the more common ways in which we are inclined to think about deviant actions. One of the simplest is the idea that deviant action is any unusual action. This, basically, is a statistical definition of deviant activities. It presumes that we can arrange people according to how far they stand from some average level of performance or character. If they are significantly above or below the average, they are deviant. Such an approach has the advantage of being simple and the quite marked disadvantage of being too inclusive. If we go by this definition, then everyone is deviant in one fashion or another. We are either "too" tall or "too" short, "too" fat or "too" thin, "too" bright or "too" stupid.

This, of course, produces the logical impasse of making abnormality a normal condition. More seriously, it bypasses what is usually a central concern with the problem of deviance; that is, it ignores the relationship existing between social norms or rules and the violation of those rules. When we view social deviations as problems, we generally do so because such deviations threaten the social order. Statistical definitions of deviance do not take social context into account.

A man who is seven feet tall is a statistical deviant. Unless his height threatens an existing socially relevant norm, however, we are not especially concerned with his deviance. We might add the obvious observation that the relevance of context to any consideration of deviance is quickly made apparent by considering what it means to be seven feet tall when you want to join a submarine crew or a basketball team.

Another approach to deviance is to view it as something harmful or dangerous or pathological insofar as the smooth operation of the community is concerned. This is an attempt to apply a medical analogy to the social body. The deviant individual or group is viewed as something potentially or actually injurious. The deviant, from this perspective, is akin to a cancer cell in the healthy body; if deviance is allowed to proliferate, organized maintenance of the body will eventually become impossible.

There are several serious limitations to this argument. It presumes to know what constitutes a healthy social body. Such "healthiness" is generally defined in terms of the existing or prevailing power structure. Strangely enough, the "healthy" society always manages to look much like the status quo. Therefore, from the perspective of those who define deviance as pathology, anything that sustains the status quo is "healthy" and anything that does not is "pathological." This form of defining deviant activities obviously has social control implications. Anyone who is rocking the boat is deviant. To be deviant is to be pathological.

By this procedure, it is possible to confuse those who are engaged in serious political and social reform or change with those who are suffering from a real illness and are, in fact, pathological cases. As Abraham Maslow has observed, a person who did not go along with the Nazis in Germany during the 1930s was considered pathological by them. Obviously, if "pathological" people are in charge, then being labeled "pathological" by such an authority suggests something to the contrary.

Labeling a deviant person or group "pathological" can generate problems. First, it disguises the possibility that a person is being so labeled simply for not going along with the existing system. Psychiatry has been condemned by a number of critics on just this ground. There was a good deal of criticism of psychiatric practice in the former Soviet Union. It seems, according to the criticism, that the Russians on more than one occasion found it expedient to label intellectual critics of the government as people who were psychotic or pathological. It is an old game. We do it in a smaller and more common way when we call someone crazy simply because he or she has the temerity to disagree with us.

Second, and more important, this labeling tends to locate the "pathological" character of the deviant person within himself or herself. The person is thus made the source of culpability for his or her deviant actions. There is possible trickery here, insofar as attention may be shifted away from the possible pathological character of the situation in which the person is involved and turns, instead, toward the person.

It is difficult to track down collective causes of individual actions. No one, for example, in any concrete and positive fashion really knows why a teenager steals a car—there are thousands of possible reasons. Whatever the reasons, the majority of them are lost in a complex past. Yet when things go wrong, an explanation is sought. It is not easy to make large groups or organizations culpable. Culpability for complex happenings must be concretized. This is done by selecting an individual or a relatively small number of people who can then be held personally accountable for events that otherwise would be almost impossible to account for. The best example we can think of is the popular inclination to blame Hitler for the complicated socio-economic and political factors that resulted in World War II.

A general illustration of the tricky nature of the medical analogy lies in current problems revolving around understanding the nature of paranoia. Much psychiatric thinking about paranoia has tended to focus on the individual and his or her aberrant fantasy life. Paranoia, according to this point of view, is something that comes about when individuals' imaginations begin to lead them to believe people are out to destroy them. Some specialists, for example, have referred to the "pseudocommunity" the paranoid person constructs in imagination, and to the person's overwrought fantasy life.

More recently, however, psychologists have considered the possibility that people who are paranoid may have good reasons for seeing the world as they do. Others really may be out to get them. Or, at least, the paranoids' delusions of persecution may not be totally unreasonable interpretations of the situations in which they find themselves. The point we are trying to make is that people cannot be understood independently of the circumstances in which they are enmeshed. Yet a purely individualistic approach to human concerns inclines us to dismiss the contexts within which people are acting out their lives.

A third and final (for purposes of this discussion) reason for being careful with the concept of social pathology comes out of its implicit endorsement of the "healthy" parts of the system. There is always the possibility that pathological developments within a society arise out of weaknesses or deficiencies whose origins are in the apparently "nonpathological" parts of the society. The simplest illustration is to be found in the so-called "race" problem. Older approaches to this "pathology" concentrated on the nature and character of black life in America. But by the close of World War II, most of the attention being given to the problem turned toward the nature of racial bigotry. The bigot was then viewed as a semipathological type, and various books and articles explored the unfortunate consequences of having an "authoritarian" personality.

Today neither of these approaches is adequate. The race problem is certainly not just a black problem, but a white problem as well. White bigots, moreover, are not simply accidents. They are not merely occasionally path-ological people. They are people who serve the interests of others who may or may not, in themselves, possess negative racial attitudes. In brief, it is just too simple to attribute the racial issue to a pathological element. In so doing, we may be shifting the blame from hidden and subtle characteristics of the morally substantial elements in the community and loading it onto the backs of those who have achieved a kind of visibility. When we do this, we engage in a double irony. The victims of inhuman practices are the ones blamed for the inhumanities they must suffer. It is a galling experience.

Let us add one further comment. The medical analogy is more than misleading. It is an attempt to add to the moral stigmatization of the poor and indigent, the crazed and degenerate, the rebels and dropouts, by impos-ing a stigmatization that carries the authority not of the church but of the sterile—and prestigious—laboratories of medical science. Because the stig-matization of people is difficult to avoid in even the most carefully constructed descriptions of human social action, this in itself would not be an especially damning indictment of the medical analogy as an approach to the study of human affairs. However, the more serious aspect of this form of stigmatization is that it removes from consideration the possible complicity of those who do not see themselves as pathological. It is, in brief, an arrogant perspective hiding its arrogance behind the benign appearance of medical altruism.

❖ *The Social Nature of Deviant Activity*

Neither the statistical approach nor the medical approach, then, is adequate even for defining the nature of deviant actions. Becker turns to another point of view for dealing with so-called "social problems" or "deviant activity." This point of view sounds disarmingly simple and reasonable at first glance. Its implications, however, lead us far afield from the directions we might take with statistical or medical approaches to deviance. Becker opens his arguments with the following statement:

> The central fact about deviance [is that it is] created by society. I do not mean this in the way it is ordinarily understood, in which the causes of deviance are located in the social situation of the deviant or in "social factors" which prompt his action. I mean, rather, that *social groups create deviance by making the rules whose infraction constitutes deviance*, and by applying those rules to particular people and labeling them as outsiders. From this point of view, deviance is not a quality of the act the person commits, but rather a consequence of the application by others of rules and sanction to an "offender." The deviant is one to whom that label has successfully been applied; deviant behavior is behavior that people so label.[7]

As we have just said, there is a disarming simplicity in this. It is easy, for example, to agree with Becker that no matter what we mean by deviance, we are talking about something that violates the existing rules of the society—whatever those rules may be. When women were not "permitted" to smoke, those who engaged in such actions risked acquiring the status of "deviant." This, of course, parallels present times, when anyone who participates in the use of marijuana risks acquiring the status of "deviant." It makes little difference whether he or she is otherwise a good and proper citizen of the community. It makes little difference whether the person indulges heavily or hardly at all. (Confessing to even a single marijuana experience, even today, can in certain places be damaging to one's career progression.)

Participation in such action, because it is illegal, always means there is the possibility that the participant will be apprehended and informed that he or she is no longer a good and proper citizen. People can be labeled as deviants even if they are engaging in activities that are indulged in commonly, though covertly, by virtually everyone. (A simple example is the fear of exposure of masturbation by men and women at the turn of the century, despite the fact that it was and is practiced by nearly everybody.) So it is, then, that those who acquire the "deviant" label may constitute a small proportion of the total population engaging in the activity that is illegal or negatively sanctioned. The large numbers of those who are not labeled as deviants suggest that trying to see deviance exclusively in terms of personality characteristics is a misguided effort. This contention will be developed further.

So far, the argument is elementary. Part of understanding the nature of deviant activities must include a consideration of those rules that are, in themselves, the defining mechanisms of deviance. Understanding deviant action, then, calls for more than giving attention to the person who has been labeled as deviant. It means that attention must also be given to an analysis and understanding of the rules defining the activity as deviant. To do this adds complications to the examination of social problems. At the same time, it avoids the ultrasimplistic formulations of either the statistical or medical approaches. Deviant activity, from this perspective, is seen in part as a symbolic process that *always* involves at least two parties—the person who is labeled as deviant *and* the person who has the authority or the right to invoke the label.

Even a brief consideration of the implications of Becker's arguments brings several new complications into the study of social conduct in general and the problem of deviant actions more specifically. We cannot consider deviance as simply a manifestation of a particular configuration of personality traits; it is not exclusively a psychological problem. The reason is obvious: The process of labeling people as deviants is not infallible. (Even medical tests are not above criticism. Tests, such as urinalysis testing for drug use, have been heavily criticized for their tendency to label innocent people as drug users.) Those who have not engaged in deviance of a particular kind may be given the label,[8] while others who have engaged in such deviance may not be so labeled. In other words, the total group engaging in the action considered to be deviant is not the same as the group labeled as deviant. This happens because there are difficult problems involved in the accurate and certain identification and labeling of deviants. For practically any class of deviant action, there are large proportions of members of the class who pass as nondeviants.

The greatest difficulty and the most obvious one, then, results from the fact that people are able to disguise or hide their deviant characters. Homosexuals pass as "straight." Drug users learn that they can get high and still go shopping at the supermarket and no one notices. An unknown number of men (but probably a surprisingly large one) practice transvestism and, while dressed as women, make use of women's public restrooms. The ability of people to disguise deviant actions accounts for a part of our interest in such activities, yet at the same time makes it nearly impossible for us ever to have a truly solid body of empirical knowledge dealing with the issue.

The point of the discussion, so far, is to reorient thinking about deviant actions. Becker would like us to change from a psychological view, in which we are inclined to see deviance as something within the deviant, to a more sociological point of view, in which we see deviance as something residing in a more complex relationship between the person who is labeled deviant and the person who is doing the labeling.

If we want to control deviance, we may be able to deal with it in part by raising this question: To what extent is it necessary to label any particular pattern of social action as deviant? The question, in itself, suggests that one way of reducing or "solving" so-called "social problems" is by dismissing them as problems. From this perspective, one of the sources of social problems is the group that somehow acquires the capacity to define a situation or happening as a problem.

It adds more breadth to Becker's work if we recognize that more is going on here than simply a discussion of social problems. Becker is moving toward the central issue of what constitutes a social structure. One way of defining such a structure is to see it as consisting of patterned and stable ways of defining people, so that a particular group acquires the right to define others as "problems." We are then called on to act in terms of the definition established by this group. One way of defining power is to see it as having the ability to so define relationships and human qualities.

❖ Control Agencies

As we have mentioned before, deviant activity, considered at its most abstract and elementary level, involves at least two components: (1) an agency or authority that has acquired the power to define an action or condition as improper and to act in terms of that definition; and (2) an event or occurrence that enables those in authority to label an individual as a deviant person.

This treatment of deviance forces us to consider the qualities of the agency that takes upon itself the task of defining actions considered deviant.

When we do this, otherwise inexplicable aspects of the way we deal with deviants become more understandable. For example, the Catholic church, during the medieval period, took upon itself the task of defining those forms of conduct to be labeled "sinful." Masturbation was among those actions. At the same time, masturbation was (and still is) a common pastime. Today it is looked upon as a modest indulgence practiced by almost any healthy person on occasion. It is apparent, without belaboring the issue too much, that such impossible ideals of virtue and proper conduct produced as much sin as they curbed.

The church, being in a position to absolve sinners of their sins, found it expedient (unconsciously, we like to think) to create sinners. The church then generated a supply of sin with which it could concern itself. The modern analogy is the tendency in psychiatry to set up situations where it is nearly impossible for a person not to express a neurotic pattern. Once the neurosis is apparent, psychiatry can step in with its services. *Deviant actions, then, can be created to maintain the agencies that exist to control the deviant activities.*

This is a fairly common device. We do not want psychiatrists to think we have singled them out for special abuse. Teachers, for example, sometimes operate on the principle of making people feel stupid or ignorant. Since we are all ignorant of a lot of things, we are vulnerable to such treatment. Teachers are then able to provide the commodity for which they have created, as it were, a demand. During the 1972 presidential campaign, there were efforts to make certain radical groups look unusually violent by infiltrating them with agents who provoked such violence. The official establishment then could justify its existence by suppressing a condition for which it was in part responsible. This process is a lot like what some psychologists have referred to as "protective provocation": You provoke a response permitting you to do what you intend to do.

However, the relationship between the defining agency and the deviant is still more subtle. For example, once a pattern of deviant actions has been defined by a controlling agency, the existence of these activities, now defined as deviant or bad, is threatening to the agency. On the other hand, if the deviance does not exist, that also is threatening. Or, as Becker phrases it: "Enforcement organizations . . . typically oscillate between two kinds of claims. First, they say . . . the problem they deal with is approaching a solution. But, in the same breath, they say the problem is perhaps worse than ever . . . and requires renewed and increased effort to keep it under control."[9]

This may help account for why enforcement agencies often make much of those whom they manage to get their hands on and label as deviant. The existence of the problem must be made apparent to all. The public must be kept aware that deviants are around and enforcement agencies are on the job. Thus it comes about that the label of "deviant" is given considerable precedence over most others. For example, individuals who are arrested for a crime soon find that their criminal status preempts practically every other consideration. They have a "record." They are criminals first and anything else second. Their status as criminals becomes a "master" status, and other statuses are subordinated to it.[10] Job applicants learn that undergoing psychiatric therapy in the past can give them a master status as an "unbalanced" person. Application forms for civil service jobs at the University of Colorado, for example, ask the applicant to indicate any psychiatric treatment received during the past three years. It is difficult to believe that anyone who honestly admitted to such treatment would not be under a handicap in getting a position.

We are suggesting, then, in keeping with Becker's arguments, that deviant activity is not something that exists independently of enforcing agencies and for which such agencies came into being. Social deviation is intricately related to more general problems that leaders encounter with regard to maintaining social order. There is more to deviant conduct than a failure of character or a flaw in personality. Becker expresses his argument in the following way:

> When the deviant is caught, he is treated in accordance with the popular diagnosis of why he is that way, and the treatment itself may likewise produce increasing deviance. The drug addict, popularly considered to be a weak-willed individual who cannot forego the indecent pleasures afforded him by opiates, is treated repressively. He is forbidden to use drugs. Since he cannot get drugs legally, he must get them illegally. . . . Hence the treatment of the addict's deviance places him in a position where it will probably be necessary to resort to deceit and crime in order to support his habit. The behavior is a consequence of the public reaction to the deviance rather than a consequence of the inherent qualities of the deviant act.
>
> Put more generally, the point is that the treatment of deviants denies them the ordinary means of carrying on the routines of everyday life open to most people. Because of this denial, the deviant must of necessity develop illegitimate routines.[11]

The claim made here is not especially new. Particularly since marijuana smoking has become so common, people are more aware that the attempt to curb a social problem can possibly be more damaging than the problem itself. Indeed, marijuana smoking, *in and of itself*, may not be a socially serious problem at all. Consider, for example, drinking as a social problem. In a similar fashion, drinking, *in and of itself*, is not a serious matter. Properly constrained, enjoyed in the appropriate atmosphere, it can be a pleasant part of life. When drinking interferes with other routines, its problematic nature begins to reveal itself. However, this is a more complex concern than simply drinking per se.

❖ Deviant Conduct as a "Career"

To make his general ideas more specific and give them substance, we shall turn to one of Becker's early studies. The publication of "Becoming a Marihuana User" helped establish Becker as a leading advocate of a more sociological approach to such activities. The study, originally published in 1953, is now dated (as the spelling of "Marihuana" in the title indicates). However, this gives it, we believe, an added interest. Because there is much argument at present over the pros and cons of marijuana and its effects on both individuals and the community, it is informative to look at earlier studies. To appreciate Becker's effort, we should keep in mind the extent to which public sentiment toward marijuana smoking was less liberal then than it is today.

The value of Becker's study lies in the twist he gave to older approaches to the understanding of deviant conduct. He attacked the idea that deviant activities of this variety are caused by personality traits or motivation. The older concern was with this question: Why would anyone do something like smoking marijuana? Popular forms of speculation in response to this question rely heavily on the idea that people must do it because they have a personality trait (for example, a need to escape or live in fantasy) that predisposes them to such conduct. Or, to use more current terminology, they suffer a loss of self-esteem and this leads them into drug use. Becker turned this conception around, in both his original paper and his later book *The Outsiders*.

> To put a complex argument in a few words: instead of the deviant motives leading to the deviant behavior, it is the other way around; the deviant behavior in time produces the deviant motivation. Vague impulses and desires—in this case, probably most frequently a curiosity about the kind of experience the drug will produce—are transformed into definite patterns of action through the social interpretation of a physical experience which is in itself ambiguous. Marijuana use is a function of the individual's conception of marijuana and of the uses to which it can be put, and this conception develops as the individual's experience with the drug increases.[12]

While reviewing this interpretation of marijuana smoking, we should keep in mind that Becker's original paper was published in 1953. The ideas behind the paper were formulated more than three decades ago—during a time when marijuana smoking was looked on by nearly everyone, including college students and certainly nearly all of their teachers, as a degenerate activity. Perhaps it is an easy matter to conclude that people who indulge in degenerate activities have degenerate characters or personalities. Becker argued, to the contrary, that personality is not an appropriate concept for the examination and understanding of marijuana smoking. Instead, what takes place is something akin to the development of a "career progression" in which the individual, once he or she forms an association with others who smoke marijuana, comes to learn the techniques of smoking and otherwise ingesting marijuana. More significantly, however, the new user acquires a set of "understandings" about the drug and those who smoke it. The progression of this *career*, rather than motivations or personalities, is the proper focus of concern.

Although this career progression is probably still typical for people who take up marijuana smoking, it is not as necessary today as it was in the 1950s and earlier. Today it is possible to purchase manuals in bookstores providing detailed information on how to find, hide, prepare, grow, smoke, cook, and eat marijuana. Much more significantly, however, such manuals provide information with respect to how the drug experience should be interpreted. Current movies also show audiences what it is like to use marijuana. An individual can thus get an education in the use of marijuana without relying on close associates.

As Becker found in the early 1950s, marijuana smokers go through a career that, in brief outline, appears to develop in the following way:

1. They learn about the existence of the drug and display a generally interested attitude toward it—wondering how it would affect them, speculating whether they could take it without "cracking up," and otherwise showing a general and vague interest in it.
2. Then, by happenstance, they gain access to the drug and those who are familiar with it. They come upon an opportunity to try it. This is generally done in the presence of associates and friends who are encouraging and who are already experienced in marijuana usage.
3. They are introduced to the techniques of smoking and the differences between smoking tobacco and smoking marijuana. (If an initiate does not learn the procedures for acquiring sufficient amounts of the drug to obtain an effect, he or she discontinues its use.)
4. They begin to recognize the relationship between the ingestion of the drug and the effects that are a consequence of its ingestion. This is an important step in the "career" of marijuana smokers. Even if effects are produced, unless the initiates are able to associate them with smoking, they will not continue using the drug. *The initiates turn to the more experienced users and seek information concerning how they might reasonably expect to feel.* Here is an excerpt from an interview with a person who recounts his early experiences with the drug:

   > I didn't get high the first time. . . . I don't think I held it in long enough. I probably let it out, you know, you're a little afraid. The second time I wasn't sure, and he [smoking companion], like I asked him for some of the symptoms or something, how would I know, you know. . . . So he told me to sit on a stool. I sat on—I think I sat on a bar stool—and he said, "Let your feet hang," and then when I got down my feet were real cold, you know.
   >
   > And I started feeling it, you know. That was the first time. And then about a week after that, sometime pretty close to it, I really got on. That was the first time I got on a big laughing kick, you know. Then I really knew I was on.[13]

5. With a recognition of the relationship between ingestion of the drug and physical responses, users come to interpret their reactions, finding in them something interesting to talk about—interesting both to

themselves and to others. They reach a point where they probe the nature of the effects they experienced and become sophisticated about the character of these effects. They learn that they can appear in public when high and not be detected. They begin to believe that they can drive a car safely while experiencing effects that previously seemed incapacitating.

6. In the final stages of the career, the users become connoisseurs. They are able to detect differences between lower and higher grades of marijuana. They also probably spend time with friends who are sophisticated in the use of marijuana, and they themselves are active in introducing others to the drug and helping them become sophisticated in its use. In this career development, the significant feature of the process is the manner in which newcomers to the scene are given information by the more experienced practitioners of the art. They not only must ingest the drug, but also must come to define its effects as pleasant. They *do not do this alone.*

One of the central concerns of this point of view is to develop the argument that the circumstances leading to deviant actions are, in their general form, much like the circumstances leading to normal conduct. If this sort of argument can be sustained, it tends to weaken the position that deviant people are the products of deviant motivations or deviant personality structures. Instead, it generates the idea that deviant people are much like nondeviant people in their personality and psychological characteristics. The primary difference between deviants and nondeviants lies in the career path they take, and this can be a matter of chance. Once the path is taken, deviant activities will produce deviant motivations; it is not the other way around.

One other aspect of deviance has led Becker to the conclusion that it should not be viewed as the exclusive product of "warped" or abnormal personalities. He presumes, first of all, that there is a great deal of so-called deviant activity being engaged in continuously within the greater society. Whether one must go through the process of being labeled as deviant and dealt with as such depends upon whether one is singled out as a deviant and presented before others in this light. This is a highly capricious matter. It is difficult to ascertain the proportion of various offenders of conventional morality who get caught, relative to all of those who engage in the offense. In the case of marijuana usage, for example, perhaps twenty million or so persons in the United States violate the conventions. The number who are brought to public attention for this practice, however, is much smaller. Becker wryly comments, at one point, that being caught is about like being hit by lightning.[14]

This being the case, the position taken by those who seek to label the marijuana user as an abnormal person possessed of a predisposing deviant nature find their argument weakened. They must, if they are to establish their point, be able to impose such qualities on relatively large and hidden populations. Rather than turn to deviant or abnormal personalities, Becker adds a couple of new considerations to the problem of deviance. We must, as was suggested earlier, consider how the rules defining deviant activities are established. If, for example, a ruling power comes to the conclusion that being Jewish is wicked and anyone possessed of Jewish qualities should be exterminated, we quickly comprehend the unreasonable nature of the rule. It is unreasonable because the rule, in and of itself, condemns people whom most of us would be willing to accept as "normal" or "good." But the establishment of rules that might actually possess abnormal or deviant qualities within themselves is not always so evident. Indeed, somehow the imposition and execution of rules generally seem reasonable. Certainly history is littered with the detritus of absurd rules that were once the pride of the nations that spawned them.

The entire machinery of lawmaking institutions and the police agencies enforcing the laws are given a rationality or reasonability by the very fact that this machinery is supported by the state. The majority of Germans believed that the "Jewish problem" was being handled properly in the late 1930s. At the same time, the institution of rules defining deviant categories may, in and of itself, be the source of the problems that the rules seek to curb. Or, to put it more simply, one way to reduce crime, deviance, and other such social ills is to reduce the number of rules defining such problems. For example, one way to solve the "social problem" of homosexuality is simply to redefine it as not being a social problem.

If this sounds improper, consider the historical fact that at one time in Western culture, avarice and usury (lending money for interest) were considered social problems. In those times, social problems were called sins. Today, few people in this culture would consider avarice or usury either a problem or a sin. Our society relies on greed and credit to function economically. What was once a problem is now an essential aspect of the culture. By redefining greed as "consumerism," we have altered the nature of the problem. Incidentally, in all of this we gain a further insight into the fact that so-called "social" problems are in fact as much social as psychological.

Becker suggests, then, that an examination of the process by which various agencies come to define actions as deviant should be an integral part of the study of deviance. Another feature of Becker's approach is his concern with deviance as a kind of "career," which can, like any other career, bring about changes in motivations, perceptions, attitudes, tastes, values, and other qualities of the person. Rather than conclude that a person has deviant motives, which lead to deviant conduct, Becker argues that the existence of the career pattern is the most significant objective fact about a given deviant action. Deviance is a sociological as well as a psychological condition. This is, perhaps, a cliché in its straightforward form; if so, it is a cliché that leads to more subtle forms of understanding.

This chapter on Becker and his work has tried to offer an impression of the possibilities that exist for combining practical interests—such as deviance, social problems, and the control of such problems—with theoretical perspectives congenial to a symbolic interactionist point of view. Although Becker is certainly not the only writer to carry off such a venture, his work reveals that it is possible to make good use of theories that are often viewed as irrelevant to the concerns of those who deal with "real" problems.

❖ *Careers as a Uniquely Human Activity*

If we come away from Becker's work with the feeling that it is a specialized study of deviant people—marijuana smokers, drug users, criminals, and other "outsiders"—we miss a lot of what his writing offers. The deceptively simple nature of his observations, along with the specialized topic of drug use, can lead a reader to conclude that his thinking is relatively restricted to the study of deviant actions. This would be wrong. His ideas are more broadly applicable than we might at first suspect. Indeed, this is the central purpose of the sociological imagination—to enable us to see in our personal and professional lives aspects of social control and human social practices we previously were not aware of. Sociology, at its best, is a form of applied vision.

Becker's insights into the nature of deviant actions rely on quite ordinary terms. Concepts such as "career," "career progression," "labeling," "master status," "control agencies," and so forth are not particularly mysterious or esoteric. What Becker asks of us is to use these terms with a deeper understanding of the extent to which they embrace a broad spectrum of human activity. Whereas we commonly think of a "career" person as someone entering into business or the professions, Becker recognizes that virtually any kind of routinized conduct implies a "career" of one kind or another.

Becker's work offers us yet another way of looking at human activities. This becomes more apparent if we once again briefly indicate what Becker has done. The central theme in his work on the marijuana smoker is that such people become involved in this activity in much the same fashion as one enters any other career. There is no need to rely heavily on the idea that the deviant person is psychologically different. If the social context is appropriate, quite normal individuals will find themselves engaging in what are generally thought of as "abnormal" activities. In other words, how people become "outsiders" is similar to the manner in which people become "insiders." The process, in its general form, is much the same. Because the form is general, it can be applied to just about any class of actions we might be interested in.

With certain types of actions, the career process is not commonly talked about or thought of; in other instances, it is a matter of common understanding. For example, we are aware, in at least a vague way, of how a boy or girl in high school is drawn into sports and then eventually accepts a career in athletics as a way of life. In a similar fashion, we are aware of how a person gets drawn into music, soldiering, literature, journalism, teaching, or any of the other accepted careers available to us.

Other activities, however, are difficult to comprehend as careers; we do not think of them as such. Yet the concept of "career" fits them rather well. How, for example, does one become a skilled safecracker or male striptease dancer? Becker suggests that it happens, again in a general sense, similarly to how one enters into any other career. There must be an initial curiosity, and then an encounter with those who understand the career; next, under the care and guidance of those who are already skilled, the individual acquires not only the skill but a set of attitudes and "meanings" that lead to a different mentality with respect to practicing the skill.

This last part of a career progression is possibly the most significant part. The drug user, for example, must encounter not only those who are knowledgeable about drugs, but those who will encourage their use by suggesting that drugs are "cool," "cosmic . . . consciousness-expanding," or whatever other term might be used to enable the user to interpret new experiences in a positive fashion. So it is, then, that we can approach nearly any kind of activity in which we might be interested and look at it in terms of Becker's conceptualization of the development of a career as a uniquely human activity.

Encounters with Social Thought

Studying American Schools

We mentioned earlier in this chapter that Howard Becker has been deeply interested in schooling in America throughout his own academic career. His dissertation completed in 1952 was a research on the effects of social class on the teacher-pupil relationship. He has noted that over the decades of the twentieth century social scientists in various disciplines have been studying schools and education, not the least of them, anthropologists such as Margaret Mead. Anthropologists like to employ a research methodology prominently known as *ethnography*. (This should be differentiated from *ethnomethodology* which we discuss in depth in Chapter 15 in connection the work of Harold Garfinkel.) Ethnography is an anthropological method for studying a group of people in their environment and cultural surroundings. It has been characterized by various anthropologists as a meticulous and highly organized attempt to record and describe the culturally significant behaviors of a particular society or group of people. During the past decade this research strategy has been gaining favor with educational researchers in the study of specialized groups of students such as ethnically and linguistically different children; students at risk; pupils with disabilities;

and professional school students such as those training for legal or medical careers.

In an article about the effectiveness of using the anthropological strategies of ethnography in studying schools, Becker discusses the draft of a study on medical students that he, Blanche Geer, Everett Hughes and Anselm Strauss prepared. He relates that the more thoughtful and dedicated medical professors wanted the researchers to make recommendations for improving their teaching from the outcomes of the investigation.

> For instance, we described (apparently convincingly) how students studied for exams. Student study methods were the usual ones; cram as much factual material as you can into your head just before the test and forget all afterward. That appalled teachers. They wanted students to take a more professional attitude toward their work. We explained to them that they provoked this sort of studying by the kind of exams they gave, which called for exactly that sort of fragmented factual knowledge. "If you want students to study differently," we said, "you can do it by giving them a different kind of exam. What do you want them to know?" They wanted students to be able to make a physical examination, take a medical history, establish a diagnosis, and plan a course of treatment. Our ethnographic knowledge immediately suggested how this could be done: give each student one or two patients to examine and treat, and then let the teachers evaluate how well they had done it.
>
> The faculty looked glum when we said that. What was wrong? *That*, one said, would take a lot of time. . . . Our solution would work, of course, but it wasn't *practical*.[15]

Becker points out that sociologists and anthropologists can produce "solutions" to the problems that educators incur, but these solutions and remedies may not be the ones that teachers and school administrators are willing to take up or implement to ameliorate the dysfunctional situations.

Another social science methodology that is frequently employed in educational research are questionnaires and surveys developed by teachers and school administrators themselves. The following scenario is becoming more frequent and more familiar at all educational levels in recent times:

> Seated around the conference table in the principal's office is a small group of five men and women. They are the members (mostly appointed, not volunteers) of the subgroup of their elementary school's Diversity Taskforce. Their task is to develop a questionnaire to assess the degree of multiculturalism, including gender and life-style awareness, in the curriculum and in the teaching "atmosphere" throughout the school. But this group of people are at a stalemate in the fulfillment of their assignment. They have realized that in order to create an ap-

propriate instrument to distribute to the school staff with questions and other items about the degree of diversity awareness and the actual application to teaching practice in the classroom, there has to be an introduction, some background, some explanation of what the project is all about.

Just to compose the first paragraphs of the questionnaire, the members of this Diversity Taskforce subcommittee have been meeting for over a month, at least once a week, struggling with how to define diversity and multiculturalism in America today. How can the "diversity" questionnaire be presented to the respondents, the teachers, so that meaningful and useful answers will be obtained? How can the concept of what is THE American culture and who is considered to be included in this American culture, be portrayed so that the Diversity Taskforce will be able to assess what is currently being taught about ethnic groups in America? What instruction is going on about diverse life-styles? gender issues? religious diversity? And isn't being "differently abled" (formerly handicapped) and concerns about the aged, all part of the Diversity Taskforce assignment to assess the condition of multiculturalism in the curriculum? So contentious and illusive are these issues in America today, that this subcommittee of merely five people cannot find even one area of complete agreement after struggling with their project week after week.

The task confronting educators and educational researchers, who examine and discuss the current social conflict in American schools, is being vastly complicated by worldwide diversity and cultural pluralism. How can we describe and discuss the interdependent, global society that is evolving currently if we cannot identify what constitutes our own American heritage, values, traditions, customs and life-styles?

Why do social thinkers continue to encourage researchers to do ethnographic studies, naturalistic investigations, and the development of controversial and problematic questionnaires and surveys? Becker asserts that it is because they are loyal to the traditions of the social science disciplines that tell all of us that this is a kind of information worth having, the only kind that will work in the long run.[16]

Putting Social Thought to Work

1. The astronomer Galileo found that people would sometimes refuse to look through his telescope to see what he had seen. They thought it was a "trick." If Galileo ran into difficulties showing people the planets, what kinds of problems do sociologists encounter when they try to tell people about what they know? What right does a sociologist have, anyway, to presume to know more than anyone else about human social affairs?

2. On a more basic level, there is the issue of how we get social information that we regard as valid. In simpler social systems, such information was provided primarily through the family and one's associates. In complex societies, we rely on the experts and people who specialize in informing us about the social world—journalists, entertainers, teachers, psychologists, sociologists, philosophers, ministers, counselors, novelists, and a variety of other people. How do we evaluate the merits of what we are being told? Whom, in other words, can we trust? How do we know we can trust them?

3. One social issue of concern to people is the question of "deviant" actions. What constitutes deviant action? What should we do about it when we encounter it? Why do Americans tend to associate deviant action with a deviant personality? For example, if a person steals a car for a lark, he or she is likely to be labeled a "thief." This is viewed as a quality of the self. Is such labeling explanatory, or is it directed more toward problems of social control? A person once labeled as a thief is vulnerable to continued identification as such. Moreover, other people, assuming that they view such a label negatively, will be influenced against acting in a similar manner.

4. Becker notes that in order for deviance to occur, at least two people are needed—one to engage in an action and another to label the action as deviant. This suggests that so-called "social problems" have at least two possible sources. One may lie in the activities of the group labeled deviant, the other in the activities of those doing the labeling. What are some examples from contemporary society of this observation by Becker?

5. We have noted, in our discussion of Becker's work (see note 8 at the end of the chapter), that people who are "normal" or "sane" and get themselves admitted to mental hospitals for research purposes find themselves having considerable difficulty in getting the doctors and staff members of mental institutions to release them after they are falsely admitted as mentally ill. In these studies, there is also evidence suggesting that the patients of such hospitals are more perceptive of the real condition of the planted "fake" patients than the doctors are. What are the implications of this with respect to the use of rational approaches to dealing with deviant actions? Is it possible to establish purely rational means for dealing with deviance?

6. Becker's work is a modern treatment of an ancient philosophical question: Is evil located within the heart of the individual? Or is evil a product of the communities in which we live? Becker, of course, argues that when a community needs "dirty work" done, the community will get the work done. In so doing, he sustains the argument that people are basically good and it is society that generates badness. A psychologist might argue to the contrary. Is it possible to progress toward a

modern complex social system in which there are no "dirty careers"? How would you design such a system, if you think it is possible? If you do not think it is possible, what are the moral and ethical implications of your position?

7. Do you agree with Becker that teachers and administrators, both in the schools and at higher education levels, really do not want the advice, solutions and suggestions for change that researchers offer them as a result of the in-depth, ethnographic, or other naturalistic methods employed in school research recently? Have you read about or do you know of any instances or examples of studies of individual schools or classrooms? Have you been a part of any such studies during your school career? If so, describe and discuss your experiences with others.

Endnotes

1. Laud Humphreys, *Tearoom Trade: Impersonal Sex in Public Places* (Chicago: Aldine, 1970).
2. The major works of Howard S. Becker include *The Outsiders* (New York: Free Press, 1963); *Making the Grade: The Academic Side of College Life*, with Blanche Geer and Everett C. Hughes (New York: Wiley, 1968); *Sociological Work: Methods and Substance* (Chicago: Aldine, 1970); *Boys in White: Student Culture in a Medical School*, with Everett C. Hughes and Blanche Geer (Chicago: University of Chicago Press, 1970); *Campus Power Struggle*, 2d ed. (New York: Transaction-Society Books, 1973).
3. Howard S. Becker, "Social Class Variation in the Teacher-Pupil Relationship," *Journal of Educational Sociology* 25 (1952), 451–465.
4. Howard S. Becker, "Becoming a Marihuana User," *American Journal of Sociology* 59 (1953), 235–242.
5. Becker et al., *Boys in White*.
6. Becker et al., *Making the Grade*.
7. Becker, *The Outsiders*, pp. 8–9. Italics Becker's.
8. It has been known for quite a while now that "normals" who get themselves admitted to mental hospitals for purposes of research will be accepted as mentally ill by doctors and hospital staff members. Once a person is labeled as having a kind of mental malfunction, it is difficult to convince the staff that he or she is actually normal and should be released. See D. L. Rosenhan, "On Being Sane in Insane Places," *Science* 179 (1973), 250–258.
9. Becker, *The Outsiders*, p. 157.
10. Becker acknowledges an indebtedness to Everett C. Hughes for the concept of "master status." See Everett C. Hughes, "Dilemmas and Contradictions of Status," *American Journal of Sociology* (March 1945), 353–359.
11. Becker, *The Outsiders*, pp. 34–35.
12. Ibid., p. 42.
13. Ibid., p. 50.
14. Becker, *Sociological Work*, p. 333.
15. Becker, "Studying Urban Schools," *Anthropology and Education Quarterly* 14, 2, pp. 107–108.
16. Ibid. p.108.

Sociology as Bad Faith

The Social Perspectives of Peter L. Berger

❖

❖ Analysis and Sentimentality

One of the more expressive writers in modern sociological literature was, at one time, a professor at a seminary in Connecticut. Perhaps his research and writing in the field of religious institutions have made him more receptive to humanistic issues than is common among sociologists. Possibly the fact that he came from Europe in his late teens led him to acquire a humanistic bent before going into sociology. Whatever the reason, Peter L. Berger has produced several books graced by style and dramatic quality.[1] In the work to be discussed here, Berger achieves this dramatic effect by bringing several incompatible ideas together. The result is like the one arising from the meeting of a cold weather front with a warm front: There is a stormy period before the air clears again.

In Berger's most general work, *Invitation to Sociology*, two sets of incompatible ideas are brought together. First, he presents us with a sharply drawn sketch of what might be called classical sociological thought. He pares away the academic issues that float about sociology and lets us take a look at its essence; thus we see sociology stripped of those qualifications that can hide its fundamental character. Then Berger confronts us with existentialist thought—the warm front that clashes with the colder views of sociology. Both positions have legitimacy, and both certainly have a large number of followers; yet the two seem to be in opposition. Sociology, for example, is analytic and deterministic; existentialism is personal and volitional. Sociology relies on a scientific approach to people; existentialism is more subjective and even sentimental. Let us see how Berger describes the conflict between these ways of thinking by beginning with his consideration of sociology.

❖ *Traditional Sociological Thought*

The traditional sociological view comes close to reducing people to the level of being victims of their society.[2] A person is simply born into society and then controlled by it. We are, as Berger nicely puts it, prisoners of society. Society forms the walls of our imprisonment in history.[3] Furthermore, we are guarded closely; even seemingly harmless acts, such as growing a beard or mispronouncing a word, are apt to bring ridicule or some other form of social constraint.

Society is an external force, as coercive and constraining as the physical and biological environments with which we must cope. Moreover, society is internal as well as external. Not only are people within society; society is within people. The very ways one comes to see oneself, the daydreams one has, the aspirations and longings that come to dominate one's thoughts, are not random or independent of society. They are subjective social actions paralleling the larger society. Thus one might daydream of military exploits as a jet pilot, or intellectual attainments as a writer, or business successes as an industrialist—or one might dream of murder.[4] Even so, the form of the daydream—distorted by the individual's ignorance and desires—will conform generally to the model provided by the society. It is in this sense, then, that Berger makes his first point. The sociological view of people reveals them as victims of their society. They are controlled by it from without and from within.

Let us examine this matter of social control in more detail. We need to get a better sense of the extent to which the sociological "cold front" is in fact "cold."

A person is born into a social system and eventually is compelled, in various ways, to meet its demands. An idea of what is taking place might be obtained by imagining human bodies as a form of money that must be distributed and allocated throughout a banking system. Some money must go into certain kinds of activities, and other money must go into yet other kinds of activities. But it is the banking system that does the allocation. In the case of actual money and banking systems, we are dealing with an inanimate element, money, which goes wherever it is directed; the problems of allocation are not disturbed by any presumptions existing within the money itself.

But in human communities the problem is different. When we allocate human beings to different activities, we find ourselves working with a more truculent and complex agent in the process of distribution. Yet the problem of allocation is there, and if society is to retain its integrity as a system, the means of allocation must be efficient enough to protect the system from disruption by the irritable qualities of human beings themselves. The problem, in brief, is to make certain, within limits, that people do what they are told while preventing either rebellion or withdrawal. Anyone who has ever tried to organize a group of people consisting of more than three or four individuals knows just how difficult this can be. If small groups often fall apart, then how is it that large groups manage to hold together? This question, simple to ask but difficult to answer, is the primary question in social philosophy.

❖ *Social Control*

In order to achieve reasonable certainty that people will, in fact, do what they are told, society depends on a variety of devices. The range and character of these devices impress upon us the extent to which we are subject to control from others. Furthermore, as Berger notes, the control coming from others has at the same time an effectiveness and yet a remoteness that can induce a feeling of helplessness on the part of an individual. For example, lower-class people talk about having to do things the way an impersonal "they" want them done. Blacks refer to being exploited by "the man." Not only is one's history on this planet narrowly circumscribed by the social milieu into which one is born, but that milieu is composed primarily of strangers—people one has never met and never will. Even though the demands may come from distant (and usually long dead) strangers, the devices society uses for controlling people are sufficient to see that the demands are met. What are these devices?

The most common and fundamental device is a reliance on violence. People are kept in their place by either the threat of injury to their physical beings or an actual act of violence. No matter how sophisticated a society may be, it nonetheless shares with primitive clans a reliance on this form of social control. The police officials of a modern state are unique within the general population, insofar as they are granted the legitimate right to engage in violence—to use physical force to bring order and stability into the community. The resort to violence to insure control is generally effective. But it is not, of itself, sufficient; it is not the only device upon which a society must rely.

The threat of violence is the demand that the individual conform or suffer. But there are times when the individual would rather suffer any form of physical injury than conform. For example, Sir Thomas More chose to have his head cut off rather than bend wrongfully, as he saw it, to the authority of King Henry VIII. The Romans fed many a Christian to the lion, but they could not kill Christianity. Men and women have gone to the stake and the scaffold. They have stood smiling in front of firing squads. They have taken themselves and their families into confrontations with spitting mobs. They have been tortured with the thin edge of the razor. Yet, despite these physical horrors, they kept their integrity. They did not give in. They did not sell out when the ultimate pressure was brought to bear.

For this reason, violence is insufficient as a control device. There is yet another reason. Violence, for all its dramatic simplicity, does not control the individual other than by outward manifestations. People who are forced to do something, or else have their heads bashed in, may do it, but their attitude toward the whole procedure will probably be one of scheming to find ways to escape. When the Union, through military power, defeated the Confederate states in the Civil War, it was able to dictate its terms. But a military defeat does not always mean a defeat of spirit. The South, even today, manages to retain much of the sentiment and many of the culturally prescribed ways of acting that existed long before the Civil War.

Violence may be necessary, but it is limited as a social control device. It produces a minimal outward conformity, but at the price of generating hatred toward the conformity-inducing agent. It would be better to achieve conformity and, at the same time, to have the conforming individual love the coercion and even become unhappy if the coercive pressures are removed. If necessary, one can always physically threaten a potential nonconformist. However, it is better to win the person's loyalty. Then he or she conforms and, at the same time, brags about it.

Society can win a person's loyalty by means of a second device it has to achieve control. This device consists of controlling an individual's beliefs. At birth, a person is perfectly vulnerable with respect to what he or she can believe. This fact provides the community with an opportunity to use belief as a means of controlling individuals and seeing to it that they fit into their place. Most significantly, they will fit into their place because they believe it is a true and proper place.

A good example of the relationship between belief systems and social control appears in Malcolm X's autobiography.[5] Malcolm X was a leading spokesman for black pride in the 1960s; he was assassinated in 1965. In his autobiography, Malcolm X described his experience when he received his first "conk." Conking is a process whereby a black person's hair is straightened to look more like the hair of a white person. What is important to note here is that black persons who conk their hair believe that straight hair is better. Conking is, then, just one way of acknowledging the natural superiority of whites. Malcolm X described his experience thus:

My first view in the mirror blotted out the hurting. I'd seen some pretty conks, but when it's the first time, on your own head, the transformation, after the lifetime of kinks, is staggering. The mirror reflected Shorty behind me. We both were grinning and sweating. And on top of my head was this thick, smooth sheen of shining red hair—real red—as straight as any white man's.

How ridiculous I was! Stupid enough to stand there simply lost in admiration of my hair now looking "white," reflected in the mirror in Shorty's room. I vowed that I'd never again be without a conk, and I never was for many years.

This was my first really big step toward self-degradation: when I endured all of that pain, literally burning my flesh to have it look like a white man's hair. I had joined that multitude of Negro men and women in America who are brainwashed into believing that the black people are "inferior"—and white people "superior"—that they will even violate and mutilate their God-created bodies to try to look "pretty" by white standards.[6]

Malcolm X was influenced by belief. He later came to believe differently, and at that point he became more truculent toward white domination. His description of conking reveals how far the white belief system was able, at one time in his life, to induce conformity to its ideals.

To the threat of violence and control by belief, we can add a third device available to society—ridicule. Ridicule is essentially a veiled threat to withdraw affection. For example, one teenager might say to another, "If you don't take the turn at eighty-five, you're chicken." The threat of ridicule exists, then, if the taunted person does not respond. This is a common enough way to control the actions of another person. The surprising thing is that such a taunt works. Logically, ridicule of this sort is saying, "If you don't take the turn at eighty-five, we will place you in the class 'chicken.' We do not like people who fall into the class 'chicken.' Therefore, if you don't take the turn, we won't like you any more." Ridicule is, therefore, an indirect assertion of possible dislike or disaffection, but the indirection of the statement seems to make it more effective. In any event, ridicule is an effective means for controlling conduct. We might add here that Japanese parents use it as a means of curbing their children by cautioning them with the admonition, "People will laugh at you."

A fourth and quite common device is the use of fraud. If you cannot force or persuade or ridicule people into conforming, you can try tricking them. (The pervasive use of fraud in everyday life as a means of gaining control over others is the basis of much of Erving Goffman's approach to human social conduct.) The following frustration of the effectiveness of fraud took place during World War II in North Africa. Allied interrogation officers wanted to determine the identity of new German divisions just entering the North African campaign. The use of force and of intimidating threats was not effective. Finally, one interrogation officer suggested that the German prisoners be taken outside into a compound. He then had a variety of numbers put up on stands in an assembly building. After setting up the situation, he told the guards to march the prisoners into the building on the double—with the order that the prisoners were to line up by their division numbers.

The prisoners were then rushed rapidly into the assembly hall and, as the interrogation officers watched, a number of prisoners ran over and stood beside their division numbers. What force was unable to extract, cunning did. (We cannot vouch for the particulars of this illustrative anecdote. It came from a naval intelligence officer several years ago. We like the story because it illustrates, as well as any we know, how fraud can be used to control human actions.) Again, the point is that fraud exists as a device enabling control to be maintained over others. The German prisoners tried to avoid giving information to the enemy; nonetheless, they were coerced into an action contrary to their individual preference or choice.

This illustration might make it appear that trickery or fraud is an occasional device. This would be an erroneous conclusion. Any society relies on deceit, deception, and trickery, in one form or another, rather constantly. Certainly, modern complex societies are studies in the use of what we are broadly referring to here as "trickery." In the chapter on the works of Erving Goffman that appears later in this book, the reader will get an opportunity to consider an approach to human social conduct that gives great emphasis to this feature of human communities.

A fifth device used by society to achieve compliance is the threat of ostracism. Ostracism includes elements of physical violence or injury and elements of ridicule. Yet it is sufficiently different to warrant separate consideration. Ostracism says, in effect, that if you do not "shape up" and do what you are told, you will be asked to remove yourself from the group. In earlier times, ostracism could be an occasion for a ceremonious pronunciamento. An example is the excommunication of the philosopher Baruch Spinoza, which read, in part: "We order that nobody should communicate with him orally, or show him any favor, or stay with him under the same roof, or within four ells of him, or read anything composed or written by him." This statement also demanded that Spinoza "should be cursed by day and night, lying down and rising up, going out and coming in." Spinoza was excommunicated from the Catholic church for suggesting in the seventeenth century that the origins of religious doctrine were located in human historical processes rather than in divine miracles.[7]

When we ostracize people today, we make less show of it, perhaps, but it is still an effective social control device. It appears to be popular at colleges and universities. A student is not subjected to physical violence, nor is he or she especially ridiculed or tricked into doing what is required by the school. The primary social control mechanism is ostracism: If the student does not study and do what the teachers require, he or she will be asked to leave the organization. As a matter of fact, the student will be *required* to leave it. This threat is usually sufficient to maintain at least an approximation of order.

A sixth device for promoting conformity is occupational control. If one does not conduct oneself properly, there are ways of seeing to it that the better jobs are somehow made unavailable. An interesting manifestation of this appears in the following quotation from the *Congressional Record*. In this quotation, we witness an attempt to control religious belief by using occupational controls.

> Mr. Ashbrook (R.–Ohio): Mr. Chairman, I offer an amendment [to the Civil Rights bill]: ". . . it shall not be unlawful employment practice for an employer to refuse to hire and employ any person because of said person's atheistic practices and beliefs."
> Mr. Elliot (D.–Ala.): We leave the right of an atheist to believe, or not to believe, as may be his choice. All this amendment does is preserve for the American employer a freedom to insist that his employees be under God.
> Mr. Jones (D.–Mo.): It would be interesting to see how many people are going to stand up here and be counted, and say they feel an employer is compelled to give consideration to the hiring of an atheist, when he is trying to run a business that is based on good moral grounds.
> Mr. Wickersham (D.–Okla.): You might even require the churches and lodges, clubs and businessmen and Congressmen to hire atheists unless this amendment is accepted.
> The question was taken, and on a division demanded by Mr. Celler, there were—ayes 137, noes 98.[8]

It seems, from the account above, that religious freedom extends only as far as the right to believe in a particular religion or other; it does not extend all the way to having the freedom to believe atheistically or the freedom not to believe in orthodox ways. The amendment considered in this debate is interesting, because it permits the discussants to feel they are permitting freedom ("the right to believe . . . as may be his choice"), while at the same time invoking a possibly severe penalty if the individual is so naive as to tell a Christian, Jewish, or other employer that he or she is an atheist. So occupational control is yet one more device available for inducing conformity and compliance from people who might otherwise act "badly."

A seventh device referred to by Berger in his discussion of the force society can bring to bear on the individual is control coming from the "sphere of intimates." This is a subtle but effective form of control. Studies of soldiers in combat show that the ordinary soldier is not motivated to fight by lofty political ideals and moral philosophy. He fights because his buddies are fighting. Another illustration of what Berger means by influence coming from the "sphere of intimates" is suggested in the following passage from Vance Packard's *The Hidden Persuaders*:

> A young New York ad man taking a marketing class . . . made the casual statement that, thanks to TV, most children were learning to sing beer and other commercials before they learned to sing the Star-Spangled Banner. Youth Research Institute, according to *The Nation*, boasted that even five-year-olds sing beer commercials "over and over again with gusto." It pointed out that moppets not only sing the merits of advertised products but do it with the vigor displayed by the most raptly enthusiastic announcers, and do it all day long "at no extra cost to the advertiser."[9]

Finally, there is an eighth way in which the actions of the individual are directed and controlled by others—through systems of mutual obligation. This is essentially a contractual variety of relationship stating, either explicitly or implicitly, "If you do such-and-such, then I shall do so-and-so." The point here is that once the contract is entered, the actions of the individual become controlled by it. Even when a person may prefer a different course of action, he or she can still be coerced into conforming through the stipulations of reciprocal contractual agreements. For example, many of the letters addressed to Ann Landers and Dear Abby have to do with a problem arising from a reciprocal obligation that went sour. An example, that occurs more frequently than we think, was described in a letter to an advice columnist. The letter related how a product salesman came to the home to demonstrate a household device and before the homeowner knew it she had signed a contract to buy the device on monthly installments for two years. She realized that she now had to inform her husband about these monthly installments. Further, she really did not need the product and could not afford it anyway. The letter writer was appealing to the advice columnist to ask if there was some way she could get out of the contract?[10]

Society relies, then, on at least these eight devices for assuring itself that any given individual will not step far out of line. So when Berger says a person is the prisoner of society, he identifies the bars of the prison: threats of violence, belief systems, ridicule, fraud and deception, threat of ostracism, occupational controls, the influence of intimates, and reciprocal obligations. These are effective constraints, and people are kept in line by them. But they still do not exhaust the extent to which a person is "held" by society. We must not only see the person in society; we must become aware of the extent to which society is in the person.

❖ Social Identity

Society enters a person by providing him or her with an identity. Identity is related to the social class into which one is born; more specifically, it is related to the social roles one is required to play as a member of the social system. Berger phrases it succinctly:

> This significance of role theory could be summarized by saying that, in a sociological perspective, identity is socially bestowed, socially sustained and socially transformed. The example of [a] man in process of becoming [a military] officer may suffice to illustrate the way in which identities are bestowed in adult life. However, even roles that are much more fundamentally part of what psychologists would call our personality than those associated with a particular adult activity are bestowed in a very similar manner through a social process. This has been demonstrated over and over again in studies of so-called socialization—the process by which a child learns to be a participant member of society.[11]

The belief system into which children are born has, in addition to providing them with ideas about the world around them, the special capacity of providing them with certain notions about themselves. It is in this sense that society is able to enter a person's character and thereby "victimize" that person. The socially derived conceptions people acquire about themselves are relatively enduring. Beliefs related to major organizational elements of a society are especially connected to concepts of self. For example, in India, caste has been a central organizational feature of Indian society. It is essential that people born into the different subcaste levels acquire beliefs about themselves that permit the caste system to operate relatively smoothly. In order that a member of a depressed caste will in fact feel inferior and unworthy, the caste system imposes the following restraints on lower-caste persons, requiring that they:

1. cannot be served by clean Brahmins
2. cannot be served by barbers, tailors, and the like who serve caste Hindus
3. may pollute those with whom they come in contact
4. cannot serve water to caste Hindus
5. cannot use public conveniences such as ferries, wells, or schools
6. may not enter Hindu temples
7. must engage in a despised occupation.[12]

After being worked over in this fashion, it is not surprising that individuals, as they mature, take on an identity that fits them into the caste system. They accept the allocated slot—no matter how wretched the slot might be.

It is, however, an oversimplification to see society as a static structure with various positions to be filled and people placed in these slots to remain there throughout their lives. Two complicating factors should be taken into account. In the first place, positions that once were functional in a society may lose their meaning or value. Thus, with the advent of the automobile, people trained as blacksmiths had to change their occupation. In the second place, it is generally necessary for a person growing up to make various modifications in social position. After all, one cannot be treated like a child all one's life. These two simple qualifications require consideration of the problem of identity changes. Berger refers to more pervasive and durable forms of identity change as "alternation." Thus, a student who comes to college with strong religious faith as an integral part of his or her identity and then becomes an atheist in the senior year has undergone alternation.

❖ *Alternation and Lack of Character*

Alternation can be a relatively gentle process or a violent one, depending on the extent to which the individual must be protected from further alternations. For example, if it is necessary to create a definite cleavage between a boy and his mother when the boy reaches adulthood, a society is likely to achieve this through rigorous and painful tests of manliness. Any future alternation away from a manly identity is made less probable by such tests. Where alternation is not as much of a problem, initiation rites are less severe. Alternation suggests that social identity is subject to change. A person can be one thing at one time and something else at another.

Berger is more descriptive: He uses the term "lack of character" to refer to this feature of human actions. People lack character insofar as they are able to undergo changes in identity. The pacifistic civilian can be transformed into a bayonet-wielding marine. In an example used by Berger, "The Nazi concentration-camp commander who writes sentimental letters to his children is but an extreme case of something that occurs in society all the time."[13]

For the sociologist, lack of character is not a cause for a diatribe on hypocrisy. It is, rather, a cause for emphasizing more fully the social character of self. If lack of character is typical (and observation seems to support this view), then to whatever extent character exists, it is implanted there by the social performance required of the person. Identity, self, and character are sustained by social demands and cannot exist independently of such demands. Thus, jazz musicians who play before "square" audiences feel themselves possessed of a corrupt character that later must be washed away by ritualistic musical performance.[14] Or we find the sadistic Nazi storm trooper being brutal in one context and gentle in another.

These are not insincere or hypocritical performances. When Berger says that people suffer from a lack of character, he does not mean that they are entirely without character of any kind. He means, instead, that the characters people possess are highly responsive to the social situations in which they find themselves. These characters can vary considerably from setting to setting, and yet the individuals can retain a sense of sincerity in their actions.

> That is why insincerity is rather a rare phenomenon. Most people are sincere, because this is the easiest course to take psychologically. That is, they believe in their own act, conveniently forget the act that preceded it, and happily go through life in the conviction of being responsible in all its demands. Sincerity is the consciousness of the man who is taken in by his own act. Or as it has been put by David Riesman, the sincere man is the one who believes in his own propaganda.[15]

The individual responds, then, to group opinions and can, within certain latitudes, adhere to contradictory identities and act accordingly. What an individual "really is" amounts, in the final accounting, to an enumeration of the situation in which he or she is one thing and those in which he or she is another.[16] The fact that people lack character means that they are susceptible to identities imposed on them by others. The illustrations just given are concerned with making the point that social identities do in fact have a social locus because they are subject to change. If, for example, the Nazi commander were cruel in all circumstances, we would have reason to suspect that his character reflects a genetic or inborn quality. However, because he is gentle toward one group of people and cruel toward others, submissive to his superiors and belligerently domineering toward his inferiors, we can conclude that his character is actually quite variable—responding to the demands made by particular social occasions and relationships.

We lack the ability to give meaning to ourselves in isolation from others. Others provide us with an identity, and we have little recourse but to respond accordingly. This identity, furthermore, has a "real" quality. A woman who, as a result of an indiscreet love affair, finds others referring to her as a "slut" and a "tramp" might find the alternation being demanded of her impossible. She might react by becoming depressed or perhaps even going so far as to attempt suicide. Thus, the identity problem is sufficiently intense or real to produce reactions that can run contrary to the naturally grounded demands of biological survival.

❖ The Mechanical Conception of People

Let us now pause for a moment and pull a few ideas together. Berger first attempts to overwhelm us with an extreme statement of what sociological determinism means. It means, in a metaphorical way, that we are the prisoners of society. Society uses a variety of devices to make certain we remain in line. The devices are generally successful because, by and large, people do conform. Look around you. In their public appearances, at least, people show a surprising "standardization." They talk alike, they dress much alike, and they generally keep out of trouble. Berger indicates why. Nonconformity is socially disruptive and will invoke controls over the individual. If one becomes too recalcitrant, one will be removed from the picture—sent either to an asylum (a prison within the prison) or to eternity.

So people are prisoners of their society. But this is not all: They are willing prisoners. They come to want what society wants them to want. They are not only controlled by external forms of coercion; they are controlled by internal coercion, which takes the form of social identity. A person is granted a certain identity and comes to view the self accordingly. Eventually, the person attempts to respond as he or she believes someone with such a character ought to respond.

We now are more aware of the extent to which sociology presents a cold and virtually mechanical conception of people. Whatever we are, we are by virtue of the fact that we exist within a greater social structure. Our character and our fate are determined by where we happen to be born within the structure. All else is irrelevant to the sociological quest.

❖ A Discussion of Freedom

Overdrawn as this picture is, there is much truth in it. Still, it is a disturbing kind of truth, and we find ourselves longing for alternatives that might yet allow us to view ourselves as creatures with heroic qualities. We want to think of ourselves as more than pawns or agents of social force. Berger examines a possible alternative by entering into a discussion of freedom. To what extent can people break free from the constraints of society and still survive as individuals? What means are available to a person for finding freedom and individuality?

We can begin by considering a characteristic of the mechanical conception of sociology outlined in the previous pages: In at least one respect, it bears a striking resemblance to instinct theory. Behavior in an ant is channeled by instincts; in a person, it is channeled by institutional directives. Both the ant and the person behave because of coercion. The only difference, it would seem, is that the coercion to which the ant is subjected comes from "inside"; that to which a person is subjected comes from "outside." The ant responds to instinct; the person responds according to social character.

So both the ant and the person, when asked why they act as they do, might respond, "Because I must." However, such a reply is perfectly correct only in the ant's case. People deceive themselves when they say, "Because I must." We employ the phrase "I must!" to hide from ourselves the fearful thought that it might be otherwise—the thought that we have chosen to act the way we are acting. We may be only pretending that something is necessary when, in fact, it is not. Jean-Paul Sartre refers to this as "bad faith." Berger describes it in the following way:

> To put it very simply, "bad faith" is to pretend something is necessary that in fact is voluntary. "Bad faith" is thus a flight from freedom, a dishonest evasion of the "agony of choice." "Bad faith" expresses itself in innumerable human situations from the most commonplace to the most catastrophic. The waiter shuffling through his appointed rounds in a café is in "bad faith" insofar as he pretends to himself that the waiter role constitutes his real existence, that, if only for the hours he is hired, he *is* the waiter. . . . The terrorist who kills and excuses himself by saying that he had no choice because the party ordered him to kill is in "bad faith," because he pretends that his existence is necessarily linked with the party, while in fact this linkage is the consequence of his own choice. It can easily be seen that "bad faith" covers society like a film of lies. The very possibility of "bad faith," however, shows us the reality of freedom. Man can be in "bad faith" only because he is free and does not wish to face his freedom. "Bad faith" is the shadow of human liberty. Its attempt to escape that liberty is doomed to defeat. For as Sartre has famously put it, we are "condemned to freedom."[17]

With this statement, Berger seemingly reverses himself and, by doing so, throws everything into a state of confusion. Until now Berger has spent a great deal of effort confronting us with a sociological conception of humanity that finds people "locked" in society. Now he turns around and tells us that Sartre is correct when he says we are "condemned to freedom." What is going on? If we stay with Berger a little longer, we will find that he is not being as contradictory as it might first appear. The existentialist position of Sartre can, if we think about it more carefully, mesh with the arguments and perspectives of the sociologist. For the moment, let us return to a further consideration of the existentialist position.

> Sartre has given us a masterful vista of the operation of "bad faith" at its most malevolent in his portrayal of the anti-Semite as a human type. The anti-Semite is the man who frantically identifies himself with mythological entities ("nation," "race," "Volk") and in doing so seeks to divest himself of the knowledge of his own freedom. Anti-Semitism (or, we might add, any other form of racism or fanatical nationalism) is "bad faith" *par excellence* because it identifies men in their human totality with their social character. Humanity itself becomes a tacticity devoid of freedom. One then loves, hates and kills within a mythological world in which all men are their social designation, as the SS man *is* what his insignia says and the Jew *is* the symbol of despicability sewn on his concentration camp uniform.[18]

Society "imprisons" people. However, it can do this only when people permit the deceptions foisted on them by society to take on the quality of reality. What Berger suggests, as a sociologist, is that people are kept prisoners by society only to the extent to which they permit themselves to remain ignorant of its influence. With knowledge and understanding of the nature of their communities, people can begin to free themselves of its controls when those controls are not beneficial. They can begin to comprehend the extent to which choice is available. We can play various social roles knowingly or blindly. When we play them blindly, we are the victims of society. When we play them knowingly, society becomes the medium through which we express our volition.[19]

This conception of freedom suggests that social awareness is a means toward attaining personal freedom. Social awareness prevents us from being "duped" or overwhelmed by the social fictions surrounding us. It would then seem reasonable to conclude that sociology—one way of obtaining a more sophisticated understanding of social reality—would be a certain route to the attainment of greater freedom. Unfortunately, it is not possible to make such claims for sociology. This discipline can be used as an academic justification for existing inhumanities, or it can be an approach to a morally critical understanding of our injuries to each other. There is nothing within sociology itself that dictates the use to which it might be put. Berger states the problem thus:

> Sociological understanding itself can become a vehicle of "bad faith." This occurs when such understanding becomes an alibi for responsibility. . . . [F]or example, a sociologist located in the South may start out with strong, personal values that repudiate the Southern racial system and he may seek to express these values by some form of social or political action. But then, after a while, he becomes an expert, qua sociologist, in racial matters. He now really feels that he understands the system. At this point, it may be observed in some cases, a different stance is adopted *vis-à-vis* the moral problems—that of the coolly scientific commentator. The sociologist now regards his act of understanding as constituting

the sum total of his relationship to the phenomenon and as releasing him from any of those acts that would engage him personally.[20]

Berger is aware that the socially responsible use of sociology is not easy to describe. The cool and dispassionate scientist described in the quotation above can be exemplifying bad faith while acting on sound moral principles. Whether it is bad faith or morally responsible action must rest, in the final analysis, on the social scientist's careful evaluation of whether, by maintaining a dispassionately analytic point of view, the outcome will be the attainment of humanistic ends. There is always the possibility that the detached objectivity of the sociologist is a way of appearing to be interested, when, in fact, objectivity takes the place of personal commitment.

❖ *Sociology as a Humanizing Effort*

In his final evaluation of sociology, Berger finds it to be a humanizing endeavor, although, of course, it is not necessarily such: Sociologists can promote inhuman or dehumanizing activities as well as humanizing ones. It depends totally on the manner in which sociology is to be used. As Berger puts it, it is not easy to find a humanistic dimension in research that is trying to find the optimum crew composition of a bomber or seeking ways to entice a somnambulant consumer into buying a particular breakfast cereal.[21] Even so, the typical or general effect of sociological sophistication is to bring about a more humanistic sense. The kinds of understanding sociologists bring to such matters as the social meaning of race, sexual conduct, and capital punishment have liberating moral implications. For example, studies by criminologists that show there is no relationship between capital punishment and indulgence in crime tear at the fiction that capital punishment is necessary. If we retain capital punishment, we do so now more from choice than from necessity.

The important thing Berger gets at, however, is a recognition of the fact that sociology is not *necessarily* morally liberating. A sociological understanding of the race problem can result in profound comprehension of why, for example, the African American has been held in bondage for centuries. Berger is well aware, as we have already seen, that such comprehensive understanding can produce a feeling of acceptance—it is simply the way things are. The powerful and grinding interplay of vested interests, ingrained social beliefs and fictions, the processes of intergroup conflict and struggle, social differentiation, role demands, and the needs of a greater social system can, as one begins to comprehend them, generate the attitude that it is only *natural* for people to suffer in any social system.

If a sociologist or a student of human activities gets no further than this, then he or she is likely, in a real sense, to employ sociology as a form of bad faith. Existing inhumanities are justified in scientific terms, and there is nothing we can do to correct them. We can lecture about them, or we can research them, or we can write books about them; however, when it comes to improving someone's lot, there is nothing to do but stand aside and assume the cool and quite patronizing attitude of the dispassionate observer. Berger, of course, does not endorse this attitude, and he goes considerably outside the limits of formal sociological scholarship to find a way of avoiding sociology as bad faith. It is for this reason that he touches on existentialist philosophy. The sociologist must not become the apologist for the existing system. He or she must not be the Western equivalent of the articulate and educated Indian who says that the caste system is good because it permits the maximum amount of social differentiation with the minimum amount of friction.

Sociology and existentialism seem so fundamentally different in character that we need to attempt a resolution of these differences before bringing this chapter to a close. A partial resolution, at least, can be achieved by comprehending the differences in what each approach seeks to achieve. Sociology is analytical. Essentially, it takes events after they occur and asks the question "Why?" Once an event occurs, it is really quite foolish to rely on concepts like "choice" or "freedom" or "volition" as ways of bringing understanding to the matter. If a race riot tears apart a Los Angeles black ghetto, then it gets us nowhere to say, "They did it because they chose to." After Adolf Eichmann sent hundreds of thousands of people to their deaths in gas chambers, it would be ridiculous to say that he was expressing his volition. We now know that. He did what he decided to do, and we know he decided to do it because he did it. This gets us nowhere at all. We still want to know *why* he chose this particular course of action over alternative courses of action confronting him.

In response, historians and sociologists might point to such conditions or influences as the cultural reaction of Germany as a nation to the insulting demands of the Versailles Treaty, the charismatic qualities of Hitler, or the ability of the Nazis to dominate the military but less brutal *Junker* class. Psychologists might concentrate on the personal life of Eichmann, his relationship toward his Jewish friends, and his own fears and anxieties. So it continues, and out of the past comes at least a partial understanding of people's inhumanity to others.

If concepts like "choice" and "freedom," are useless within a sociological context, how do they acquire validity within an existentialist context? Existentialism is able to maintain a validity of its own when it uses terms like "choice" and "freedom," because it is concerned with getting people to recognize that before an event occurs one does have choice. There is a place in the mental realm of human beings that cannot be touched by science or analysis—and this place is the subjective anticipation occurring prior to taking a course of action.

The point is that, prior to acting, the individual is free to act in a contrary fashion. There is still available the possibility of conducting oneself in a fashion that a psychologist or sociologist would not be able to anticipate. Existentialist thought tries to make the individual face up to the possibility of choice in life. Existentialism attempts to turn the individual toward the coming moment rather than the past determinant. Existentialism attempts to reconstruct a philosophy of individual responsibility. Above all, existentialism, as Berger is concerned with it, attempts to bring us to an awareness that inhumanity cannot be rationalized. When we impose suffering and misery on others, we do so through choice, not through necessity. After the fact, perhaps, we can explain away what was done. But before the fact, we choose our course of action.

A trivial but common enough example may help clarify several aspects of this discussion. Teachers who isolate themselves from students, who curtly dismiss those in trouble as "stupid" and "worthless," and who take pride in the high percentage of failures in their classes are acting in an inhuman fashion. They may rationalize their conduct by pointing to the necessity to do research or sustain "standards." The point is, however, that they choose from several alternatives the one they find self-gratifying. There is no necessity. The dehumanizing use of epithets like "stupid" and "worthless" may be a device protecting the teacher from the moral sense of conscience this decision implies. "They" are stupid; "I" am wise. "They" are wrong; "I" am right. It is this kind of attitude that the existentialist fights, forcing the individual to see such conceptions of others as a matter of choice and personal responsibility. Sociology also fights such an attitude, but from another vantage point. The analysis of the past reveals, time after time, the social fictions that have caught people up and led them into frightfully inhuman acts. Possibly, then, sociology and existentialism may have a meeting place after all.

Sociology, by emphasizing the "fictional" nature of much social conduct, provides the basis for seeing human actions as "constructions." They are not something immutably determined by "human nature" or our genes. The hope exists that, with greater knowledge, human beings can create social systems offering greater opportunity for the full expression of human life and consciousness. We can modify the set of fictions that surround us and bind us. To do so, however, we must sense the possibility of escape. It is this sense of possibility that existentialist thought offers. Sociology provides the blueprints and plans revealing the outlines of the structure of the prison containing us. Existentialism presents the possibility—indeed, the moral necessity—of an escape into something better.

Sociologists like Peter L. Berger add a further dimension to sociology. In their hands, it becomes not only an instrument for analysis; it takes its place between science and the humanities. It becomes a further means of developing a humanistic perspective. Berger is not willing to let the sociologist say, "Sociology for the sake of sociology." Unless sociology is used for humanity's sake, it is worse than an empty effort. Its use becomes an institutionalized and legitimized form of bad faith.

❖ *Political Implications of the Idea of Freedom*

This brief review of one of Berger's more popular works underscores an ancient philosophical puzzle. In effect, the puzzle consists of determining whether or not people are free agents with the ability to choose their destinies, or instead are much like everything else on this planet—driven by constraining forces over which they actually have little real control. Are our lives determined, or can we choose our fate? Strong arguments can be made on either side of the issue.

Berger is correct in suggesting that Western social science emphasizes the belief that our lives are determined. Indeed, the task of any science is essentially to find the determinants of whatever condition we might be interested in. Medicine, for example, could not get very far by assuming that people simply choose to get sick. Physics does not even consider the possibility that subatomic particles choose to disintegrate. A botanist does not assume that a growing plant has freely chosen to become a rose instead of a daisy. It is only when we get into the realm of human affairs that the concept of choice or freedom begins to make itself strongly felt. It is a most significant and human concept. We cannot conclude this discussion of Berger without at least mentioning a few of the problems into which the concept of freedom leads us.

We have already suggested that freedom is a concept that is antithetical to explanation. If an individual chooses a given course of action, then choice, in and of itself, is the sufficient accounting for the action. It makes no sense to attempt to determine why a person has chosen a given action, because then you have introduced a set of determinants. If there are determinants, then the person obviously did not choose the action, but was instead led into the action by causal influences.

All of this might sound like abstract metaphysical meandering. It is, however, metaphysics with a real bite to it. Whichever way we turn between the alternatives of determinism and choice, we run into vital, practical, and serious political and human problems. For example, Western criminal justice is based on a philosophy of choice. Indeed, unless we believe a lawbreaker broke the law willingly, we cannot invoke punitive sanctions. The present practice of excusing people from punitive sentencing because they are mentally defective is a case in point. In such instances, the individual is presumed to be under the influence of a powerful determinant that relieves the person of responsibility for his or her actions.

Carried to the extreme, a philosophy of freedom or volition moves into a sentimental realm of discourse. In such extreme applications, all pretense of understanding determinants is ignored. The individual becomes the sole repository of the forces leading to the decision to act and becomes the responsible agent for the action. For example, a young boy steals a car. Why did he steal the car? If we then answer "Because he chose to," we close off all further discussion. The individual is the exclusive determining agent and the final locus of responsibility. It is only through concepts such as "volition," "freedom," "choice," and related terms that we are able to assign responsibility to the individual.

In social philosophy, overreliance on the idea of freedom, curiously enough, transforms freedom into a strangely repressive device. The point can be made with an anecdote. One of us (R. P. Cuzzort), during a stay in Colombia, visited a grotesquely impoverished barrio. Later, during a conversation with one of Colombia's wealthiest businessmen, he mentioned his trip to the barrio. "Oh," said the wealthy Colombian, "those people who live in that horrible place. I really do not understand them. It makes no sense why they would want [i.e., choose] to live in such a wretched way." For the businessman, the people of the barrio were there by choice. It was obvious to him that they chose their fates because it was equally obvious that they were living in the barrio. Notice that this belief relieved the businessman of any sense of responsibility or concern. If they wanted to live that way, it was their own business. There was no accounting for it.

In responding to Berger's writing, we must attend to his own admonition to use the social sciences—and, indeed, our fullest lives—to the end of humanizing ourselves and those around us. Berger should have warned us that freedom is a concept that can dehumanize as well as humanize. It is a term that, properly used, calls for a great deal of careful thinking. Rarely is it properly used.

Encounters with Social Thought

The Environmental Problem—Choice or Constraint?

To a greater degree than is characteristic of most sociologists, Berger's writing moves us back to a consideration of broad moral issues. Western social science, in its quest to achieve a science of social reality, has tried to bypass the question of moral concerns. The ideal endorsed by the social sciences is to be as objective as possible in all things and concentrate on analysis rather than argue over what people ought to do. The objective ideal in Western social science is nothing less, and certainly nothing more, than to deal with "what is" rather than "what should be." The discussion of freedom and constraint appearing in Berger's *Invitation to Sociology* reintroduces the objective ("what is") versus the moralistic ("what should be") issue. The proper application of Berger's ideas, or at least the ideas we have drawn on here, is a matter of coming to recognize complex moral issues that force themselves into any kind of objective analysis or description we might make of human events. In the course of such efforts, we begin to acquire a better awareness of what moral systems within human communities are actually doing. We also begin to see the virtual impossibility of being purely objective when it comes to human communal concerns. No matter what we are doing when we act as humans, we cannot avoid the question of moral implications.

To illustrate, through an application, the direction in which an understanding of Berger leads us, we now turn to what is a growing and universal problem—the deterioration of the environment of the planet. In the course of the following discussion, we shall presume that the reader is generally familiar with the dismal statistics and arguments recently coming out of atmospheric, oceanographic, and urban studies. The ozone layer of the earth itself is possibly being seriously depleted. There are strong and serious indications of a warming of the earth's atmosphere, leading to the melting of the polar ice caps. The major cities of the world currently sit within dense clouds of poisonous smog. Cities such as Tokyo, Mexico City, Los Angeles, Phoenix, and other urban centers, grow more and more polluted. The oceans themselves appear incapable of absorbing the huge loads of trash and nonbiodegradable plastics now pouring into them from continental land masses. The picture is a grim one. However, dismal though the picture is, we are not concerned with filling in its details.

We shall, for the moment, presume the possibility of an ecological disaster capable of possibly destroying the planet as a locale for human life. The question is not whether this will or will not happen. Rather, if we had a sense that it would happen, could we freely undertake to turn the situation around, or, instead, are grand socioeconomic forces now set in place that will force us to capitulate to our own excesses? The question, in and of itself, offers a sense of the humanistic scope of the concerns to which Berger has dedicated himself. There are severe implications coming out of how we respond to this question.

If, for example, we conclude that it is a hopeless business—if we conclude that the populations of the world will ravage the planet until it is ultimately exhausted—then, within a few short generations, the planet Earth will join its planetary mates in a lifeless cycle of solar orbits. It will become a dead globe in which geological weathering will erode all but a few traces of what were once grand and vital civilizations. This position, incidentally, appears to be one taken by most observers, especially those who like to think of themselves as political and economic "realists." That is to say, the economic and institutional forces in which we are now caught up are so vast and so controlling that we cannot hope to change them before it is too late. If this is the truth of the matter, then the idea of "freedom" is nothing more than empty rhetoric. What does a word such as "freedom" mean if we are not even free to save our tiny planet in order that our children and our children's children may be able to breathe and live? The term "freedom" then becomes absurd, and we are consequently absurd to think of ourselves as "free" men and women.

There is yet another dimension, a more personal one, in how we respond to the question of whether we are free to solve the "ecoproblem." If we presume, along with the realists, that the socioeconomic and institutional forces are so vast as to be beyond our ability to turn them around, then we are absolved of any kind of moral responsibility for what happens. What will come will come. It is society's fault, or the economy's, or something else's. We have no say in the matter, and, having no say, have no responsibility. Curiously enough, this frees us to act however we might wish. The race to consume can be joined without guilt.

The ecological problems facing the world today are no different in form from the basic Malthusian problem with respect to population growth. As noted earlier in this book, Thomas Malthus argued that populations grow more rapidly than the systems on which they depend for support. As a consequence, the fate of humankind is to suffer and die. The only natural checks on population growth, he argued, are famine, disease, pestilence, and war. This is a natural and unavoidable fact of life. We cannot choose to do much about it. Contraceptives and other forms of population control offer us possible freedom from the melancholy fate predicted by Malthus. Still, the world's population grows despite our modern freedom.

The ecological problem is not so much a consequence of population growth, which is subject to the checks Malthus talked about. It is a consequence of the astonishingly rapid proliferation of our ever hungry and ravenous machines. Machines, like people, must consume resources in order to survive; unlike human populations, they exhale vast quantities of lethal waste. The pure air and resources of our planet are transformed into industrial feces—the waste products of engines. Unlike organic feces, the waste products of machines and engines are not part of a vital ecological recycling process. The excesses are now obvious. The demographic dynamics of machines are as lethal as the old Malthusian demographics. The question becomes one of whether we should or should not stop their growth. If not, there is no problem. If so, then there is yet another problem: Can we stop them? To put Berger's perspective slightly differently, do we control our machines, or do our machines control us?

It makes a difference, then, both morally and practically, whether we endorse a philosophy in which we see ourselves as being controlled by circumstances or in control of our circumstances. There is more than a hint in Berger's arguments that modern Western social science, particularly as it has appeared in the United States in the past, promotes an objective stance and a philosophy based on determinism rather than volition. It shies away from moral concerns on the grounds that such concerns are not scientific. This attitude, found in economics, psychology, social psychology, sociology, and (possibly to a lesser degree) anthropology and political science, is based on the belief that all human actions are caused by determinants. It is the task of the social scientist to ascertain the nature of these determinants.

Berger's discussion of freedom inclines us to wonder about this sentiment. We must consider not only whether it is possible to establish the causes of human actions, but what the consequences might be if we did. Could human social life, as we now know it, continue if we determined, down to the last factor, why we do the things we do? Remember, if this endeavor were successful, it would mean that people have no choice (or even the illusion of choice) in their lives. As individuals, we would be reduced to the level of all other things in nature—blindly blowing before the winds of complex causal forces.

At the apex of respectability among the American social sciences stands the field of economics. Like the other social sciences, it is a field that strongly endorses a policy of objectivity, detachment, statistical description, mathematical studies, analysis (as opposed to synthesis), and a focus on purely economic matters. When we examine the major efforts of economists, we find that the predominant economic studies describe what is taking place within an economic system without commenting in any serious, sustained, or profound manner on the moral implications of that economic activity.

In the United States, for example, this means an endorsement by economists of the peculiar idea that economic growth must be sustained. A survey of economic books and articles quickly reveals that the concept of growth is accepted by all but an extremely small and generally disregarded body of economic writers.[22] There are policy disputes in economics, of course, but these take the general form of arguing over which policy will be most effective in generating growth. Productivity, with its economic corollary of consumption, is accepted as a bedrock fact of economic life. It is natural to produce, and it is even more natural to consume. There is little in Western economic thought challenging this assumption. There is, on the other hand, much that sustains it.

The result of this institutionalization of economic awareness is the massive support of a point of view that looks on economic processes as forces apart from the free expression of men and women. The immediate rejoinder to a comment such as this, of course, is to point out that Western economic practice is grounded in the dynamics of a *free* market. The market and its economic repercussions are, however, unchallenged. An economy based on the free expression of market demands is an economy rooted, in the final analysis, in the free expression of consumption. So it is that Western economic philosophy looks on unbridled consumption as an aspect of the human condition even more solidly rooted in nature than Malthus's notions about the growth of organic populations.

Economics offers us a vision of our economic nature as one in which freedom is merely the freedom to consume. Other alternatives are closed off. Moreover, the productive system, being dependent on consumption, must encourage consumption. Each nation, as it moves into this cycle of economic conduct, follows the Western model of economic thought in which growth is viewed as essential. Yet growth is a concept that lends itself to simple mathematical expressions. It was Malthus who pointed out that even quite modest rates of unchecked population growth lead to populations that, in relatively brief periods of time, are easily capable of covering every inch of the entire planet across all of its oceans and mountains.

In sum, the idea of unchecked economic growth, like the idea of unchecked population growth, is one that leads to quite absurd ultimate consequences. World economics cannot continue growing without exacting a terrible price. Just as it can quickly be seen that any kind of organic population growth must be checked, it is also the case that any kind of economic growth must also be checked. For example, we can no more have an infinite number of automobiles occupying the planet than we can have an infinite number of people. What, then, is the equivalent of the "positive checks" that Malthus spoke of with respect to population growth when we consider checks on economic growth?

It might be argued that it is absurd to talk about an infinite number of automobiles, because people do not need an infinite number of cars in their garages. The question then becomes this: How many do they need? There are Americans who own more than twenty cars, and owning five or six is certainly not uncommon. If each person in the world were eventually to come into the ownership of even one automobile, we would have some five billion personal vehicles on the roads of this small planet. That number of vehicles would contribute thirty-five times as much pollution into the atmosphere as is now generated by the automobiles traveling the roads and highways of the United States.

We must return to the central concern of this discussion. The problem of economic growth has been introduced as a nice case study in how we are influenced by whether we think of the moment as one that is determined or one that we can alter. Present-day economics (and, more broadly, present-day social science) emphasizes a deterministic mentality. As a consequence, we are drawn into a sense of the inevitability of events. It is, for example, inevitable that the world's economic state must rely on ever-growing levels of productivity, despite the growing evidence that such a policy can only lead to disaster.

The question Berger raises as we examine global economies is whether we are free to do anything about where we are headed. Let us presume for the moment—and it is an assumption that, in the long run, makes good sense—that continued economic growth is both a logical and a practical impossibility. Let us presume further that it might be a good idea to begin thinking about changing things around. Can we do it? Are the forces of economic and social control greater than the forces of good sense? How might we exercise freedom of choice in this situation?

The very least that is necessary for freedom of choice is to have an idea of the existing options before making a choice. To have no sense of options is to be without choice. Modern economic philosophy offers little in the way of a sense of fundamental options. We know of only a few works in mainstream economic literature that talk about no-growth or balanced economies. It offers us a sense of the extent to which social control pervades our beings as we become aware of how difficult it is for us even to imagine an economy that is in a state of equilibrium between its consumptive and productive forces.

Both the significance and the weaknesses of Berger's treatment of the idea of freedom begin to appear in this brief consideration of the problem of global contamination of the air and the oceans. First of all, it is significant insofar as it directs our attention toward the manner in which we think of ourselves. Modern social science, by endorsing a philosophy of objectivity and determinism, tends to withdraw from moral and ethical problems. In so doing, it opens the door to fatalistic sentiments, leading to a feeling that there is not much to be done. A proper rejoinder to this assertion might be to argue that Western social science claims that the only effective way to control a problem is to find its determinants and control them. It is a good argument. However, social science leaves implicit the question of whether or not the determinants of a problem should be controlled.

At the same time, the treatment of freedom Berger offers us is more tantalizing than substantial. It is a food that fills the bowl but somehow leaves us hungry for more. The significance of Berger's essays on freedom are not that they resolve the problem of freedom, but that they once more introduce the concept into discussions of modern social and political philosophy. It is difficult to ignore the concept. At the same time, establishing its meaning and value is not as easy as it might first appear to be. Once again, the issue of global pollution quickly reveals a few major weaknesses.

First of all, Berger's discussion of freedom concentrates almost exclusively on the individual as a free agent. However, the issue of global pollution is not an individual problem, but a corrective one. It is not the consequence of any single person's actions, but, rather, the consequence of billions of people acting in concert. Each of us, of course, is perfectly free to consume as much or as little as his or her circumstances permit. If you are a wealthy American, you can (as many have) exploit the resources of the land in an extravagant and wasteful manner. You can also choose not to exploit those same resources. However, if the problem of global contamination of the environment is to be checked, it means that the free expression of consumption must be changed for hundreds of millions of people in a relatively short period of time.

This means that somehow great numbers of people must suddenly elect to choose the same policy of ecological conservatism. However, the concept of freedom is awkward when we begin thinking about large numbers of people suddenly doing something alike. If everybody is doing something, does it mean that they have all somehow just elected to do it out of choice, or have they been led to make the same choice? If they have been led to make the same choice, then are they free?

If nothing else, we come away from Berger's treatment of control and freedom with a new awareness of the profound difficulties that exist in this most ancient of arguments. Are we really free agents? Are we the pawns of forces raging within us and about us? What do we really mean when we say we are "free"? Perhaps the darkest question of all is to wonder whether we really want to be free in any serious way. Berger opens up a new domain of questioning for modern students of social philosophy by turning to the oldest questions of all. We should not despair because the questions have not as yet been solved or answered. We should continue to pursue these aggravatingly human riddles because, in the questioning, we begin to liberate ourselves from the belief that we knew the answers to begin with. And that, so it turns out, amounts to a small victory for freedom.

Putting Social Thought to Work

1. Berger offers us an opportunity to consider the observations and general arguments of sociology together with some of the observations and general arguments of modern philosophy, particularly existentialist philosophy. He begins with a consideration of the extent to which we are virtually prisoners of the historical epoch into which we are born— the extent to which we are the children of our cultures. We grow up and we acquire language, attitudes, ideas, knowledge, understandings, and all-too-solid perceptions of the world around us that are derived from the culture. Given the forces of social control, it is surprising not that people conform, but that they manage to display whatever eccentricities they do. Why are Americans so concerned with the problem of conformity? Why do high school and college students idealize nonconformity and, at the same time, show a high degree of conformity in dress, speech, interests, and tastes? Why are people generally so quick to condemn even slight deviations from orthodox patterns of conduct? Given the American adulation of freedom, is this a form of hypocrisy, or is it evidence of the extent to which people conform unconsciously while consciously praising the free life?

2. Is violence, or the treatment of violence, the most effective means for achieving conformity? Why do Americans subscribe to violence in movies and television as a device for resolving problems, and at the same time condemn it? Are Americans, much like the German people of recent times, supportive of violent systems of control so long as they do not have to be a direct part of them? Are minority group reports of police and criminal violence exaggerated? To what extent are Americans concerned with controlling the life of the individual?

3. The American system subscribes to "freedom" and, at the same time, has created the most massive legal code in the world directed toward controlling the affairs of the individual. The problem of control cannot be avoided in any social system. For example, young people who do not wish to be controlled by their parents must in turn exercise some kind of control over the parents if they are themselves to avoid control. Is it possible to have a conception of freedom that does not involve, at the same time, an implicit form of control over someone?

4. If I am seeking to drive my motorcycle down city streets at one hundred miles per hour, then my action will control the efforts of those who are attempting to negotiate traffic in a less sensational manner. Does this imply that the quest for freedom is actually only another way of phrasing the question of who is to control whom?

5. Berger makes a surprising statement for a sociologist: He argues that any attempt to identify people in their totality with their social character is an act of bad faith. Yet the foundation stone of sociological thought is to locate the nature of people in those values derived from the fact of their social existence. Is this contradictory? Is sociology a "human" way of trying to understand ourselves? Why or why not? If a scientific approach to human affairs implies a kind of "inhumanity" through its deterministic and analytic approach, then how do we achieve a more "human" understanding of human actions?

Endnotes

1. Peter L. Berger's major works include *Invitation to Sociology: A Humanistic Perspective* (Garden City, NY: Doubleday, 1963); *The Human Shape of Work*, edited by Berger (New York: Macmillan, 1964); *The Noise of Solemn Assemblies: Christian Commitment and the Religious Establishment in America* (Garden City, NY: Doubleday, 1961); *The Precarious Vision: A Sociologist Looks at Social Fictions and the Christian Faith* (Garden City, NY: Doubleday, 1961); *The Sacred Canopy: Elements of a Sociological Theory of Religion* (Garden City, NY: Doubleday, 1966); *The Social Construction of Reality*, with Thomas Luckmann (Garden City, NY: Doubleday, 1966); *Sociology: A Biographical Approach*, with Brigitte Berger (New York: Basic Books, 1972); *The Homeless Mind*, with Brigitte Berger and Hansfried Kellner (New York: Random House, 1972); *Facing Up to Modernity: Excursions in Society, Politics, and Religion* (New York: Basic Books, 1977); *Speaking to the Third World*, with Michael Novak (Washington, DC: American Enterprise Institute for Public Policy Re-

search, 1985); and *The Capitalist Revolution: Fifty Propositions about Prosperity, Equality, and Liberty* (New York: Basic Books, 1986). A collection of Berger's ideas appears in *Making Sense of Modern Times*, edited by James D. Hunter and Stephen C. Ainlay (Boston: Routledge & Kegan Paul, 1986). The prolific writing of Berger is only suggested by this bibliography, which is a partial one.

2. For academic and well-developed criticism of this point of view, see Dennis H. Wrong, "The Oversocialized Conception of Man in Modern Sociology," *American Sociological Review* 26 (April 1961), 183–193.

3. Berger, *Invitation to Sociology*, p. 92. This is Berger's expression.

4. It might seem, from one point of view, that dreams of murder are antisocial. Yet, in a sense, they follow a model provided by society. Though we disagree with many of his particulars, Frederic Wertham is correct in general as he develops this theme in both *Seduction of the Innocent* (New York: Holt, Rinehart & Winston, 1954) and *A Sign for Cain* (New York: Macmillan, 1966).

5. Malcolm X, with the assistance of Alex Haley, *The Autobiography of Malcolm X* (New York: Grove Press, 1964), p. 55.

6. Ibid., p. 54.

7. This account of the excommunication statement appears in Barrows Dunham, *Heroes and Heretics* (New York: Knopf, 1964), p. 335.

8. A fuller treatment of this debate appears in the February 8, 1964, issue of the *Congressional Record*. Although much of the *Congressional Record* is not exciting reading, there are more than occasional passages that surpass *Alice in Wonderland* when it comes to whimsy and fantasy.

9. Vance Packard, *The Hidden Persuaders* (New York: David McKay, 1957), p. 159.

10. This anecdote was taken from a "Dear Abby" column as it appeared in the Boulder *Daily Camera*, February 9, 1967. Permission for use given by the Universal Press Syndicate, Kansas City, Missouri.

11. Berger, *Invitation to Sociology*, pp. 98–99.

12. Kingsley Davis, *Human Society* (New York: Macmillan, 1949), p. 380. We are aware, of course, that India is at present concerned with doing away with such caste constraints. But India, like the United States, finds the process of removing the inequities and inhumanities of caste a slow and troublesome one.

13. Berger, *Invitation to Sociology*, pp. 108–109.

14. William Bruce Cameron, "Sociological Notes on the Jam Session" *Social Forces* 33 (December 1954), 178.

15. Berger, *Invitation to Sociology*, p. 109.

16. The phrasing here is Berger's.

17. Berger, *Invitation to Sociology*, p. 143.

18. Ibid., p. 144.

19. This idea appears in Richard Kim's taut novel *The Martyred* (New York: Braziller, 1964). Kim contrasts two Christian ministers. One believes in the validity of his God and, in the final moments before he is executed by a Communist firing squad, abandons his faith and his God. The second does not believe, but finds in his role as a minister a way of bringing aid and assistance to a suffering humanity. The second minister acts out of choice rather than a sense of constraint.

20. Berger, *Invitation to Sociology*, pp. 153–154.

21. Ibid., p. 169.

22. Ernst Friedrich Schumacher, *Small Is Beautiful: Economics as if People Mattered* (New York: Harper & Row, 1973).

Chapter 14

Erving Goffman
Born: 1922 · Died: 1982

Life as a Con Game

The Dramaturgic Vision of Erving Goffman

❖

❖ Symbols within Symbols

In the course of growing up, we learn the language of the culture in which we live. It is a thorough and surprisingly exact form of teaming. We learn a language so precisely that phonetics experts, like the fabled Professor Higgins in Shaw's *Pygmalion*, can identify a person's birthplace merely by listening to the idiosyncrasies of dialect. The learning is not only precise, so that we are instantly attuned to a slightly mispronounced word, but it is extensive. By this, we simply mean that we learn a complex and vast amount of material. The typical child entering school between the ages of five and six already has a vocabulary of some two thousand words at his or her command.[1] Moreover, mastery of the art of language is virtually universal within a culture; even men and women of low intellectual endowment generally acquire at least a working knowledge of the language of their culture. Though this mastery is an astonishing feat of memory and learning, it is so common that we take it for granted. Only when we try to learn a foreign language do we discover how much we have learned of our mother tongue. Only when we cease taking language for granted do we become aware of its deep influence in our lives.

Learning language is obviously important in becoming "human," and it is also obviously necessary for maintaining the elaborate social and cultural systems within which we operate today. However, just what is it we learn when we learn a language? Certainly we learn more than spoken or written words. What symbols, words, or meanings are involved in human social exchanges? How does language work? What are the effects of language? We shall explore these questions throughout this chapter and arrive at some engaging conclusions and observations. The most general and significant conclusion we shall come to might be stated in the following manner.

Suppose we begin by accepting the fact that human beings are symbol-using creatures. (Walt Kelly, creator of the comic strip *Pogo*, once said that people are "symbol-minded." It is an expressive way to put it.) If we recognize at the same time that symbols are, in a sense, "false" because they are never the same as the reality they represent, then people are, in a sense, "false." Unlike the nonsymbolic animals around them, people cannot merge with nature. We are, by the very nature of language itself, separated.[2] This separation is a product of the deceptive and imperfect nature of language. To begin to dwell on the implications of people as symbol-using creatures leads us to at least begin to view people as deceived by their own words. We deceive ourselves and deceive others. There is no way out of this situation. To be human is to use and be used by language.

It is this feature of the human condition that receives the attention of Erving Goffman. Essentially, all Goffman does is to make evident the fact that in the course of social action, people influence each other by means of elaborate symbolic devices. In itself, this is nothing new. It certainly does not seem, at least at first sight, to be especially shocking or probing. Nonetheless, Goffman's works[3] form the foundation for a view of humankind even more disenchanting than that emanating from Darwin's theory of evolution or Freud's conception of human beings as impulsive animals held in an uneasy state of control by society.

Darwin left open the possibility that if people are creatures of low heritage, at least they are intelligent ones. If humans are animals, they are nonetheless animals capable of building vast cultures. Above all, Darwin permitted us to view people as beings standing at the apex of an evolutionary process, the origins of which are lost in time. Darwin allowed us to keep intact our view of people as something special and privileged in nature's realm. Freud, on the other hand, disenchantingly left us to the mercy of unconscious and devious impulses. Even so, the Freudian picture is a dramatic and thoroughly romantic one. Although Freudian man or woman may be crushed by a repressive morality, he or she never admits defeat without a fight. The fight may take place within the unconscious, but it is always a fight. Freud saw people embroiled in combat with their communities throughout the entirety of life; it is an invigorating and even flattering conception—every person a kind of embattled hero or heroine.

But Goffman leaves us, at first glance anyway, with practically nothing. He appears to divest us of our sanctity by suggesting that we are all incorrigible con artists. Worse yet, we have no choice about the matter. We must be con artists. Moreover, the same tricks that make a con game work are basically the devices used in the act of being "human." Goffman argues that we must deal with the fact that we all give off impressions. At times we are unaware of the impression we are making. For the most part, however, we try to "manage" impressions. These impressions, grounded in the meanings we give to appearances, gestures, costumes, settings, and words, are all that a person *is* as a social being. Strip these away, and we lose much that makes us seem "human." Conversely, clothe people with those fragile devices that enable them to maintain an impression before others, and we give them the shaky essence of humanity.

The perspective that Goffman develops in his writing reduces humanity to an act or performance; moreover, it is a performance based on remarkably flimsy devices. At the same time, to become aware of the devices being used to sustain a performance causes us to respond to the performance with a different (and generally more negative) attitude than before. A child who discovers an uncle hiding behind Santa's false whiskers may continue to play the game, but more from choice than from a belief that he or she really is playing with Santa Claus.

It is in this sense, then, that Goffman appears to leave people more naked and alone than did Darwin or Freud. The distinctive feature of human activity resides ultimately in things that amount, in the final analysis, to little more than a Santa Claus outfit. To be human is to perform, like an actor, before audiences whom we con into accepting us as being what we try to appear to be. Our humanity is the costume we wear, the stage on which we perform, and the way we read whatever script we are handed.

❖ Two Aspects of Language: Content and Style

When we try to impress others, two somewhat separate kinds of language or symbols are involved. We impress others by *what* we say; and, of course, we impress others by how we say it. Usually we do not think of how we say something as a form of language. We reserve the idea of language for the content of what we wish to express. How we express ourselves we generally think of as "style" or "technique." Goffman suggests that what we commonly consider to be style is, in actuality, another manifestation of language.

In fact, it is a form of language that serves the significant purpose of validating whatever it is we wish to express as content.

A simple illustration quickly makes clear what Goffman means when he refers to the validating properties of styles in human performances. The difference between a performance of *Hamlet* by Laurence Olivier and one by a not particularly talented high school student is certainly not a difference of content. Both individuals read the same words or lines from identical scripts. However, the performance of Olivier is believable. It impresses us as authentic. It appears to be a valid characterization. That of the high school student may appear lifeless, dull, artificial, stilted, stiff, or unreal. We know that the high school student is not "really" Hamlet, but Olivier can "con" us into accepting that he is Hamlet. The difference, of course, rests in the style of the performance. But if style can communicate a sense of validity, then it must be seen in itself as a form of language. Moreover, its importance must not be overlooked; lack of control of the language of style may mean the difference between having one's message or performance accepted by others or having it rejected.

❖ *Symptomatic Action*

Goffman uses the term "symptomatic range of action" to refer to what we have called the language of style.[4] By this he means that certain actions are symptomatic of a valid performance. For example, an erudite and competent professor who comes to class the first day with trembling hands may lose his or her audience because students will see this as symptomatic of fear or nervousness; if the professor is confident in his or her knowledge, then the hands should not reveal a nervous tremor. The fact that the professor suffers from an incurable neurological disorder does not prevent the tremor from symbolizing something quite different to the class. In this illustration, the neurological disorder is viewed by the audience as symptomatic of a person who does not possess valid claims to the performance being staged. Conversely, a calm, poised, and steady bearing is symptomatic of a valid claim to the performance.

We have identified two classes of symbolic action so far. One of these is the content of the performance, and the other is the symptomatic action that validates or lends reality to the performance. The relationship between these two classes of symbols is summarized in Table 14–1. The first and fourth cases in this scheme are self-evident. The second and third cases are the interesting ones. Consider the second case, in which a person may control content but lacks mastery over symptomatic action. Such a person, despite control over content, may not be able to disguise ineptness with regard to symptomatic impressions.

The lecturer whose hands shake illustrates this condition. A specific and actual case in point was the platform conduct of Thorstein Veblen, the great American economist and social analyst. Although his brilliance was widely

Table 14–1 The Relation Between Content and Symptomatic Action (Style)

Content	Symptomatic Action	Audience Reaction
1. Positive	Positive	Performance accepted
2. Positive	Negative	Performance damaged
3. Negative	Positive	Performance accepted if content cannot be checked
4. Negative	Negative	Performance rejected

recognized, and although hundreds of students flocked to his classes, the end of the semester would find the classroom nearly empty.[5] Students would abandon his courses by the hundreds. Veblen's lack of concern for classroom oratorical devices eventually proved more than his audience could bear.

❖ *The "Phony" Performance*

The third case represents a type we usually refer to as a "phony." The person is capable of manipulating appearances to make the performance look like the real McCoy. However, the performance is invalid because the performer does not possess content. We witnessed a case in point during an amateur performance of *The Merchant of Venice*, when an actor momentarily forgot his lines. His stage presence was impressive, however, and he continued talking and gesturing as though nothing were wrong—all the while spouting a phony form of Shakespearean dialogue that he invented as he went along. Eventually he recalled his lines and continued with his part. The attention of the audience was retained, and it appeared to us that few people were the wiser.

In this instance, the performer was able to disguise the fact that he momentarily lost mastery over the content of his performance. So long as the disguise was effective, the incongruity between loss of content and retention of symptomatic control never became apparent. We cannot, of course, presume that the phony is superior to the person who lacks control over symptomatic actions. Loss of either aspect of a performance is threatening to the maintenance of the performance. The phony is more likely to be effective, simply because it is generally easier to disguise lack of content. Students, for example, commonly prefer a teacher who is a kindly-appearing old phony over an ominous-appearing recognized authority, simply because they cannot distinguish between the two on a professional basis.

It is apparent that a phony performance will be successful only to the extent to which the performer is capable of concealing from the audience the fact that he or she does not possess control over the legitimate content of the performance. But concealment in other forms is involved in situations where the performance is not a phony and not careless or incompetent. Several of these usual or workaday situations are identified by Goffman:

> First . . . the performer may be engaged in a profitable form of activity that is concealed from his audience and that is incompatible with the view of his activity which he hopes they will obtain. . . .
>
> Secondly, we find that errors and mistakes are often corrected before the performance takes place, while telltale signs that errors have been made and corrected are themselves concealed. In this way an impression of infallibility, so important in many presentations, is maintained. . . .
>
> Thirdly, in those interactions where the individual presents a product to others, he will tend to show them only the end product, and they will be led into judging him on the basis of something that has been finished, polished, and packaged. In some cases, if very little effort was actually required to complete the object, this fact will be concealed. . . .
>
> A fourth discrepancy between appearances and over-all reality may be cited. We find that there are many performances which could not have been given had not tasks been done which were physically unclean, semi-illegal, cruel, and degrading in other ways; but these disturbing facts are seldom expressed during a performance. . . . We tend to conceal from our audience all evidence of "dirty work," whether we do this work in private or allocate it to a servant.[6]

Concealment is a necessary element in practically all social performances, and it poses a rather trying dilemma for the actor. If one is honest and open—that is, if one refuses to engage in concealment—then one risks losing the audience. If one engages in concealment, then one is practicing deceit. All human social performances, from Goffman's perspective, involve a constant weighing of the costs of losing one's audience against the cost of losing one's integrity by acting in a deceptive manner. Doctors, for example, have to convince their patients that they are more certain of the effects of a given therapy than they may be in fact. Teachers need to conceal from their students the many doubts that plague them as they present a lecture. Salespeople must conceal their contempt for some customers. So it is, then, that all social performances have a "phony" element about them. Not only does the fraudulent performer conceal his or her ignorance, but also the legitimate performer conceals items of information that would, if they became known, cause rejection by the audience.

This human dilemma can be seen in an overly cynical manner. Such a view is depicted, for example, in J. D. Salinger's novel *The Catcher in the Rye* when Holden Caulfield discovers that people all around him practice a variety of deceits. He concludes that people, especially adults, are "phony." Caulfield's rejection of these "phonies" is based on his feeling that phony actions betray a great weakness in the character of the person. Goffman suggests something different. "Phony" action is a product of the relationship existing between the performer and those who observe him or her. If retention of the audience is important, then deceit may be necessary. Thus, the teacher who is committed to the ideal of educating young people can do so only by retaining the attention and the acceptance of the students, who are of immediate concern. This can be achieved only through performances that convince the audience of the worth of the performer. Such performances will necessarily conceal errors, hidden pleasures, "dirty work," and tedium. On these occasions, the performer typically cannot escape an awareness of the deception that he or she is practicing.

Goffman locates phony presentations not within the actor, but within the complex of social relationships containing the actor. Consider the following situation. If an organization in which a person is located demands adherence to several conflicting standards or ideals, the individual will probably hide unavoidable violations of one of the ideals. A person will usually hide those violations that are easiest to hide. The act of hiding violations of the ideal, however, serves the purpose of keeping the ideal intact. Goffman gives the example of an attendant in an asylum for the mentally ill who must maintain order and must, at the same time, conform to the ideal of not physically injuring patients. Violations of the latter ideal are more easily disguised than those of the former. Therefore, the attendant may indulge in such practices as "necking" a patient, which is forcing the patient to act properly by the act of throttling with a wet towel—a practice that leaves no mark.

We are inclined to criticize the actions of the attendant. Goffman suggests, however, that such conduct is an attempt to maintain the ideals of the social organization. If keeping order and not physically injuring the patient are both legitimate ideals and, at the same time, difficult to achieve simultaneously, then the only way they can be kept intact is to hide the fact that one of them must be violated. The demeanor of the attendant, when viewed in terms of conflicting legitimate ideals of the organization and the endeavor to preserve these ideals, is at least easier to understand (if still not acceptable). The point that Goffman makes is that critical response to the individual in a situation such as this is misdirected. Attention should be given instead to the ideals of the organization and the means made available to the individual for supporting those ideals.

A similar situation can be found in the typical grade school. Among its varied concerns, the school must deal with imparting knowledge, and it must also maintain a semblance of social control or order. Of these two concerns, the loss of order in the classroom is more readily apparent than are problems with respect to imparting knowledge. If one or the other ideal must be sacrificed, it will be the ideal of imparting knowledge. Thus the teacher who insists on order, regardless of whether teaching is taking place, is responding to structural features of the situation in which he or she has been placed. It is important to note, in all of this, that Goffman does not locate phoniness or deception or inclinations toward concealment as qualities of personality. They are, instead, qualities that arise out of the demands of performance. People cannot be understood apart from the greater social situations in which they are located.

❖ *Cynical and Sincere Performances*

Goffman shows us, perhaps more sympathetically than any other observer of human activities, that there is a large element of phoniness in all human interaction. We pose, as it were, behind a variety of masks used to frighten, intimidate, implore, awe, beg, or otherwise elicit from others the kinds of reaction we seek. On some occasions, we do this self-consciously; at other times, we may be unaware of the extent to which we use these devices.

Goffman calls consciously manipulative conduct a "cynical" type of performance, whereas an unconscious use of manipulative devices produces actions that are "sincere." It is worth noting that this places sincerity and cynicism within the subjective awareness or in the mind of the actor. It is impossible to detect it from outside. For example, a cynical man may consciously and knowingly act ineptly in order to convince the woman he is trying to seduce that he is sincere. A sincere lover, unknowingly, may act in a similar manner. The performances are virtually identical; the difference is subjective. Goffman's concern with the subjective differences in a given action highlights the significance of the performance itself.

The cynical performer or the phony is a threat not because he or she performs less effectively; on the contrary, the threat or concern exists because the performance is so good! The effective cynic or phony demonstrates that it is not necessary to be friendly in order to act as a friend; it is not necessary to be in love in order to be a lover; it is not necessary to be respectable in order to appear respectable. There is a real problem, then, in everyday conduct when it comes to evaluating the sincerity or value of a performance. If two performers are equal in skill, the only difference being that one is legitimate or sincere and the other not, then how is legitimacy to be established?

This problem is solved by the institutionalization of labels that give the performer a legitimate claim to the performance he or she is conducting. We establish licensing agencies to perform the service of providing documentary evidence that an individual has the right to engage in certain types of performances. In effect, this is one of the major services provided by educational systems. It is well known that people (quite large numbers of them, in fact) come out of such systems with little more knowledge and enthusiasm than when they went in. It is also known that people can acquire an education of considerable merit without attending school. Nonetheless, all college graduates get a certificate that legitimizes their level of learning; the self-taught person does not. It is especially important to see that an effective fraudulent or phony performance conducted by an "illegitimate" performer threatens the legitimizing agency.

Consider, for example, the following instance:

> A victim of his latest ruse calls "Dr." Arthur Osborne Phillips "one of the most remarkable medical phonies of all time." And from his jail cell, "Dr." Phillips replies: "I'm a genius. I had to be a genius to do all that I did with no formal

medical education." "All" he did was hoodwink the federal government and authorities in 10 states during a 40-year career as a phony doctor.

The 70-year-old man's latest caper was working on delicate research into the surgical use of the laser light at the University of Colorado medical center in Denver. His associates there said he "did competent work."

According to prison records, Phillips' career began when he worked as an orderly during World War I for a Dr. James Herman Phillips of Doro, Ala. The real Phillips died in 1920 and the phony Phillips, according to the records, took over his name, medical shingle and license.

While working as a "surgeon" with the Civilian Conservation Corps in Wyoming, Montana and Idaho in the 1940's, Phillips performed 32 successful appendectomies.[7]

In this case we are confronted by a person who, according to his colleagues, does "competent work." But if his performance is competent, even though he did not attend medical school, then what is the point of medical school? It is in this sense that the phony performance is threatening. Let us make explicit once again that the legitimacy of the performance is not determined by the adequacy of the performance. Legitimacy is external and is bestowed on an actor by an established legitimizing agency, such as a school, military system, church, political party, or family heritage.

The phony or illegitimate performer is threatening only to the extent to which the performance is competent. After all, if the phony is incapable of performing competently, then the problem of identifying the illegitimate performer is simple, and the need for legitimizing agencies is reduced. This appears to be pretty much the case with professional athletics. In the athletic contest, the claims of the performer are expressed in the performance, and the criteria for evaluating the performance are clear-cut. The only problem here is to assure that a performer is not lying when he or she claims a lack of skill. In situations where the performance is the criterion of adequacy, the phony may be a person who is pretending to be less skilled or experienced than he or she is in fact. An example of this is the "hustler" in golf or pool who makes a living by leading an unsuspecting "pigeon" into a wager that the pigeon cannot hope to win. Legitimizing devices must exist, therefore, to assure that a person who claims a lower level of skill does not, in fact, possess a higher level. For this reason, performances such as those given by the athlete are divided into amateur and professional categories, and elaborate means are taken to insure that professionals do not pose as amateurs.

There is one other area where legitimizing a performance introduces several interesting problems. Where no professional legitimizing agency exists, and where the criteria for competency are not clear, other lines may be drawn for distinguishing between the "true" performer and the performer whose actions are suspect. This occurs in the theater, where people who live by acting will make much of the distinction between themselves and actors who do not make a living by performing. Presumably the claims of the person who does not make any money by acting are suspect, and this may be the case regardless of the quality of the performances given by the amateur.

The scheme is now sufficiently developed to let us see, along with Goffman, that social performances are fragile and delicate matters. The problem of making your audience believe you really are what you are trying to be involves several layers of symbol—the content and symptomatic actions—and it may involve legitimacy as well. To the extent that a person has control over these elements, the performance is affected accordingly. Some social roles make it easier to control these elements than others do. This is especially important to note, because it forces us to recognize that human activities are not a simple manifestation of personality or "inner" character. Rather, real social action is a complex exchange of symbols and meanings between, at the very least, two people. Commonly, in this exchange, a person is required to perform a routine that lacks dramatic quality. To recognize that such a performance is required implies that it is not a simple product of personality. At the same time, the fact that the performance is lacking a dramatic quality produces an interesting problem for the individual. Let us see how Goffman describes this problem.

❖ *Dramatic Realization*

Some kinds of social performances are defined in such a manner as to convince audiences easily and quickly of the reality of the performances. That is, the person is readily seen as being what he or she is trying to appear to be. Moreover, the performer is able to do this easily. Other kinds of performances do not easily dramatize themselves. In such situations a person may, even though doing the work or whatever is appropriate to the role, have difficulty impressing others that this is so. We can, therefore, talk about the extent to which a role permits "dramatic realization."

Goffman offers the example of the medical nurse and the surgical nurse to illustrate what he means by this. The duties of the surgical nurse are such that the performance is quickly accepted. As the nurse stands beside the surgeon, masked and attentive, no one is doubtful about the work performance. The case of the medical nurse is different. In this instance, the nurse may come to the door of a patient's room and casually converse with the patient. While conversing, the nurse may be observing changes in the patient's skin color, breathing, voice, and so on. Each of these observations may provide pertinent information about the progress of the patient's condition. Even so, the nondramatic character of these actions may cause the patient to conclude that the nurse is simply "messing around" or "goofing off."

The medical nurse, to avoid this, commonly invents or develops routines that lend dramatic quality to the performance. However, these actions, because they are added merely for this reason, are likely to interfere with the task that has been assigned. Therefore, a "dilemma of expression" develops. The dilemma rests on the following horns: (1) If the nondramatic task is adhered to exactly, it may result in the actor's being rejected by the audience;

however, (2) if dramatic elements are added to the task in order to retain the audience, they will interfere with the proper conduct of the task. The performer is required to create a balance between impressing people and getting the job done. Goffman puts it this way:

> A *Vogue* model, by her clothing, stance, and facial expression, is able expressively to portray a cultivated understanding of the book she poses in her hand; but those who trouble to express themselves so appropriately will have very little time left over for reading. . . . And so individuals often find themselves with the dilemma of expression *versus* action. Those who have the time and talent to perform a task well may not, because of this, have the time or talent to make it apparent that they are performing well. It may be said that some organizations resolve this dilemma by officially delegating the dramatic functions to a specialist who will spend his time expressing the meaning of the task and spend no time actually doing it.[8]

❖ *Role Expectation*

Any performance, whether on a theatrical stage or in everyday life, requires at least a general conception of what is expected of the performer. Sociologists refer to this as "role expectation." Goffman suggests that role expectations may be "realistic" or "idealized." The difference between a realistic and an idealized conception of a role seems to hinge on whether or not the conception derives from the experience of an "insider" or the credulity of an "outsider." Goffman gives the following examples of what he means by "idealization," and this characterization probably still holds for much of American society.

> American college girls did, and no doubt do, play down their intelligence, skills, and determinativeness when in the presence of datable boys, thereby manifesting a profound psychic discipline in spite of their international reputation for flightiness. These performers are reported to allow their boy friends to explain things to them tediously that they already know; they conceal proficiency in mathematics from their less able consorts; they lose ping-pong games just before the ending. . . .[9]

Goffman quotes a girl who is concerned with how she impresses her boyfriend:

> "One of the nicest techniques is to spell long words incorrectly once in a while. My boy friend seems to get a great kick out of it and writes back, 'Honey, you certainly don't know how to spell.' "[10]

The realities of a woman's role are known best by women. In the instance cited above, however, the woman is not "being herself." She is putting on a performance. Moreover, it is a performance that fits the myths and stereotyped images of women that characterize American culture. It is in this sense, then, that the woman is acting out an idealized conception of her role.

Girls who misspell words, blacks who put on a show of stupidity for the benefit of whites, and virginally proper college boys who pretend to be rogues are all engaging in performances that involve idealization. In such instances, the form the idealization takes may be to play down certain attributes the actor possesses. In the examples just given, the girls play down their knowledge, the blacks play down their abilities, and the college boys play down their secret commitment to old-fashioned sexual morality.

Idealization may work in the other direction. College students who complicate their prose because they think intellectuals write in an incomprehensible manner are doing this. The housewife who usually prepares common meals for her family but presents guests with an elaborate feast is indulging in a form of role idealization. In such cases, the performer expects to lead a credulous audience into an acceptance of the performer on the basis of the performer's conception of how the audience feels the role should be played. Moreover, the performer is playing up certain abilities that, in actuality, he or she may either lack or be less inclined to exercise.

The relationship of idealization to performances is significant, because it forces us to recognize that human social activity involves (1) our own understanding of how our role should be played; (2) the conceptions others have of how the role should be played; and (3) the possibility of discrepancies between these conceptions. Severe discrepancies will result in performances that are bizarre and ineffective. Lower-class people who think that upper-class people are arrogant and snobbish and who try to emulate this pattern as they strive to be upwardly mobile will in all likelihood simply lose their friends.

There is an important difference between roles played on the stage and those played in everyday life. The former are well defined. A script is provided to the actor, and the performance is directed in a manner that reduces errors of which the actor might not be aware. Of course, there are instances where everyday roles are also very well defined. Take, for example, the role expected of us when we are called upon to participate in certain rituals. A priest conducting a high mass goes through a set of role responses as well defined as those in a play. On the other hand, the response expected of us when we are introduced at a party is, within considerable limits, subject to a variety of possibilities. Actors are on their own. They may feel they are supposed to be congenial and amusing, but how they elect to do this must come from their own background, abilities, and preconceptions of the responses others will make to their actions.

In such circumstances, a person has an opportunity to "ad-lib" and play the role creatively in terms of his or her interpretation of that role. This allows the performer to engage in role idealization. We may attempt to upgrade or downgrade ourselves, but in doing so we conform to a conception of how such downgrading or upgrading should take place. One has, in other words, a model of performances that one follows in order to achieve the particular effect one seeks. In this respect the person is never, in performances before others, completely independent of social roles and the definitions that society has given to these roles.

This view of people as performers before audiences they are trying to impress seems cynical. It suggests, as we have said before, that much of what is human is, at bottom, little more than a kind of show. Humanity is a matter of putting people on. A deceptiveness and a phoniness characterize much of human conduct. Goffman gives us a picture of human beings that emphasizes this "artificial" quality in our actions. However, it is necessary to be careful in this evaluation of Goffman. In the first place, although in much of his writing he views people as "phony," he does not judge this as "bad." On the contrary, Goffman forces us to see this aspect of human activities as an unavoidable consequence of our attempts to please others; such actions usually facilitate those affairs of daily life necessary for survival and comfort.

A "cynic" is defined as a person who thinks that any action is motivated by the worst of motives. Goffman is cynical insofar as the motivation he gives to human action is that of the "con." But Goffman, unlike a thoroughgoing cynic, does not consider this the worst of motives; the con more often than not is altruistic. The con or phoniness is certainly universal, and we are on dangerous ground when we begin to criticize others for their phony conduct.

Above all, Goffman probes deeply enough to make us see that what we consider a "real" performance has elements identical to those involved in the phony performance. This requires us to think in new ways about the essential nature of humanity. When we see the larger conception of human nature that Goffman reveals, we find that it will not permit us to define humanity simply in terms of the trappings people use to frighten and awe each other. In this sense, Goffman is the most humanistic of the authors discussed in this book. He views sardonically the shows people put on before each other, and he views them as an outsider would. But throughout his work, there can never be any doubt that his basic conception of humanity cuts through to the inner experience and understanding of the world that any individual human being has. He is concerned with how one's relation to others and to society affects the understanding of oneself and the world. In other words, Goffman relates society and the person; but of the two, the person is always the more important.

❖ The Problems of Stigma

Goffman's humanism is brought out by the unique treatment he gives to the problems experienced by people suffering from stigmata of different kinds.[11] Goffman defines "stigma" in the following way:

> While the stranger is present before us, evidence can arise of his possessing an attribute that makes him different from others in the category of persons available for him to be, and of a less desirable kind—in the extreme, a person who is quite thoroughly bad, or dangerous, or weak. He is thus reduced in our mind

from a whole and usual person to a tainted, discounted one. Such an attribute is a stigma.[12]

It is important at this point to see that stigmata are not purely physical defects—even when the manifestation of the stigma is, let us say, a scar that runs from a person's ear to his or her mouth, resulting in a twisted, leering expression. A stigma must be viewed always in terms of a language of relationships. What the scar, in this case, is defined as being (much as what a word is defined as being) determines whether or not the relationship between the person with the scar and those without it will take a certain form. If, for example, the scar is obtained by a German university student who is a member of a *Schlangende Verbindung*, or dueling society, he may define it in terms of virility, courage, and military values, and wear it as a badge authorizing him to assume an arrogant stance toward those without it. If, on the other hand, the scar is obtained in an automobile collision in the United States, and the victim is a woman, the whole thing will be interpreted quite differently.

Our reactions to a person possessing a stigma are influenced by the common theories we rely on regarding the nature of that stigma. Goffman points out:

> By definition, of course, we believe the person with a stigma is not quite human. On this assumption we exercise varieties of discrimination, through which we effectively, if often unthinkingly, reduce his life chances. We construct a stigma-theory, an ideology to explain his inferiority and account for the danger he represents, sometimes rationalizing an animosity based on other differences, such as those of social class. We use specific stigma terms such as cripple, bastard, moron in our daily discourse as a source of metaphor and imagery, typically without giving thought to the original meaning. We tend to impute a wide range of imperfections on the basis of the original one, and at the same time to impute some desirable but undesired attributes, often of a supernatural case, such as "sixth sense," or "understanding."[13]

Stigmata fall into three broad classes: gross physical defects, defects in character, and membership in a social class or group that is not acceptable. A stigma may be acquired at birth or at any time during the life of the individual. Although there are variations caused by the kind of stigma or the time of its acquisition, most stigmatized persons share a number of common problems and common strategies for meeting these problems. Goffman sees stigmatized persons generally as humans who employ strategies designed to meet a particular difficulty—that of managing the "spaded" identities they have somehow acquired. But that identity is not inherent in the manifest form of the stigma. A stigma is, in Goffman's term, a "perspective."

> May I repeat that stigma involves not so much a set of concrete individuals who can be separated into two piles, the stigmatized and the normal, as a pervasive two-role social process in which every individual participates in both roles, at

least in some connections and in some phases of life. The normal and the stigmatized are not persons but rather perspectives.[14]

A stigma does not determine the type of performance required of the person having it, but it does help determine the extent to which a person will be forced to accept whatever role is given. Goffman is saying that a stigma such as epilepsy, for example, does not in itself produce a particular way of life for the person having epilepsy. On the other hand, it does not, in itself, establish the manner in which the epileptic is to be viewed by persons who are not epileptic. However, once norms are generated that define how an epileptic is to relate to others, then the epileptic will experience a greater likelihood of encountering these requirements. Thus, in cultures where an epileptic is believed to possess divine powers, the probability of encountering this expectation is increased for the epileptic, to the point that he or she is likely to conform and accept the role of shaman. On the other hand, in a society where epilepsy is degrading, the person having this condition is more likely to encounter perspectives that lead to a self-derogating view.

Goffman's treatment of stigmatized people is concerned with the extent to which certain signs or manifestations of character increase the likelihood that these people will be coerced into social performances that set them at a disadvantage. The social relevance of stigmata is that they move individuals into playing social games with the cards stacked against them. A reasonable reaction for stigmatized people is to attempt to minimize the extent to which they will be injured or suffer loss by such circumstances. There are several things they can do. They can attempt to withdraw and not play the game. They can try to withhold information and thereby avoid getting themselves into a position where they must play against the stacked deck; or they can develop ways of meeting the situation directly. It might be possible, for example, to take advantage of the fact that the other players feel a sense of guilt because they know the deck is stacked.

Withdrawal as a means of coping with the situation does not mean that the stigmatized person is completely isolated. The person may withdraw by encapsulating himself or herself within a group of individuals who know about the condition and will not use it against the person. One such group may be those persons who share the stigma; another may be those who are normal but sympathetic. Normal yet sympathetic people know about the condition of the stigmatized person, and at the same time act in a manner indicating that the stigmatization does not matter. In the company of such people, the person with a fault need feel no shame nor exert any special form of self-control. Goffman cites an example from the world of prostitutes:

> Although she sneers at respectability, the prostitute, particularly the call girl, is super-sensitive in polite society, taking refuge in her off hours with Bohemian artists, writers, actors and would-be intellectuals. There she may be accepted as an off-beat personality, without being a curiosity.[15]

There are differences between groups sharing the stigma and those composed of the sympathetic. Perhaps the most significant is that the stigmatic group dramatizes the stigma through formalized organizations or journals devoted to a treatment of how to live with the stigma; stories are told of individuals who have achieved outstanding success despite possession of the stigma. Contrary to this, groups made up of the sympathetic are more inclined to reinterpret the stigma in a way that minimizes its existence; for example, the call girl is seen as an "off-beat personality."

A second way in which stigmatized persons can avoid playing against the stacked deck is to attempt to control their identity so that the stigma will not be perceived by others. Thus, illiterates may wear the trappings of the literate. Goffman cites the following illustration:

> When goal orientation is pronounced or imperative and there exists a high probability that definition as illiterate is a bar to the achievement of the goal, the illiterate is likely to try to "pass" as literate. . . . The popularity in the group [of illiterates] studied of window-pane lenses with heavy horn frames ("bop glasses") may be viewed as an attempt to emulate the stereotype of the businessman-teacher-young intellectual and especially the high status jazz musician.[16]

Identity control may or may not be effective, of course. If it is effective, the stigmatized person is able to "pass" for a while as a nonstigmatized person. But the matter is more complex than merely a successful disguise of a stigma. Between people who can completely cover their stigmata and pass without fear of discovery and those who can never cover their stigmata lies a great range of cases.

> First, there are important stigmas, such as the ones that prostitutes, thieves, homosexuals, beggars, and drug addicts have, which require the individual to be carefully secret about his failing to one class of persons, the police, while systematically exposing himself to other classes of persons, namely clients, fellow-members, connections, fences, and the like. . . . Secondly, even where an individual could keep an unapparent stigma secret, he will find that intimate relations with others, ratified in our society by mutual confession of invisible failings, cause him either to admit his situation to the intimate or to feel guilty for not doing so. In any case, nearly all matters which are very secret are still known to someone, and hence cast a shadow.[17]

Within this range, stigmatized people retain several alternative modes of information control. They may pass, or they may attempt to convert the stigma into a lesser form. Some blind people wear dark glasses, which immediately identify them as blind, but which may simultaneously disguise or hide facial disfigurements that accompany the blindness. Finally, the stigmatized person is confronted with unique problems in the realm of audience management. In these cases, the stigmatized person has to play the game, but he or she attempts to minimize the handicap by playing on the meanings that others give the condition.

"Breaking the ice" exemplifies what is meant here. Initial contacts are important in determining how an interaction between two or more persons will continue. The stigmatized person can be either an object of pity (and thereby subject to those subtle forms of discrimination reserved for objects of pity), or the person can establish individuality and rights as a human by how he or she handles initial meetings with others. For example, a man who has lost both hands and is served by artificial limbs may, on a first encounter with others, take out a cigarette and light it regardless of whether or not he feels like smoking. This ostentatious display of skills within a stigmatic context is sufficient to warn the audience that there is no need to go beyond the normal set of social understandings.

❖ *Goffman as Scientist and Humanist*

Whether it is a person with a stigma or a normal individual coping with a common problem in everyday life, Goffman concentrates on how people manage the impressions they try to convey to others. Goffman is not, in the usual meaning of the term, a "scientist." His work does not rely on elaborate measurements. His major works are not based on questionnaires or even structured interviews. He is not at all hesitant to make use of literary examples if they help illustrate a concept or idea.

Yet it would be a mistake to discount Goffman as a scientist. There is in his writing a more dispassionate and unbiased reporting of human events than is to be found in many studies more heavily armored with quantitative data and statistical analysis. Goffman's methods, which consist largely of careful observation combined with extensive scholarship, flow from his general conception of human conduct. Human activities, for Goffman, are not a series of discrete actions that result from biologically derived urges or drives. Nor is such activity a manifestation of an inner condition like "personality." Instead, human actions are distinctly complex and consist for the most part of an elaborate progression of symbolic performances.

This conception of humanity forces us to see our conduct as though it were a work of art. We are artists—con artists, Goffman might suggest, but nonetheless artists. If this is so, then the important thing is to see the total impression created by whatever we might do. But this cannot be done unless we try to evaluate or understand the complete performance. We would have a very limited understanding of a painting by Picasso if we were informed only of the percentage of the painting that is blue. Yet, in effect, that is what attempts at quantifying social actions commonly amount to.

Goffman stands back and observes, through the perspectives of science, the artful performances of people. The effect is powerful. The large following Goffman's work enjoys today in sociological and psychological circles, as well as the growing ranks of qualitative researchers, is a result of the fact that he brings together the synthetic powers of the humanistic artist with the analytic and objective powers of the contemporary social scientist. To read Goffman is to be brought directly and cleverly to a perception of people as role players and manipulators of props, costumes, gestures, and words. Goffman is able to suggest, indirectly, the injustices that such role playing can produce—as when, for example, we deny a person status as a warm and intelligent human being because he or she is deformed and dwarflike.

But if Goffman is able to penetrate into the most subtle irrationalities of human conduct, he simultaneously is generous in the extent to which his conception of humanity embraces all of us. Goffman's writing asserts that no person is more human than others, but that one person may be able to give a certain kind of performance better than another. If so, then in purely human terms, a beggar is the equal of a king. Goffman finds people caught up in myriad con games; at the same time, the objective and cold vision of this social scientist upholds in a devious way one of the most sympathetic of human values—the fundamental equality of all human beings.

Encounters with Social Thought

The Drama in Nuclear Weapons

Erving Goffman wrote his major works in the 1960s and 1970s (just before his death at age sixty), a period in Western civilization's history when the theatrical arts achieved a prominence beyond anything in the past. Until the first quarter of the twentieth century, theater was reserved for special groups—urban men and women of wealth and leisure. By the third quarter of the twentieth century, theater was virtually totally democratized in all industrial nations. Now it is no longer a privilege; it is virtually an essential human right. American prison systems, for example, are expected to provide television entertainment to inmates (observers from the Middle East look on this as an astonishing indulgence). Theater, in one form or another, is a constant element in modern culture. Surveys note that Americans' television sets are turned on over forty hours a week, on the average.

This is an era in which both political and economic forces have discovered the necessity to play up to and manipulate audiences that number in the hundreds of millions. Out of this necessity has come the public relations specialist who manipulates images for the political campaigner. Out of this necessity has come the advertising specialist skilled in creating little moments known as "commercials," which sell products through theatrical devices.

Given the ubiquity and influence of drama in American life, it is surprising that so little attention was given to the dramatic arts by sociologists and political scientists before Goffman. As early as the 1920s and 1930s, American social scientists studied the impact of film on American morals, and they conducted other minor studies dealing with the dramatic arts. But it was Goffman who forced the attention of an entire generation toward the dramatic arts as a central element in human social relations and conduct.

This was a radical position to take, because the dramatic arts, by definition, are quite different from the rational sciences. The social sciences have sought to find the rational forms that are the underlying forces in human social communities. To turn to the arts for interpretive inspiration, as Goffman did, seemed almost heretical at that time. There is the implication that social conduct is an artful process. The fundamental view of Goffman is that we are forced to deal with others who are audiences to our performances. Our primary task, as social beings, is to retain those audiences by relying on actions that positively impress those who are watching us.

What does this have to do with an issue as deep and as physically real and threatening as nuclear weapons? How can Goffman provide us with yet another way of seeing the issues posed by "the bomb"? It is obvious that nuclear weapons are dramatic devices. Those men and women who are associated with their production, their design, their deliverance, their refinement, or their procurement are people who perforce must be taken seriously. To put it another way, when the nuclear physicist Edward Teller speaks, people listen. Given the fact that we live in what appears to be the most dramatically oriented society or culture in human history, a dramaturgic perspective should be especially insightful with respect to any number of topics. Certainly there is a dramatic relevance to weapons. Nuclear weapons, in a sense, are the ultimate dramatic device.

In this sense, then, we might, from a Goffmanian view of the world, come to the conclusion that the bomb, by its inherently threatening and total nature, provides "dramatic realization," to use Goffman's term, to its keepers and caretakers. Since people evidently value that which enables them to acquire and retain audiences, nuclear weapons must be valued by those whose lives are involved in their production and utilization. Nuclear weapons are not only a defensive system against the dreaded nightmare of an ememy nation's assault; they are also the most impressive sort of dramatic "prop" any actor could ever wish to rely on as a device for capturing the attention of people. Or, to put it another way, the bomb has given significance to the lives of a great number of people. There is more to the bomb than simply the argument that it is necessary to protect our nation's interests. It is also necessary to protect the social significance of those who continue to develop it.

Prior to the explosion of the first nuclear weapon in New Mexico in 1945, intellectuals, scientists, physicists, and other types of "eggheads" were considered more or less harmless intellectual eccentrics. Their audiences were limited pretty much to their own kind. After the devastation of Hiroshima and Nagasaki, physical scientists became more than celebrated figures; "eggheads" took on the mythic qualities of Superman. Although individual scientists are not able to "leap tall buildings in a single bound," their creations are, in many ways, superhuman. Scientists achieve social recognition through their creations, and their most impressive creation has been nuclear weaponry. Goffman cannot provide an answer to the question of whether or not scientists would be willing to give up their newfound social recognition if it meant giving up, as well, the rockets, the laser beam weapons, and the thousands of hydrogen warheads that now fill up the arsenals of the world. However, the question in itself suggests the extent to which we grant the dramatic priority over the practical.

Although there is much that is humane and deeply sympathetic to the human condition in Goffman's writing, there is also a cynical streak, an acceptance of the hypocrisy and the inevitable demand for posing and posturing that constitute the price we must pay as social beings. If we draw on the cynical side of Goffman's view of humanity, we may conjecture that nuclear weapons, though they are feared by all of us, hold a dramatic fascination for us at the same time. Those who work with them must find their lives enhanced by the serious purpose and socially dramatic implications of what they are doing, regardless of protests to the contrary.

The weapon—knives, rifles, pistols, machine guns, cannons, swords, bows and arrows, bombs, clubs, whips, fists—has been a central prop, at least in American entertainment and drama. The holstered six-gun of the gunslinger of the western, the tommy guns in violin cases carried by hoods in gangster movies, the esoteric devices portrayed in James Bond films, and other examples of the weapon as a dramatic device *in itself* suggest that, on the world scene, the nuclear weapon is an astonishingly dramatic prop. It cannot be carried on the hip or in a violin case, like the small weapons used in western and gangster films. It can only be carried abstractly. But there are those who maintain control over these weapons. They cannot wear them as a police officer might wear a pistol. However, "wearing" abstracted power, such as that offered by nuclear weapons, enhances the dramatic realization of anyone's performance.

In this sense, being associated with the bomb is similar to being associated with great wealth. Status and significance are acquired through the fact that one is associated with matters that are inherently significant. So it is, then, that Goffman's work leads us to view the nuclear situation from yet another angle—the manner in which it is desired and is of dramatic social value to those who attend to its development and its progression. It is obvious that nuclear weapons serve economic interests and that there are many people who want nuclear technology to continue because it means jobs and money. Goffman approaches the situation from a slightly different angle: The bomb serves the human social need to impress others with the seriousness and the propriety of our actions.

Is it possible that even if the "aggressor" nations were to abandon the bomb, there would be a fair number of individuals in our own society who would still want it around? Or, conversely (since the Russians, Chinese, or Pakistanis are not immune to the dramatic moment), if we abandoned the bomb, would there be numerous people of influence who would still want it? To what extent is there an inherent intranationalistic motive, as it were, to retain these devices simply because they grant social significance to people?

Questions such as these remain speculative. It is difficult to penetrate into the inner sanctum of the caretakers of the bomb. The mystifying powers of secrecy add further dramatic significance to whatever it is they do. However, the questions seem worth the asking. The situation that confronts us is terrifying enough as it is. If the caretakers of the bomb are not in a love-hate relationship with it and would happily abandon it, even if it meant losing money and status and power, then we should concentrate on the ways in which international tensions are the primary factors underlying the arms race.

But if the implications of Goffman's work are correct and the caretakers of the bomb are wedded to their creation, like Dr. Strangelove in the film of the same name by Stanley Kubrick, then the problem becomes still more profound. We are left with the possibility that the world powers could come to the most peaceful of understandings, and yet, within each power there would be those who would still find reason to continue their work on ever more destructive and powerful technological systems.

We can only raise questions. These questions suggest, however, even without any complete answer, that possibly we face two enemies—the enemy from without and the enemy from within. There may come a time when we shall solve the terrible, terrible problems that nuclear weapons pose for the modern world. To do so will require that we come to see such weapons in more than technological terms. We must move beyond seeing them simply as a response to the needs for defense. We must move beyond seeing them simply as devices that serve military and economic interests. These mighty weapons, in addition to the above-mentioned functions, grant dramatic significance and importance to people who quite possibly would otherwise find themselves engaged in less socially significant work.

If this encounter with Goffmanian thinking has any validity, then we appear to be in a situation where we shall have to live not only with the bomb, but with the continuing refinement and development of an

ever greater and more devastating weapons technology. The social motivations, as well as the economic and military reasons, for this technology are without any known or definable limits. Perhaps we shall
"solve" the nuclear arms race. From a dramaturgic perspective, it does
not appear likely so long as men and women are concerned with socially impressing each other. That is to say, it does not appear likely
at all.

Putting Social Thought to Work

1. Few writers offer a better opportunity for questioning the properties of
   human social behavior than Erving Goffman. His works provide a basis
   for entering into a discussion of such matters as "phoniness," hypocrisy, sincerity, and the "reality" of social action. How do we, in fact,
   determine whether a person is phony, and why are we so worried
   about phony actions? How do we determine whether or not a person
   has the "right" to do whatever he or she is doing? Is our intense interest
   in such things as movies and popular magazine literature associated
   with our desire to be able to identify and deal with social performances?

2. Although we tend to condemn "phoniness," we also seem to want it.
   That is to say, we like to be conned or "smooth talked." We are also
   aware of the extent to which we feel impelled at times to "put on an
   act." Goffman raises the question of the place of phoniness in social
   relations and refuses to permit us to dismiss it as an easy issue by
   saying that phoniness is bad and we do not want anything to do with
   it. How do we differentiate the phony from the sincere act? More important, to what extent has "phoniness" become an important part of
   modern American society? What culture or society would produce a
   book such as Goffman's *The Presentation of Self in Everyday Life*?

3. Perhaps phoniness is an essential part of human conduct, and Americans are simply too idealistic. For example, it is probably necessary to
   "pose" for a while in a social role before coming to the point at which
   one is competent in the role. A student has to pose as an intellectual
   for a while before really becoming one. The interval of posing may be
   relatively short in the case of a brilliant student or quite long in the
   case of someone less competent, but, for a while, the "pose" is necessary. This raises the possibility that some of the anxieties of youths in
   our culture—and young people seem to be the ones most concerned
   with phoniness—are products of the fact that young people must pretend to occupy roles that are not fully legitimated. In what ways is
   phoniness a problem for people, young or old, and in what ways is it
   necessary? Is it possible to get through a day in the company of others
   without engaging in occasional phony actions?

4. Goffman is referred to as a "dramaturgic" sociologist. That is to say, he relies on the metaphor of drama and dramatic action to interpret the world around us. To what extent do people "build" drama into their lives? How important is drama to us? Does drama incline us toward irrational action? What does it mean to be "dramatic"? How is drama transformed into reality—that is to say, how do we realize drama? How does stigmatization influence dramatic performance?

5. Football players engage in high drama on Saturday and Sunday afternoons. They also have a high probability of injuring themselves. What does this suggest with respect to the question of whether or not people prefer drama over physical welfare? Is risk an essential part of drama?

6. To what extent is our modern economy based on an ideology of drama? That is to say, to what extent are such economic factors as labor, commodities, land, and capital dramatized? We look down on the Russians for being "drab" and "unexciting" people. Does this reflect on the extent to which we have become "hooked" on the dramatic form? Who have more dramatic control in life, wealthy or poor people?

Endnotes

1. Fred J. Schonell, *The Psychology of Teaching and Reading*, 4th ed. (New York: Philosophical Library, 1961), p. 36. The total vocabulary of twelfth-grade high school students ranges from 36,700 to 136,500 words. D. McCarthy, "Language Development in Children," in L. Carmichael (ed.), *Manual of Child Psychology* (New York: Wiley, 1946), p. 59; cited in the student manual, *Stereotypes*, prepared by Sociological Resources for Secondary Schools, 1966, p. 7. Figures such as these are not very reliable. Even if they were, they would not give a good indication of the full complexity of speech and language. For example, the sentence, "You know what I mean," has five different words, but it can be given many different meanings by changing intonation or word order. Thus, we might say, "What *I mean*, you know." Or, "You mean I know *what*?" For a gracefully written exposition of such complexities of language, see J. R. Firth, *The Tongues of Men* (London: Oxford University Press, 1964), p. 34.

2. We are again indebted to Charles K. Warrener of the University of Kansas for warning us against giving the impression of a false dichotomy. One can, for example, view symbols as enabling people to merge more consciously with nature. A debate on whether symbols enable us to merge with nature can quickly turn into a profitless metaphysical dispute. We are only trying to suggest, through this phrasing, that labeling an object or event has the capacity to separate us from other qualities that this object or event may possess.

3. Possibly the most significant of Erving Goffman's books is *The Presentation of Self in Everyday Life*, which was first published as a monograph in the Social Sciences Research Centre at the University of Edinburgh in 1956. This chapter is based on materials appearing in the Anchor Books version (Garden City, NY: Doubleday, 1959). Goffman's other major works include *Encounters* (Indianapolis, IN: Bobbs-Merrill, 1961); *Asylums* (Garden City, NY: Doubleday, 1961); *Behavior in Public Places* (New York: Free Press, 1963); *Stigma: Notes on the Management of*

Spoiled Identity (Englewood Cliffs, NJ: Prentice-Hall, 1963); *Interaction Ritual: Essays on Face-to-Face Behavior* (Chicago: Aldine, 1967); *Frame Analysis* (New York: Colophon Books, 1974); and *Gender Advertisements* (Cambridge, MA: Harvard University Press, 1979).

4. *The Presentation of Self in Everyday Life*, p. 2. Goffman's emphasis on the symbolic nature of social interaction places him among those sociologists who refer to themselves as "symbolic interactionists." The foundations of symbolic interactionist thought were laid by George Herbert Mead and Charles Horton Cooley.

5. A student of Veblen's is quoted as having said, "Why, it was creepy. It might have been a dead man's voice slowly speaking on, and if the light had gone out behind those dropped eyelids, would it have made any difference? But we who listened day after day found the unusual manner nicely fitted to convey the detached and slightly sardonic intellect that was moving over the face of things." Even so, Veblen's classes dwindled, and one ended with only a single student. See Robert L. Heilbroner, *The Worldly Philosophers* (New York: Simon and Schuster, 1953), p. 214.

6. Goffman, *The Presentation of Self in Everyday Life*, pp. 43–44.

7. A United Press International news item that appeared in the Urbana, Illinois, *News-Gazette*, January 20, 1966, p. 12.

8. Goffman, *The Presentation of Self in Everyday Life*, pp. 32–33.

9. Ibid., p. 39.

10. Here Goffman quotes Mirra Komarovsky, "Cultural Contradictions and Sex Roles," *American Journal of Sociology 52* (1958), 186–188, in *The Presentation of Self in Everyday Life*, p. 39.

11. *Stigma* traces the problems and involvements that arise when an individual is forced to play the social game, while at the same time wearing a mask that is marred or reading a script that is flawed.

12. Goffman, *Stigma*, pp. 2–3.

13. Ibid., p. 5.

14. Ibid., pp. 137–138.

15. Goffman quotes J. Stearn, *Sisters of the Night* (New York: Popular Library, 1961), p. 181, in *Stigma*, p. 28.

16. Goffman takes this example from H. Freeman and G. Kasenbaum, "The Illiterate in America," *Social Forces 34* (May 1956), 374. See *Stigma*, p. 44.

17. *Stigma*, pp. 73–74.

Chapter 15

Studying the Commonplace

The Work of Harold Garfinkel

❖

❖ Introduction

The great preponderance of the social actions in which we engage from day to day are commonplace events. These are the ordinary, the usual, the routine, the obvious patterns of activity that we have little cause to question. If we do question them, we tend to come up with commonplace observations. The significance of the commonplace and ordinary actions of day-to-day existence is that we do not question them. They acquire a taken-for-granted quality that removes them from our examination and consideration. This gives them a hold over us that most other events, those falling outside the commonplace, do not have.

But how can we approach the commonplace without coming up with observations so banal and commonplace in their own way that we are prevented from achieving intellectually interesting results? It is not difficult to imagine writing something interesting about events taking place in the White

House or explorations on the surface of the moon. To gain access to such unusual arenas of human activity virtually assures a reporter of a good story. But what about reporting on how people walk down the sidewalk, or how they pass through the checkout counter at the supermarket, or what happens when two people greet each other in the halls of a building on campus?

Our experience has been that students believe that writing a paper about commonplace experiences is an easy assignment. After all, the material is available and "human." They feel they can rely on immediate and direct observations. When the completed papers are turned in, however, they usually consist of extremely ordinary and uninteresting observations; they lack intellectual depth. Now it is possible to study the commonplace in an uncommon way, but it takes an unusually well-trained mind to move beyond the obvious and apparent features of such activity. It requires being able to question that which few people ever question during their entire lifetimes. It requires, in a way, the ability to become a stranger in an unstrange land.

Granting these difficulties, there are still several reasons why common, ordinary, day-to-day events are particularly significant for advancing our understanding of human social behavior. In the first place, most human activity is of the ordinary variety. Even people who acquire the label "extraordinary" spend most of their time in commonplace activities. If we ignore the commonplace, we bypass most of what is going on among human beings. In the second place (and this is by far the more important and interesting consideration), the fact that a social relationship is commonplace tends, as we have said, to make it impervious to deeper examination. After all, it is not worthy of analysis or examination; it is something that can and should be taken for granted.

Yet it is this very taken-for-granted quality of the commonplace event that gives it a special power over us. It is significant because it is not examined. It has a hold over us because we accept the demands of the taken-for-granted moment without question or conscious consideration.

But do commonplace events really have to be beyond intellectual question, or is there something to the mundane events of day-to-day living that is a key to the "higher" moments of our lives? Is there perhaps a special way to approach the commonplace so that more is revealed than the taken-for-granted matters of the moment?

This, in part, is the question to which Harold Garfinkel has turned his attention. It is a profound matter, in the final analysis, because it has to do with how we come to accept as "real" various features of our social and physical world. How does one penetrate a reality so "obvious" to those who are caught up in it that they cannot even begin to question it? One way in which Garfinkel has attempted to delve into the structure and character of the commonplace is by the simple device of disrupting it. The disruption does not have to be especially profound to achieve its effect. Garfinkel has obtained revealing responses merely by interrupting an ordinary conversation with an innocuous question. What Garfinkel has often done is to have his students ask a person with whom they are talking to elaborate on something he or she has just said. Students are instructed, however, to make this request at a point in the conversation when everyone involved is inclined to think that what has been said is perfectly clear and obvious.

For example, a student may be talking with someone in the hall just outside the classroom before a lecture begins. The conversation may go something like this:

Friend: That sure was a great party at your place last night. Everybody had a really great time. You know what I mean?

Student: No, I'm not certain I do know what you mean.

Friend: Come on. You know.

Student: No, when you say that everybody had a great time, just what are you talking about?

Friend: You know. They really had a good time.

Student: Yes, you said that before; but I want to know what you *mean* by a good time.

Friend: Jesus! What's gotten into you? You know what I mean. They had a good time!

This may sound like a bit of minor sadism on the part of Garfinkel's students, but the response of the friend is revealing. The friend is puzzled. The normal expectations around which ordinary day-to-day forms of expression take place have been challenged.[1] Still, it is not *unreasonable* to ask for an elaboration of a statement—or is it?

When do we have the right to question, and when does the act of questioning interfere with a process that is not supposed to be questioned? A number of people who were questioned like the friend in the conversation above became distressed, upset, or otherwise flustered over the disruption of what appeared to them to be a perfectly normal sequence of events. If you tell someone that you recently had a flat tire, and that person asks you what you mean by "having a flat tire," it is likely that you will respond the way one person did when questioned by a student of Garfinkel. That is, you will wonder aloud why anyone would ever question what you meant. Everyone should "know" about such things. You can act in a predictable, ordinary way with others only if you can presume they share a common background with you. If something takes place that disrupts your trust of that common background, then suddenly your interaction is forced into new and uncertain pathways. You may begin to wonder about the other person's sanity, perhaps, and in some instances you may begin to wonder about your own.

Another way in which Garfinkel has often attempted to move behind the ordinary conventions that buttress our day-to-day social affairs is to have his students report on some social scene or event as though they were not really an integral part of it. For example, students have been asked to write a description of a holiday visit at home as if they were outsiders rather than members of the family. How would they view their parents, for example, if they were only boarders in the house instead of being their children? Several of the papers Garfinkel has received from this assignment have a bizarre quality to them. There is a detachment and objectivity to the observations, and the identities of the people involved get shifted around in strange ways. It is one thing to see your mother as your mother; it is something else to see her at any one time simply as a woman who is serving a meal.[2] Garfinkel literally asks his students to do what social scientists call "making it strange."

What is the point of such an exercise? Fundamentally, the point is to ascertain the difference between the reality that confronts us in its purely objective form and the reality that we experience as a result of how we have come to construct our world. The exercise has as its aim nothing less than to show that the same event can be seen as having variant forms of reality. Or, to put it in a slightly different way, what we "do" to reality transforms the reality we are responding to. Reality is not an objective state, but is instead an interaction between the state and the observer. It is, in sum, relativism pushed to its most radical extreme.

❖ *Elaborative Experiences*

The process whereby people create the kinds of reality to which they then respond is nowhere better delineated than in a simple demonstration that we consider to be one of the most clever and also profound demonstrations to be found in modern Western social science. In this study, Garfinkel was able to show empirically how people elaborate on their experiences until eventually the experiences "make sense." We presume that patterns exist in reality, even when they are not there, and we somehow manage to find them. (We have a way of drawing support from whatever we find around us.)

In this particular demonstration, students volunteered for psychiatric counseling about their personal problems. Each student provided the "counselor" with background information on some problem and then asked a question that could be answered "yes" or "no" by the counselor. The student and counselor were separated by an opaque screen. After the student heard the counselor's reply to his or her question, he or she recorded reactions to the counselor's reply into a tape recorder. The counselor could not hear the reactions. When the student was ready with the next question, he or she addressed the counselor, asked the question, and then continued with an evaluation of the counselor's next "yes" or "no" response. Here is a modified transcript of one such counseling session.[3]

Subject:	I happen to be of the Jewish faith and I have been dating a gentile girl. My dad is not directly opposed, but at the same time he will come up with digs and sayings that make me feel very ill at ease. My question is, do you feel that I should continue dating this girl?
Counselor:	My answer is no.
Subject:	No. Well, that is kind of interesting, I suppose, or maybe it is easier for an outsider to see certain things that I am blind to at this moment. I would like to ask my second question. Should I have further discussion with Dad over this subject about dating the gentile girl?
Counselor:	My answer is yes.
Subject:	Well, I feel that is reasonable. I guess we should have a discussion based on what the future possibilities might be and how he would feel about that. He may not be too strongly opposed now because we are only dating, but perhaps he sees future complications that he would really like to get off his chest at the moment. I am ready for my third question now. If Dad says to continue dating her, but he really does not want me to date her, but he is only doing it because he wants to be a good dad, should I still date the girl?
Counselor:	My answer is yes.
Subject:	Well, I am actually surprised at the answer. Even though he might have said, "Go ahead and date her," I perhaps would feel guilty in knowing that he really did not want me to continue to date her, though I don't know that it would actually help the situation. I am ready for the fourth question now. Do you think it would be proper for me to have my mother have a serious talk with him, and therefore try and get a truer reaction to Dad's opinion on the situation?
Counselor:	My answer is yes.
Subject:	Well, this seems fair to me. I feel perhaps that he would be honester with Mother about the situation. She would be a little more liberal about things like this. At least I feel that we are moving along some way. I am ready for my fifth question now. Do you feel that I should tell the girl that I am dating the problems that I am having at home over her religion?

Counselor: My answer is no.

Subject: I am surprised. Of course, that might depend on how much you care for the girl. I feel that it is only right to tell her. If she feels that this will be a block, then I feel perhaps that would end the situation right there. I am ready for my sixth question. If we planned to marry, do you feel I should ask her to change her religion?

Counselor: My answer is no.

Subject: Well, this has me stymied. No, unfortunately, I have never seen a family with a split in religion that really has been able to make a success out of it. I think that perhaps I would be tempted to ask her to change. I don't think that I would be able to really. I am ready for number seven. Do you feel that it would be a better situation if we bring our children up in a neutral religion other than the two that we believe in?

Counselor: My answer is yes.

Subject: Well, perhaps this would be a solution. If we could find a religion that would incorporate our two beliefs to a certain extent—I guess I should follow this along a little bit further and see exactly what happens. I am ready for number eight. If we were to get married, would it be best for us to live in a new community where we will not be in contact with our parents if we were getting a lot of family pressure over religious differences?

Counselor: My answer is no.

Subject: Well, I kinda tend to agree with this answer. I feel that you wouldn't be accomplishing too much by running away from the issue. So we best remain there and try to work it out. I am ready for number nine. If we did get married, would we just bring the children up in this new religion that we talked about and let them believe that that is what we originally believed in?

Counselor: My answer is no.

Subject: I tend to agree here too. If they did find out that there was this difference that we once had, they would feel that we were sneaking. This would not be the best situation, either. I am ready for number ten. Do you feel that our children would have any religious problems because of our difficulties?

Counselor: My answer is no.

Subject: Well, I really don't know if I agree with that or not. I kinda feel that if their religion was a wholesome one which supplied the needs of a religion, there would not be any problems with them. I am finished with my comments now.

The session was then closed, but the subject was asked to make some comments about the counseling he had received. Among his comments were some of the following statements:

Subject: The answers that I received were for the most part aware of the situation as we moved along. They had a lot of meaning for me. His answers as a whole were helpful. He [the counselor] was completely aware of the situation at hand. I feel that it had a lot of sense to me and made a lot of sense.

As readers may have guessed by now, the interesting feature of this study is that the counselor's advice consisted of random "yes" or "no" responses. The "counselor," actually an experimenter, was replying to each question, in effect, by tossing a coin and saying "yes" if it turned up heads and "no" if it turned up tails. This did not make any difference, however, for the subjects. They believed the answers showed that the "counselor" was "aware of the situation," "helpful," and "made a lot of sense."

But what is the point of all this? Garfinkel gets people to tease their friends by asking them to elaborate on the meaning of commonplace utterances. Students describe what it is like to see their own households from the perspective of a boarder. People make sense out of counseling that is random and unrelated to the questions they ask. At first, Garfinkel's work seems playful and prankish, like something the creator of the once popular television program "Candid Camera" might have pulled on people. But the tricks played on people for the television program were simply pranks, putting people in situations that were amusing. The idea behind this television show (and more recent copies of the same format) was to entertain people. Garfinkel, on the other hand, is singularly humorless in his writing. His style is cumbersome and tortured—a virtual necessity to prevent the reader from concluding that he is simply messing around. When Garfinkel plays a "joke" on people, it is for the sake of trying to uncover the devices that enable them to carry off complex and abstract actions.

Moreover, these actions are so taken for granted that challenging them can be a disturbing experience. So Garfinkel disturbs people slightly in their ordinary routines and then looks for what is revealed by these disruptions.

❖ *Interpreting the Commonplace*

As we have argued before, the problem with the commonplace is that it is commonplace. When people are questioned about their commonplace activities, they (curiously enough) are not as well able to describe what they are doing as when they are engaged in not-so-commonplace activities. The paradox of the commonplace moment is that the actors feel their actions are unproblematic, despite the fact that they can be extremely vague in describing what they are doing. We cannot come to grips with familiar and ordinary conduct by asking the persons involved in it to tell us about it. They are too immersed in the familiar to be able to recognize it or articulate it. Somehow, the imaginations of the actors and the events within which they find themselves become a single, reasonable happening. They are able to take whatever is there and transform it into something that "makes sense." But, more significantly, it can make so much sense that there is little point in discussing the matter. It simply takes place.

A brief digression may make this discussion, if not clearer, then at least more relevant to our day-to-day affairs. One theory of religious practice is that it came out of people's awed response to their world. We begin discussions of this theory by asking students in our classes how they feel about the classroom and the moment they are in. They usually reply by asking, "What do you mean, 'How do I feel'? What is there to feel anything about?" The casual, matter-of-fact response of students to the peculiar circumstances in which they move—their striking lack of awe—illustrates not only a weakness of the "religion as a response to the awesome" theory, but also Garfinkel's concern with "matter-of-factness." The surprising thing about people is not that they are awed but that they are so little awed—that they take so much for granted. In an infinitely awesome and mysterious world, we accept our trifling human accounts of events as reasonable.

What is the power or influence we find in the "reasonableness" of the ordinary event? What gives it its hold over people? How is it possible to investigate and understand what happens at the point where imagination and reality join together to create the acceptable social act? Because the acceptable social act is so acceptable, the people caught up in it cannot articulate readily what it is they are caught up in. They may, however, give some clues about the forces that contain them if the smooth operation of those forces is interrupted. So it came about that Garfinkel's approach to the study of human social events is similar to that used by the physicist trying to fathom the nature of physical matter. The "building blocks" of social reality are examined by a process of subjecting them to collisions that reveal their hidden subjective nature, much as the collisions between particles in a cloud chamber give clues to the nature of matter.

Garfinkel is explicit about his method of approach to the subjective state. He argues that we should expose commonplace, everyday, familiar interchanges between individuals to intense examination. What is "really" going on when people sit down together for breakfast, or walk across the campus, or talk together in the halls? Some would argue that we do not need to know about such matters. After all, they pretty much take care of themselves, and it is silly to analyze something that is not a problem or a source of trouble.

Garfinkel, however, insists that the commonplace is important and that the way to study it is by disrupting it and then observing carefully how people deal with the disruption. It is in dealing with the disorganizing moment that the structure holding the interaction together is revealed.

It is possible, after all, that the commonplace has implications for the not-so-commonplace. The processes that lead us to accept the reasonability of an ordinary encounter may offer clues as to why we think it is "reasonable" to engage in war or ravage the resources of our planet or send a condemned person to the gas chamber. Garfinkel's work is a relatively pure form of social research. It will take some time before we can judge its full implications for the promotion of our understanding of human social behavior.

Garfinkel is interested, then, in producing moments of small madness. To the extent that we can understand such madness and produce it at will, we might be able to understand greater madnesses, also. However, Garfinkel is little concerned with whether his work will have such beneficial effects. The task, as he sees it, is to observe and to struggle to understand ourselves, regardless of whether such efforts promote humanistic values or a "better" society. He is quite explicit about this:

> Ethnomethodological studies are not directed to . . . arguing correctives. . . . They do not formulate a remedy for practical actions, as if it was being found about practical actions that they were better or worse than they are usually cracked up to be. Nor are they in search of humanistic arguments. . . .[4]

Another way of looking at Garfinkel's work is to see it as an attempt to separate individuals momentarily from the social supports that hold them up and give a "natural" quality to the commonplace action. When individuals begin to act truly as individuals, we may be able to compare their conduct with the way they act when sustained by their ordinary social backgrounds. Garfinkel suggests that much can be gained from observing those moments when individuals are pulled free and then have to act relatively independently of whatever constitutes their social nature. In the contrast, we uncover the difference between the social actor and the individual per se. As a uniquely sociological procedure for investigation, Garfinkel suggests that people be placed in circumstances where they are denied their normal reliance on social understandings and must struggle with the situation on their own.

This kind of observation of the individual as individual can be achieved through a variety of devices. One device is to engage in an apparent breach of convention during a social happening. This is the case when Garfinkel has had students press someone with the question "What do you mean by that?" Another device is to have the observer attempt to divest himself or herself, through an act of imagination or by changing identity, of the social background normal to the usual circumstances of his or her life. This is the effort in the case of the students who are asked to view their personal households as if they were boarders. Still another device is to have the individual unwittingly engage in a relationship that he or she has interpreted one way but that is moving along some other avenue of development, more or less independently of anything the person is doing. This was the case with the students who were being "counseled" by random "yes" and "no" replies from the "counselor." In each of these situations, people are placed in circumstances where they continue to act socially. But the form of the social action is revealing in what it does *not* offer them. More significantly, it is revealing in how they respond to that lack.

These observational devices are designed to allow the researcher to "observe" the ways in which people attempt to reconstruct a relationship that looks as though it is going "sour." Relationships are based on commonly understood rules that enable the participants to make sense out of the relationship and the world around them. This is what "common sense" is all about. If you are enjoying a conversation with someone and your common sense is thrown into doubt, it is a disturbing experience. Not only is the relationship threatened, but there is the potential for a threat to one's total understanding of the way the world is supposed to be ordered.

❖ What is Ethnomethodology?

Garfinkel refers to his work as "ethnomethodology." *Ethno-* refers to "people." *Method-* refers to "method." And *-ology* refers to "study." Ethnomethodology, then, is an examination of the methods people commonly use to sustain some kind of consensus about the world and to solve problems characterized by highly irrational features. Garfinkel, for example, was, at one point in his career, interested in how people came to conclusions about the motives and events leading up to the deaths of people who were thought to have committed suicide. Garfinkel observed that no matter how vague the clues might be, people who had been assigned the task of commenting on a suicide were invariably able to say something about it.

One of the fascinating features of social activity is that it operates on the basis of uncertain knowledge. To present as simple an example as possible, students and instructors in a typical college classroom do not know much about each other's lives. Students do not have any truly good awareness of the past experiences and understanding of the instructor, and it is much the same for the instructor's understanding of the students' lives. This does not, however, prevent both the students and the instructor from constructing understandings of each other and then acting on the basis of those understandings. It is this process that interests Garfinkel.

❖ Implications of the "Counseling" Study

We can gain further insight into what Garfinkel is trying to do by returning to the "counseling" study. The experiment with the "counselor" provides us with an explicitly developed set of findings. These findings offer us a way of entering into the vision of human social activity generated by an ethno-methodological approach. We would like to suggest that these findings also offer insights into the nondeterminant or "artful"[5] and complex nature of human social activity in even its simplest and most commonplace forms.

There is a bit of paradox in the fact that Garfinkel's investigations of commonsense understanding of the world are probably not especially commonsensical. A great deal of sophistication is required to follow Garfinkel's interpretation. In the material that follows, we have listed the findings from the Garfinkel study separately in much the same way as they have been presented by the author. We have somewhat modified the order of presentation, and we have deleted comments outside the range of a book of this kind.[6]

We have also taken the liberty of suggesting concepts of our own that we think may help the student comprehend a little better the thrust of what is being talked about. These concepts—"loading," "patterning," and so on—do not appear in the original work of Garfinkel and are intended, again, only as devices to help the student. We have added some commentary to underscore how an ethnomethodologist looks at what is going on when people seek to construct meaning in their social affairs. Although the findings are drawn specifically from the "counseling" demonstration, they apply more broadly to the general interpretations of social actions subscribed to by ethnomethodologists. (Page references are to *Studies in Ethnomethodology*.)

Finding 1. "Typically the subjects heard the experimenter's answers as answers-to-the-questions. Perceptually, the experimenter's answers were motivated by the questions" (p. 89).

This sounds like a peculiar "finding." One's first reaction, we should think, would be to say, "Of course they did, you fool." But such a quick reply would miss the point, and it is a basic point from an ethnomethodological slant. First of all, it is necessary to keep in mind the simple fact that the answers were *not* answers to the questions. If this is kept constantly in mind, then what Garfinkel is saying becomes a reasonable foundation for much of what follows.

We shall refer to this aspect of human social behavior as "naive perception." That is to say, people tend to respond to symbolic definitions of events as "reality," unless there is good reason to suspect otherwise. In other words, symbolic realities are "real." The students saw their "counseling" as "real" counseling, despite the fact that it was not. The value of the counseling did not come from the stimulus event per se, but rather from what the students subjectively perceived and manipulated as a stimulus event.

So, on the one hand, there were "counselors" who were essentially commenting at random at the request of other people. The people making the request were "set up" to deal artfully with those random comments—and they did so! (We have used the term "set up" to convey some sense of what Garfinkel is talking about, even though he does not use this term.) They began to create a set of "meanings" around the random commentaries of the "counselor." These meanings acquired their value not from anything intrinsic within the counselor's comments, but from something more complex. For the moment, we shall call the source of the comments "background."

The background in any situation involves not only the various recalled experiences and knowledge of the person, but also the sets of rules that determine how information will be used in encounters with others. Although experiences vary considerably from individual to individual, it is possible that the rules that are part of the *common* sense of experience are similar. If so, then we may be able to describe the normative regularities that underlie complex social relationships. In this sense, then, despite the apparently eccentric nature of Garfinkel's work, it falls definitely within the conventions of scientific investigation. That is, it is empirical, and it is concerned with uncovering regularities in its object of study.

Finding 2. "All [subjects] reported 'the advice that they had been given' and addressed their appreciation to that 'advice' " (p. 89).

This observation underlines Finding 1, with the perspective changed only slightly. Garfinkel is particularly interested in the extent to which a social exchange involves what, for want of a better term, might be called "loading" or "overloading." The "yes" and "no" responses in the experiment were just that—"yes" and "no" statements coming from a predetermined random process. But they were invested with particular meanings by the subjects, who "loaded" them with an understanding that was not within the statements themselves. The subjects had been "set up" to deal with the responses in a manner that overlaid them with meanings the subjects were able to elaborate in terms of their own conceptions. The important thing to remember is that the subjects were creating a social relationship—even against a random event. They were loading the responses of the "counselor" with meanings they could then respond to. This is common in all human social communications.

Once more, we must emphasize that we are using terms that are not used by Garfinkel, but that we hope convey the spirit of his interpretations. It is extremely significant to note here that Garfinkel is adding a dimension to a problem raised by Émile Durkheim. Durkheim was concerned with the intensity of human punishment, which usually far transcends the often banal qualities of the crime for which it is imposed. He believed that the extreme nature of much human punishment came from the augmenting of human motivations by the powerful "collective conscience." The collective is bigger than the individual, not only in size, but also in its capacity to generate and sustain emotion. Durkheim, however, was not able to say how this process worked. It seemed reasonable to conclude that the intensification of emotion comes somehow from involvement with and within the "collective conscience." But how? Garfinkel has suggested the answer in a simple demonstration, in which students gave much "deeper" meanings to an event than the event contained within itself.

The individual is capable of elevating the meanings of symbols and situations by endowing them with qualities that, as they become part of the situation, are then responded to by the individual. In other words, we respond to our own creations. A stimulus event is never simply a stimulus in and of itself, but a stimulus as it comes to be elaborately defined *and then* further responded to. The picture of a parakeet pecking at its image in a mirror comes to mind here, but it is much too simple. Although each participant in a social interaction loads the responses of others with materials from his or her own personal background, the individual is responding to much more than an immediate self-image.

In ordinary and not-so-ordinary social moments, the constant operation of this inclination to overload messages sustains social behavior and, at least in part, provides it with continuity. Terms such as "black power," "freedom," "love," and almost any other socially significant concept far transcend the simple meaning of "yes" or "no." They are invitations to persons using them in social discourse to project background interpretations upon the concept. It is in this process that the social act is generated and the peculiar meeting between the individual and the greater society takes place.

Finding 3. "Over the course of the exchange the assumption seemed to operate that there was an answer to be obtained, and that if the answer was not obvious, that its meaning could be determined by active search, one part of which involved asking another question so as to find out what the adviser 'had in mind' " (p. 89).

We shall refer to this as "searching." That is to say, the students came into the "counseling" with a sense of an answer that was presumed to be there and that would be ascertained with a proper search. The character of the stimulus event was anticipated prior to the moment when a student encountered the stimulus. Garfinkel is impressed by the "artful" nature of the sustained social event. When a person is "set up" for an engagement, the general theme of the engagement is carried through in terms of premises that give the engagement meaning. *Again, this meaning is sustained by the actor's capacity to continue to interpret the responses of the other as relevant to that meaning—regardless of whether it really is.* In this finding, Garfinkel begins to display the extent to which a common social interaction relies on conditions far removed from the persons involved, but "brought into" the situation to "fill it" and retain its continuity.

Finding 4. "The identical utterance was capable of answering several different questions simultaneously, and of constituting an answer to a compound question that in terms of the strict logic of propositions did not permit either a yes or no or a single yes or no" (p. 90).

We shall refer to this as "compounding." Garfinkel demonstrates that people are often quite satisfied with what are, in the final analysis, totally illogical responses. In the "counseling" study, a student asked, "Should I marry my girlfriend, or should I go to Europe and forget all about it? Or maybe it would be better to go to work." The counselor replied by saying, "My answer is yes." The student asked a compound question and was satisfied with a simple response. Apparently the counselor's response was not related to the student's question in any strictly rational or mechanical manner.

This is one of those findings common to sociology, insofar as it appears to be something that everyone has known all along. However, one of the peculiarities about things we have known all along is that we often do not really know them. This finding underscores a conception of people as rather irrational and certainly illogical creatures. Garfinkel concedes that human beings are not logical in much of their social interaction. However, he sees most of this interaction as a response to quite rational concerns. That is, the individual does engage in "searches" for support of a particular position he or she has taken.

The rational conduct of the person engaged in day-to-day social discourse is not, however, the same as scientifically rational actions. In the final section of the work being discussed here, Garfinkel goes to great lengths to explain the way in which a purely scientific rationality would destroy any sense of social relationship among people. For our purposes, however, it is sufficient to note that social activities, as seen by Garfinkel, are not necessarily logical in their nature. Again, we see a kind of overloading of terms with meanings they cannot, in a strictly logical sense, actually have.

Finding 5. "More subjects entertained the possibility of a trick than tested this possibility. All suspicious subjects were reluctant to act under the belief that there was a trick involved. Suspicions were reduced if the adviser's answers made 'good sense.' Suspicions were least likely to continue if the answers accorded with the subject's previous thought about the matter and with his preferred derisions" (p. 91).

We shall refer to this as "test resistance," although the term does not do Garfinkel's observation justice. Garfinkel is interested in the fact that students rarely made tests of the situation they were in. Garfinkel suggests that evidently the students found their own constructions of the "sense" of the situation sufficient. It is important to underscore, once more, that the students were responding as much to their own creations as they were to the external and "real" situation. For as long as the students could sustain a correspondence between their comprehension of the situation and what they were doing, they refused to test the situation and accepted it for what it appeared to be.

This is the world as "taken for granted." Garfinkel is interested in the extent to which most of us are unwilling to test certain kinds of rules or possibilities inherent within a particular moment or situation. In a different demonstration, Garfinkel had students go out as potential customers and show an interest in some item worth no more than two dollars. Then they were to bargain with the salesperson, beginning with a very low opening bid.

Garfinkel discovered, first of all, that students found this difficult to do— particularly if the assignment called for the student to try to bargain only once. Where students were to make the effort three or more times, there was a greater tendency for them to carry through with the assignment. Interestingly, the students found that by the third time they were able to enter a bargaining stance with salespeople and enjoyed "dickering" with them over the price of an item. They even discovered, somewhat to their surprise, that more often than not they could get significant bargains by this process. For Garfinkel, however, the significance of their efforts lies in more general possibilities. One of the qualities of whatever is taken for granted is that it does not get tested. Many rules operate, he suggests, not because they have withstood some test of time but rather because they simply have not been tested. "Indeed, the more important the rule, the greater is the likelihood that knowledge is based on avoided tests."[7]

Among the students who were being "counseled," the possibility that a trick was in progress was more likely to be considered than tested. Interestingly enough, the judgment as to whether deceit was involved rested on the congruence between the background expectations and interpretations of the student and the pattern of random responses being presented by the counselor. Garfinkel suggests here (though he does not pay much further attention to the possibility) that paranoid or suspicious qualities in an interaction arise out of incongruencies between expected backgrounds. That is, paranoia is not specifically a personality characteristic in many cases, but comes instead out of qualities of the interaction between persons—with the most significant aspect of the interaction being the matching or mismatching of backgrounds.

Finding 6. "Throughout there was a concern and search for pattern. Pattern, however, was perceived from the very beginning. Pattern was likely to be seen in the first evidence of the 'advice' " (p. 91).

We shall refer to this as "patterning." The students in the counseling demonstration believed that they were able to deal with the entire range of stimuli. They would indicate this with statements such as, "Ah, I see now how it *all* fits together." In other words, stimuli were not discrete "yes" or "no" responses, but were manipulated by the students into organic patterns of stimuli. This is a major feature of Garfinkel's work. It is an overriding premise that pervades the whole of his thinking about the nature of human social actions. Garfinkel is interested in the consequences of the fact that people come into social relationships with a preestablished sense of pattern. How does this pattern influence the interaction? What is its source? What are the consequences of even minor disturbances in the pattern? How can the nature of the pattern be ascertained by disrupting it?

There is a strong temptation to draw parallels between the Gestalt school of psychology and Garfinkel's work, with Garfinkel representing an unusual form of Gestaltist sociology. The concept of pattern underlies both points of view. Unlike psychologists, however, Garfinkel is not especially interested in pattern as it affects the individual's purely sensory perception. He is interested in pattern as it relates to the ordered manner in which people conduct their ordinary social affairs.

The idea of a preestablished pattern of ideas about an interaction sounds similar to the older social-psychological concepts of attitudes and prejudices. In their older usage, these terms either had a pejorative quality (it is "bad" to be prejudiced) or restricted application (one has attitudes about some relevant issue of the time, such as the election of a Catholic president or the use of fluorides in drinking water). Garfinkel finds that apparent patterns are a constant and necessary condition for *any* social interaction. In this sense, his work is an extension of already well-established concepts in the fields of social psychology, sociology, and cultural anthropology.

We can gain an appreciation of the extent to which Garfinkel does not accept the taken-for-granted aspects of social actions as we progress into some of his evaluation of the finding that social interaction is grounded in the "search for pattern." He comments, for example, that the subjects found it difficult to deal with the fact that they had been given random counseling. When they were informed that this was the situation, they shifted their interpretation of the counselor's comments from "advice" to "deceit." Again, keep in mind that during the period when the subjects were naive, they had accepted the random advice as advice. *In other words, the character of the advice itself was not what determined whether it was acceptable as advice.* Some other condition or background factor determined this.

So the character of the advice received in the study was not a function of the advice being given, but rather the conceptualization of the advice by the recipient. The random responses, seen as an event, provided documentation for an established pattern. Once the pattern was established, the documentation process took place with some insistence. The underlying patterns might shift, but the constant process of documenting the pattern from the givens of the interaction remained as an integral part of the person's social concern.

Finding 7. "Subjects assigned to the adviser as his advice the thought formulated in the subject's questions. For example, when a subject asked, 'Should I come to school every night after supper to do my studying?' and the experimenter said, 'My answer is no,' the subject in his comments said, 'He said I shouldn't come to school and study.' This was very common" (p. 92).

We shall refer to this as "projection." This general concept is an old one in psychology, where it is commonly used to describe defensive behavior. For example, a disturbed person may project his or her disturbance onto others. This sometimes happens with a person who is inclined toward homosexuality but, at the same time, fears homosexuality. The person then accuses others of making advances toward him or her or otherwise acting homosexually. The homosexual fears have been projected. Garfinkel goes further. He suggests that such projection is not simply a defensive psychological device. Instead, it is a purely natural and common aspect of any human interaction. People are constantly projecting, as it were, those backgrounds they bring into a given social moment.

This seventh observation has a great number of implications. It suggests, among other things, that (1) the meaning of messages in social interchange cannot be isomorphic (that is, show a one-to-one correspondence) unless the backgrounds of the participants are isomorphic; (2) distortion is a natural part of ordinary social events; (3) a message does not exist as an isolated event and cannot be given any value as such; (4) messages that carry no meaning in themselves can establish a meaning through the process of communication; and (5) understanding any message that is presented within a group (where such understanding is sought by some outside observer) calls for comprehensive knowledge of the social and cultural backgrounds of all members of the group, including how those backgrounds influence the messages received. There are other implications in this observation that space does not permit us to consider. We urge the reader, however, to note how commonly this matter of projection occurs in day-to-day interaction with friends and associates.

It is also important to note here that people are not generally cognizant of the extent to which they are shaping and influencing the situation that is also shaping and influencing them. When students were informed, after the "counseling" sessions, that they had contributed a great deal to the "advice" they received, they were astounded.

Finding 8. "Subjects made specific reference to various social structures in deciding the sensible and warranted character of the adviser's advice. Such references, however, were not made to any social structures whatever. In the eyes of the subject, if the adviser was to know and demonstrate to the subject that he knew what he was talking about, and if the subject was to consider seriously the adviser's descriptions of his circumstances as foundation for the subject's further thoughts and management of these circumstances, the subject did not permit the adviser, nor was the subject willing to entertain, *any* model of the social structures. References that the subject supplied, were to social structures which he treated as actually or potentially known in common with the adviser. And then, not to *any* social structure known in common, but to normatively valued social structures which the subject accepted as *conditions* that his decision, with respect to his own sensible and realistic grasp of his circumstances and the 'good' character of the adviser's advice, had to satisfy. These social structures consisted of normative features of the social system *seen from within* which, for the subject, were definitive of his membership in the various collectivities that were referred to" (pp. 92–93).[8]

This lengthy, tortured, and at first obvious-sounding "finding" has some not so obvious and even lengthier implications. First of all, Garfinkel is probing into what constitutes individuals' determination of the validity of information they are receiving from others. However, rather than seeing it as a "psychological" or "personality" matter, Garfinkel finds that the individuals' actions are a peculiar working out of institutional directives. The individuals begin to appear as people who are relating to others in terms of rules of which they are uncertain and are attempting to define as they go along. However, they define the rules by referring to what they consider the central rule-making agencies, which they believe others in the relationship also accept. We shall refer to this as "social validation." The important thing to note here is that the process of validating the situation rests essentially on a determination of the social character or identity of the other persons.

From this perspective, then, individuals become the representatives of a not-very-well-defined institutional system, and *they attempt to establish the reality of that institution through their conversations with others*. In the case of the students and the "counselor," the students attempted to make the "counselor" a proper and valid representative of the system of rules that constituted the foundation for the judgments and aspirations of the students. It is as though they were involved in some kind of game situation in which they knew it was proper to play the game, but they could not be certain just what rules were involved and whether the other person also understood the rules. So, some parts of the interchange between the students and the "counselor" involved attempts by the students to make certain that the "counselor" was properly representative of the game and knew about its rules—even though the students themselves were not certain of them. They then made use of replies from the "counselor" that they perceived as supporting their feeling that the "counselor" was "with it" and could therefore be used to validate the norms or rules of which the students were uncertain.

This is a conception of people as creative agents who fashion within each social moment affirming conditions, which then move on to become the "real" institutionalized complex of lifeways they can turn to as justification for their particular actions. Though it sums up matters much too briefly, Garfinkel suggests here that what individuals shore up, when they engage in what is commonly thought of as ego-supportive behavior, is actually their conception of central institutional structures with which they see themselves significantly involved.

Finding 9. "Through the work of documenting—i.e., by searching for and determining pattern, by treating the advisor's answers as motivated by the intended sense of the question, by waiting for later answers to clarify the sense of previous ones, by finding answers to unasked questions—the perceivedly normal values of what was being advised were established, tested, reviewed, retained, restored—in a word, managed. It is misleading, therefore, to think of the documentary method as a procedure whereby propositions are accorded membership in a scientific corpus. Rather, the documentary method developed the advice so as to be continually 'membershipping' it" (p. 94).

This final observation and conclusion coming from the "counseling" study by Garfinkel summarizes all that has gone before. In the course of conversation and ordinary discourse, people behave in terms of social norms and manners. However, this "puppet on a string" approach is much too simple for Garfinkel. People do not merely reflect some psychological–personality characteristic, nor do they simply respond mechanically to a given social-normative-cultural demand. Individuals, from an ethnomethodological perspective, are constantly in need of other people as agents through which they can continuously confirm their own uncertain and hopeful (or fearful, or both) sense of what they represent within the community.

Garfinkel observed that students did not passively receive information and act on it. They "managed" the information they received. We shall therefore refer to this as "information management." (There is an interesting parallel here with Erving Goffman's notion that people are forced to manage the impressions they must present to others.)

We are all familiar with the gross management of information depicted in George Orwell's novel *1984*. It is apparent that people often distort information or otherwise use it for some special purpose other than its original intention. What is unique about Garfinkel's perspective is, again, his awareness of the extent to which this is a constant and natural feature of virtually any human interaction. Information management is something all of us engage in, and it is probably something we must engage in throughout our lives. It is a much "deeper" element of the human condition than we can possibly comprehend.

❖ Rationality, Science, and "Ordinary" Conduct

So it comes about, from this point of view, that individuals move as creative and actively "documenting" agents within any social setting. They reinterpret the comments and actions of others, and then incorporate them within a preexisting body of conceptions of how the world is and, more specifically, how people are. Individuals become unwitting and uncertain propaganda agents. That is, whatever information they receive is employed to sustain the already established sense of moral order they bring into their interactions with others.

The "reasonableness" of people is not a function of what they are or even what they are doing. It is axiomatic for the kind of sociology that Garfinkel develops that it is actually quite impossible to know what people are or what they are doing! That is, it is impossible to know this without creating a meaning or imposing one on the situation. But created or imposed conceptions of what people are or are doing force us to consider the process of creation or imposition, and the question of what people *really are* begins to lose its salience. The "reasonableness," then, of what others are and are not doing does not come directly from them or from their actions. It comes, instead, from the extent to which we can accept what they do as valid in terms of our diffused understanding of what is required of us as participants with the greater community.

After dealing with human actions in commonplace situations, Garfinkel closes his work with a discussion of rationality, science, and "ordinary" conduct. It is a discussion that reviews the interpretations and observations that have gone before and relates them to one of the dominant forces of modern culture—science. In his discussion of science and common day-to-day social living, Garfinkel views both realms of action as data and not as methodologies. That is, science is something more than simply a method. It is a socially viable point of view, and is competitive as such with other social doctrines. At this point, science begins to press upon us as a way of life and as a way to achieve rational social relations. However, Garfinkel comes to the conclusion, after comparing science as a social fact with what takes place in common social interaction, that science cannot be an integral part of "ordinary" social activities. To attempt to be social requires that specifically scientific thoughtways be set aside.

Because the issue of science and the place that science occupies in modern life are now approaching overwhelming dimensions, it is worth spending time on Garfinkel's view of this sector of human life. The discussion reveals, at one and the same time, the general character of Garfinkel's mode of understanding human social activities and the pressing relevance of his concerns.

The term "rational" has come to have great influence within both the academic world and the world of everyday affairs. What is a rational person? How did our belief in rationality come to amass its current overwhelming support? Why do we seek to produce rational social orders, educational programs, and models of war? Is there any difference between rational conduct in ordinary situations and rational behavior within the context of scientific investigation? If there is a difference between scientific rationality and the rationality of ordinary social events, then where does the difference appear? Finally, is there any necessary conflict or interference between rationality as it operates within the moral program of science and rationality as it operates within the moral order of human social relations?

Garfinkel concludes that there are significant differences between rationality in science and rationality in common affairs. He also concludes that the two forms of rationality are in serious conflict. He makes a plea at the end of his work that the relationship between science and human affairs should not be taken dogmatically as something given. It would be unwise to hold that science can give form and substance to human affairs. It cannot do this. He suggests, instead, that the imposition of a scientific rationality on ordinary daily life would probably result in a multiplication of the anomic or disorganizing features of human relations.

One of the distinguishing features of daily social interaction is the extent to which it cannot rely on a purely scientific rationality. Scientific rationality, for example, requires being neutral or even skeptical toward the idea that things are what they appear to be. In daily social activities, rational positions are almost the opposite of this. One must take a position that is not neutral. Things must be accepted for what they appear to be. Although doubt can be entertained, it is the exception rather than the rule. So, for example, it is a "social," though not scientific, form of rationality to accept the belief that one's teacher is an expert or that the president is unusually dedicated to the affairs of the country. A scientific stance toward such aspects of the "social" realm would, by its very dedication to doubt and neutrality, tear at the social fiber and generate anomie and disorganization. Thus, Garfinkel claims that the proper study of the sociologist is the examination of how people generate the means (the folk methods) whereby doubt is minimized and a sense of "things as they are" is sustained.

There are further implications in this statement by Garfinkel. The most significant, given the trend of our times, is that any kind of attempt to impose a rational-scientific mentality on people as a whole would defeat its purpose. The kind of rationality necessary to sustain social interaction simply is not the same kind of rationality that is necessary for the solution to scientific problems. In a day and age that subscribes so totally to science as a problem-solving device, we must be kept constantly on guard lest we abuse and misuse, through oversubscription, this most powerful of thoughtways. Garfinkel's studies, eccentric as they seem to some readers, have a profoundly humanistic theme at their center. How far can we go with science before we have done more damage to ourselves than good? There is no easy answer to this question. A review of *Studies in Ethnomethodology* will offer any serious student of these issues an introduction to the complexities that surround the dream of producing social behavior that is more scientifically rational than we have been able to achieve in the past.

For those students who lack the patience or background to cope with Garfinkel's major works, there is an engaging alternative. One of Garfinkel's best-known students is the author Carlos Castaneda, the author of a popular series of novels involving the character of an old Yaqui Indian named Don Juan.[9] These novels have been extremely well received and widely read, especially among college-age people. The thing that is interesting about the old Yaqui Indian is that he really talks more like a modern phenomenological or ethnomethodological sociologist than one might expect. This has led to some speculation that Don Juan is really a romanticized and fictionalized characterization of Castaneda's teacher, Harold Garfinkel. Whether this is true or not we are unable to say. We can, however, suggest that one can get at least a charming introduction to some of the major ideas behind Garfinkel's work by thoughtfully reading about the adventures of Castaneda and his friend Don Juan.

In concluding this all-too-brief introduction to one of the more controversial developments in modern sociological thought and writing, we would like to suggest that Garfinkel's work, for all of its detached and abstract character, is rich in practical implications for those who wish to find them. We have received more than a few letters and comments from students and instructors in which we were informed that we had imposed too much impractical theorizing on the reader. Students want something more immediate and direct, something useful. The paradox of understanding, however, is that often the route to truly practical efforts calls for a deeply thoughtful examination of what is going on. To the ordinary mind, the most practical way to get to the moon would seem to be to build a simple rocket, aim it in the right general direction, and then set it off. We are all aware today that to accomplish such a task required the development of innumerable theories and observation in the fields of mathematics, physics, metallurgy, pressurized systems, waste control, communications, and so on, and so on.

It is the same with modern understanding of and work in the realm of human social and cultural affairs. If nothing else, Garfinkel warns us that projections, loadings, distortions, information management, and other irrational features of social communication are inherent, in all probability, in any social discourse. Moreover, they cannot be removed. To be placed on one's guard, even when the circumstances are commonplace and ordinary, is to move toward a more practical understanding of these capricious and irrational forces or processes that can, if not understood, lead to gratuitous forms of injury and damage. But Garfinkel is not interested in the practical. The extent to which his work can be given practical value will have to be left to those who take the time to study his ideas.

Encounters with Social Thought

The Unique Status of Pets in America

I had said, "How are you, little coyote?" and I thought I had heard the animal respond, "I'm all right, and you?"[10]

Back in 1978 the United States was estimated to have a dog population of roughly fifty-two million animals. The cat population, at the same time, was estimated to be around thirty-six million. There is, then, approximately one cat or dog for every two and a half Americans. The numbers indicate the significance of the pet in the life of the American in more ways than one. Obviously, pets are common. In a mass society, commonness means not only large absolute values, but all of the consequences that are a result of dealing with mass events. If we can presume that what it takes to feed so many animals would feed fifty million human beings, then we provide enough food for our pets in one year to accomplish the following:

Feed all the people of Argentina for almost two years.

Feed all the people of Australia for three and a half years.

Feed all the people of Canada for two years.

Feed all the people of Sweden for six years.

If we skimped a little on the rations, we could feed the entire population of the world for about a week on what Americans give their dogs and cats. In this sense, then, the population of the United States is not some 220 or 230 millon people, but more like 300 millon beings. Pets are excluded from the dependent population count, but it might make sense to include them. If they were, then the dependent population would go from roughly seventy-five million people (aged fourteen and under or sixty-five and older—the dependent people) to well over double that in terms of dependent beings.

Viewed from the perspective of absolute scales, the cost of the American pet is not in the least inconsiderable. Food alone is estimated to run around three to three and a half billion dollars a year. Medical costs are also worth considering. There are other costs, of course, besides food and medical costs. There are costs associated with housing, animal control, toys for pets, pet books, grooming items, and so forth. The well-stocked pet shop offers a surprisingly broad diversity of goods.

We are aware, however, that these figures of ours are slippery. They are slippery not only because obvious problems go with trying to make such estimates; they are slippery in a more profound way. This can be shown quickly, just by turning things around, so to speak, and taking a look at relative data. When we do so, the pet becomes the insignificant little beast that it is. If we take the three billion dollars spent on animal or pet food in a year in the United States as a proportion of total national income, it amounts to only about one-tenth of 1 percent of the income received by Americans in that year (1978). Even if we deal only with wages and salaries as income, the amount spent on pet food is hardly three-tenths of 1 percent of income received through wages. At the most, it would appear, pets do not cost Americans more than 1 percent of the income they receive. Pets, then, are cheap. They are cheap, that is, when seen in a relative sense. They are expensive in an absolute sense.

The marked difference of understanding that comes from looking at the relative and absolute effects of an event leads us into a trying intellectual issue. Any aspect of modern mass society can be seen in terms of its absolute and/or relative effects. These effects can be readily stated—as we have just done with some basic data on pets. For many of us, the political and economic absolute consequences of mass events cannot be comprehended, because they are easier to deal with at a local or relative level. That is to say, most of us know that our cats or dogs are not an especially costly part of our lives. They give a great deal of pleasure (and aggravation) for small sums of money. We are hardly cognizant of the fact that each of us, in the owning of an animal, adds to a collective event that, overall, is massive in its costs and effects.

That pets are political is known more by the extent to which they are immune from control than by the extent to which they are controlled. The Chinese, forced by extremely severe circumstances, were eventually brought to the point where now the only dogs or cats to be found in the country are found in zoos. If any politician in the United States were, even jokingly, to suggest that pets be put in zoos, that politician would likely find himself or herself put in an asylum in some remote part of the hinterlands.

New York City introduced a law some years ago which made pet owners responsible for pet droppings in public areas. Owners were (and still are) required by law to use some kind of "pooper scooper" as they follow their animals around—this resulted in a furor. (Again, it is the relative versus the absolute perspective in conflict. A little dropping from one's beloved pet does not seem, to the doting owner, to be that much of a problem. The amusing thing, in a way, is that the owner's perspective is essentially a correct one. After all, what is a dog dropping in the grand cosmic scheme of things?)

If we come back to absolute considerations, it turns out that the problem is that we do not easily see how one small thing can lead to another until it is no longer a small thing. Using our earlier rule of thumb, the city of New York may have as many as four million dogs and cats. Although our statistical entertainment now verges on the indelicate, it is still necessary to move from the relative, back into the absolute mode of seeing the world. If each pet produces eight ounces of droppings a day, then this results in two million pounds of refuse. This is a thousand tons of animal deposits. In a year, of course, that amounts to 365,000 tons of animal droppings. Obviously, the situation can get out of control.

These quasi-statistical amusements provide their own information and have a kind of intrinsic interest. But there is still another feature to all of this, which we shall now consider in at least a preliminary manner. We want to suggest that there are two kinds of "reality" that come from seeing things first in terms of absolute values and then relative values. It is patently evident that the picture obtained from either reality is, first of all, quite reasonable and valid. Second, it is equally obvious that we get contradictory understandings of "reality" from these perfectly valid perspectives.

From the relative perspective, the pet is insignificant—just a little creature serving one's emotional needs. Evidently, most other countries look on the pet in this manner. In even the most desperately impoverished barrios in South America, there are pets. There are dogs wandering around—starving, mangy, drooping, and sick—competing for food with children who suffer from kwashiorkor and other diseases of malnutrition. In the barrios, the approach to the dog is relative. In China, as we have just noted, the approach to the dog is absolute: On the larger scale, they consume food in competition with people, and therefore must be controlled severely. (Two different views of "reality" lead to quite different practical consequences.)

If simple statistics can give us two different views of an event that is, in itself, quite ordinary and commonplace, what happens when we move into more subtle and abstracted aspects of the world around us? Is there one reality confronting us that we can understand in some singularly convincing manner; or are there many realities, all valid, as it were, yet different and contradictory? To accept the second possibility is truly a wrenching act of the mind, and possibly a uniquely modern perspective. In any event, modern philosophers and social scientists are considering moving in the direction of accepting the idea that there are multiple realities.

Although the "Don Juan" novels of Carlos Castaneda, mentioned earlier, are not as well known today as a decade ago, there are still many college students familiar with Castaneda's works. (At this point we seem to be drifting from the topic of pets, but bear with us.) What is interesting about Carlos Castaneda is that he is certainly the best-known of the students of Harold Garfinkel. Garfinkel, in turn, is the best-known of a group of modern sociologists who subscribe to the belief that reality is not singular in nature, but instead has multiple forms. We are—any one of us at any point in time—caught up in our particular confrontation with reality, which is our unique sampling of it. And it is "real." It is something we come to take for granted. Garfinkel talks a lot about the "taken-for-grantedness" of the world. So does Castaneda, and so too does the old Indian, Don Juan. Here is a brief passage in which Castaneda talks about Don Juan in the introduction to *Journey to Ixtlan*:

> For Don Juan, then, the reality of our day-to-day life consists of an endless flow of perceptual interpretation which we, the individuals who share a specific *membership*, have learned to make in common.

The idea that the perceptual interpretations that make up the world have a flow is congruous with the fact that they run uninterruptedly and are rarely, if ever, open to question. In fact, the reality of the world we know is so taken for granted that the basic premise of sorcery, that our reality is merely one of many descriptions, could hardly be taken as a serious proposition.[11]

So, here in the Don Juan novels we have a series of tales in which the significance of the ordinary is heightened to the point where it becomes dramatically fascinating. Don Juan talks with teakettles and wolves and rabbits. He is able to discern death in an approaching mist. The smallest rock takes on a magical significance. Don Juan has great control. The charming feature of Don Juan Matus is his ability to involve himself with all that is about him in a living way. Here is an example. Castaneda speaks first, then Don Juan:

> "Do you think that one can stop smoking or drinking that easily?" I asked.
> "Sure," he said with great conviction. "Smoking and drinking are nothing. Nothing at all if we want to drop them."
> At that very moment the water that was boiling in the coffee percolator made a loud perking sound. "Hear that!" Don Juan exclaimed with a shine in his eyes. "The boiling water agrees with me."
> Then, he added after a pause, "A man can get agreements from everything around him."[12]

If one is familiar with Garfinkel's work, one can almost hear him making the very same statement in his lectures. The kind of "agreement" that is being talked about here is no simple matter, however. Stated another way, and all too lightly, there is an agreement between each of us and the reality we experience. But in some peculiar way, a great deal of this agreement appears to arise out of what we believe reality is. If, like a paranoid schizophrenic, we come to believe that the world is out to destroy us, we will find agreement coming from the world itself. If, like some truly, truly holy person, we come to believe the world is all good, then the world demonstrates its goodness—no matter how vile it might be. There are, then, to use Castaneda's way of putting it, "separate realities."

We must now come back to our original subject. One kind of reality Americans deal with is something known as "the pet." Pets are rarely the subject of serious philosophical discussion, but they serve, as well as any other feature of the world around us as a way to illustrate some of the points phenomenologists are fond of arguing. The term "phenomenon" comes to us from the writings of the eighteenth-century German philosopher Immanuel Kant. Kant distinguished two features of reality: "noumena" and "phenomena." *Noumena* comes from a Greek term referring to things being perceived. *Phenomena* comes from a Greek term referring to appearances. So, a noumenon is something in itself, the essential self, or, to use Kant's German expression, *Ding an sich*.

The pet, then, can be an object in and of itself, and it can also be an appearance—a phenomenon. This kind of argument proves difficult with people, because it is not, initially, a simple matter to begin to comprehend the extent to which the Kantian distinction has relevance in our daily lives. In a sense, this is what Garfinkel has tried to do. Just as John Calvin took the Christian work ethic out of the monastery and made it a part of every individual life, Garfinkel appears to want to take Kantianism out of the academic cloister and bring it into the day-to-day world of practical living. The most ordinary events and happenings are examined for their "strangeness" or their apparent nature. There is a kind of "sorcery" in suddenly discovering that the teakettle might, after all, be telling you something more than you had previously suspected. To step out of the taken-for-granted nature of the world is to experience a kind of "magic."

To begin to see what phenomenologists are talking about, let us consider one common feature of the relationship of a person to a pet, particularly in Western culture. (This certainly does not necessarily hold true in some Middle Eastern and Oriental cultures.) We refer now to the fact that most people talk to their pets. This is more than offering signals that control the pets' behavior. People *talk* to their pets. The most extreme and intellectually interesting form of such talk, although it is generally viewed as plain silliness or foolishness, takes place when a pet owner speaks to his or her beast in special dialects, the most typical of which, probably, is something called "baby talk." ("Widdy snook-ums wookums not eat him din-din? Is our widdy petty tickie in him tum-tum?")

It is only when such actions are pulled out of their context—their taken-for-granted, in-the-moment context—that they appear, objec-tively, for what they are. That is to say, they are not only silly, they are also intellectually fascinating. What is really going on here? Why do people talk "baby talk" to dogs and cats and goldfish? Are there other contexts within which a similar pattern occurs but is still less obvious?

In talking with animals, we seek to leap the subjective barriers that separate us from our pets. We accept the animal as a kind of dull child that might, if we are patient enough, someday learn the forms of com-munications we humans rely on. We address the pet as though it were a human baby. It is not, of course. It is an animal whose levels of sym-bolic awareness are actually impossible for us to grasp. We create the mentality of the pet and then respond to our own creation. The pet, from this perspective, is a kind of middle agent to ourselves. The pet gives us an indirect means of reacting to that which we have created. When a pet dies, for example, our mourning—and it can be a serious form of mourning—is as much for the demise of what we have created in the pet, as for what the pet in fact might be.

Phenomenology is concerned with the problem of how appearances can take on the character of "reality" when they are not the same as the reality from which they spring. What we think is in a dog's mind and what is actually there are two quite different things. In fact, we can never, ever by any currently known means, establish what is in a dog's "mind." Yet we treat our pets as though they have minds, and anyone who has tried to argue this point with a class of college students knows that there are a lot of people ready to fight over the contention that they do not know what their dogs are thinking. It is something pet lovers take for granted.

We must broaden the pet problem slightly. At the moment, we have been talking about the relationship between the individual and his or her dog or cat. We have suggested that the mentality of the pet is created by the pet's owner. This mentality acquires a kind of "reality." We take it for granted that we know our pets and our pets know us. This is at the individual level. At the collective level, we display common sentiments or understandings of reality. That is, we share a common "reality." Americans, for example, tend to look on dogs in a common way. We do not, as a case in point, see dogs as such dirty animals that they should never be allowed in the house. There are cultures where the thought of allowing a dog to sleep in the same bed with a child would be considered outrageously irresponsible.

So, at the collective level, reality must be somehow "coordinated." Yet reality is a matter, for the phenomenologist, of appearances. Appearances, then, must be coordinated. This is a matter of becoming involved in the subjectivity of others. Now, if reality, noumena, were precisely what they appear to be, then the problem of bringing about such subjective coordination would not involve any problems whatsoever. Assuming that people are similar in their intelligence and sensory capacities, the world should look the same to all people. Noumena should equal phenomena. As we are aware, however, noumena do not equal phenomena.

In our relations with others, we bring with us an important presumption—that they share appearances with us. That is to say, we assume that they are responding to the same reality we are responding to. It is obvious that if this assumption is violated, then all kinds of mischief can take place. We quickly begin to call each other "crazy." Making some kind of subjective "connection" with other people is important. To come back to pets, this concern with the subjective carries over into a realm where it begins to verge on the ludicrous.

Here is a handy example of what we are talking about. We have all seen cat food commercials that sing praises of the superiority of one cat food over the other. With voices singing a familiar ditty in the background, we are urged to buy the cat food that cats "like" best—the "taste" that cats have shown they prefer because continual testing has proven this is the brand of cat food most desired by kittens and mature cats!

No profound intelligence is required to observe that Americans, or at least a fair number of them, are virtually pathologically neurotic about their pets' appetites. The eating habits of an animal are the most readily accessible indicator of whatever its subjective state might be. American pet owners want their animals to have a quality that they themselves think of as a part of reality—being happy.

But happiness is a supremely subjective quality. Is one's "snook-ums wookums" happy? The owner can talk to the little beast and ask it the question, but he or she is not likely to get much in the way of an articulate reply. There are no external signs of inner grace, so to speak—purring, jumping about, and tail wagging are limited gestural responses. The pet, then, is a daily confrontation with a grand subjective abyss that people have longed to bridge for thousands of years. Nothing is more phenomenological than the fantasy of Dr. Dolittle (the Hugh Lofting character) or Don Juan Matus bridging the gulf by talking to animals in a casual and magical way.

The American pet is more assiduously fed and pampered than is good for its health. So it is that American industry has created pet foods designed to protect the pet from the implications of the peculiar meaning that pets have for their American owners. If the pet is happy, it will indicate this in at least one way—by having a good appetite. A pet is an animal that *should* eat. Intersubjectivity, in this instance, is obviously a projection of the subjective understandings held in the head of the pet's owner. Moreover, it is a subjective state shared with pet owners throughout the nation.

This means the American pet, like its owner, is likely to get fat on the food made available to it. Twenty years ago this was the common fate of American pets, and it evidently is the fate of American pets today. However, a new style has appeared in America, in which fat bodies are viewed as something to be disciplined by dieting and exercise. So it is that this subjective quality is now played on as the pet owner purchases foods that have the unique ability to offer the pet a tasty meal while, at the same time, providing a low-calorie diet—thereby keeping the animal trim.

In all of this, we are trying to point out that the pet is not something responded to in itself, but is instead responded to in terms of the "membershipping" of animals. That is, our memberships in commonly perceived realities permit us to incorporate the pet into that reality and then to deal with it from that perspective rather than dealing with the animal as a "thing in itself."

Pets, by their nature, are not intelligent in the same sense human beings are—although this is disputed by pet owners who swing to the extreme of claiming that pets are more intelligent than people. They may have a point, but we are not going to argue the matter here. We shall note only that the imperative to be intelligent in America is only slightly less urgent than the imperative to be beautiful. Americans look for signs of intelligence in their pets. Somehow they manage to find them. (The world has ways of agreeing with us.) There is tradition behind this, as there is with most of the ways we go about looking at the world, which we think we are seeing with objective and fresh vision. We can only briefly mention one outstanding moment in this tradition, the case of Clever Hans.

In 1904, an eight-year-old stallion named Hans, who belonged to a Berlin schoolteacher named Wilhelm von Osten, amazed scientists and just about everybody else by being able, among other things, to do arithmetic problems of a complex nature. He could spell by tapping an alphabetic code with his hoof. He could tell time. He could recognize the photographs of people. He was more than a horse genius; he was the long-sought bridge across the subjective abyss.

Eventually it was shown, by extremely careful study, that Hans was just a horse. Evidently Hans was a perceptive horse, capable of responding to the most subtle cues from his owner, but he could not do arithmetic or anything else. What is especially interesting is that his owner, von Osten, was at first furious with the horse for proving to be something less than a horse genius. Later, however, he returned to his earlier belief and rejected proofs of the animal's ordinariness. Von Osten went the phenomenological route. He was overcome by appearances.

A much more ordinary form of the Clever Hans phenomenon is the pet that has the extraordinary ability to evaluate fundamental qualities of human character. The animal "knows." More correctly, the owner believes that the animal knows. We have to approach such creatures with concern, because we can never be certain how they are going to react. If the animal takes a dislike to someone, the pattern is set forever; the owner, at the very least, jokes a little about the matter while making a mental note that this person needs to be watched carefully.

There are two things about this kind of experience with someone's pet that are interesting. First, the owner is willing to "load" a sign from the pet that leads to eventual embellishments on the other person's character. The second is that the other person also finds it difficult to shake off the sign. When this happens, it is as nice an example as the world can offer of a triadic phenomenological moment—pet, owner, and victim caught up in a little dance where the music is supplied by something other than what is real. The music comes from something other than the bedrock of reality, and that "somewhere else" is what interests the phenomenological philosopher.

Putting Social Thought to Work

1. Garfinkel's theories help us realize that we are so much a part of whatever place in our day-to-day lives that we rarely have an opportunity to comprehend the extent to which much of what we do is constructed by ourselves, or by friends and others. Usually, events are constructed in an informal manner rather than formally. We daily reconstruct and reestablish social reality. We bring a great amount of background material into a social interaction, which is then incorporated into the moment. Whether this information is valid or false is not so important as whether it "works." Many groups rely on someone who takes the role of "butt" or scapegoat in the group. By what procedures is such a person identified? What methods are employed to keep the person in the group, and at the same time to sustain his or her identity as the least able member of the group?

2. Ethnomethodology seeks to make us more aware of the devices we employ in creating the realities to which we respond. Often those realities are not "outside" us so much as they are "inside" us. Ethnomethodology, of course, raises a host of questions concerning the nature of reality. Particularly significant is the problem of the nature of social reality. How is it constructed for us, and how do we participate in its construction? The question is not an academic one.

3. How we develop particular conceptions of social reality can have a variety of effects. The example is given earlier in this chapter of the extent to which asserting the right to bargain for an item in a store can have beneficial economic consequences for those who do it. On a deeper level, the way in which economics, as an institutionalized "method," has defined the economic behavior of the culture as a whole has also had consequences. One comes to "see" the economic features of the society as more basic than the noneconomic features. American economists tend to emphasize commodities over values. Is this one reason for the recent problems that economists have encountered in trying to deal with such contemporary difficulties as inflation or the national debt?

4. Garfinkel's "counseling" study is both simple and devastating in its implications. What happens to us when we seek counseling—whether it is from a professional or from a friend? What are we doing when we "counsel" someone who has come to us for help? What are the implications of Garfinkel's counseling demonstration for those who would like to reduce social behavior to genetics? What are the implications of this for such practices as divination through astrology or tarot cards?

5. How does Garfinkel solve the problem of why astrology continues to thrive in an age of science? In what areas of our lives might random decision making work about as well as any other kind? (Hint: Garfinkel

might suggest that the areas are broader and more inclusive than we are at first likely to believe.)

6. The application of ethnomethodological ideas in this chapter has consisted of a brief examination of the pet in American life. How might Durkheim, Marx, Weber, a structural-functional thinker, or a dramaturgic theorist consider the same topic? Each of these perspectives or pathways of social thought gives us a different "slant" on whatever topic we may be interested in. Does this mean that one of the perspectives is correct and the others wrong? Or is it possible that each theory provides us with an opportunity to examine a different aspect of a segment of reality?

Endnotes

1. Details of such conversations will be found in Harold Garfinkel, *Studies in Ethnomethodology* (Englewood Cliffs, NJ: Prentice-Hall, 1965), pp. 42–44. This book, the major work by Garfinkel, consists in large part of material originally published in other sources, including the following: Harold Garfinkel, "Studies of the Routine Grounds of Everyday Activity," *Social Problems* (Winter 1964), 43–113; and Harold Garfinkel, "Common Sense Knowledge of Social Structures," in J. Scher (ed.), *Theories of the Mind* (New York: Free Press, 1962), pp. 689–712.
2. Again see Garfinkel, *Studies in Ethnomethodology.*
3. Based on material in Garfinkel's "Common Sense Knowledge of Social Structures." Garfinkel refers to the "counselor" as an "experimenter" for reasons that will become apparent. The dialogue reported here is a modified account of a similar dialogue reported by Garfinkel.
4. Garfinkel, *Studies in Ethnomethodology*, p. viii.
5. Garfinkel uses the term "artful" several times to describe social behavior. He begins his preface, for example, with a reference to the ordinary artful ways of social accomplishment. See *Studies in Ethnomethodology*, p. vii.
6. Our discussion follows the general character of Garfinkel's "Common Sense Knowledge of Social Structures," reprinted in *Studies in Ethnomethodology*, pp. 89–94. *Studies in Ethnomethodology* combines many of Garfinkel's works, and the student will probably find it easier to use for that reason.
7. *Studies in Ethnomethodology*, p. 70.
8. Italics are Garfinkel's.
9. A few of Carlos Castaneda's "Don Juan" novels are as follows: *The Teachings of Don Juan: A Yaqui Way of Knowledge* (New York: Simon and Schuster, 1968); *A Separate Reality: Further Conversations with Don Juan* (New York: Simon and Schuster, 1971); and *Journey to Ixtlan: The Lessons of Don Juan* (New York: Simon and Schuster, 1972).
10. Castaneda, *Journey to Ixtlan*, p. 296.
11. Ibid., p. 25.
12. Ibid., p. 32.

Chapter 16

Building a Global Civic Culture

Elise Boulding and Strategies for a Peaceful World

❖

❖ *The Invisible World of Women Social Scientists*

Until the very close of the twentieth century the names, the publications, and the professional reputations of outstanding women in the social sciences were scarcely known or even recognized by the academic community, let alone the general American public. The earlier editions of this volume, *Twentieth-Century Social Thought*, did not contain one chapter on the work of a woman social thinker until the career of Margaret Mead was added to the book. Further, it was not until 1988, by the time of the fourth edition, that the authors felt an obligation to carefully edit and revise any sexist terminology or the constant use of the male pronoun ''he'' when referring to the work of various social thinkers—especially when presenting those men who lectured and wrote at the close of the nineteenth and in the early twentieth century—Durkheim, Marx, Weber, George Herbert Mead, and C. Wright Mills.

One of the most famous figures in the discipline of psychology, Sigmund Freud, has achieved such a degree of disdain for women that he has been singled out as the social theorist whose writings were the most outrageously sexist, focusing on hysterical women and penis envy. Some feminist social scientists currently eschew even a reference to Freudian theory or the work of his disciples, including his famous daughter, Anna Freud, in the attempt to erase his existence in the social sciences altogether.

In this volume, as we move into the later decades of the twentieth century to discuss the social theories of our contemporary colleagues, Robert Merton, David Riesman, Howard Becker, Peter Berger, Erving Goffman, and Harold Garfinkel, we find a changing style of social thought with efforts to include the other half of society—women—in the research, theorizing, and the writings. Yet it has still been the names of "famous" *men*, who continually appear in textbooks, research monographs, academic journals, and those more widely read, popular magazines and newspapers. Now, as we approach the twenty-first century, it is imperative that the accomplishments of women social thinkers, those who have worked and written alongside their male counterparts but have remained "invisible," unheard of, unrecognized, be acknowledged. In just the past decade a number of these magnificent women social thinkers have been recognized and their contributions to modern social thought and the advancement and enlightenment of human beings revealed. Along with anthropologists Margaret Mead and Ruth Benedict, we now are teaching about the writings of sociologists Jessie Bernard, Alva Myrdal, Mirra Komarovsky, and historians Barbara Ward and Mary Beard. Therefore, it is most fitting and appropriate to close the fifth edition of this book with an examination and discussion of the work, accomplishments, and the example to humanity of the career of Elise Boulding.

Distinguished sociologist, eminent international educator, celebrated women's studies scholar and notable futurist, Elise Boulding exemplifies the precepts of Margaret Mead. When Mead identified and delineated the leaders of the prefigurative culture, the culture of future societies, she was envisioning the lifelong career of an individual such as Elise Boulding. In Chapter 9 we quoted Margaret Mead as stating that where women's experiences had traditionally been fenced off from contributing to the high-level planning of the world, they can now be used in the attack on such problems as the unfair distribution of food resources, the fouling of the environment, and the overall quality of life in human settlements. Elise Boulding is and continues to be such a trend-setter, participating on a worldwide level, seeking the peaceful world community for women, men, and children that has always been so elusive. Over the decades of her remarkable career as a sociologist, international peace activist, and women's studies specialist, Boulding has traveled across the United States and around the world again and again, all the while researching, writing, and lecturing for the betterment of human beings. Not only has she been inspired and mentored by Margaret Mead, Jessie Bernard and Alva Myrdal, she readily attributes much of her success in social science to the stimulation and support of her lifelong partner, her late husband, Kenneth Boulding, the world-renowned economist and peace researcher.

❖ *Life as a Quaker Sociologist*

Elise Boulding speaks of herself as a person with high energy. Such people are often characterized as pursuing multiple careers and this is certainly true of Elise Boulding. She began an academic career at the age of forty-five, after a quarter-century of homemaking, child rearing, and community activism, by taking a doctorate at the University of Michigan. This was followed by a family move to Colorado from Michigan, and a faculty position for her at the University of Colorado, jointly in the sociology department and the Institute of Behavioral Science, followed ten years later by an appointment to chair the sociology department at Dartmouth College.

Next, one can look at her outstanding commitment to peace research, which involved Boulding in the founding of the International Peace Research Association in the 1960s, an organization she served as secretary general in the late 1980s. She also founded and chaired the North American affiliate of IPRA, the Consortium on Peace Research, Education and Development. After retirement she continued her affiliation with Dartmouth as senior fellow of the Dickey Endowment, and with the Center for Conflict Analysis at George Mason University as senior associate.

Over the past twenty-five years she has been honored for her research and writings on conflict resolution, international understanding and future studies. These honors include: the National Woman of Conscience Award, the National Woman Who Made a Difference Award, and the Institute for Defense and Disarmament Award for a Lifetime of Work for Peace and Democracy; and in 1990 Elise Boulding was nominated for the Nobel Peace Prize by the American Friends Service Committee. Boulding continues to work actively on an international basis on problems of peace and world order. Among the organizations to which she has devoted her time and energy over the years are the United Nations University, the U.S. Institute for Peace, the World Order Models Project, and of course the above-mentioned IPRA and COPRED. In the activist realm, she served as international chairperson of the Women's International League for Peace and Freedom in the late 1960s and has worked in various ways with the American Friends Service Committee over the years.

When interacting with her, one is continually impressed with yet another major aspect of her life. Always in the center of her writing, teaching, and research as a sociologist, feminist and futurist is her role as wife and mother of five adult children, and her deep religious commitment as a member of the Society of Friends (Quakers). In an inspiring, elegant and touching book, *One Small Plot of Heaven: Reflections on Family Life by a Quaker Sociologist*, Boulding expresses her joy, fulfillment, and lifelong devotion to her family and community of faith in both essays and poems. Her deep sense of religious commitment and vision of a better world for the future, through family and community, are revealed in this book on Quaker family life that describes the family as a small society, as a practice ground for making history, and as a way into the future. She reminds us with clarity and honest forthrightness:

> How did women ever get into the position where they felt the need to belittle the amazing experience of bearing and rearing children? Yet already, the women's movement has come full circle, and people are rediscovering the importance of mother (and fathering). . . . Increasing appreciation of individual differences among women and among men now makes possible a choice of lifeways based on capabilities and preferences. This has made the marriage relationship both richer and more complex. In my youth, a woman expected to adapt her lifeway to that of her spouse. Now the adaption goes both ways, and parenting is shared in a way we could hardly have imagined in the 1940s.[1]

Later in this book about her life as a Quaker sociologist she writes that during her years as a college professor with a number of national and international committee and task force assignments, she increasingly came to feel the relevance of her previous twenty-five-year apprenticeship in homemaking and community activism.[2]

A prolific writer and researcher, her publications span three decades, beginning with her translation from the Dutch of Fred Polak's classic work, *Image of the Future*, in 1961. She has authored myriad articles, readings, chapters in books, pamphlets, monographs and research reports.

However, one of the most significant and portentous pieces of scholarly work that Elise Boulding has undertaken, which she began during a year spent in solitude at a hermitage in the mountains near Boulder, Colorado, is her 800-plus-page tome, *The Underside of History: A View of Women Through Time*. This major contribution to women's studies and future studies, as well as feminist theory, originally published by Westview Press in 1976, has been reissued in 1992 by Sage Publications in a revised two-volume edition. The new edition highlights the impact of the tremendous surge in women's activism at the close of the twentieth century and the promise of social transformation to a postpatriarchal order in the twenty-first century.[3]

❖ A History of Humankind as Viewed by Women

In describing her inspiration for undertaking such a mammoth project, a macro-historical account of women's roles from Paleolithic times to modernity, Boulding tells us that it was really a venture for her into the search for meaning in human existence. In the preface to *The Underside of History*, she relates that as a woman activist in the twentieth century she could not avoid identity struggles because society gives a person so little ground to stand on. "Because I am a sociologist as well as an activist, I saw that struggle in historical terms. Women have for millennia had to work for the public good from privatized spaces. Why?"[4]

◆ Sampling the Invisible

From her disciplinary viewpoint of the sociologist, rather than from that of the historian, Boulding discusses the framework and theoretical perspective which she employed in *The Underside of History* in the first chapters of the work. In presenting the concept of women's adaptations to the ever-increasing levels of societal complexity and technological advances through the centuries, she proposes the concept of the "underlife" for women's roles as opposed to the "overlife" of men. She points out that the role of women in many societies, in the past and still today, can be likened to that of the inmates in total institutions, as Erving Goffman has so astutely characterized them (see Chapter 14). The home and the household can be construed as a total institution imprisoning women and children. Boulding goes on to make us aware of the consequences of this disempowerment using Goffman's analogies to prisoners and mental patients in total institutions.

> [I]t is true that women in most societies are, *to a degree*, stripped of identity, autonomy and privacy as Goffman describes that stripping for inmates of total institutions. . . . [W]omen in every part of the world are treated in part as prisoners, mental patients, and dependent children. Their names come from their fathers or their husbands. Their obligations to provide twenty-four-hour domestic service to their fathers, husbands, and children leave them perpetually on call at any time of day or night. There are substantial limitations on their rights to transact business and get credit in their own names, and they have limited rights in courts of law.[5]

To illustrate in even more striking detail the concept of the underlife of women, Boulding brings to our attention the writings from the French of Evelyne Sullerot, who labels these situations of everyday life *dedans* (the within) for women and *dehors* (the without) for men. Sullerot, in turn, draws her terminology from the works of the ancient Greeks, namely Xenophon, whom she quotes to supply us with this classic justification for the servitude of women. Elise Boulding provides us with the translation of Xenophon's statements: "The gods created the woman for indoors functions, the man for all others. The gods put woman inside because she has less endurance for cold, heat and war." Boulding goes on to explicate this metaphor further:

> The *dedans* concept is simply descriptive to the extent the women's major workplace is in the household. What turns the *dedans* into a victimage concept is the notion of confining women to the home at all times, and denying her other worksites. This application of the *dedans* concept is indeed suggested by Xenophon in the passage quoted, although it was never practiced by more than a

small group of urban middle-class women, even in Xenophon's time. Another way to think of the underlife/overlife, within/without dichotomy is in terms of private versus public spaces. The kitchen and the courtyard, society's service areas, are for women; the agora where the public interest is defined and acted on, is for men.[6]

Thus, we are presented with both historical and sociological evidence from the opening of this important contribution to feminist thought with the sources of its title as well as its theoretical premises.

> This is an exciting time in women's studies, one filled with challenge, diversity, and conflict and one that will test our analytic and sisterhood skills to the utmost. . . . It is important that you know you are standing "on the shoulders of giants" but giants in a different sense than male scholars have conceived them. These giants are the heroic women of the underside, peasants and poets, jugglers and queens, *hetaira* and nuns, adventurers and scientists, and always mothers and daughters from the time of knowledge-seeking Eve to the current time. These giants have not only provided history with its hidden undergirding structures but have unfailingly passed on to each succeeding generation the love, courage, and imagination that has helped to keep humanity, with all its failings, open to new beginnings. *Sisters, climb up where you belong so you can see where to go!* [Emphasis added].[7]

The first volume of *The Underside of History: A View of Women Through Time* covers women from the Paleolithic period to the year 1000 C.E. (Common Era). In this imaginative reconstruction of prehistoric and early historic times she shows how the sharing of the same physical spaces and experiences by women and men during the hunting/gathering nomadic phase of human existence, generated a quality of egalitarianism in female-male relationships that disappeared with the shift toward settled agriculture. As humans began staying in the same place to raise food (and accumulate possessions) it was the women who farmed, while the men remained hunters, exploring farther-off terrains unfamiliar to the women. Male mobility created privileged knowledge about distant resources and peoples and led to the creation of male-organized trade networks in which women had only secondary status. With the rise of city-states and empires, control of land remained a source of power for women, but organization acted to close them off from public spaces, walling them inside domestic spaces.

The second volume of *The Underside of History*, taking women from the beginning of the second millennium to the modern era, is in two parts. First the Middle Ages and the ensuing excitement of the Renaissance, the Enlightenment and the age of queens and revolutions—all of which did so much for men and so little for women; second, the awakening of women to the political realities of the nineteenth and twentieth centuries, and their growing response to those realities, as women move from *dedans* to *dehors*.

Part I opens the theme of the developing underlife of women in the chapters on the European Middle Ages, 1000–1450 of the Common Era. As people moved from the countryside to the growing cities because of major changes in the mode of production, the men continued to move where the jobs were, but women, with childcare responsibilities, were not so readily mobile. Women who had formerly worked side-by-side with their men in the fields and home-based workshops, now worked the fields alone, or took in piecework to help support the family. The growing differentiation of women's and men's spaces in urban settings meant that even though women were increasingly entering the wage labor market, wage differentials became ever more pronounced. "Through their relative immobility, women had no bargaining power, so the complaints of wage discrimination began early—and they were found everywhere."[8]

Following the ideas of *dedans*, the sociologist discusses how a growing urban middle class of merchants established workplaces outside the home. Family-based economic partnerships of the previous centuries were disappearing, and wives were left to create a more leisurely life-style centered in the home. The more women were relegated to the private sector of the home, the more their participation in legal and business matters was limited.

> Law is an overlife institution. Custom is not. Women did not participate in the new regulatory process. . . . The all-important equity law, which was developed to deal with the inadequacies and injustices of the common law at first protected women from the consequences of the shift to national codes. But the more the legal profession specialized and expanded with the expanding economy, the more it became evident that this new public arena was a man's world.[9]

In the later centuries of this period—the 1600s and 1700s—the rise of domesticity meant a decline in the status and opportunities for women, Boulding notes, even though famous queens such as Isabella of Spain, Elizabeth the First of England, Catherine the Great of Russia, and Victoria of England were powerful in their respective nations. By 1800, and the reign of Victoria in England, the British Parliament was totally composed of men and only elected by men (Beard, 1946; in Boulding, 1992 p. 183).

◆ Women and the "as if" Life in the Transition Centuries—the 1800s and 1900s

The economic gains from the Industrial Revolution fueled the flowering of the arts and humanities of the Renaissance and the Reformation which led to new discoveries about the nature of "man" and the state as an organization of men, rather than a commonwealth of families. In this section the sociologist furnishes the reader with a gripping realization. For all the emphasis on the traditional family during these pivotal times in the Western world, "single," "widowed," or "separated" are the categories historical data provides for nearly half the women of Europe.

> A historical picture is beginning to emerge of a society organized "as if": *as if* every household consisted of a husband, wife, and children; *as if* every household

must have a woman at home at all times; *as if* there were no lesbian households; *as if* there were no single women, no illegitimate children; *as if* all productive labor were carried out by men and all significant civic arrangements created by men.[10]

Further, because women not partnered with men have been seldom documented or researched, we have very little information even on their existence. Popular belief, even today, reinforces the myth of the universal model of living as a "traditional" family.

Boulding goes on to write that by the nineteenth century many women were no longer willing to support the old fictions of male guardianship of the female, which held that women were not men's intellectual, social, and legal equal. She notes that the legal regulations labeled "the doctrine of included interest," which held that a husband and wife were one person and therefore the legal existence of the woman was suspended while she was married, was challenged. However, many women were, and are still today, caught up in conflicting loyalties, as well as myths about reality.

> Many are frightened at the thought of having rights instead of protection. Others feel no need for more autonomy than they already have. Counterfeminist movements evolved in the nineteenth century and continue in the twentieth, representing women who are content with traditional patterns and who fear that feminism will destroy the family life they cherish. Women who have lived in private spaces do not see the social whole objectively. It is hard for them to see the broad spectrum of social arrangements that can enhance the lives of women, men and children, both inside and outside of traditional family households. The absurdity of the privatization of a woman's world within the larger society is by no means evident to Western women generally.[11]

From the Middles Ages up to the twentieth century, Boulding's focus has been largely Eurocentric. The author is very aware of this, and apologizes to her "sisters in the Two-thirds World" as she terms them—the women of Africa, Asia, and Latin America—for her reporting of events and movements from a "One-third World" perspective. She is well aware that the device of including a chapter titled "An Historical Note on the Underside of the Two-Thirds World," which crams into a few pages what she herself considers an amazing and heroic story of the struggle of women to create and maintain their own spaces in the face of the onslaught of Western imperialism, is hardly an adequate way to deal with their story. Yet she knew that she could not begin the twentieth century story without some indication of what had been left out. The concluding chapter and the Epilogue of Volume II do finally treat contemporary women's movements in a genuinely global context.

◆ *Women in the Postpatriarchal Order of the Future*

Boulding points out in the final chapter that there are really many women's movements, not just one, and that they continue to unfold in highly diverse ways on the five continents and in the 180 countries that now comprise the international system. These contemporary women's movements are trans-national in membership and goals although they differ in ways of working. She points out, however, that a great gap remains between the Western-style women's groups that tend to think of Western values as universal values, and women's organizations from the Two-thirds World who have suffered economically, politically, and spiritually from a kind of Western feminist imperialism.

In concluding, Boulding offers us a visual representation of women's situation. In Figure 16–1, "The Agents of Oppression for Women," she shows how women, at the center of the circle of life, are surrounded by the forces of the patriarchal culture; the church, the school, the polity, the marketplace, the workplace, the media, and the household. In Figure 16–2, "The Agents

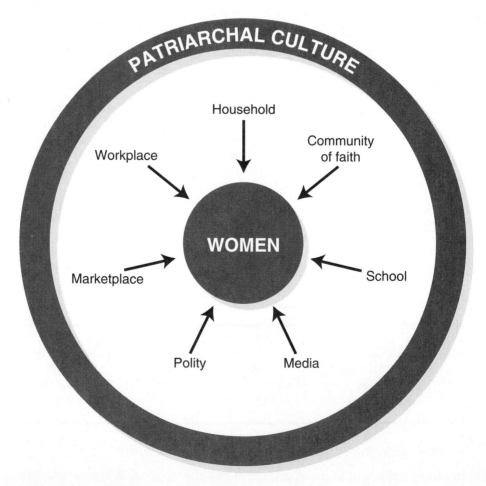

Figure 16–1. The Agents of Oppression for Women[12]

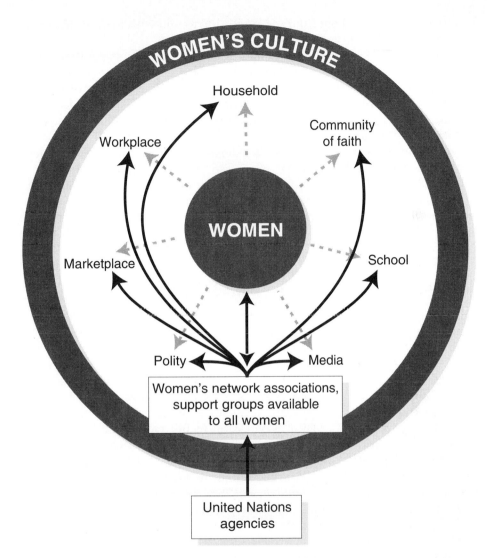

Figure 16–2. The Agents of Social Transformation to the Postpatriarchal Order[13]

of Social Transformation to the Postpatriarchal Order," women at the circle's center are ringed by a women's culture, a culture handed down from generation to generation that reflects how women can initiate action to change their life situation and the nature of society itself. Women's individual initiatives are shown by the dashed lines leading to each institution from women at the center of the circle. The support system for women comes from networks and organizations that collectively act as a great multiplier empowering individual women. Boulding posits that over time women's strategies will bring them from the underside to join with men in shaping a more humane and peaceful world order.

In the epilogue, Boulding envisions the future. She points out that women's writings about what a new feminist-inspired social order could be are not widely available, although there are indeed a growing number of women futurists. Margaret Mead, of course, is one, and we have described Mead's futurist thinking and her vision of the prefigurative culture in Chapter 9. Women teachers are increasingly becoming practicing futurists, Boulding believes, offering postpatriarchal role models to their students—from kindergarten to the university campus.

We have described here a few of the major points of Elise Boulding's *The Underside of History; A View of Women Through Time*. We urge the reader to obtain the two-volume version (Sage, 1992) and peruse for him- or herself this stunning record of women's journey through time into the twenty-first century.

❖ *Human Rights and the Wheel of Life*

Another important contribution by Elise Boulding to family and community studies in an international context is the volume entitled, *Children's Rights and the Wheel of Life*, published in 1979, not long after the first edition of *The Underside of History*. In that book Boulding focuses transnationally on the life situations of the young (those under twenty-one) and the old (those over sixty), and how their experiences are impacted by customs, tradition, extent of technological advancement, and legal status in the culture in which they live. This book marks a logical progression in her work from her doctoral dissertation on the effects of industrialization on the participation of women in society, to her 1977 publication of *Women in the Twentieth Century World*, which translates into actual country situations the UN data compiled in the publication, *A Handbook of International Data on Women* with Shirley Nuss, Dorothy Lee Carson, and Michael Greenstein.

This book on the rights of children and the aged is not merely the amassing of international data on many aspects of living for these targeted groups. It also provides interpretations and implications for the future that such data hold for either a peaceful or a strife-ridden world. Selected tables and figures on children and youth presented in *Children's Rights and the Wheel of Life* include:

The economic activities of children and young adults.

Military service requirements by age and length of service.

Number of births per females aged 15–19.

Percent of births to females aged 14–19 that were out-of-wedlock.

Death rates per 100,000 by cases of children and young adults.

Death rates per 100,000 by accidents, poisoning, and violence for children and young adults.

Age of majority in the five continents of the globe.

Selected tables and figures on aspects of the aged include:

Normal retirement age for men and women in cross-cultural comparison.

Death rates specified by sex and age.

Community services for the elderly in eight countries.

Participation by age in the labor force in industrialized and nonindustrialized societies.

Representation of status of the aged by degree of modernization in the society.

Persons below the low-income level by age.

Boulding provides not only the data but also insightful analyses intended to motivate social scientists and policymakers to perceive children, youth, and the aged as coparticipants in the shaping of society, not merely as its victims. Attention is focused on the phenomenon of age sorting and how gender and age interact to limit participation of youth and the aged in the mainstream of a society. These targeted groups are often deprived of rights and benefits based on age without regard to capability. Boulding asks that age be recognized as an important category in the United Nations Declaration of Human Rights, so that neither the young nor the old will be excluded from social and political decision making at local, as well as national and global levels.

❖ *Education for a Global Civic Culture*

Elise Boulding has also turned her scholarly and activist efforts toward research, writing, and curriculum development in the field of education directed toward the empowerment of coming generations for the creation of peaceful futures. Her books, articles, and pamphlets, as well as chapters and readings from edited books she has authored on the topic of education are listed in the endnotes.[14]

To date, her major work for teachers in peace education is *Building a Global Civic Culture: Education for an Interdependent World*. The text is divided into two parts. In the first part, the sociologist gives teachers and educators reasons to examine their techniques for teaching the conventional school subjects of civics, geography, and history. She asks that the teaching of civics and history be viewed from a world perspective and imbued with new meanings, rather than taught by the humdrum and tedious methods that have been practiced in American public schools over the decades. In this initial section of the book, Boulding asks teachers to expand their sense of time and history, to consider that our planet is in transition. She describes and discusses a mapping of the planet based on the tracing of intergovernmental networks (IGOs), the United Nations and its agencies, common market and other treaty groupings, and the international nongovernmental networks (INGOs), ranging from cultural and humanitarian INGOs (e.g., OXFAM), to occupational and scientific networks (e.g., International Peace Research Association).

The second section of the book considers what new methods and curriculum materials teachers need in order to present ways of knowing the planet as a whole for children growing up in a high-tech global culture. Boulding goes on to provide such ideas and strategies for learning and teaching about the worldwide society that *is* reality today. She labels this reality the "sociosphere" and urges teachers to imbue education with local, national, and worldwide content, as they recognize the impact of gender and ethnicity. She cautions:

> How do we know about the world? How do we find out what it is like? In the urban and suburban settings of the countries of the North, and for some elites of the South, children grow into adulthood without ever discovering anything about the physical and social environment beyond their own personal daily path, except through programmed secondary sources such as television, radio, the telephone, the computer, and of course, books. They live in technologically shielded settings that cut them off from feedback about the larger environment in which they live. In fact, it is considered progress NOT to have to bother with getting or dealing with that feedback.[15]

In writing on educating for our interdependent world, Boulding calls attention to the importance of conflict management in the face of wide-ranging diversity and cultural pluralism found in every country, as well as between states. She presents strategies and methods for developing skills that are needed to deal with the conflicts that diversity brings. No one society can create or impose *the* universal social order. It is incumbent on societies to find creative ways of working together that acknowledge our human diversity within an overall context of peacefulness. Destructive strategies that deny our differences must be avoided. Creative strategies that educators can use in their classrooms are workshops for peace learning through imaging a peaceful world, and the development of "The Portfolio of Global Experience" by students. Both of these educational strategies are described below:

◆ The "Imaging Peace" Workshop

This experiment in peace learning was first developed by Warren Ziegler of Futures Invention Associates based on the work of the Dutch sociologist, Fred Polak, whose book, *Images of the Future*, Elise Boulding translated into English. Boulding describes the imaging workshop as an activity in freeing oneself from the present time, and the willingness to take a leap into the future.

> Focused imaging is a combination of free-floating fantasy and daydreaming and a kind of night-time aware dreaming which is called 'lucid dreaming.' It is *intentional*; the participant engages with a group of colleagues in a purposive use of the imagination on the behalf of normatively defined social goals. There is a powerful contradiction between the invitation to enter into the free-flowing inner world of mental imagery with its evanescent material that can hardly be handled like a potter's clay, and the instruction to *see* community in which previously stated goals have been realized. Yet people find their way through that impossibility. The imaging is first done individually and then shared in small groups. . . .
>
> After the fantasy material has been reported and discussed, people shift to the analytic mode and ask 'how' questions of the imagery. How does this world work? What has to be in place in this future society, for what was seen to be possible? Only after details of this world have been crafted as far as possible in the time available (the workshop can take one to three days) does the most important work of all take place; imaging a history, backwards from the future, that brought such a world into being. The imagined history generates new ideas for social action in the present, which is the real purpose of the workshop.[16]

In an important appendix titled "A Workbook for Imaging a World Without Weapons" in the book, *Building a Global Civic Culture*, Boulding describes the procedures for peace-imaging workshops in detail. She lists these seven stages:

1. The goal statement, i.e., checking out one's own hopes for the world.
2. Exercising the imagination through memories.
3. Moving into the future.
4. Clarification of the experienced imagery.
5. Consequence mapping and world construction.
6. Working from the future back to the present (reconstructive history).
7. Action planning for the present.

The futures that emerge from the workshops are varied; some represent high-tech urban-centered societies; others a low-tech decentralized "green" world. All images are characterized by nonviolence, egalitarianism, and an absence of hierarchy. "Most workshop participants see some form of world cooperation that does not erode localism."[17] She notes that while the imaging-peace workshops were originally developed for peace movement groups, they have been held for others such as physical and social scientists, military personnel, diplomats and policymakers, educators, and intergenerational community groups.

◆ *The Portfolio of Global Experience*

This unique questionnaire (pages 394–397), created by Boulding to help teachers and students become aware and tap into aspects of their lives that

PORTFOLIO OF GLOBAL EXPERIENCE[18]

In our study of global systems, we want to build on the background of world experience and perceptions of the planet you already have. Preparing this portfolio will make it easier for you to utilize your own experience in understanding a global perspective.

I. EXPERIENCE OF RESIDENTIAL MOBILITY

List all the home addresses you have had since you were born, including moves within the same town. These addresses must be for places that were your home for six months.

	Town (or farm)	State	Country
1)			
2)			
3)			
4)			
5)			
6)			
7)			
8)			
9)			
10)			

Comments:

II. TRAVEL EXPERIENCE

List all the regions of the U.S. and foreign countries you have been in, with indication of length of stay.

	Region or Country	Under 7 Days	7–30 Days	1–6 Months	Longer (specify)
1)					
2)					
3)					
4)					
5)					

6) ＿＿＿＿＿＿   ＿＿＿＿＿   ＿＿＿＿＿   ＿＿＿＿＿   ＿＿＿＿＿

7) ＿＿＿＿＿＿   ＿＿＿＿＿   ＿＿＿＿＿   ＿＿＿＿＿   ＿＿＿＿＿

8) ＿＿＿＿＿＿   ＿＿＿＿＿   ＿＿＿＿＿   ＿＿＿＿＿   ＿＿＿＿＿

9) ＿＿＿＿＿＿   ＿＿＿＿＿   ＿＿＿＿＿   ＿＿＿＿＿   ＿＿＿＿＿

10) ＿＿＿＿＿＿   ＿＿＿＿＿   ＿＿＿＿＿   ＿＿＿＿＿   ＿＿＿＿＿

11) ＿＿＿＿＿＿   ＿＿＿＿＿   ＿＿＿＿＿   ＿＿＿＿＿   ＿＿＿＿＿

12) ＿＿＿＿＿＿   ＿＿＿＿＿   ＿＿＿＿＿   ＿＿＿＿＿   ＿＿＿＿＿

Comments:

III. EXPERIENCE WITH SUBCULTURES IN U.S. OR ELSEWHERE

Indicate the subcultures (ethnic, racial, religious, political) you have been part of or known. Check one of the three columns on the right for each.

Type of Subculture	Been Part Of	Been In Close Interaction With	Had Some Exposure To
1)			
2)			
3)			
4)			
5)			

Comments:

IV. LANGUAGES YOU CAN USE (BESIDES ENGLISH)

Language	Read Only	Speak Only	Read and Speak		
			Poorly	Well	Fluently
1)					
2)					
3)					
4)					

V. MEDIA EXPERIENCES THAT SHAPED YOUR WORLDVIEW IN SOME CRITICAL WAY

1. Books in English:

2. Books in Other Languages:

3. Radio, TV, Theater:

4. Other:

VI. PERSONS IN YOUR LIFE WHO SHAPED YOUR WORLDVIEW IN SOME CRITICAL WAY

1. Parents, older siblings, or other relatives; mention only if particularly relevant to your global understanding, and give example of type of influence for each:

2. Other persons you have known; again, give typical example of influence for each:

3. Public figures you have only known through the media:

4. Radio, TV, Theater:

VII. EVENTS IN YOUR LIFE THAT SHAPED YOUR WORLDVIEW IN SOME CRITICAL WAY

1. Can you remember the very first time you ever had a vivid impression of the planet as a *whole*, as an interdependent community of peoples? Describe, and give your age at the time:

2. List the five major events since your childhood that have affected your country:

a) _____

b) _____

c) _____

d) _____

e) _____

3. List the five major events since your childhood that have affected the world:

a) _____

b) _____

c) _____

d) _____

e) _____

4. Describe any other world-orienting events that were personally significant to you, and your age:

are really global in nature, is printed in *Building a Global Civic Culture*. The futurist notes that most of us have grown up and currently live in communities filled with instant communications and international media broadcasts. Hence, preparing a portfolio of global experience helps make each person more aware of living in a global society.

Elise Boulding's writings offer new resources and new thinking on education for a worldwide culture, the empowerment of women and men, and the young and the old in a global society bursting with diversity. As Margaret Mead has urged, we must work toward attaining a world order in which social conflicts can be handled by less than ultimate forms of threat and counterthreat. We have no choice in the matter. All societies must work to solve these social conflicts or witness the end of human cultures as we have known them. Boulding carries on the work and traditions of Margaret Mead in showing how a "global civic culture" can be built through lifelong learning in school and community.

❖ Envisioning a Peaceful World

In this chapter we have characterized Elise Boulding as a social thinker who has extensively contributed to the literature on family and community studies through comparative and cross-national research. A tireless investigator and scholar, Boulding has worked in the areas of conflict resolution, peace education, future studies, and women's studies. As professor of sociology, she directs her work toward social learning for all ages from preschoolers to senior citizens. Her recent research has focused on ethnic identity. An article in the volume, *Global Visions Beyond the New World Order* (1993) examines the dynamics of ethnic groups and ethnic identity in the closing decades of

the twentieth century. She calls for a new term to describe these groups—
identity groups—as a viable approach to examining their place in the tumul-
tuous political future of the twenty-first century. The term identity group
can refer to all groups that have some sense of common history and fate,
including, for example, Gypsies and Jews, who can be found on all continents, yet have recognition everywhere as subcultures with common historical roots.

We cannot bring to a conclusion this discussion on the contributions of
Elise Boulding to the literature of the social sciences without including a
sample of her subtle but attention-grabbing use of gender in academic writing. Beginning as early as the 1970s, a decade before gender-neutral language and guidelines for nonsexist usage were promulgated in academic
circles, Elise Boulding composed articles in the following style:

> Identity groups, to the extent that they are able, still practice the traditional trust-
> establishing ways of dealing with the stranger, and there is no reason why these
> should not be more widely recognized and accommodated. The Bedouin, meet-
> ing a stranger in the desert, feeds her first and asks no questions until an inter-
> personal relationship has been established through conversation. Some tribes
> have the practice, when a stranger looms on the horizon, of sending one person
> out to greet her, and to engage in a dialogue about places and people until some
> contact point through mutual knowledge of a person, place, or event has been
> established. If none can be discovered, the two in dialogue create a fictive point
> of contact. The point of contact established, the greeter brings the stranger back
> to the group and introduces her; she can then be welcomed as a distant relative,
> a member of the tribal family. . . .[19]

Even at the close of the twentieth century one is startled and wont to
stop to reread such a passage using the female pronoun, "she" to replace the
use of the traditional "he"—especially when describing events in an Arabic
culture like that of the Bedouin! Just a few decades ago it took the courage
of a Joan of Arc to carry on one's academic career in this style. Elise Boulding
always had such courage.

In her role of futurist, the sociologist predicts that in the twenty-first
century pluralism and diversity in the arena of international politics will
increase, as states adapt to a variety of constitutional arrangements, offering
greater participation to diverse identity groups "in global networks pursuing
an unimaginable variety of peaceable human adventures."[20]

Encounters with Social Thought

Becoming a Citizen of Planet Earth

Multiculturalism and Diversity in American Schools

The following scenario is becoming more frequent and more familiar to teachers at all educational levels in recent times:

Seated around the conference table in the principal's office is a small group of five men and women. They are the members (mostly appointed, not volunteers) of the subgroup of their elementary school's diversity task force. Their task is to develop a questionnaire to assess the degree of multiculturalism, including gender and life-style awareness, in the curriculum and the teaching "atmosphere" throughout the school. But this group of people is at a stalemate in the fulfillment of their assignment. They have realized that in order to create an appropriate instrument to distribute to the school staff, with questions and other items about the degree of diversity awareness and the actual application to teaching practice in the classroom, there has to be an introduction, some background, and some explanation of what the project is all about.

Just to compose the first paragraphs of the questionnaire, the members of this diversity task force subcommittee have been meeting for over a month, at least once a week, struggling with how to define diversity and multiculturalism in America today. How can the "diversity" questionnaire be presented to the respondents—the teachers—so that meaningful and useful answers will be obtained? How can the concept of what is *the* American culture, and who is considered to be included in it, be portrayed so that the diversity task force will be able to assess what is currently being taught about ethnic groups in America? What instruction is going on about diverse life-styles? Gender issues? Religious diversity? And aren't being "differently abled" (formerly "handicapped") and concerns about the aged, all part of the diversity task force assignment to assess the condition of multiculturalism in the curriculum? So contentious and illusive are these issues in America today that this subcommittee of merely five people cannot find even one area of complete agreement after struggling with their project week after week.

In her article, "The Passions of Pluralism: Multiculturalism and the Expanding Community" Maxine Greene of Teachers College, Columbia, a philosopher and educator, urges renewed attention to the growing diversity in school populations at every level of our educational enterprise. With eloquence, Greene writes:

> There have always been newcomers in this country; there have always been strangers. There have always been young persons in our classrooms we did not, could not see or hear. In recent years, however, invisibility has been refused on many sides. Old silences have been shattered; long-repressed voices are making themselves heard.[21]

She urges that we open up the curriculum to expose every aspect of schooling to the wide diversity that now exists in communities across America. Like Elise Boulding, Maxine Greene does not see an inherent danger of particular ethnic traditions replacing mainstream American cultural characteristics and value orientations. "To take this view is not to suggest that curricula should be tailored to the measure of specific cultural groups of young people," Greene cautions. She notes that there is no question that what history has overlooked or distorted must be restored for such groups as African Americans, Hispanics, Asians, women, Jews, Native Americans, the Irish, and Poles. But, "as time goes on more and more African American literature and Hispanic American literature and women's literature are diversifying our experience, changing our ideas of time and life and birth and relationship and memory." Additionally, there is always the danger of stereotyping, which seems to be inherent in multicultural education and a pluralistic approach to the school curriculum. Teachers and other educators could fall into the trap of characterizing *these* children as Asian American or *those* children as Native American or Hispanic American, as though there was not wide diversity and extensive difference found in any of these broad categories of ethnic/racial groupings.[22]

A Portrait of Multiculturalism in One Primary School

School communities characterized by extensive ethnic, racial, and religious diversity, resulting from both "domestic" differences (i.e., Asian Americans, Hispanic Americans, etc.) and recent "foreign" immigration are not uncommon in the United States today. A detailed portrait of one ethnically and linguistically diverse school of young children and their teachers follows, demonstrating the role of the school in America in fostering cultural continuities, value orientations, and the cultural dialogue. The school described is in a public school system of a large city in the American Southwest. It is typical of many neighborhood public schools in communities where the once culturally homogeneous neighborhood of the 1950s, 1960s, or even the 1970s is a thing of the past and probably will never return again. In this neighborhood of single-family homes (some built at the turn of the century) adjacent to the campus of a private, 150-year-old university, a multiethnic, multilingual primary school enrolling approximately 400 children, ages four to eight years, has evolved. As new, young families—some from countries and cultures from the far corners of the globe—moved into the more spacious homes of this older residential area the neighborhood began to take on an international, multicultural atmosphere. In recent years, languages such as Arabic, Italian, Turkish, and Korean could be heard on the streets and in the park areas of the community. The all-white residents were replaced by people of many skin hues, and their general appearance was altered as well by fascinating and colorful dress. This community also attracted local residents of differing ethnic and racial backgrounds who decided to move into the community because the neighborhood school offered educational experiences and a curriculum suited specifically for very young children.

By the end of the 1980s the children in this school hailed from twenty-six countries around the globe and included at least seventeen different languages. The school offered special assistance to these many diverse speakers through its English for Speakers of Other Languages program. We have described the multiethnic character of the school neighborhood, but further, to add to the student diversity, this school was "paired for busing" with an upper elementary school, grades three through five, that increased its highly pluralistic school population also. Hence, the ethnic composition of the school was recorded as 38 percent Black, 6 percent Hispanic, 8 percent Asian, 1 percent Native American, and 47 percent other ethnic groups at the close of a recent academic year. Further, the children came from varying socioeconomic levels, from lower to upper middle class. Many of the students lived in single-parent homes. The majority of the remaining group had families in which both parents were employed. There was, however, extensive family involvement. Parents' high esteem for the principal, the school staff, and its multicultural educational programs found expression in their willingness to volunteer in the classrooms, the library, the computer laboratory, for field trips and art classes, and for special events and school-wide programs, such as the unusual "International Images" project.

This International Images project evolved from the proposal for a mini-grant submitted by one of the primary grade teachers to a local philanthropy interested in funding innovative educational programs. It was an intensive six-week integrated interdisciplinary project designed to promote international awareness and appreciation of multicultural arts at the early elementary school level. Organized and implemented by the teacher of the gifted and talented, these multidisciplinary, cross-cultural arts activities involved the entire school—all the staff and students. It was led by and centered around a local artist, ceramicist and painter, the mother of two children in attendance at the school. After presenting slides and discussions to each classroom in the school on the development, history, and techniques of mural making, the artist and the teaching staff proceeded to have each child create a ceramic tile depicting the various countries and cultures they had been studying about in their classes, many of these cultures represented by the children and their families themselves. The project covered three months of activities, including discussions, creating and coloring the tiles with the use of special glazes, collecting the tiles from each class and then firing them at the artist's studio. Finally, this mother–artist-in-residence designed a tile mural and assembled the tiles on the walls at the entrance of the school, where children, parents, teachers, and visitors could view and enjoy this unique expression of International Images. The impetus and stimulation for this particular outpouring of effort by the teachers and parents for teaching about multiculturalism and international perspectives to such young children had been an ongoing commitment at the school for a number of years. It was displayed on every corridor wall and especially in the areas of the school's kindergartens, where both of these early childhood teachers specialized in dealing with differences, global education, and cross-cultural perspectives for five-year-olds.

When Elise Boulding stressed that teachers at all grade levels are really futurists, she had in mind the teaching staff in this school. The kindergarten teachers traditionally began the school year with the theme of "friendship" and the idea that the world is an interesting place because of differences, yet it is our similarities that tie us together as human beings. "This makes dealing with difference a matter of seeing that differences are all right," said one of the kindergarten teachers. "We give children a global feeling from the beginning by studying a different country each week, along with learning a different letter of the alphabet each week. I provide an artifact, or song, game, or some words for each country we study." Visiting these kindergartens, one could not help but notice and be impressed by the wide-ranging internationalism displayed in every corner of the rooms—signs in many written languages—Hindi, Arabic, Greek, as well as English; photos, drawings, ceramics, clothing, and objets d'art of every description to instill global awareness. Parents were an intimate and essential part of this kindergarten curriculum for global awareness and multicultural education. Children were assigned "homework" every weekend, which involved activities with their families, to promote research and project development on the current topics and themes in the kindergarten classroom. These kindergarten teachers asserted that children in their classes learn that they are not powerless to do something vital on a worldwide scale. Each spring the yearlong activities on global awareness and learning were culminated by the creation of a cloth quilt to which each child contributed and that parents assisted in assembling. The quilt was then raffled off and the money raised donated to help alleviate the hunger of children worldwide, impressing upon the kindergartners that they can make a difference in the world.

English and the Many-Other-Languages Classroom

The English for Speakers of Other Languages teacher on staff would rather be known as a teacher of "biliterate" students. She said, "Most of our students are 'biliterate'; they are learning to read and write in their home language and in English." Her classroom and the adjacent corridor area overflowed with the internationalism and the cross-cultural atmosphere that reflected her educational philosophy and methods for teaching children who speak many different languages and represent a myriad of cultures—Farsi, Arabic, Korean, Vietnamese, Laotian, Hmong, Cantonese, Cambodian, Turkish, Greek, Italian—and on around the globe. She encouraged these children, most of them from recently arrived refugee families, to learn in both their mother tongue and in English. Using parents, siblings, family members and international students from the nearby university, this teacher brought her pupils from their assigned classrooms for periods of time into her classroom for specialized instruction in science, social studies, and mathematics. She used many ways of communicating, learned over her twenty-four years of experience in cross-cultural, international, and multilingual teaching in the United States and abroad. Her techniques included the use of flashcards, charts, games, music, artwork, and media materials, as well as the many human resources she attracts to her fascinating classroom with its diversity of multilingual students. "But careful and detailed planning is the key to teaching non-English-speaking children, who also need to learn about a new culture and a whole new way of life," she reiterates. This teacher's creativity and commitment permeated the entire program at the school and set a standard of caring about diversity that exemplifies life in a global civic culture that Boulding predicts for the future.

One international graduate student from the People's Republic of China who worked for several months with the "other languages" teacher, wrote accounts of her experiences with this "biliterate" program. From the journal of this perceptive and highly experienced Chinese teacher came the following descriptions of life in an American classroom for non-English-speaking children:

◆ This academic quarter I had the chance to gain some experience about multicultural and diversity education at the school close to our campus. I have been to different classrooms and participated in many classroom activities, but I write here about my experiences in Mrs. P.'s class most especially. To describe this classroom and the general environment of the area of the building I begin on the stair landing outside the classroom on the second floor. Here there is a poster with the title

"Our Umbrella of Friendship." Three children of black, white and yellow skins stand under the umbrella. The caption says: "Our umbrella of friendship keeps us safe from the storm of prejudice. There is room under the umbrella for your friends—umbrella of sharing, caring, kindness and understanding. Anger, prejudice, fear and hatred are all kept out of the umbrella." Alongside this poster is a map of the world, photos of the school's children from different countries in the world are attached on both sides of this map with colored yarns indicating the children and the countries of their origins. This helps these children remember their own heritage and makes them feel proud of who they are. This also helps the Anglo-American children see that the world is made up of different countries, different peoples and cultures, each with its own value and uniqueness. . . .

◆ Mrs. P. is a teacher of English for Speakers of Other Languages and during my practice period at this school, I have been with her for more time than I have with any other of the teachers. She teaches children with different cultural backgrounds. Inside her classroom she has collected and displayed different toys, objects, and many pictures of cultures all over the world where the children can see their cultures reflected. On January 16th Mrs. P. had a celebration for the birthday of Dr. Martin Luther King, a famous black American who fought for rights for black people during his lifetime. Mrs. P. showed the children in her class the video tape of last year's celebrations and activities for Dr. Martin Luther King's Birthday. Last year the ethnic students at this school performed their own traditional dancing and singing—Laotian, Thai, Chinese, Malaysian, Indonesian, Russian, Arab, Korean. The dancing and singing provided the children a chance to see that other cultures are just as unique as their own. No culture is superior or inferior to another. Mrs. P. took every possible chance to talk about the people to the children, making them realize the world is made-up of these different people.

In the afternoon of the same day, a school assembly was held. The school principal, an African American woman, made a speech in memory of Dr. Martin Luther King. Then each teacher brought up to her the two or three "Best Citizens" chosen from her class list, making them known to the public, explaining why she had chosen them as the "Best Citizens" for their good manners, their gentle ways, their affection and help to classmates and teachers. I could see how the rest of the students admired them when the principal shook hands with each child. . . .

◆ Another thing that amazed me was how the children learned the American spirit of independence from a very young age. In the early childhood education classrooom, the children were assigned a free choice time to do different things—literacy, art, carpentry, housekeeping and so on. They were to make decisions by themselves. Some made up their minds right way, some seemed to hesitate, and they looked around the room to see different activities before making their decision. I think it is good to start training early to make choices, especially for those children who are from a different cultural background. I would not have realized this if I hadn't come across an experience on February 13th in Mrs. P.'s classroom. This day she held a small party for the Lunar New Year's Day of the Chinese tradition. After the party, Mrs. P. asked the school principal to enjoy the Chinese Lunar New Year's happiness, too. So I prepared a tray with some lucky cookies, a piece of rice cake, a Chinese dumpling, a calendar, a red envelope for lucky money. Then Mrs. P. and I and the new Chinese girl student, Min Chao went to present the tray to the principal.

I had been holding the tray when Mrs. P. said, "Don't you want Min Chao to take the tray?" I told her: "I'll let her take the tray when we get to the office because I'm afraid she will fall down or drop it." Mrs. P. was very thoughtful. She did not give me a direct criticism, instead she said, "The children themselves take their own lunch on trays all the way upstairs and downstairs." It came to me immediately that what Mrs. P. was telling me was that children should learn to be independent from a young age and be trusted to do things that adults can do.[23]

These excerpts from the journal of a mature, international graduate student in teacher education correspond to a number of points in the previous discussion of the writings of Elise Boulding and the creation of a global civic culture in American schools. It is revealed in the descriptions above that the American school is shaping, inculcating, and socializing students in the traditions, heritage, folkways, values and customs of the majority American culture. Excerpts from the international teacher's journal that describe the most recent addition to our national holidays, the Martin Luther King Day ceremonies, held by the principal and the English for Speakers of Other Languages teacher, demonstrate that educators can incorporate opportunities for children from very diverse cultures to dance and sing in their familiar ways of celebration for an American holiday. The school's physical appearance, the corridor walls, and inside the classrooms were decorated with international images so children and school visitors could experience the respect for, and recognition of, our contemporary world's diversity. The teaching staff and the administrator demonstrated concern, coupled with understanding of the uniqueness of individual students and their families, by acknowledging the wide differences within ethnic and nationality categories in their teaching, planning, and yearlong school programs. This school, which we must reiterate is not an unusual example of American public elementary schools currently, is sensitive to those identity groups Boulding describes, while acknowledging the global civic culture by accommodating diverse ways and traditions, allowing conflict and individual expression.

Implementing the Portfolio of Global Experience with Students—an Example

We had the opportunity to use Elise Boulding's *Portfolio of Global Experience* with undergraduate and graduate students for seminars in a department of education of a major university in the American Southwest. One of the courses where this questionnaire was given to college students to fill out and discuss was titled "Education in International Settings." Here is some information and details about this higher education offering and the Portfolio we used:

Title: Education in International Settings

Course Enrollment: Upper division undergraduates and graduate students, ages twenty years and over, both American-born and international students.

Purpose: This course presents issues and theories, underscored by examples, case studies, research findings, curriculum materials and resources to encourage students to bring global perspectives and world awareness into the educational setting and the curriculum of elementary and secondary schools.

Objectives: to develop world awareness and a sense of global responsibility in teachers for infusion into all aspects of education; to identify promising practices and exemplary curriculum materials for teaching global perspectives and world awareness; to discuss educational philosophies that undergird international educational trends; and to provide field experiences and face-to-face interchanges with international educators, teachers, and students in the promotion of education in a global arena.

Texts: Elise Boulding. *Building a Global Civic Culture: Education for an Interdependent World.* Teachers College Press, 1988; Edith King. *Building a Borderless Planet: Classroom Curriculum for World Awareness.* Unpublished manuscript, 1992; and readings provided by the instructor from books, journals, and articles.

Assignment: *The Portfolio of Global Experience*—prepare your responses and fill out the portfolio. Discuss and go over the individual items in class.

Results of the Responses to the Portfolio of Global Experience

The university students who responded to the items in the *Portfolio of Global Experience* represented both American-born men and women and international students. Their ages ranged from twenty to forty years. These students were mainly enrolled in teacher education programs or international studies programs at a large university in the American

Southwest. As indicated above, the students were asked to reply on the questionnaire to the items presented as a required assignment for a seminar in international education.

We present the responses here of a representative sample of these respondents, item by item from the *Portfolio.*

Item I. Experience of Residential Mobility—a listing of all the home addresses you have had since your were born at which you have resided for at least six months. Students responded with between four and sixteen different locations where they lived. There appeared to be little variation in number of home addresses between American-born and international students.

Item II. Travel Experience—to regions of the U.S., as well as foreign countries. All the respondents listed over ten different regions or countries to which they had traveled including North America and many "foreign" locations. One student responded: "I traveled around the world for eight months through most of Europe, the Middle East, Africa, the Far East, Australia, and South America."

Item III. Experience with Subcultures in the U.S. or Elsewhere—a listing of the subcultures—ethnic, racial, religious, or political that you have been part of or known, with indications to degree of participation. The American-born students listed from a minimum of five to a maximum of fifteen different subcultures and groups, while indicating varying degrees of experiences with these groups. In contrast, the international students listed very few different groups and commented that since their countries were highly homogeneous they have had little experience or exposure to groups different from their own.

Item IV. Languages You Can Use (besides English)—this item was further qualified: Read Only; Speak Only; Read and Speak. Responses ranged from none to two, with one student indicating fluency in three different languages. Both the American-born and international students noted their limited "other" language facility.

Item V. Media Experiences that Shaped Your Worldview in Some Critical Way—including books, broadcast media, or other. Here the students, both American-born and international, produced a wide variety of answers, but the television broadcasts by CNN stood out and were listed by almost every person; also noted were the radio broadcasts on National Public Radio and newspapers such as the New York *Times.*

Item VI. Persons in Your Life Who Shaped Your Worldview in Some Critical Way—including your parents and relatives; other individuals; public figures. Respondents, both American-born and international, usually listed *either* their mother or their father, but, most interestingly, not both their parents as the strongest influence upon their worldview. Next came specific mention of a teacher, a coach, or a special friend. When identifying public figures drawn from the media, students cited many different individuals; however, most often mentioned were: astronauts, Martin Luther King, Jr., Ghandi, and John F. Kennedy.

Item VII. **Events in Your Life that Shaped Your Worldview in Some Critical Way**—especially world-orienting events that were personally significant to you. This item elicited the most extensive responses, both in writing and in class discussions. There was a wide range of answers focusing on wars—such as the recent Gulf War, the Vietnam War, and the possibility of a nuclear holocaust. Frequently cited was the collapse of communism and the break-up of the Soviet Union; the end of the Berlin Wall, the massacre in Beijing, the destruction of the rain forests, and the AIDS epidemic. Both American-born and international students had many comments and incidents to relate in response to Item VII. Some touching anecdotes included:

"The assassination of the musician John Lennon personally distorted my vision of world peace. A man struggling for world peace who is shot down for no reason was utterly senseless and confusing to me. I was fifteen years old at the time."

"I remember watching Neil Armstrong walk on the moon and how the camera panned back to the Earth, capturing the smallness of the globe in the Universe."

"When I was six years old, I remember seeing the Coca-Cola commercial on television. The commercial portrayed people from all over the world singing together 'in perfect harmony.' I realized at this age that all people are basically the same."

We have presented merely a brief recounting of some outcomes from the use of Elise Boulding's provocative strategy for teaching about world awareness and peace education, the *Portfolio of Global Experience.* Additionally, we described programs and projects in American elementary schools that promote conflict resolution, peacemaking, and the sense of global responsibility that Boulding has promulgated over the decades in an effort to create better human relations in this troubled world.

Putting Social Thought to Work

1. In portraying the lifework of sociologist and futurist Elise Boulding, we described the multiple careers which she has pursued simultane-

ously. Do you know of others who have successfully engaged in occupations or professions which they have carried out concurrently? Describe these individuals, either in writing or in oral discussions with your colleagues. What personal attributes are characteristic of these people? Do you admire them? Envy them? Would you want to be like them?

2. In this chapter we brought out and emphasized the concept of the *underlife* of women versus the *overlife* of men. The French terms *dedans* (inside) versus *dehors* (outside) were also employed to describe the private world of the home and family where women have traditionally been situated, versus the public world where men have been placed. Do you find agreement with the historical evidence that has been presented about this situation of gendered life? Do you disagree? What information, examples, anecdotes can you bring to support or refute the concept of this private versus public life that differentiates the sexes?

3. It was stated in this chapter that, even as long ago as the fifteenth century, the more women entered the wage labor market the more wages dropped for them because they had no bargaining power due to their limited mobility. Do you think this is a valid statement? What evidence can you bring to support or counter the assertion that when women enter the job arena wages or salaries in that job or profession immediately start to drop?

4. Discuss the historical "as if" myth of the family that arose in the 1800s and 1900s in Europe and America. The myth, as presented in Elise Boulding's writings, holds that every traditional family or household must be made-up of a husband, who goes out to work and provides the financial support for the family, a wife who stays at home at all times, and their children. Do you think that the "as if" myth is still widely held today? Do you think the "as if" myth still influences young adults in shaping their lives and their careers? How appropriate do you think it is to assert that some women and men still want the "as if" myth of family life to prevail because they fear that the women's movement will disrupt this cherished paradigm?

5. Discuss Elise Boulding's models as presented in Figures 16–1 and 16–2: the traditional situation—"The Agents of Oppression for Women," and the futurist's prediction—"The Agents of Social Transformation to the Postpatriarchal Order."
   Do you concur with the traditional model depicting the agents of oppression for women? Do you support the futurist's model of the postpatriarchal order? Why or why not?

6. What insights on society do we gain from researching and studying the life conditions of youth and the aged as presented in Boulding's book, *Children's Rights and the Wheel of Life*? Are you familiar with other materials, such as books, pamphlets, journals, television program series,

films, or other media presentations on this topic of concern for the human rights and equal participation in society of targeted age, gender or ethnic groups?

7. In your estimation, how important is it for teachers and educators to implement a global perspective and cross-cultural awareness in the school curriculum? Do you think we live in such a technologically shielded society that children today receive the majority of understanding of world society, not firsthand, but through the media—primarily television and computers?

8. Consider mounting an "Imaging Peace" workshop. Refer to the description in this chapter or obtain the sources cited here for the strategies to design and implement such a project.

9. Elise Boulding's instrument, the *Portfolio of Global Experience*, is reprinted in Chapter 16. Fill out the Portfolio and share your responses with others.

Endnotes

1. Elise Boulding, *One Small Plot of Heaven* (Wallingford, PA; Pendle Hill Publications, 1989), p. 85.
2. Ibid., p. 159.
3. Elise Boulding's extensive writings range from the 1940s to the present. We list here selected publications and major articles, chapters and pamphlets:

    BOOKS: *Image of the Future*, 2 vol. translated from the Dutch, *De Toekomst is Verleden Tyd* by Fred Polak (Utrecht; W. De Hann N.V. , 1953); English translation published by Oceana Press, 1961; abridged edition (San Francisco: Jossey/Bass/Elsevier, 1972). The *Handbook of International Data on Women*, with Carson, Greenstein and Nuss (New York: Halsted Press, 1977); *Women in the Twentieth Century World* (New York: Halstead Press, 1977); *From a Monastery Kitchen*, with Daniel Marshall (New York: Harper & Row, 1976); *Children's Rights and the Wheel of Life* (New Brunswick, NJ: Transaction Press, 1979); *The Social System of the Planet Earth*, with Kenneth Boulding and Guy Burgess (Reading, MA: Addison-Wesley, 1980); *Women and Social Costs of Development: Two Case Studies*, with Elizabeth Moen, Jan Lilleydahl and Risa Palm (Boulder, CO: Westview Press, 1981); *Building a Global Civic Culture: Education for an Interdependent World* (New York: Teachers College Press, Columbia, 1988); *Peace, Culture, and Society*, with Clovis Brigagao and Kevin Clements, eds. (Boulder, CO: Westview Press, 1990); *New Agendas for Peace Research: Conflict and Security Reexamined*, E. Boulding, ed. (Boulder, CO: Lynne Rienner Publishers, 1992); *The Underside of History: A View of Women Through Time* (Boulder, CO: Westview Press, 1976; revised edition Beverly Hills, CA: Sage Publications, 1992); *Futures and What Makes Them Happen*, with Kenneth Boulding (Beverly Hills, CA: Sage Publications, 1994).

    CHAPTERS, READINGS, ARTICLES: "Warriors and Saints: Dilemmas in the History of Men, Women and War," in *Women and the Military System*, Eva Isaksson, ed. (London: Harvester Wheatsheaf, 1988); "Building Utopias in History," in S. Mendolvitz and R. B. J. Walker, eds., *Towards a Just World Peace* (London: Butterworths, 1984); "Two Cultures of Religion and Obstacles to Peace," in *Zygon*

21, no. 4 (December 1986): 345–366; "Image and Action in Peace Building," in *Journal of Social Issues 44* no. 2 (1968): 17–37; "The Concept of Peace Culture," in *Peace and Conflict Issues after the Cold War* (Paris: UNESCO, 1992); "Ethnicity and the New Constitutive Orders," in *Global Visions Beyond the New World Order*, J. Brecher, J. G. Childs, J. Cutler, eds. (Boston: South End Press, 1993).

4. Elise Boulding, *The Underside of History: A View of Women Through Time* (Boulder, CO: Westview Press, 1976), p. xvii.

5. Ibid., pp. 18–20.

6. Ibid., pp. 18–21. Boulding cites Evelyn Sullerot, *History and Sociology of Women's Work*, vol. 2 (Paris: Société Nouvelle des Éditions Gontheir, 1965), p. 34.

7. Elise Boulding, *Underside of History*, vol. 2 (Beverly Hills, CA: Sage Publications, 1992), pp. xi–xii.

8. Ibid., p. 87.

9. Ibid pp. 90–91.

10. Ibid., p. 256.

11. Ibid., p. 257.

12. Ibid., p. 334.

13. Ibid., p. 335.

14. The following articles and readings by Elise Boulding are among those she has written specifically on the topic of education: "The Role of Education in Building a Peaceful World Order," *The New Era* (London) (1964); "Education for Inventing the Future," in *Alternative to Growth I: A Search for Sustainable Futures*, D. L. Meadows, ed. (Cambridge, MA: Ballinger Press, 1977); "Schooling and the Creation of Human Futures," in *Sharing for Global Understanding*, (Grand Blanc, MI: People for the Promotion of Global Understanding, 1977); "Children's Rights," *Society 15*, no. 3 (1978); "Learning to Make New Futures," in *Educational Reform for a Changing Society*, L. Rubin, ed. (Boston: Allyn and Bacon, 1978); "World Security and the Future from the Junior High Perspective," *Peace and Change xix*, no. 2 (1981); "Education for Peace" (1982); "Peace Education as Peace Development," *Transnational Associations*, no. 6 (1987); "Strategies for Learning Peace," in *Human Rights, Education and Global Responsibilities*, J. Lynch, C. Modgil and S. Modgil, eds. (London: Falmer Press, 1992).

15. Boulding, *Building a Global Civic Culture*, p. 77.

16. Boulding, "Strategies for Learning Peace," in *Human Rights, Education and Global Responsibilities*, p. 212.

17. *Building a Global Civic Culture*, pp. 113–115, and Appendix B, pp. 172–176.

18. Ibid, Appendix A, pp. 167–171.

19. Boulding, "Ethnicity and New Constitutive Orders," p. 216.

20. Ibid., p. 229.

21. Maxine Greene, "Passions of Pluralism: Multiculturalism and the Expanding Community," in *Education Researcher* (Jan–Feb. 1993): 13.

22. Ibid., p.16.

23. Yan Xia Zhong, unpublished project, University of Denver, College of Education, 1992.

Chapter 17

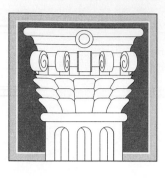

Epilogue

Social Thought for a Global Society

❖

Whatever people have become; whatever we might mean by civilization, progress, or cultural evolution; whatever we happen to achieve in the way of controlling nature; and whatever we imply when we talk of being better off—all of these are consequences of human social organizations. To be human is, one way or another, to be a member of an organization. There is no more elementary social fact than this. American society, with its extremely powerful individualistic ideology, leads all too many people to think that organizations are either bad or unnecessary, or both. We cannot determine whether organizations are good or bad for people; this is too complex a moral problem for a small work such as this. That organization is necessary, however, is difficult to dispute. At the very least, a minimal form of organization—that of the family—is required for the survival of the individual.

If we move only a little further, we find that extraordinarily elaborate forms of organization become necessary for even the simplest of modern conveniences and life "style." Today, the woman or man who drives a car (constructed, designed, and distributed by organized groups of workers numbering in the millions), who listens to electronically augmented music on a stereo system (all of which evolved out of a history embracing still more millions of artists, engineers, and workers), and who is working toward a degree in law (a totally collective and organized activity) can nonetheless subscribe to a belief that the individual is everything and that social organization should not ideally be necessary. Or there might be a grudging concession that social organizations are necessary, but hardly worth the effort of serious study.

Sociology grew out of the recognition that social systems are as much a part of our fate as are the physical and biological systems that grant us life. We live within a "sociosphere," as Elise Boulding has pointed out, as well as an atmosphere and a biosphere. There is nothing new in this recognition. Philosophers, humanists, priests, politicians, and generals have been aware since the dawn of history that people are social animals and that their strength is derived from their ability to organize themselves into larger systems. Before the social sciences came along in the nineteenth century, the perplexities of social life were discussed and evaluated in every literate society through philosophy, literature, and religion. Whether we like it or not, the social world bears closely on our personal fates. To understand ourselves, we must understand the communities upon which we grow more dependent every day.

We would like to drive the point home with one more observation. This is an age of psychology. We are inclined to turn to the individual as the locus of action problems. A careful assessment of the human condition, however, reveals that nearly any kind of individual problem has a sociological aspect as well. We are sociological as well as psychological beings. Indeed, we are more likely to violate our biological selves in the name of a social cause than to violate a social cause in the name of our biological selves. The extreme example of this, of course, is the person who, because he or she cannot somehow find social acceptability, commits suicide. An examination of our progression through even the most ordinary day reveals our ongoing concern with social position and our relationship to those whose respect we seek. If, as Margaret Mead pointed out, young people today find adolescence a trying time of life, it is not because they are psychologically "messed up." It is because they live within cultures and societies that are "messed up." In other words, adolescence is a sociological as well as a pychological condition. We would be inclined to suggest that it is more of a sociological than a psychological condition.

Modern social thought moves us toward a more rational, systematic, or "scientific" mode of interpretation of human affairs. As we have observed in the chapter on Émile Durkheim, social forces in earlier and simpler societies were dealt with in terms of myth and religious expression. Religion has been, and still is, one way of making evident the subtle and indirect forces of the community. The quest now, in economics, sociology, and political science (as well as in history and anthropology), is for a reasoned understanding based on logic and data. The statistical approach to the study of society is fairly recent. The current effort to find mathematical regularities that will uncover basic processes in human social conduct is an extreme extension of this faith in logic.

Whether we approach society from a mystical point of view, through myth, ideology, propaganda, or through rational understanding, it is something we must live with and it is something we must understand in some fashion if we are to survive. Sociology and the social sciences in general are essential. We have no choice with regard to whether we will or will not be involved with social theory. We can only choose to try to do the job well or poorly. We can either improve our understanding or regress. History is replete with examples of what happens if we regress.

❖ The Study of Society: A Paradox

The study of society seems easy, because almost anything one may say about it makes some kind of sense, and, paradoxically, anything one may say about it can also be viewed as the purest nonsense. For example, there are theorists in academic sociology who emphasize the extent to which human societies are stratified; such social differentiation makes for conflict and internal stress and exploitation. This, of course, was one of the central themes of Karl Marx. On the other hand, the writings of sociologists such as Robert Merton and Émile Durkheim emphasize the idea that society is composed of various functioning elements and that these elements seem to work together; they are structurally interrelated in such a manner as to sustain the entire organization. Such a point of view accentuates the extent to which cooperation is a part of human social systems. However, Merton does note that dysfunctions arise and unanticipated consequences can enhance or impede human social actions.

Almost any kind of metaphor is likely to work when we talk about something so remote from our direct comprehension as the social order. If so, then the analysis of society, in any manner (whether rational or irrational), is all too easy. We can speculate however we wish and can always find examples to fit our speculations. We can argue and debate, but we can never hope to resolve any social issue in the same clear way that we can solve an equation in algebra. The analysis of society can become a pettifogging sort of game—a bit of fun, perhaps, but not something to be taken too seriously.

So, one barrier to the study of society is that it is really too easy. It might seem that there is little need for it because people know what their societies are about. But there is another barrier: Sociology, seen on the one hand as obvious and easy, can also be seen as impossibly difficult. This is the more astute and also the more serious observation. It seems that we can never make sense of the human social realm in the same fashion that we can, for example, make sense of chemical reactions. Einstein's intellectual concerns involved probably no more than ten or twelve fundamental variables—space, energy, mass, time, and other similarly fundamental dimensions of reality. For any social issue, however, the number of complicating factors, events, dimensions, and variables is as large as anyone might wish to make it. Unfortunately, any one of those variables can have a significant role in the outcome of a historical happening. And so, one concern of the social scientist is to select what is singularly important or basic and eliminate the extraneous.

This was a critical matter for C. Wright Mills and, indeed, for the entire idea of a social science. It is true, Mills argued, that minor and unforeseen happenings can alter the course of history; examples include the assassination of John F. Kennedy or the misinterpretation of Japanese phrases during peace negotiations that led to the atomic bombing of civilian populations. However, despite these particular moments, there are broader social and cultural processes at work that can be delineated and become the basis for simplifying the great variety and complexity of human social behavior. In this respect, the general concept of "culture" is to society in all of *its* complexity as the simple and general concept of "mass" is to the physical world in all of *its* complexity. The process of trying to find general and relatively universal elements of social reality becomes, in itself, an important intellectual task.

If, then, people avoid the study of social organization because it is on the one hand too easy and on the other too difficult, it appears that sociology is damned if it moves in one direction and damned again if it moves in the other. Certainly, sociology offers to the serious and involved student as much challenge as any other discipline or field can offer; just as certainly, we cannot ignore the study of society.

❖ *Limitations of Social Science*

The limitations of social science, as science, are quickly made apparent by the inability of its research efforts to move beyond relatively weakly established relations. Sociological research (and that of the social sciences generally) is pleased when it establishes relationships that explain half of whatever problem is under study. This is seen as a major accomplishment. More commonly, social research accepts correlations that explain only 10 or 20 percent of a problem.

Such research has its uses, but the severity of its limitations can at least be suggested by considering how other sciences would be affected if they had to rely on such weak correlations. For example, how would an aerodynamics specialist design a rocket or an aircraft if he or she had to deal with mechanisms that could be counted on to work only half the time? 10 percent of the time? 20 percent of the time? If aircraft were designed on the basis of data and relationships that social scientists find highly acceptable, would we want to fly in them? Actually it is a moot question, because there is little likelihood that such an airplane would ever get off the ground.

More profound than the problem of the level of acceptance in social research findings is the fact that sociologists have not solved the problem of "subjectivity." The natural sciences deal with reality as "object." When people are dealt with as objects, we must ignore the very reality we want to explore—what they are like as thinking and feeling individuals. But to introduce such factors as "thinking" and "feeling" into our studies means that we have to deal with subjective elements. As we introduce subjective factors, we move away from objective scientific concerns into something else. In sum, it appears that the more rigorously scientific we become in the social sciences, the more we remove ourselves from what we want to understand. The more we tolerate subjective human qualities, the less scientific we are.

So, on the one hand, we want the power and certainty of scientific knowledge. We desire, in the social sciences, the reliability of scientific methods. On the other, we want to know ourselves and our societies. The two ambitions are difficult if not impossible to combine.

Although the basic observations of the natural sciences are generally true regardless of context, those of the social sciences are not. Astrophysicists have spent much time and effort determining whether hydrogen that exists in the remote regions of the universe is different from hydrogen on earth. It is not. Whether hydrogen is in our galaxy or one billion light years from here, it appears to be the same stuff. But where are such universally established conditions to be found in the social sciences? When Sigmund Freud developed the concept of the Oedipus complex and implied that it was a universal human experience, his critics—specifically, cultural anthropologists—quickly pointed out that possibly it was only a part of Western culture. Or when Margaret Mead went to the South Seas to study the adolescence of girls in Samoa, her major social science breakthrough was the discovery that young women in Samoa do not go through the same adolescent experience as those in the United States or Europe.

Even defining the context within which a social action takes place can be extremely difficult. In recent times if a person is arrested by the police for "driving under the influence," DUI, what is the proper context, what are the actual circumstances surrounding such an event? On the one hand, there are continual newspaper reports about chronic alcohol- and drug-addicted individuals who evade the law time after time, but finally, in a drunken state ram into a carload of children on their way home from a school function, killing several of them, while the drunken driver escaped without a scratch! The DUI laws in many states currently mete out severe penalties in such situations once the drunken driver is apprehended and his or her record of DUIs is revealed. But on the other hand, in hundreds—possibly thousands of cases nationwide—an individual, after having a glass of wine at an evening business function, could be driving a friend home, and is stopped by the police for "swerving in the lane." Immediately all the procedures for the DUI are applied to the driver. The individual is handcuffed, rushed to the police station, given a Breathalyzer test (which can be made to register over the legal limit), booked, and jailed. The ensuing entanglements with the law, sometimes for years, including loss of driver's license with the consequences of loss of employment as well, can ruin an individual's life. All of this has occurred because the law-abiding, innocent citizen had one glass of wine but fell victim to a "police trap to ensnare drunken drivers."

At the close of the twentieth century, such occurrences are becoming more and more frequent so that it is easily possible that each of us knows of a friend, relative, or acquaintance for whom the "Jean Valjean" situation (as told by Victor Hugo in *Les Miserables*) becomes reality. If we were to do a statistical study of five hundred DUI arrests in any one state, we would have to recognize that they were not identical events. However, we can and we must, if we are to do a statistical study, read them as such; yet when we do so, are we being rigorous or judicious in our use of data? Are they really similar events, or do the unique circumstances or contexts within which these transgressions of the law occur make each situation something different? How can we sift through the data to discern those who are truly irresponsible and criminal from those who have been victimized and persecuted due to no fault of their own?

Another limitation or problem in the study of society is that of deception. There is, of course, the problem of conscious deception, which takes place when a respondent in a study does not want the researcher to know the truth of things. More significantly, there is the deeper problem of deception when neither the respondent nor the researcher is aware.

A natural scientist need not be concerned with whether physical objects will act in some uncharacteristic manner because they want to deceive the scientist. However, deception of a sort begins to plague researchers as soon as they take on the task of dealing with living beings other than humans. Psychologists, for example, report that the way in which mice are returned to their cages can have an effect on how they perform in experiments. A psychologist, pleased with a mouse that has just run a maze because it behaved according to expectations, may fondle the mouse and stroke it as it is taken from the maze and returned to its cage. This mouse has been given an additional "reward," and it might perform even better the next time. Its behavior, in a sense, has become deceptive.

In dealing with human subjects, the problems of deception are compounded. The social science literature is replete with anecdotes, case histories, and long-standing debates concerning how subjects—whether they are contemporaries or preliterate peoples fulfilling the roles of informants—have "deceived" social science researchers. Among some of the more famous of these social science "scandals" have been the case of Sir Cyril Burt in Britain,[1] and more recently the extensive flap over Margaret Mead's research in Samoa that arose after her death.[2]

But even when an informant wants to tell the truth, is the respondent capable of it? Any number of studies demonstrate that people distort what they know of an event immediately after they have observed it. This is not all necessarily malicious or attributable to tendencies to lie, or falsification. It is simply not possible for people to recall an event with much accuracy.

Distortion is inherent in perception itself. We believe we have seen something or have not seen it, and the truth of the matter may be quite different. Lawyers have relied for centuries on this simple quality of the human condition. When we are told about matters that someone else has seen, our understandings of the world become even more distorted. Keep in mind that *most of what we know about our social worlds is what we have been told, not what we have observed directly.* At the very least, more than 90 percent of our social knowledge is what we have heard about or read about. Such information is invariably subject to serious distortion.

Small wonder, then, that social information is a mishmash of deceptions, distortions, and misunderstandings. It is, in general, a potent web of misconceptions. It is a marvel that human social systems operate at all. This is an extremely difficult problem for the development of a rigorous science. The primary difficulty lies in the fact that deception in the social sciences can never be rigorously disproved. No matter how authentic a work may be, its authenticity can always be claimed to be a product of extremely ingenious deception. There is no way around this problem. This means that the scientific integrity of such research is forced to remain a matter of conjecture. Social research depends, much more than does research in the physical or natural sciences, on the good will of that which it studies.

The social sciences are sometimes accused of being "soft" or "easy" in contrast to the natural sciences. There is certainly nothing easy about trying to understand the nature of human social systems. They are virtually impossible to figure out in any rigorous manner. If there is "softness," it lies in this matter of deception. It is simply easier to get away with deception in the social sciences than in the natural sciences. So, not only do the social sciences depend to a considerable extent on the good will of the people they study, they depend also on the trustworthiness and honesty of the social scientists themselves. If a physicist fudges data, the corruption will be discovered by those who review the study. If a social scientist fudges data, it is often difficult to determine whether the original researcher, or the critic, or anybody is really at fault. To put it more bluntly, it is easier to get away with being a fraud as a psychologist or sociologist than it is as a natural scientist. This is not a small concern.

Is it possible to circumvent the problem of either conscious or unconscious distortion? Unfortunately, we cannot prove or demonstrate in a truly rigorous fashion that any response to any question asked by any social scientist is not a deception. There is one exception. Questions that have to do with physical actions or attributes can often be checked. For example, if we ask a person about his or her age and the person lies, we can sometimes check the matter by referring to court records (though the records might be forged or falsified).

We are forced to assume that most responses are honest and straight-forward and, in some sense, meaningful; however, this can never be proved. The social data we obtain are reasonable because they seem to be reasonable, and we have to accept them as that. When we are no longer willing to accept them as reasonable, we can readily find means to challenge their validity. It is for this reason that no matter how a particular group may try to establish a social argument, another group can undermine it. This is as true of socio-logical claims to social knowledge as it is for any other group.

In sum, the social sciences cannot endow their research with the rigor and the intellectual integrity so often characteristic of the natural sciences. They may sometimes appear to do this, or assert that they do it, but we think it is better to acknowledge at the outset that such claims are based more on hope than attainment.

❖ *Rewards of the Study of Society*

If the social sciences are faced with such problems—if they produce knowl-edge that is only relatively certain—then why bother? After all, one school of thinking argues that people should only devote themselves to solvable problems and let everything else slide. Why waste one's time with matters that cannot be given exact and specific solutions? We think this argument is worth examining, because how we respond determines whether we shall continue the quest for better social knowledge or give up. If we give up, what can we turn to for social understanding? Does giving up mean going back to primitive and simplistic social dogmas? We have to develop "theo-ries" of one kind or another and rely on these "theories" to deal with the demands of day-to-day social life.

One of the more difficult features of learning what modern social thought is about is that from the time we first become aware of the world around us, we begin to develop a sense of how to relate to other people. We begin to obtain that solid sense of what the community is like and how it works. We come, then, to the study of sociology or anthropology with the notion that we already know how human societies work. If sociologists tell us something that does not correspond with our established beliefs, we can casually dismiss the sociologists' arguments—we know better. In this case, we are likely to look on the social scientist as a pointy-headed intellectual who is not really "with it." If what the social scientist tells us agrees with our beliefs, we then can conclude that the sociologist is simply telling us what we already know. This makes the social scientist appear to be an empty-headed intellectual or, worse yet, tediously boring. It is a Catch-22 situation. The social scientist cannot advocate ideas that are either too unusual or too common without risking total rejection.

Not only do we have fixed notions about human societies before we begin the study of sociology, but these notions have a solid sense of "cer-tainty" about them. If we are of a conservative bent, we know that criminals are trash and that the way to prevent crime is to build more prisons. If we are liberal, we know that criminals are people driven by desperation and poverty into acts that violate the rules of the community. Either view is, of course, astonishingly simplistic. Crime is a complex issue. It happens among the "best" of people, and it is common to all societies. Nearly everyone engages in criminal actions at some point in his or her life. The study of criminology leads us away from our solid and certain ideas into a more open frame of mind. It is here that social science is of the greatest value. It does not provide us with a sense of certainty, but, rather, with a sense of the complexity of life and the options that stand before us with regard to understanding our lives. It liberates us from the prisons of simple beliefs as Robert Merton has so eloquently pointed out. The liberation comes at a cost, however. To be freed from the prison of simple belief means learning how to live with uncertainty and true freedom. Freedom, after all, has its own demands. Most people, so it seems to us, prefer the various comfortable prisons of simple belief to the grander but more bewildering mansions of free thought.

To begin with, then, we already function as social thinkers. We acquire a variety of ideas about social systems from the time we are born. This knowledge is essentially folk knowledge. It is biased. It is simple. However, the world is not simple. We can no longer afford to rely on knowledge that is biased and simplistic. Or, to put it a little differently, to rely on folk knowledge is not enough. We need something more comprehensive and carefully thought out. It is the task of the social sciences to think through issues and obtain information when folklore is willing to trust knowledge obtained at an earlier time under different circumstances.

Social knowledge that we get from folklore and "common sense" tends to move toward "hard" understandings. We begin to believe that our group, whatever it may be, is good and that other groups are certainly suspect and, more generally, downright evil. Social scientists have a phrase for this: "In-group virtues are out-group vices." That is to say, what we do is "morally proper." If *they* do the same thing, it is "wicked." For example, we are "ambitious," but *they* are "pushy." We are "a proud people." *They* are "uppity." We enjoy "a high standard of living." *They* are "a bunch of pigs." And so forth.

People fear the unfamiliar, the alien, the stranger, the outsider, the person who is not a member of the "in-group." We are not saying that such fear is always unreasonable; however, it is not sensible to turn against people simply because they are outsiders. We can do as much damage by fearing what we should not fear as we can by not fearing that which is dangerous. (A most dramatic instance, of course, occurred when Germany ousted thinkers of the magnitude of Albert Einstein from their midst because the Nazis had an irrational fear of the Jews.)

Fear plus simple explanations lead people to develop inflexible attitudes and beliefs. Carried to the extreme, this becomes authoritarian thinking. Authoritarian thinking is characterized by extreme rigidity and a sense that there is one correct way of doing things and all others are wrong. If social science has discovered any general principle with regard to sociocultural systems, it is that people have developed a great variety of ways of living together that have proved extremely effective. No single system is inherently superior to all others.

People commonly dislike the idea that social and cultural communities can be radically different from their own and yet be perfectly acceptable to those who live in them. We accept our own system as best, and others, for the most part, accept their own system as best (though even this has been challenged in the breakup of the Soviet Union and other European communist nations at the close of the twentieth century). Sociologists refer to this as "ethnocentrism," the inclination of people to think that the world, so to speak, is centered within their ethnic group. It is not. Ethnocentrism, carried to the extreme, leads to the belief that our own culture is superior to all other cultures. From this sort of thinking, it is but a short step to conclude that it is our task, then, to subordinate all other people to our way of thinking.

❖ *Concluding Comments*

Despite the fact that people seem as socially troubled in this century as they were at any previous time, there is still the prevailing sentiment that the study of society is the easiest and the simplest of intellectual undertakings. This little epilogue has been concerned with making it apparent that the accomplishment of effective and "truthful" sociology is almost beyond the capabilities of human beings. The social realm may, by virtue of qualities unique to it, resist the kinds of rational and naturalistic investigations that have proved so successful in the physical sciences.

However, we are concerned with more than simply making the point that sociology is a difficult effort when taken seriously. We are also concerned with the general problem of defining or expressing what we are dealing with when we talk about "social" actions or the "social system." We have suggested that social actions reside in symbolic interchanges between people and that these interchanges are subject to a variety of interpretations. Interpretive behavior is itself a part of the social process. It is difficult to separate social theory (viewed broadly as various efforts to interpret society) from society itself. We become social when, in confrontation with other people, we exchange points of view and acquire a particular "slant" on things. These perspectives are invariably presumptuous and generally based on collectively sustained ideas of what constitutes the "right" way of labeling people and responding to them.

It is the task of social science—sociology in particular—to ask serious questions and promote questioning. We cannot, as the natural sciences have done, provide solid and "hard" answers to much of anything. Indeed, this should not be the task of the social sciences. We come to the study of sociology, anthropology, and the other social sciences with "hard" answers about ourselves and the community we live in already well established. It is the task of the social sciences to promote flexibility of thought, not certainty and dogmatism.

In conclusion, let us say once again that we do not mean to imply that thinking about society is an ineffectual or impossible effort. In view of the massive obstacles confronting it, the study of society has been surprisingly successful and worthwhile. As we have reiterated in the previous chapter of this fifth edition of *Twentieth-Century Social Thought*, we must work toward attaining the peaceful resolution of human conflicts in what has become a worldwide society or we will see the end of human cultures as we now know them.

We have no choice, really, as to whether we are going to be social thinkers. Each and every one of us, as we act within the community, must make a number of sociological assumptions and rely on them every day. We label some people "immoral" and others "moral" because we believe in a particular theory of how social affairs should be arranged. We condemn some people as not fit to belong to our group and actively seek the membership of others because we have very definite theories about how such membership will influence the group. The importance of the group itself is enhanced by other theories or presumptions that we have about how the group serves the society as a whole. Our sense of personal worth and what we are as human beings is related to the "folk" theories we subscribe to and attempt to enforce. There is no way we can avoid being social thinkers. We can only be ignorant or knowledgeable about the alternatives facing us. This book is predicated on the simple belief that it is better to be knowledgeable than ignorant about these alternatives.

As our social and economic systems grow larger and more complex, the effort to understand them becomes increasingly difficult. The future may well find the social sciences increasingly at odds both with those not trained in them and with each other—economists versus sociologists, anthropologists versus psychologists, "hard-headed" quantifiers versus "soft-thinking" humanists. It may prove to be a time of crisis. We may hope, however, that if the social sciences can continue to attract dedicated and serious students, this time of crisis may prove instead to be a period of lively debate in which it is discovered that human society is complex enough to tolerate many approaches.

We may eventually discover that there is a delight in freedom. We may even eventually be able to grant freedom a deeper and more wholesome meaning than we have been able to do up to this point in our history. After all, our current notions of freedom are limited to being *free from* some disliked coercion. When the coercive pressure is lifted, we all too often find ourselves free but at a loss as to what to do next. We shall not have explored the true dimensions of freedom until we understand what it means to be *free to* act in ways not dictated by blind belief and simple dogma, but in ways created through an awareness of the complexity of the world.

To reach this higher conception of freedom, the social sciences must move in a new direction. The social sciences must, of course, continue to provide people with the best, most reliable, and most carefully obtained social information possible. At the same time, they must, in addition, reveal to people the range of possibilities inherent in social thought. We must abandon the quest for some final, ultimate truth about the social order. We must come to accept the more exciting possibility that there are many different views, each with its strengths and limitations, which the imaginative thinker can draw upon and use for deeper understandings of what it means to be a human being at this time in history. This ideal can be reached only when the social sciences accept as their central task the stimulation of controversy and discussion, in a spirit of recognition that human social affairs can never be encapsulated by any kind of rigorously precise empirical "laws."

Endnotes

1. See "The Cyril Burt Affair" in *The Intelligence Controversy* by J. H. Esenyk (New York: Wiley, 1981), pp. 99–105; and Leon Kamin, *The Science and Politics of I.Q.* (Potomac, MD: Erlbaum, 1974).
2. See Derek Freeman, *Margaret Mead and Samoa: The Making and Unmaking of an Anthropomorphological Myth* (Cambridge, MA: Harvard University Press, 1983), and Lowell D. Holmes, *Quest for the Real Samoa* (South Hadley, MA: Bergin & Garvey, 1987).

A Glossary of Social Thought

❖

This glossary contains terms that may be unfamiliar to the reader. Often the definitions include concepts that are not likely to be found in the ordinary desk dictionary.

Abstracted empiricism. A term used by C. Wright Mills to refer to factual studies that concentrate on some part of a process and, as a result, lose their grasp of the whole. For example, voting studies have demonstrated that wealthy Americans tend to vote Republican. These studies are empirically or factually sound. At the same time, the abstracted nature of such data leads us away from a consideration of the more complex political machinery that makes such facts significant. Mills used this term to criticize what he thought was one of the central limitations of empiricism as it exists in sociology—its tendency to destroy comprehension of the complex unity of human social action.

Altruism. Behavior revealing a concern with the welfare of others, unselfish conduct, subordination of one's interests to those of another. See *Altruistic suicide.*

Altruistic suicide. Suicide resulting from altruistic motives. Durkheim saw in altruistic forms of suicide a means of indirectly assessing the nature of the social bond. Collective sentiments have the capacity to enable the individual to overcome his or her own fears of death. Altruistic suicide is self-destruction in the

424

interest of socially established goals. An example of such conduct would be the self-immolation of Buddhist monks in Vietnam.

Ambivalence. Having feelings or reactions of both a positive and negative kind toward some object, event, or condition. For example, intellectuals in America are probably viewed with ambivalence by many people. On the one hand, their knowledge is admired and recognized as the source of many cultural accomplishments. On the other hand, they are viewed with some suspicion and hostility as a threat to established values and traditions.

Analogue. A condition or event similar to some matter one wishes to understand that, because of the similarity, can promote such understanding. For example, since the computer is in many ways analogous to the human brain, one can understand some aspects of human thought by turning to the computer. Most social theories rest ultimately on some kind of analogous reasoning. In some theories, the biological organism is implicitly taken as an analogue for society; society is then seen as having a circulatory system, intelligence centers, digestive mechanisms, and so on.

Anomic suicide. Suicide resulting from being placed in a situation where the regulative controls of the social order have been weakened or removed. Émile Durkheim saw, in the higher suicide rates found among divorced people, evidence supporting the proposition that anomie is conducive to self-destruction. The divorced person, he argued, finds intolerable the anomic conditions existing after being freed from domestic responsibilities. See *Anomie*.

Anomie. Literally, "without name or identity"; the condition of not knowing what one's social character is supposed to be. The subjective character of anomie is similar to the feeling that comes when one is supposed to go someplace but has no map to tell how to get there. This term was coined by Durkheim to identify situations in which individuals are, or feel, only loosely united with the community or social order.

Atavistic stigma or **stigmata.** Marks (stigmata) that identify people as reversions (atavisms) to primitive physical types. Cesare Lombroso, an Italian criminologist, believed that many criminals have a primitive physical appearance. American white racists believe that American blacks can never really be civilized because they are physically a primitive type and that, moreover, this is proved by the blacks' physical appearance—their atavistic stigmata. Physical anthropologists, we should note, have convincingly demonstrated that Caucasians share as many physical traits in common with the gorilla as do the members of any other race.

Biologism. As used in this text, the belief that the social nature of people is inherent within, and explainable in terms of, biological nature. In its crude form, biologism argues that our major institutions are a reflection of biologically endowed instincts. If we followed this line of reasoning, the Bank of America would have to be seen as a genetic phenomenon arising from an acquisitive instinct found in all people. Another naive form of biologism is the argument that a superior society can be created by producing a biologically superior form of human. In a more sophisticated form, the modern biologist argues, quite reasonably, that we must not ignore people's animal nature. This form of biologism concedes that some aspects of the social order are not simple manifestations of biological urges or drives. Social and biological forces interact with each other. Thus, Konrad Lorenz, after exploring the biological nature of aggression in subhuman animals, very tentatively explored the possibility that the lessons learned at such a level might be applied to the aggressive nature of human beings. Note, however, his use, in the following quotation, of both biological and sociological or anthropological concepts.

> The ganging up on an individual diverging from the social norms characteristic of a group and the group's enthusiastic readiness to defend these social norms and rites are both good illustrations of the way in which culturally determined conditioned-stimulus situations release activities which are fundamentally instinctive. (*On Aggression*, translated by Marjorie Kerf Wilson [New York: Harcourt, Brace, 1966], p. 259)

Sociologists for the most part have eschewed biological approaches to human behavior.

Bureaucracy. A large-scale organization, hierarchically structured, and dedicated to efficiency in the pursuit of goals, with duties prescribed by a written set of regulations, pesonnel selected on the basis of examinations, and power resting within the concept of an "office" rather than in the individual. A modern bureaucracy can be almost incomprehensibly large. Bureaucracies, because of their reliance on codified rules, are also highly legalistic in nature. Bureaucratic modes of organization in modern societies tend to diminish the influence of traditionalistic and kinship systems of organization.

Celibacy. For an adult, the state of living without a sexual partner. Dictionaries define celibacy as being single or unmarried. Celibacy, however, appears to be declining among the unmarried of our time. Vows of celibacy refer to the intention to lead a life devoid of sexual experiences.

Charisma. A Greek word meaning "divine gift." As used by Max Weber, this term refers to the dramatic or exciting personal characteristics of the prophetic leader or demagogue that enable the person to retain power over a following. Charismatic power is located in the unique personal attraction of the leader. Because such power is neither long-lasting (it dies when the leader dies) nor dependable, one of the problems faced by any social organization is the need to achieve more stable modes of allocating power. Bureaucracy achieves greater stability in its power structure by placing power within an office or position rather than in the individual. Thus, people of power within a bureaucracy are often those having very little personal attraction or "charismatic" quality.

Consumerism. A social movement seeking to augment the rights and powers of buyers in relation to sellers. Historically, consumerism was begun in the Middle Ages by those who attacked deceptive selling practices and promoted the concept of "just price" rather than charging what the market would bear.

Continuum. A condition to which we can, in our imagination, assign any value as we move from its lowest to its highest extremes. A continuous variable differs from a discrete variable. The latter permits only particular values as one moves from its lowest to its highest extremes. For example, wealth is a discrete variable. Along the tremendous range from no wealth to billionaire status, one must move by a series of discrete steps resulting from the fact that wealth is an accumulation of pennies. One must go from $25.00 to $25.01; there is no stage in between. Time, on the other hand, is continuous. No matter how finely we divide a second, we can think of a still finer division.

Cultural lag. The idea that the material aspects of culture progress more rapidly than the nonmaterial or symbolic aspects. The adherents of this point of view claim that many social problems of our time arise from the inability of our moral concepts to keep pace with our technological development. Thus, while we are surrounded by atomic technology and supercomputers, we still depend upon a legal and moral philosophy that met the needs of a pastoral people who lived over two thousand years ago. Opponents of the culture lag theory argue that all aspects of culture, including the technological, are essentially symbolic in nature and that the distinction between material and nonmaterial features of culture is spurious.

Darwinism. The theory of evolution attributed to Charles Darwin. It holds that all species (plants or animals) developed from earlier forms by natural selection among chance mutations. Those forms survive that are best adapted to the environment. See *Social Darwinism*.

Dehumanization. According to Erving Goffman, the act of divesting any person of the right to employ those props, symbols, costumes, or fronts which enable that person to impress others favorably. Our conception of humanity, however we define it, is associated with group membership. A particular action that might be seen as human when carried out by a group member can be viewed as less human when performed by someone outside the group. Sociologists have summarized this phenomenon with the phrase, "In-group virtues are out-group vices." So it happens that we are "ambitious," but they are "pushy." We are "intelligent," but they are "too smart for their own good." Dehumanization is a complex form of behavior operating at a symbolic level, which requires, first of all, a set of devices for depriving some class of persons of their right to use positive forms of impression management, and second, a justificatory scheme for the enactment of such deprivation.

Demography. The study of the numbers of humans living at any time, as affected by fertility, mortality, and migration. Because mortality rates have been dramatically reduced in recent years, fertility has been the major factor accounting for variable rates of population increase in different nations. Demographers have become especially concerned with factors influencing human fertility.

Determinism. The philosophy that, in principle at least, all actions, including those of people, are the result of causes over which the acting agent has no control. Thus, a rock falls because of the determining influences of gravitational force. A human being does something because of the numerous determining forces of the situation. A person engaging in some action, placed in the same situation again, would respond in the same manner. Advocates of this point of view claim that the idea of choice or volition is entirely a matter of illusion and that in actuality we have no choice. Just as we physiologically mature and enter senility because of biological processes over which we can exercise no control, so we behave in response to the very complex conditions in which we find ourselves, which are, in their entirety, fortuitous circumstances. Even whether or not we believe we have a choice is a matter of cultural and ideological determinants into which we are thrust by the accident of birth. Critics of a deterministic position argue that determinism requires the capacity to assign causes to events. When such causes cannot be assigned, an indeterminate situation exists. When a situation is indeterminate, the future is uncertain. The uncertainty of the future offers us the opportunity to assign, in the present, the priorities we will give to future actions. This assignment of priorities is a decision-making effort and involves thoughtful choices. Thus, we can choose. The fact that a determinist cannot predict the choices that will be made is a limitation of deterministic philosophy. In summary, determinism is a concept that arises from the feeling that people will someday understand the workings of the entire universe. Meanwhile, we must live with the fact that our understanding is not sufficient to tell us whether we will survive the present century.

Dialectic. An approach taken by Marx as a way of interpreting social change. The dialectic process is one in which a given society or economic system generates its own opposition and is forced, ultimately, to change. For example, the feudal system was sufficiently successful in organizing economic affairs to produce a capitalistic system, which then modified the feudal system that brought it into existence. The term is used in argumentation to refer to the way in which a thesis can generate an attack or antithesis. The result is a synthesis, which can become a new thesis for further argument.

Dichotomy. A twofold classification of some condition. For example, we can dichotomize people as rich or poor, strong or weak, bright or stupid, good or bad. The most famous dichotomy we can think of is that pertaining to the sexes.

Dust-bowl empiricism. A term coined during the 1930s, when the southwestern areas of the United States had suffered monstrous dust storms. The term refers to arid factual studies that have had the topsoil of thoughtful interpretation blown away, leaving behind the bedrock of numerous statistical or descriptive observations.

Dysfunction. Any social action that disrupts the well-being of the greater social system. The prefix *dys-* means "bad"; therefore, we are talking about a bad function. In medical terminology, "dysfunction" refers to the incapacity of an impaired organ to maintain the welfare of the whole organism. The idea of dysfunction in social analysis implies that its user has a very good concept of what a healthy social system is. However, this would imply an ethical judgment because social structures are, as Durkheim pointed out, moral structures. But social scientists are hesitant to make ethical judgments. Thus, the concept of dysfunction places them in a bind. If they exorcise it from their terminology, then they become apologists for the status quo. If they include it, they can be accused of making hidden ethical judgments which would contradict their commitment to ethical neutrality. It is difficult to find examples of dysfunctional features of a social structure with which all sociologists would agree. Rioting, for example, would seem to be dysfunctional. However, one might reasonably claim (as would sociologist Georg Simmel) that such behavior is functional.

Ecology. A perspective that concerns itself with the interaction between organic systems and their environments. Ecology concentrates on life systems as a complex interaction producing delicate, mutually sustaining living patterns for a great variety of organisms. If this ecological system is disturbed at any point within its structure, the established equilibrium is destroyed, and the whole structure is affected. Some ecologists are coming to the conclusion that we might see, in the near future, catastrophic changes in the earth's biosphere. These changes could be very abrupt.

Egoism. A concern with one's own interests rather than with those of others; a concern with self to the exclusion of a concern with others. Egoism should be contrasted with altruism. See *Egoistic suicide.*

Egoistic suicide. Suicide resulting from egoistic motives; suicide in which self-destruction is seen as serving the interests of the persons who kill themselves. Such suicide may take quite elaborate forms, and the individuals often show a curiousness and interest in the fact of their own death. Durkheim described it thus:

> A calm melancholy, sometimes not unpleasant, marks his last moments. He analyzes himself to the last. Such is the case of the business man mentioned by Falret who [went] to an isolated forest to die of hunger. During an agony of almost three weeks he had regularly kept a journal of his impressions. (*Suicide* [New York: Free Press, 1951], p. 281)

Electra complex. See *Oedipus complex.*

Empathy. The ability to feel or experience the subjective state of others; the capacity to enter the experience of another person. Social-psychological studies have shown that students who can easily empathize with their teachers tend to make better grades than those who cannot empathize.

Empirical. Having a factual quality; based on facts and observations as opposed to logical or rational considerations. According to a well-known story, purely rational considerations lead to the conclusion that the bumblebee is aerodynamically incapable of flying. Empirical considerations force us to conclude, to the contrary, that bumblebees do a very reasonable job of flying. Sociologists argue that much of what is wrong with our understanding of human social behavior arises from the fact that we have dealt with this subject on the basis of reasoning rather than observation. Sociology owes its distinction as a field pretty much to the commitment it has made to finding ways of factually determining the nature of human social behavior. However, because social behaior is both very complex and generally symbolic in character, the application of purely empirical modes of investigation is an ideal difficult to meet. Sociologists functioning at their empirical best generally rely on official records of various events, which are then submitted to statistical analysis. Demography, usually conceded to be the most empirical wing of the sociological enterprise, is of this character.

Epistemology. The study and examination of the means whereby one can establish true or valid statements. The epistemologist is concerned with establishing the limits that hold for human knowledge. The epistemologist keeps raising the question: "But how can you be *certain* that what you say is true?"

Esthetic. Having the quality of beauty, considered pleasing to the senses; meeting cultural definitions of what is thought to be symmetrical, well formed, and artistically appealing. Until recently, at least, one could give the example of a junkyard as a place lacking esthetic qualities.

Ethical. According to sociologists, behavior that conforms to the normative structure of the society in which the individual lives. Because sociology strives to be a science, and because science is ethically neutral, sociologists try to assume an ethically neutral stance. Professional ethics thus place sociologists in the unusual position of being unethical when they write or lecture with an ethical bias.

Ethnography. A research methodolgy developed by anthropologists to study the culture of a group of people in their environment. In recent years ethnography has been employed as a research strategy in other disciplines including sociology, education, social work, and social psychology. Ethnography is characterized by its meticulous and highly organized attempts to record and describe the culturally significant behavior of a particular society or group of people.

Ethnomethodology. A term coined by Harold Garfinkel to refer to the study of the methods employed by people in everyday social relationships to sustain the relationships and make them "real" or "valid" or "reasonable" (*Ethno-* "folk"; *method* "methods"; and *ology* "study of").

Existentialism. A philosophical position of a highly varied nature, grounded in the observation that mortal beings are contained and must exist within a universe that appears to be neither for nor against them. Faced with the fact of existence in an unconcerned world, individuals must choose the meanings they will give life. Existentialism, as employed in this book, refers to a philosophy of choice that says people have the possibility of making what they will of life.

Exponent. A figure indicating how often a number is to be multiplied by itself. The exponent 3 in 2^3 means that 2 is to be multiplied by itself three times, or $2 \times 2 \times 2$. Reference to exponential forms of growth has to do with the extremely rapid increases in values that come from repeated raising of a value by a factor contained in an exponent. Thus, if the factor in the exponent is 2, we would rapidly get very large terms by repeatedly squaring any real number greater than 1 or less than 1. For example, beginning with 2, we would have $2^2 = 4$; $4^2 = 16$; $16^2 = 256$; $256^2 = 65,536$; and so on.

Feminism. The movement organized around the principles that women should have political, economic, and social rights equal to those of men. Feminists advocate equal treatment for all individuals regardless of gender.

Generalized other. According to George Herbert Mead, to become fully socialized, a child must respond to others not simply as individuals but in terms of how these individuals are interrelated as a group or community of people. Ultimately, we are influenced not simply by specific isolated others, but by the way in which those others are related to each other, that is, by a "generalized" other.

Hedonistic. Subscribing to a philosophy of the pursuit of pleasure. The hedonistic calculus, a concept used to explain preference for criminal behavior, argues that if such behavior gives more pleasure than pain, it will be engaged in. A modern revival of hedonistic theory has appeared in the works of the late B. F. Skinner, a behavioristic psychologist at Harvard. According to Skinner, any organism will reveal a greater predisposition to repeat behavior it has found rewarding. We can employ this knowledge to make an organism behave as we would like it to by rewarding it each time it performs according to our preference. Thus, we can get a dog to roll over by rewarding it quickly on any occasion when it rolls over by chance or even begins to look as if it might roll over. One of the difficulties in applying such a theory to human behavior is that we cannot always be certain just what it is we want to reward. If we give a novelist a great reward (reinforcement) for writing a wonderful novel, this does not mean that he or she is supposed to sit down and write the same novel again. Sociological theory, concerned as it is with the structural relations between statuses or roles, is surprisingly devoid of a reliance on hedonistic principles in its approach to human conduct. Sociologically, people often appear to go about role performances in a cheerless and conformistic fashion. If they experience pleasure, it is because the role they are playing tells them to; they do not experience the role because of their desire for pleasure.

Heuristic. A device or concept that, though perhaps meaningless in itself, has the capacity to promote, advance, or stimulate understanding. Many mathematical models have heuristic qualities. The late Kenneth Boulding, economist and social philosopher, told his students that mathematical models are wonderful, so long as one does not believe them. He means that one should use a model to comprehend the nature of the real world, while at the same time remaining acutely aware of the constricted and artificial nature of the model itself. Boulding was saying that the mathematical model is best seen as a heuristic device.

Hierarchical. Being arranged in a series of ascending order of power or control, with each stage having greater power than those falling beneath it. The military is the typical example of a hierarchically arranged set of statuses with each level having authority over those beneath it.

The Holocaust. The mass murder of over six million people, mostly European Jews, by Nazi Germany during the 1940s. In 1993 President Bill Clinton, along with Elie Wiesel and other survivors of the Nazi concentration camps of World War II, opened the United States Holocaust Memorial Museum in Washington, DC. This national museum is dedicated to commemorating those who died in the Holocaust. Educating the American people about the history and lessons of the Holocaust is the museum's primary mission—to ensure that future generations will never forget.

Humanistic. Being concerned with humanism; revealing a strong interest in human thought and ideals as opposed to an interest in nature or religion.

Ideational. A term created by Pitirim Sorokin to describe cultures based in an ideational mentality centered in reality that is seen as eternal, spritual, and holding unchanging values. See *Sensate*.

Idealization. A symbolic construction of an event or condition that moves it beyond reality. This can take place only because idealization is a consequence of symbolic elaborations. Erving Goffman uses the term in a more restricted sense to refer to role playing in which a person responds to some fantasy of how the role should be played rather than what the role in fact demands.

Inner-Directed. Having the ability to retain a strong and contrary sense of moral purpose when placed in circumstances where it would appear reasonable to succumb to the norms of the natives. As David Riesman, proponent of this term noted, the inner-directed nature of the British colonial administrator in the extreme heat of the tropics was exemplified by his habit of dressing in Western clothing for dinner. See *Other-Directed*.

Internecine. Referring to conflict that is mutually destructive; deadly rivalry; struggle that avails little to either side in the battle.

Latent function. A consequence that was not anticipated or planned in the course of a social development. For example, if it is true that the institution of prostitution during the Victorian period helped hold the Victorian family together, then one of the latent functions of prostitution at that time would have been that it helped maintain the integrity of the family. Latent functions are the implicit, indirect, and "unofficial" reasons for the existence of some agency, corporation, institution, status, or position. Latent functions are contrasted with *manifest* functions.

Mana. A Polynesian term used generally by anthropologists to refer to an impersonal and diffused supernatural force which has magical powers. Thus, a tree that is very fruitful might be claimed to possess *mana*. A successful and healthy man might be said to have *mana*. According to sociologist Guy Swanson, a belief in *mana* exists only in societies with a particular form of social structure.

Manifest function. A consequence that was planned or anticipated in the course of a social development. The manifest function of an aircraft factory, for example, is simply to provide a safe and rapid means of transportation for the people in a society. Manifest functions are the simple, direct, and "official" reasons for the existence of some agency, corporation, institution, status, or position. Manifest functions are contrasted with *latent functions*.

Metaphysical. Literally, "beyond physics"; speculative thought that attempts to move beyond the directly observable nature of the physical world. To be interested in the accelerative dynamics of falling bodies is a physical interest. To be interested in the question of whether God exists in the form of a perfectly symmetrical cube is a metaphysical interest. Science has abandoned metaphysical concerns on the grounds that they cannot be responded to in a manner that produces consistent and reliable results.

Methodology. The study of method. Because of the problems encountered in trying to establish reliable knowledge about the social order, sociologists have shown an especially sensitive concern over the methods they employ. Most sociology departments of any size in American universities have at least one person, and sometimes several, whose special training is in the area of methodology. Sociologists subscribe to the belief that if their methods are sound, their conclusions will be acceptable. While concentrating on the means to be employed to establish factual results, sociologists sometimes lose sight of the ends to be accomplished by their findings. The fact that the study of method is a separate and specialized area of concern to sociologists suggests that there is such a thing as a sociological method of research. In practice there are any number of procedures that, depending on the effect being sought by the particular writer, can equally well serve as a means of setting forth convincing arguments. Because sociologists subscribe to the belief that only scientific results are acceptable to the field, the study of method has concentrated almost exclusively on the application of scientific procedures that have produced valid results in other fields. A uniquely sociological method or set of methods has yet to be found.

Milieu. A French term for environment or surroundings; a more elegant way of referring to environmental influences.

Monasticism. Preference for solitary living, a form of institutionalization of solitary existence by taking up residence in a monastery, where one lives a quiet, relatively solitary, and meditative life; a belief in the monastery as a way of life.

Monotheism. A belief in the existence of one god. We often hear Christian religious beliefs described as monotheistic. This is not correct. Christian theology, contains a number of gods and godlike spirits; it is, therefore, a polytheistic religion. According to Guy Swanson, relatively few cultures contain purely monotheistic religions.

Motifs. As used in this text, themes or central ideas around which the different elements of a culture are organized; the unifying concepts of a culture.

National character. An elusive concept based on the idea that there is a correspondence between a cultural milieu and the personalities of the people brought up in that culture. The idea of a national character is a refinement of the folk awareness that people from different nationalities have different qualities, in addition to the obvious ones of language differences. In the cruder stereotypical forms that appear in common thought, German national character, for example, is viewed as militaristic, authoritarian, bureaucratic, romantically sentimental, and given to the enjoyment of heavy and fattening foods. The attempt to provide more factual bases for such thinking has proved difficult. Anthropological and sociological research has shown that there is considerable variety in personality types with any cultural system. Such variety should be kept in mind when dealing with the concept of national character.

Naturalism. The philosophical position that whatever is experienced in nature is to be explained, accounted for, or understood in terms of nature; the philosophical position that supernaturalistic or extranaturalistic explanations are mythical, fictional, or silly. The natural sciences lean exclusively toward this position, as their name suggests. One physicist put it rather badly by arguing that there is no place for God in the laboratory. Another scientist is reputed to have claimed that God is redundancy in any mathematical equation because He would have to appear on both sides of the equal sign. An extreme naturalistic position is less attractive in the human realm. However, sociology, to the extent that it assumes a scientific perspective, is grounded in the belief that *any* human institution—*any* human social action—ultimately has its origins in purely natural phenomena. Despite occasional demurrers, such a position is logically and practically antithetical to a religious explanation of human conduct.

Oedipus complex. A term coined by Sigmund Freud to refer to the tendency of the maturing male to find his mother an attractive sexual object. The son is biologically impelled to commit incest. Society, of course, is opposed to such a practice. The maturing male child thus finds himself biologically set against the demands of a constraining social order. A further feature of the Oedipus complex is the feeling of hostility developed for the father as the child becomes aware of the father as a block between himself and his mother. Thus, the son is led into a situation where he wishes to murder his father and make physical love to his mother. How the sexually maturing male child resolves these horrifying desires has an impact, according to Freud, on the course of his adult life. The term *Electra complex* was given to the same situation with the sexes reversed. Hence the sexually maturing female child would be physically attracted to her father and hostile toward her mother.

Ostracize. To ban; to make someone an outcast; to shut out from the group; to set up barriers that make normal interaction with members of the group impossible. Ostracism often implies that a person being ostracized has been a member of the group and is then found unacceptable and banned from further participation in the group's activities. Ostracism is highly varied, however, and may take many forms, including the exclusion of persons who were never a part of the group. Ostracism can also be partial in character. We know about a member of a country club who asked the management whether he could invite a friend to play a round of golf with him. When he told them that his friend was an African-American professor, he was told that the game of golf would be all right, however, his professor friend was not to go near the swimming pool.

Other-Directed. Particularly associated with the theories of David Riesman, other-directed people are extremely sensitive to the demands of others. Riesman says that other-directed people look to their contemporaries as the source of guidance; either those personally known to them or those with whom they are indirectly acquainted through friends and through the mass media. See *Inner-Directed*.

Paranoia. A psychiatric term referring to systematic delusions of persecution that have reached the point where the individual is incapacitated in the performance of normal life routines. Paranoid individuals live according to the assumption that everyone is against them. If people are friendly, it is because they want to get close enough to take advantage. Paranoid persons are often quite dangerous, insofar as they come to believe they have good justification for inflicting damage on those near to them, they must do so in order to protect themselves. At a national level, such systematic delusions of persecution and misanthropy result in internecine struggles in which no one benefits and many suffer.

Pathogenic. A medical term referring to anything that produces a disease or organic abnormality; in the context of this book, any event that leads to socially destructive behavior. In this sense, the term *pathogenic* is quite similar to the idea of *dysfunction* and has the same problems involved in its usage. Usually, whether we consider something pathogenic in a social sense involves a personal normative judgment.

Pathological. Of a diseased nature; organically dysfunctional. Sociologists, often fond of organic metaphors, sometimes refer to crime, marital discord, rioting, conflict, or other violations of humanistic ideals as "pathologies." Such metaphors should be treated with caution. They are invariably disguised value judgments. They permit the sociologist to retain a cloak of objectivity while using a term that is the equivalent of an epithet.

Patriarchy. A system of social organization that is hierarchical, in which men dominate. A patriarchy is dominated by men who hold power and are the heads of households, organizations, and corporations.

Pecuniary. As used here, showing an interest in money; relating events and people in terms of their monetary values.

Peer group. Literally, a group of one's equals. Sociologists generally use the term to refer to equals in the sense of similar age levels. Thus, an eight-year-old's peer group would consist of other children of a similar age. However, the peer group of a college professor would consist of other professors who share similar levels of sophistication and prestige, regardless of differences in age.

Peyote. A mescal cactus of the southwestern United States and Mexico that yields a drug capable of inducing unusual subjective and introspective states of mind.

Pluralism. In its most general meaning, the fact that something can exist in several forms. The term pluralistic society has become popular in recent years and have been applied especially to the American system, in which a variety of ethnic cultures have been able to share in the common expression of American ideals. We have employed the term industrial pluralism in the text to refer to the American industrial system, in which a variety of industries are allowed to produce a common product. These products are supposed to be different because they come from different plants. Everyone is aware, however, that the differences that appear to exist come more from the office of an advertising agency than from the factory.

Polygamy. Literally, the situation in which one may be married to several spouses. In common usage, this term is often used to refer to the situation in which a husband has multiple wives. This is more correctly called *polygyny*. The situation in which a woman has several husbands is referred to as *polyandry*.

Postfigurative culture. A concept developed by Margaret Mead to characterize cultures in which change is extremely slow and almost imperceptible. The concept is related to those of cofigurative and prefigurative cultures, which form a tripartite description of cultures or cultural continuities, according to Mead. Cofigurative cultures utilize the models of contemporaries as the standard for values and attitudes. Prefigurative cultures characterize our modern, contemporary situation where adults learn from children and youths. All three types of cultures can be found around the globe at this time.

Postpartriarchal Society. A concept developed by Elise Boulding that foresees a social transformation to a culture that reflects how women can initiate action to change their life situations and reverse a patriarchal society dominated by men.

Postulate. As used throughout this book, a proposition that is assumed without need of proof in order to further an argument; a statement regarded as self-evident and not in need of further verification. One of the postulates of structural-functional theory, for example, is that any social action must have social consequences and must therefore be capable of being interpreted in terms of its social functions. A basic postulate of naturalistic philosophy is that all natural events can be understood in terms of what we perceive in nature.

Pragmatic. Subscribing to the philosophy that knowledge should be evaluated in terms of its practical values; the idea that the world exists to be manipulated; the conviction that knowledge that promotes manipulation is good (the rest, being useless, is worthless); dedication to the belief that events and people should be related in terms of their usefulness.

Prognostication. An attempt to divine the future; a forecast; an estimate of the outcome of some course of action.

Proletariat. The industrial working class of the world; people who do not own any means of production other than their labor power—in other words, most of us.

Psychic. Having the capacity to go beyond natural constraints; transcending the boundaries of normal and natural mental processes. Persons who are psychic are said to be able to foretell the future, move objects by application of will, and be aware of what other people are thinking without resorting to questioning and natural forms of communication.

Racism. The oppression (both institutional and informal) of socially stigmatized groups, often backed by theories that attribute the status of these groups to inherited inferior traits rather than to the lack of opportunities and economic mobility in the society.

Replication. The act of repeating. As used here, this term refers to the practice of repeating investigations over and over in order to check the validity of initial results. The fact that a sociological study often can be replicated and maintain a consistency of results is, in itself, a strong argument for the possibility of a science of human relations.

Retreatist. As used by Robert Merton, any individual who abandons both the goals and the means endorsed by a society as legitimate and worthwhile. The dropout is a retreatist.

Ritualist. As used by Merton, any individual who becomes involved in a socially sanctioned means activity to the detriment of attaining socially valued goals. Ritualism implies a ''blind'' reliance on established modes of attaining goals even after these have ceased being effective.

Sensate. A term coined by Sorokin to refer to cultures in which emphasis is given to knowledge derived through the senses. Such cultures, according to Sorokin, have a number of common characteristics, such as sensual art forms, pragmatic philosophies, positivistic science, relative moral systems, situational ethics, and prestige systems based on external signs of worth. See *Ideational* (cultures).

Shaman. A term broadly used to refer to a person who believes he or she can interfere directly in the workings of good and evil spirits; a medicine man or woman.

Significant other. A person who is more significant to us than others with whom we come in contact, and whose favor we seek to win more seriously. (The significant other can also be an enemy whose respect for our punitive power is something that takes over our fantasies.)

Social Darwinism. The carrying of Darwin's theories into social and moral theory. Social Darwinism argues, essentially, that superior cultures are the product of adaptation to the demands of the struggle for survival. A superior culture is usually one in which an exponent of this theory is a member at the time.

Social goals. Objectives that achieve a special significance because they are collectively held. When, for example, acting was considered a rather debased way of making a living, few people felt any desire to become an actor. Today, the social significance given to acting makes it a prized social goal—an aspiration that many hold as a dream.

Sociometric. A means of recording patterns of social relationships within a group. A sociometric is typically a simple charting of friendships among people. For example, one might ask students in a classroom to write down the names of their three best friends. Given this information, one can then determine who is the most popular student in the class and who is the least popular. Lines of informal influence can be established from such data.

Sociosphere. The term popularized by Elise Boulding to describe the worldwide culture that is a reality in contemporary society.

Status panic. A term coined by C. Wright Mills to refer to the problems faced by Americans in their quest for a sense of worth. Because the standards of worth in the American system, according to Mills, are ill-defined, Americans, no matter how hard they work, can never be certain they are successful. No matter where one stands in the system, there is always someone who can be looked upon as better. Moreover, because American culture emphasizes a competitive relation with others, one is then obligated to match the worth of the person who stands above one. The fact that this is a never-ending and uncertain enterprise induces a sense of panic, the constant feeling that one is on the edge of failing.

Status quo. The existing order; the present way of getting things done; the established and accepted system of human relationships as it exists in the present.

Structural-functional theory. As used here, a sociological school of thought (structural-functional theory is also found in the biological sciences and in other social sciences) that attempts to relate particular forms of social action to the total social system within which the action occurs.

Sui generis. Literally, "of its own kind," something unique; a thing apart, having special qualities. This term was used by Durkheim in his attempt to establish the social order as something having qualities of its own. Just as life, though dependent on the physical order, is different from inert matter, so is society, though dependent on biological beings, different from biological matter. The term is a call for recognition of the special understanding that is required to comprehend the nature of social activities. A social system has dynamics of its own (*sui generis*); it is not a simple manifestation of individual human needs and character.

Symbiotic ecology. Mutually sustaining life systems. A symbiotic relation is one in which several life forms provide reciprocal benefits. A prosaic example of a symbiotic relation is that of a person and a dog. The dog, in return for its gratification of the human need for recognition and affection, is given shelter and food. (In some areas of the United States, the dog is also given psychiatric care.) See *Ecology*.

Symbolic elaboration. The ability of symbols to enlarge upon almost any subject, including the symbols themselves. In thinking about this notion, it is important to recognize that such elaboration is a property of symbols and not intelligence, curiosity, or some other psychologistic variable.

Symbolic interactionism. As used in this text, a theoretical point of view in the social sciences emphasizing the symbolic nature of human social relations; the idea that human interaction is essentially symbolic interaction; the belief that one's sense of self arises out of the capacity to view one's self as a meaningful entity apart from others (this, in turn, is based on our capacity to evaluate ourselves symbolically). A very simple demonstration of what the symbolic interactionist is trying to put across can be carried out with an ordinary television set. First, turn off the sound and watch the picture. Because this reduces the symbolic content of the picture drastically, the meaning of most of what is taking place is lost. Next, turn off the picture but retain the sound. The symbolic content carried by the physical action in the picture is now lost, but this is the smaller symbolic element. At the level of pure symbolic interaction, we can retain a good sense of what is taking place. Human social interaction takes place at a symbolic level, and this makes it distinctive. When we interact with a person, we interact with that person in terms of the values that they obtain through the symbolic meanings we attach to him or her. The symbolic interactionists, in the classical formulations of George Herbert Mead, made much of the fact that not only do individuals have the capacity to interact at the symbolic level with others, they can also interact symbolically with themselves. Individuals can assume the roles of others and then either praise or castigate themselves from the perspective of these other people. Symbolic interactionists see this as the most essential aspect of social control. Any biologically and mentally normal person is highly vulnerable to the symbolic evaluations that others make of him or her. We have no physically determinable and sensorily observable self. Therefore, what we are is what others make of us. We uncritically assume the symbolic evaluations of self that others give us. If enough persons tell us we are bad, we come to accept this evaluation. Conversely, if enough people tell us we are good, we also accept this. Our self, therefore, is located in the external evaluations imposed upon us. For this reason, society and self are only different manifestations of the same process.

Symptomatic behavior. A term coined by Erving Goffman to refer to behavior that validates one's right to act out the content of a particular role. Such behavior is symptomatic of whether one "really" is what one is trying to appear to be. For example, a professor who has a deep British accent, everything else being equal, will be more acceptable to an audience than one who has a strong Arkansas accent. The British accent is viewed as symptomatic of a person of wit, dignity, and learning. A colleague of ours once said that he mistrusted the work of a certain instructor because he had seen her at a meeting and she was deeply tanned. No *real* scholar would be tanned. As Thorstein Veblen pointed out, a suntan is symptomatic of a frivolous life in an age of office workers.

Tautology. Circular reasoning; saying the same thing in different ways; redundancy; redefining a condition and then using the redefinition as an explanation.

Transcendent principles. At the simplest level, principles that can exert an influence or are accepted across various lines of social division. Money, for example, is an obvious transcendent principle—poor people and rich, young and old, male and female, bright and stupid, educated and ignorant subscribe with more or less the same intensity to the idea that money means power.

Transcendental. Going beyond the limits of normal human experience; transcending one's natural abilities; extending beyond normal physical awareness.

Tripartite. A threefold classification scheme. Margaret Mead's three categories of cultural learning exemplify a tripartite classification or David Riesman's classification of three types of individuals—tradition, inner- or other-directed.

Typology. A classification scheme; an examination of types.

Unanticipated (Unintended) Consequences. A sociological phenomenon that arises in conjunction with the functional analysis of purposive social actions in which events or situations occur that were not expected or foreseen.

Usury. The practice of lending money at very high rates of interest.

Utilitarian. Having utility or usefulness.

Utopia. An ideal community; a place in which people achieve their most noble conceptions of life; literally, "no" (*ou*) "place" (*topos*).

Value system. A structure or ordering of action that is highly esteemed by a people; the assignment of worth to different activities in a manner that reveals an underlying common basis of evaluation of such activity.

Volition. A concept implying that people have the capacity to exercise choice; decision making. See the discussion under *Determinism*.

Worldmindedness. Worldview; a conception of events, issues, and experiences; a way of seeing society in a global perspective.

Xenophobia. Having a fear (*phobia*) of that which is strange or foreign (*xenos*); a hatred of the foreigner.

Credits

Table 2-1 (page 24). Modified version of table on page 65 of Guy E. Swanson, *The Birth of the Gods: The Origin of Primitive Beliefs* (Ann Arbor: University of Michigan Press, 1960).

Pages 26-29, 31. Quotations from pp. 72, 73, 81, 93, 100, 329; reprinted with permission of The Free Press, an imprint of Simon & Schuster, from *Division of Labor in Society* by Émile Durkheim, translated by J. A. Spaulding and George Simpson. Copyright 1933, 1961 by The Free Press.

Pages 50-51, 53-55. Quotations from pp. 50, 51, 57, 60, 83-85, 91, 105, 108, 158 of *The Protestant Ethic and the Spirit of Capitalism*, by Max Weber, translated by Talcott Parsons. Copyright 1958 Charles Scribner's Sons. Reprinted with permission of Macmillan College Publishing Company.

Pages 57, 60-66. Quotations from pp. 17, 18-27; reprinted with permission of The Free Press, an imprint of Simon & Schuster from *Administrative Behavior*, Third Edition by Herbert A. Simon. Copyright 1945, 1947, 1957, 1976 by Herbert A. Simon.

Pages 156-159, 161, 163. Permission to quote from P. A. Sorokin's *Social and Cultural Dynamics* was granted by the copyright holders, Peter P. and Sergei P. Sorokin.

Pages 172, 173. From "Macbeth's Physician" by Joseph J. Weiss, M.D., Detroit Medical News, December 24, 1990, p. 6.

Pages 181-182 and 190-194. Quotations reprinted with permission of Oxford University Press from C. Wright Mills, *The Power Elite* (1956), pp. 10-11, 105, 106, 304; and *The Sociological Imagination* (1959), pp. 52-60, 74, 89-90, 195-226.

Pages 186-189. Quotations from pp. 78-79, 81-89, 98, 125 of C. Wright Mills, *The Causes of World War III* (New York: Simon & Schuster, 1958); reprinted with permission of Brandt and Brandt.

Pages 211-215. Excerpts from pp. xvi, xxvi, 5, 7, 33, 44, 56, 64, 88 of *Culture and Commitment* by Margaret Mead. Copyright 1970, 1978 by Margaret Mead. Used by permission of Doubleday, a division of Bantam Doubleday Dell Publishing Group, Inc.

Pages 228-230, 231, 232, 235, 237, 238. Excerpts from pp. 11-12, 21-22, 56, 63, 149-150, 155, 246, 258, 259 of *The Lonely Crowd: A Study in the Chang-*

Index